REVOLUTION IN BRAZIL

BY IRVING LOUIS HOROWITZ

Revolution in Brazil
The New Sociology
Power, Politics and People (editor)
The War Game
Philosophy, Science and the Sociology of Knowledge
Radicalism and the Revolt Against Reason
The Idea of War and Peace

REVOLUTION IN BRAZIL

Politics and Society in a Developing Nation

by Irving Louis Horowitz

New York   1964
E. P. DUTTON & CO., INC.

Published simultaneously in Canada by Clarke, Irwin
& Company Limited, Toronto and Vancouver

Library of Congress Catalog Card Number: 64-13916

in memory of
ANTÔNIO VICENTE MENDES MACIEL
otherwise known as
ANTHONY THE COUNSELOR
christian mystic and revolutionary divine

PREFACE

BRAZIL IS different from the rest of Latin America. If only for the comparisons it affords, this is one nation which deserves serious attention. I must frankly admit that I came to an appreciation of this difference in an indirect manner: first, through a steady focus on the social character of Argentina, and second, through a continuing study of social development in the *Tiers Monde*. I do not mean that Brazil is special simply in terms of the obvious distinctions to be drawn between a Hispanic culture and a Luzo-Brazilian culture. Differences in language, customs, racial composition, and cultural outlooks are only the most striking, but not necessarily the most significant elements.

Contrasts between Brazil and Argentina are just as much matters of *esprit* and *élan* as they are questions of industrial production. In the world of art, Brazilians produce a unique blend of technical sophistication and folk appreciation excelled only by the Mexican muralists. Argentines, for their part, produce a unique blend also: of abstract expressionism—New York style and Parisian style. A deeper look reveals this to be a distinction between creativity and mimesis, between a society exhibiting a high degree of purpose and one convinced that society is directionless.

There is not a nation in Latin America where the plenitude of creature comforts is more apparent than Argentina. Little wonder then that a traveler to Buenos Aires can feel right "at home." On the other hand, Brazil is a nation where creature comforts remain relatively poor in quality and comparatively scarce in quantity. But this is because such commodity goods are increasingly being manufactured by Brazilian-owned factories and on Brazilian-produced machines. To this must be added the fact that consumer production is less significant at present than production of basic tools and facilities. Again, a deeper look reveals the distinction between structural development and simple modernization. For this reason, probably no place in Latin America seems (on the surface, at any rate) less "inviting" to a visitor from the United States than Brazil.

These admittedly personal remarks are not made lightly. Argentina is a nation I have known for a long while. And I have come to admire its people greatly. I can make no extensive claims of emotional attachment for Brazil. But perhaps, for this very reason, my views will strike a better balance than might otherwise have been the case. In a subsequent work on "The Rise and Fall of Peronism" I hope to make clear the precise nature of the difference between the two major powers of South America. In the present work, emphasis of a comparative nature had to give way to considerations of Brazilian internal development, and to its relationship to the major power structures as they exist at an international level.

This is not intended to be a work of personal reportage, but a social scientific examination of a major world area. Hopefully, this book offers a basic introduction to both specific data and general theoretical issues. The generosity of Brazilian scholars who allowed me the use of their studies makes this a cooperative venture in the truest sense of the term. I am particularly grateful to L.A. Costa Pinto, Gláucio Soares, Celso Furtado, Hélio Jaguaribe, for the use of their materials. Of course, neither these men nor any of the other contributors to the volume are responsible for my positions and perspectives. My intellectual indebtedness is clear, but so too, I hope, is my intellectual independence.

The translation of the materials from Francisco Julião was first made by Danielle Salti. The translation of the essays by Fernando Ferrari, Hélio Jaguaribe, and Luis Suárez were made by my wife and workmate, Ruth L. Horowitz. My indebtedness for this kind of "proletarian" labor of mind is both deeply personal and lasting. For typing assistance, I am grateful to Mrs. Hylda Webb, Mrs. Adeline Sneider, and Miss Sara M. Katz. In part, these technical services were made possible under a Ford Foundation grant to Washington University for Foreign Area Studies. I want to thank the administrators of this grant for their assistance. To Neuma Aguiar Walker and to my friend and colleague Roger Walker go my deepest thanks. Their suggestions and comments on the manuscript spared me more than a few post-mortem nightmares. Finally, especial thanks are due to the editorial efforts of Elizabeth Shepherd.

IRVING LOUIS HOROWITZ

Washington University
St. Louis, Missouri

CONTENTS

this is followed by L.C. Bresser Pereira's examination of the class structure and the industrial "take-off" period; and Neuma Aguiar Walker discusses the role of labor in this process; Luis Suárez then examines the base of Brazil's economic plight, finding it in the connection between industrialization and undercapitalization; Josué de Castro reveals the "tragic expression" of economic backwardness by showing the relationship between colonialism and hunger on one side, and industrialism and affluence on the other.

. . . in which the exodus from rural areas to the big cities is shown to be a costly, and sometimes tragic, form of progress; technocratic versus socialistic solutions to the land problem; democratic versus bureaucratic solutions to the city problem; the racial problem: the world of whites, blacks, and browns, its link to the class problem; paternalism moves from the "big house" to the presidential mansion; paternalism and revolution from above, the role and function of the Brazilian militarists; social redemption as social revolution.

. . . in which Gilberto Freyre asks whether Brazil is becoming a tropical China; Jacob Gorender gives a communist view of Brazil's problem, and Luís Carlos Prestes attacks the United States and wonders whether Brazil ought not to become a tropical Russia; this is followed by Roberto de Oliveira Campos' distinction between neutralism and independence in foreign policy; and by João Goulart's statement before the United States Congress that Brazil's destiny is in its own hands.

. . . in which the main facts in the present rupture between Russian and Chinese communism are raised, with special emphasis on the strategic character of left-wing politics in Brazil; this is followed by an attempt to assess long-range strengths and weaknesses in both the Soviet and Chinese attempts to influence Brazil's pluralistic socialism.

. . . in which alternative models for the Brazilian Revolution are
discussed; the right and the wrong way for critics to make criticisms; contradictions in a solution based on American capitalism;
contradictions in a solution based on Soviet communism; the socialist alternative; when giants clash—the shape of future United
States-Brazilian relations; proposals for the American champion
and the Brazilian challenger.

ACKNOWLEDGMENTS

Grateful acknowledgment is made to the following for permission to quote from copyright material:

Francisco Julião: *Carta de Alforria do Componês*. Translated from *Que são as Ligas Camponesas?* by Francisco Julião, Rio de Janeiro, Editôra Civilização Brasileira, 1962, by permission of the publisher.

Celso Furtado: *Reflexões sôbre a pré-revolução brasileira*. Translated from *Revista Brasileira de Ciências Sociais*. Vol. II, No. 1, Minas Gerais, March 1962, by permission of the publisher.

Jânio Quadros: *Brazil's New Foreign Policy*. Reprinted from *Foreign Affairs* (Council on Foreign Relations), Vol. XL, No. 1, October 1961, by permission of the publisher.

Horácio Láfer: *The Survival of Mankind: United Nations Not a Super State*. Reprinted from *Vital Speeches of the Day*, Vol. XXVII, No. 1, October 1960, by permission of the publisher.

José Honório Rodrigues: *The Foundations of Brazil's Foreign Policy*. Reprinted from *International Affairs* (The Royal Institute of International Affairs), Vol. XXXVIII, No. 3, July 1962, by permission of the author and publisher.

Fernando Ferrari: *Panorama político del Brasil*. Translated from *Combate*, Vol. IV, No. 21 (whole number), March-April 1962, by permission of the publisher.

Hélio Jaguaribe: *A renúncia do Presidente Quadros e a crise política brasileira*. Translated from *Revista Brasileira de Ciências Sociais*, Vol. I, No. 1, November 1961, by permission of the publisher.

Gláucio Soares: *The Political Sociology of Uneven Development in Brazil*, abridged by permission of the author from a study to be published in S. M. Lipset and S. Rokkan (editors), *Party Systems and Voter Alignments*.

L.A. Costa Pinto and Waldemiro Bazzanella: *Economic Development, Social Change and Population Problems*. Reprinted from *Annals* (The American Academy of Political and Social

Science), Vol. CCCXVI, March 1958, by permission of the publisher and the author.

L.C. Bresser Pereira: *The Rise of Middle Class and Middle Management in Brazil*. Reprinted from *Journal of Inter-American Studies*, Vol. IV, No. 3, July 1962, by permission of the editors.

Neuma Aguiar Walker: *The Organization and Ideology of Brazilian Labor*. Original paper prepared for this volume by the author.

Josué de Castro: *Colonialism, Hunger and Progress*. Reprinted from *World Marxist Review*, Vol. IV, No. 10, October 1961, by permission of the publisher.

João Goulart: *Brazil and the United States*. Reprinted from *Vital Speeches of the Day*, Vol. XXVIII, No. 14, May 1962, by permission of the publisher.

Gilberto Freyre: *Why a Tropical China?* Reprinted from *New World in the Tropics: The Culture of Modern Brazil* by Gilberto Freyre, New York: Alfred A. Knopf, 1959, by permission of the publisher.

Luis Suárez: *Reportaje en Brasil, La crisis de fondo en las ultimas crisis políticas*. Translated from *Cuadernos Americanos*, Vol. CXXV, No. 6, November-December 1962, by permission of the author and editor.

Irving Louis Horowitz: *Latin America and the Sino-Soviet Split*. Portions reprinted from *Liberation*, Vol. VIII, No. 3, May 1963, by permission of the editor.

Roberto de Oliveira Campos: *Text of Speech delivered before the Pan American Society* (December 19, 1962). Reprinted from *Brazilian Bulletin*, Vol. XIX, No. 424 (whole number), January 1963, by permission of the editors.

REVOLUTION IN BRAZIL

I
AN INTRODUCTION TO
THE BRAZILIAN REVOLUTION

... in which the four gods standing in the way of our understanding the Brazilian Revolution are dealt with: the public relations bias, the anthropological bias, the ideological bias, and the Hispanic bias; some initial guidelines to Brazilian viewpoints.

THE PENETRATION of Latin America into the consciousness of Americans represents the most dramatic shift of vision and sentiment to occur since the rise of the Cold War. The series of events beginning with the near assassination of an American Vice President on a "good-will" tour and concluding with the brink-of-war confrontation between the United States and the Soviet Union over Cuba has made the Latin "presence" a matter for general consideration and immediate decision. Never again will Latin American revolutionists be viewed as balmy and untutored bogey men. Never again will the image of the Latin be connected with the word *mañana*. Never again will euphoric assumptions about good neighbors and love between our brothers and sisters to the south of us be rhetorically entertained. The age of innocence is over. Or is it?

This is a book about Brazil rather than Latin America in general. Some significant parallels between Brazil and its neighbors exist. Differences exist as well. The astute reader will come to appreciate where similarities and differences are in evidence. But what has become evident is that in place of simplistic myths about Latin American characteristics of a bygone age, we now have sophisticated images. Ignorance has begotten cleverness. The cultural apparatus has given rise to the journalistic ideologue, while the holders of exact knowledge have joined forces with propagandists to maintain the rhetoric of oversimplification. It is not so much that celebration abounds—indeed, there is precious little to celebrate about American-Brazilian relations—but that criticism is absent. The cutting edge of intellect is absent. In its place is a dulling acquiescence in pseudo-professionalism.

The god of the public relations expert has moved in upon us. In place of the slovenly, ignorant, and indolent masses of Latin America, our image-makers now speak of "vivacious, humorous and relaxed inhabitants." In an article "produced by" a staff writer for *Look*, we are told that the people of Rio, the Cariocans, teach us the lesson: *dar um Jeito*—to find a way. The Brazilian urban dweller is reputed to live in terms of a special *telos*: "for every stone wall there is a big enough ladder somewhere, and that excitement and worry about a problem are therefore irrelevant." The evidence for this is that while "other people might riot when a president resigns; when theirs did two years ago, the people of Rio went to the beach." The fact that the resignation of Quadros had as its immediate consequence a blackout on news, machine-gun-toting policemen on the streets, and tear gas thrown into the crowd, a paralysis in government, a possible rightist *coup d'état*, and served to trigger a violent monetary spiral from which the nation has yet to recover, is conveniently forgotten. The Brazilian is seen enjoying *carnival*, dancing, sipping coffee, but above all, whiling away time at the beach. The task of the public relations expert is to change nothing about material relations, but rather to resolve matters by a transformation in images. The philosophy behind this bias is that antagonism between Brazilians and Americans rests on a failure of communication but never on a structural failure of economic and political relations.

The same article, which celebrates the virtues of *carnival* time, might have done better by taking note of the words of some of these songs:

> *Rio de Janeiro, city of delights;*
> *By day there is no water,*
> *At night there are no lights.*

Ah yes! The Brazilian is a lighthearted fellow about his fate. But his parody on *Me dá um dinheiro aí*, another *carnival* song, indicates that to find a way may prove to be more of an act of defiance than of resignation:

> *Hey, Mister President,*
> *Gimme some cash—*
> *Gimme some cash.*
>
> *He don't fork up,*
> *He won't fork up.*
>
> *Now, all together,*
> *Let's all revolt*
> *And grow us beards*
> *And grow them long.*
> *For the Alliance don't pro-gress*
> *Without those beards.*

And if the traditional irreverence of Brazilians for pomp and cere-
mony be viewed as a form of fatalism, this following verse should
set matters aright.

> *You think Alliance is dollars.*
> *No, Alliance ain't dollars, no.*
> *Alliance is Che Guevara*
> *Preaching revolt and woe.*

The Brazilian knows that if his nation is permeating the North
American conscience for the first time, this is a consequence of
the over-all radicalization of Latin America, and in particular of
the Cuban Revolution. Therefore, one way to attract even greater
attention is by continuing on a path of independence from United
States interests. But our reaction to these new winds of doctrine
which are blowing in from Brazil has been to send forth a veritable
battalion of ex-novelists, sports columnists, gourmets, and travel
writers. The collective claque, on returning home, has certainly
made Brazil a place to take a holiday—from reality.

Public relations experts are charged with the task of resolving
the American ambivalence: the need to assuage our guilt over the
history of gunboat colonialism in Latin America; and the equal
desire to glide over any real threat to North American proprietorship over the area. Little wonder, therefore, that Brazil has
acquired an enigmatic quality that serves to dull the very consciousness that the god of public relations ostensibly seeks to stimulate. Fun-loving and Yanqui-hating, militaristic and democratic,
lazy and philosophical, ignorant and ideological—it is all so con-
fusing that the urge to "forget it" tempts us once more.

But the paradoxes are more apparent than real. The consistencies of social change, the logic of development, add up to a portrait which is accurate because it begins with the Brazilian national situation, and not from public relations images of that situation. The public relations experts have a penchant for viewing any development in another society as an opportunity to fashion either embroidered myths about the "intrinsic" libertarianism of Brazilians or tales of communist subversion. For the mid-cult crowd, the key word is "happiness," while for the mass-cult crowd the magic word is "horror." Those who travel, who live in terms of "jet-set" values, must be encouraged to love; while the masses who do not travel—even from Peoria to Springfield—must be reinforced by fear, tales of subversion, and cries of treason. The god of public relations has done its job well. The false alternatives remain intact. The "image-makers" have earned their fees. Only the shock of recognition which accompanies radical change in the hemisphere preserves the more thoughtful from accepting the distortion of reality. But for the thoughtful, there are other gods to contend with.

Up until the present, serious American writings on Brazilian society have been basically in the hands of our anthropologists. As a result, the public vision of Brazil has been that of a vast quaintness, or better, of a quaint vastness. Kinship relations in Brazil have been described in great detail. The "exotic" tribes of the Amazon have been enshrined in Hollywood films and jungle-adventure tales. And such other features of Brazil as its tropical climate, speculative surges of boom and bust, pottery-making, and vast geographical expanses have all been well described.

But without intending any further extension of the conflict between anthropology and sociology (an utterly stupid and senile one) it must bluntly be said that whereas Brazil has entered the modern world, American social science in relation to Brazil remains in its pristine anthropological-archaeological form. Even where American anthropologists have attempted to make some adjustments to the new reality, these have been unsatisfactory and incomplete—reflecting more the nostalgia of our anthropology than the sociological realities of modern Brazil. Anthropologists are, after all, not simply dedicated men of science. They are also men of national dedication, men who study "primitive culture" from the vantage point of "advanced culture." The relativism is only one-way. Brazilians do not come to the United States to study our "race problem," but Americans do go to Brazil to study its "race problem." Brazilians do not examine our "overdeveloped society"; but we do examine their "underdeveloped society." Nostalgic attitudes toward Brazil abound—as if sectionalism, nationalism, socialism, could not possibly pertain to a charming world of big plantation houses and stable self-contained little communities where everyone happily spends his life in mutual service.

The situation would not be tragic if it represented only the nostalgia of anthropologists. Unfortunately, it also represents a colonialist ideology and phraseology. Brazil is said to represent a "field," an "area study." No significant attempt has yet been made to connect the revolutionary tides sweeping Brazil with the general movement of events in other parts of Latin America, Asia, and Africa. A kind of Brazilian "exceptionalism" sets in, to further advertise the unique value of "the area." This is not to deny special features to Brazilian development. The pages which follow attempt precisely such an analysis. But its unique features are special aspects of phenomena and expectations common to all underdeveloped or, better, developing societies.

American scholarship in relation to Brazil tends to concentrate on perennial social factors in a state of equilibrium. There is an attempt to speak in terms of eternal verities rather than in terms of historical variables. In this way, even when sociological studies have been made, they have been made from the point of view of Brazilian structural features at the expense of developmental features; of systems of group norms instead of processes of class, caste, and status relations. And when factors of social change are treated, they usually are confined in an ethnocentric way to show how changes in Brazilian social structure affect United States interests in the area. Invariably, social science treatments of Brazil conclude with judgments on how this or that class, or this or that ruler, has reacted to or reacts upon United States interests. Even those social scientists managing to escape the "anthropological bias" are still tied up in knots by the "ideological bias," by the felt need to evaluate any given Brazilian development by its positive or negative effects on American foreign policy. The conceit implied here is that any form of development which has no apparent parallel in United States history cannot be legitimized.

Brazil's social scientists, as well as its political statesmen **and** social thinkers, have created a perceptive literature. This has been my guide in the following pages. Before we can instruct, we must learn from Brazilians themselves. By giving over many of the pages of the book to Brazilian commentators and policy-makers, to radical and conservative points of view, I hope to show that even what is meant by the terms "radical" and "conservative" is quite different from the American or European definitions of such terms. Brazil's policy-makers are now increasingly becoming its revolution-makers. It would be sheer folly not to face the simple fact that Brazilian development is no longer uniquely determined by how officials in the Pan American Union feel or by the size of loans issued by the International Monetary Fund. Brazil has its own political and economic logics, its own framework for discussing development, its own national interests. As such, it must be studied on its own terms and not in terms of inherited ideologies. Anthropologists may continue to study pottery-making among the Amazons; sociologists may continue to discuss the demographic dangers of population expansion; economists may be intimidated by the extent of Brazilian inflation—but this only reflects a gigantic ethnocentrism. These are not topics Brazilians themselves are basically worried by, even though inflation is a disturbing factor in Brazilian working-class life. In a condition of stable economy, balanced budgets may be significant; but not in Brazil, which has an annual economic growth percentage twice that of the United States. In the Polynesian islands basket-weaving and bead-stringing may still prove revealing of the national character, but not in a country which can manufacture major cities like Brasilia in less than a decade. In an industrial community the population size may uniquely determine problems of underemployment; but not in a country which needs all the manpower it can train. In an old European nation, parliamentarianism may define democracy, but not in a new nation like Brazil.

What Brazilians are worried about, what they talk about, is how to achieve economic independence from both capitalist and communist powers; how to navigate a political course between the Eagle and the Bear; how to get an agrarian reform under way which would wipe out the latifundists; how to get a public economy uniquely suited to the needs of Brazilians. Through the use of translation into English of major statements by Brazilians, and by relating my own comments to the general tenor of Brazilian interests, I hope that the reader will become intimate and not just acquainted with the revolution in Brazil.

This is a book on Brazil; but it is also a book by Brazilians. This should be obvious, were it not for the fact that a book on Brazil is rare enough to merit attention, while a book in which Brazilian statesmen and scholars present their views is still rarer.

This brings us to the fourth misconception. Americans have come to believe in the Hispanic myth (for reasons of our own to be sure). This myth asserts that Brazil is a *big* nation, but is not a *great* nation. Brazil is a land with many problems, but also a land with passive, samba-dancing people. The reason for the propagation of this myth in South America has to do with the exaggerated "European consciousness" of Argentines, Uruguayans, and Chileans. *Pensadores,* the "thinkers" of former times, were caught in the grip of this chauvinistic view of their Luzo-Brazilian neighbor. Inferiority complexes rationalize themselves and harden into defense mechanisms—even on a national scale. One white European immigrant was supposed to be worth ten to a hundred (it depends on whom you read) Brazilian Indians, and God alone knows how many Africans. In the nineteenth century, the hot weather was elevated to a climactic-geographical view of history in an effort to prove the impossibility of Brazilian development. Interestingly, even this geographical theory was imported from European sociologists who didn't know better.

Thus it was, and to some measure still is, that North American attitudes toward Brazil have suffered from a four-pronged error: (a) from the anthropological bias in favor of "primitive man" over and against the social realities of "developing man"; (b) from the ideological bias rooted in the imagined requirements of United States foreign policy and, worse still, in the supposed needs of American private investors; (c) from a Hispanic bias, from accepting at face value the judgments on Brazil made by the Spanish-speaking nations of the hemisphere for reasons having little or nothing to do with scientific comparison; and (d) from the public relations bias more concerned with proper touristic images and a leisure *ethos* than with unpleasant facts.

There is, however, a special sense in which the geographical view of history commands respect. The size of a nation, and the wealth that invariably accompanies size, do justify speaking of Brazil in superlatives. In an overcrowded and underfed universe, geography promises the possibility of liberation. There are only four nations in the world larger than Brazil: Russia, China, United States (with Alaska), and Canada. The first three represent that triumvirate of world powers upon which nearly all political mobility and military action rest. Brazil alone among nations large and populous is a place of which one is required to speak in diminutives as well as superlatives. Indeed, the present is viewed by nearly all Brazilians as "transitional" or "developmental" or "experimental." But the future is rapidly becoming the present. The edges of time are bringing Brazil into the twentieth century, eating away at the vitals of the degenerate and the decadent social order. In part, this process of transformation is one in which the decadent old has gone into building the dynamic new. The Brazilian Revolution has no official beginning. Its leaders have yet to win their place in history. Its commemorative dates are yet to be determined. Yet to speak of Brazil is to speak of revolution axiomatically: a social revolution well under way, and a political revolution that is gathering momentum in a relatively brief period. To speak of Brazil in terms of the "natural history of revolution" is to take a jaded and jaundiced view. To see only the remnants of the past, the survivals of feudalism, as uniquely determining the social structure and the social order of the future is to miss the obvious fact of social change and social progress at present. To disguise nostalgia with scientific verbiage is to run the serious risk of being taken in by the other lingering ideological failures that inhabit rather than live in Brazil. This mistake shall not be made. We shall not confuse neutrality with objectivity.

In the past, when observers did get around to dealing seriously with Brazil, the focus usually was on how it compared with the United States. Brazilian nineteenth-century positivists and romantics were fond of drawing analogies with the democratic giant of the North. Both nations had proved stronger than their respective "mother" colonial powers: for Americans it was the English, and for the Brazilians it was the Portuguese, perhaps the most backward of colonial powers in Europe. Both Brazil and the United States moved from the eastern coastal regions westward. Our pioneers drove out the Indians, while in Brazil *bandeirantes* performed the same function, in a more humane fashion, it should be added. Both nations are fantastically rich in mineral deposits, land for agriculture, and in the natural wonders that seem to be as expansive as the nations themselves. The shrewder commentators of yesteryear even took comfort in comparing the brutalities of the American slave system with the genteel cruelties of the Brazilian feudal system.

But in the present era, such comparisons have declined sharply. The shock of recognizing distinctions has affected both countries. It has come to be seen that differences considerably outweigh similarities. The United States is a fully evolved technological-economic power; Brazil is still an underdeveloped (or at best developing) power. The United States, by virtue of its economic position, has become the leading political power of the hemisphere. Brazil, by virtue of its *potential* strength, has become the leading anti-colonial nation of the hemisphere. The United States, both its private and public sectors, has become the hemispheric bulwark for gradualism, for reform without revolution. Brazil has, for its part, become the focus for activism, for reform at all costs, *through* revolution if necessary. These are harsh words to American ears—especially the discovery that our anti-communist mission is considered by Brazilians to be rationalization, part of the rhetoric of oversimplification. Economic colonialism has been disguised as assistance for so long that our public seems shocked and dismayed at every "anti-American" outburst. But there the matter rests.

It is not that colonialism is either good or bad; or that American economic colonialization is more palatable than older varieties of military imperialism practiced by the European powers. It is simply that colonialism as a form of international political and economic relations, and as the ideological representation of these relations, is fast drawing to a close. There is neither honor in upholding what is perishing nor praise due to those who welcome the collapse of the old order of doing business. The facts are plain, and plainly sufficient to all who make the effort of comprehension. No amount of wailing about the communist threat can ward off what is in the offing: a Brazilian-United States confrontation. As the English, who have smartly managed to survive the collapse of their Empire, like to say: "Must is must."

Perhaps the most powerful evidence that Brazil is in a state of revolutionary ferment lies in the comparisons made by its statesmen and scholars. No less a figure than the conservative Brazilian sociologist and historian, Gilberto Freyre, has suggested that

Brazil might turn out to be the China of the Western hemisphere—an impossible thought for those who measure everything in Brazil by United States standards: by stable economics, balance-of-terror politics, and such lesser features of our civilization as superhighways and color television; an unpatriotic thought to those who measure everything in the hemisphere by cold-war slogans of Americanism versus Communism; an uncivil thought for those who measure democracy by the simplistic measuring rod of nations which have or do not have two political parties.

The comparison between China and Brazil introduces nagging considerations, of both similarities and contrasts. In both nations the backbone of revolutionary action has been the rural peasantry rather than the urbanized proletariat or the suburbanized bourgeoisie. However, in each case the political leadership has maintained an urban-industrial orientation and ideology. In both nations there is a racial element in the organization of the populace. In China, however, this ethnic homogeneity exists apart from economic factors, while in Brazil the racial problem largely derives from the economic definition of race. In both nations there is an effort to make the change from feudal agricultural patterns to industrial life styles in a single jump through economic stage-skipping guided by political planning. However, in China this stage-skipping has been accompanied by grotesque abuses of human careers and large-scale economic failures; whereas in Brazil (particularly in the Northeast) the model of development frequently employed attempts to strike some balance between economic productivity and human creativity. In short, China is a case where the command structure is in evidence, whereas in Brazil the consensus structure largely obtains.

Both China and Brazil have had their "long marches" in which revolutionary military bands roamed the countryside in an effort to rouse the masses lacking a history to take charge of the political future. Yet, in China, these military events were decisive to the forging of a revolutionary Communist Party machine, while in Brazil these military events were indecisive, with the Party's basically liberal demands being absorbed by the orthodox political parties. The point is not the similarities or dissimilarities of development in China and Brazil, but the fact that comparisons of this sort are being entertained—and by the very stratum of intellectual society who but a decade ago still gazed fixedly upon the wonders created by their brother American state to the North.

To understand the scope of this ferment, observe the steady radicalization of Catholic thought—its "sect"-like qualities. The words of the Catholic critic, Lourencino Puntel, are typical. He recently declared: "I admit without reservation that the most amoral aspect of the society in which we live is the exploitation of man by man." After declaring his pragmatic agreement with the socialist position, the Jesuit spokesman went on to declare that "He who professes to love God and yet continues to exploit his fellow men is a hypocrite." Another leading Catholic spokesman Tristão de Ataide declared in his book *Labor in the Modern World* that: "If by capitalism we mean an economic system in which labor is the means and capital is the end, and where profit represents the only economic criterion, then we cannot remain Christians and defend capitalism at the same time." Catholic writers who years ago cautioned activists to seek their rewards in heaven, and to bear their cross as patiently as the fictional hero, the apathetic peasant, *Jéca Tatu*, now are found urging their flock to become witnesses for the revolution, to join Zé Brazil, in their fight against latifundists. Catholicism is a world force, and it is a force in Brazil. But it is becoming plainer that the older clerical opinions are being severely challenged by those who believe that Catholicism, which has survived the horrors of Roman slavery, the betrayal of feudal princes, the growth of religious pluralism, the worldliness of capitalism, can also survive the plans of socialism— if it joins rather than crushes the developing Brazilian Revolution.

Of more immediate political concern is the growing consensus among the ruling policy-makers on closer ties—in commerce and in spirit, to the Soviet-bloc nations. Franklin de Oliveira, a leading theoretician of President João Goulart's Labor Party, wrote in his recently published *Revolution and Counter-Revolution*: "Socialist revolution alone creates the conditions for a simultaneous offensive on all fronts, and in such a way as to ensure the rapid and even development of the country." At the same time, Leonel Brizola, then governor of the State of Rio Grande do Sul, lecturing at the Law Faculty of Brazil University in Rio de Janeiro, said that what is happening in Brazil today is clear evidence of the need to break the hold of United States power in the country. His comparison

of Brazil and the United States was a comparison based on conflicting models of development, and not of a common consensus.

If the democracy we enjoy continues to be used as a screen for laws
concealing the plunder of our people and the occupation of our country by any foreign power, we solemnly declare: we reject such a system as an instrument of oppression and domination of our native land,
and we shall use the methods of struggle at our disposal. The day will
come when we shall drive out the oppressor of our people. Better to
lose one's life in struggle than for life to lose all its meaning.

Of course, the sophisticate may attribute these remarks to the
passion of the moment, or to the normal revolutionary rhetoric
politicians in Brazil use to stay in power. Nonetheless, it is interesting that the type of rhetoric now required should be so radically
different from that used in the past. Social scientists, Catholic
clergymen, political apologists, all are speaking the language of
revolution; and all are seeking out models from countries other
than the United States in an effort to create a new social and economic structure.

Perhaps the most difficult form of assistance which can be rendered to the Brazilian Revolution by those who seek to do so would
be to develop a more enlightened, a more rational atmosphere
here in the United States, an atmosphere in which crackpot war-
riors who want to send Marines to Latin America at the least sign
of a threat to American business interests can properly be held in
check. We must begin to distinguish between conspiracy and
revolution. We are no longer in the position, if we ever were, to
"save" Latin America from revolutionary tides and fortunes
through Nicaraguan gunboat "diplomacy." The question has become: Can we disentangle ourselves from the ties that bind us to
reactionary tides and fortunes? The answer to that question, and
perhaps to that question alone, will determine whether the Revolution in Brazil will be violent or non-violent, friendly to the highest
aspirations of the American people or confirmed in its suspicions
of American intransigence. To save ourselves from self-fulfilling
prophecies of doom is the American question. To save Brazil from
backwardness is the question for Brazilians. Let us temper our interest with understanding. And understanding means at the least
providing a correct definition of the social situation. Perhaps by
our doing so, the Brazilians will be better able to do likewise.

II
THE IDEOLOGY OF
PEASANT REVOLUTION

. . . in which it is explained why neither the Brazilian middle
classes nor the factory workers have been able to shake the whole
country free of its underdeveloped and exploited condition; Francisco Julião's role in developing a peasant base to the revolution of
rising expectations; the ideological moorings of Peasant Leagues;
current problems in the formation of a Brazil-wide movement for
national independence.

BRAZIL AND Cuba are geographical extremes. Brazil is the largest
nation in Latin America, approximately the size of continental
United States; and Cuba one of the smallest, about the size of New
Hampshire. In terms of population the same comparison is valid.
Brazil has more than seventy million people, while Cuba is in-
habited by seven million. But in political economy and historical
strivings they have much in common. They have a shared heritage
of the latifundia, of large feudal estates which for over four centuries have dominated so much of Latin American agriculture. In
short, they have a shared background of economic underdevelopment and political undemocracy.

Since the land is cultivated by the remnants of the slave population—by the African "filth" brought over during the slave trade,
and by the Indians enslaved by Portuguese adventurers—the conflict between landholders and landworkers is a kaleidoscope of
class struggle, racial struggle, and the more complicated competition for political power. Whatever the final consequences of
Castro's revolution may be, all knowledgeable observers agree that
the causes are rooted in the corruption of "white" politics, in the
garrison state which preserved every sort of social iniquity and
personal indignity, and in an economy which connected single-
crop production with single-minded maintenance of serfdom.

13

That such causes are factors common to all of Latin America, and particularly to Brazil, should prove a sufficient and sober warning for our Panglossian image of Luzo-America. For the twenty-five million peasants of northern Brazil, the Cuban Revolution potentially represents the pragmatic extension of agrarian reform through political revolt. Geographical differences, climatic distinctions, population sizes, count for nothing when confronted with a singular hemispheric fact: Cuba has achieved agrarian rationalization, while Brazil has only rationalized about its agricultural dilemmas.

The pathological condemnation of every revolutionary movement as a communist or communist-dominated movement quite misses the point. The point is that the historical inspiration for revolution in Brazil (as in its *origins* it was for Cuba) is the French Revolution of 1789 and not the Russian Revolution of 1917; more bluntly, it is the "bourgeois" tradition and not the "proletarian" tradition which feeds the flames of revolt. As former President Jânio Quadros so clearly put matters in his outline of *Brazil's New Foreign Policy*:

The attraction exerted by the Communist world, by Communist techniques and by the spirit of Communist organizations upon the countries but recently freed from the capitalist yoke is common knowledge. Generally speaking, all underdeveloped countries, including those of Latin America, are susceptible to that appeal. It must not be forgotten that whereas the independence of the Latin American nations was inspired by a liberation movement rooted in the French Revolution, the autonomy obtained by the new Asian and African nations was preceded by a wave of hope aroused by the socialist revolution in Russia among the oppressed classes and peoples all over the world.

Thus any trends in Brazil toward the communist-bloc nations will reflect more on the failure of nerve of traditional western conceptions of revolutionary democracy than upon the inherent necessity of communist victories in Latin America. It is within a highly flexible and fluid frame of reference that the peasant movement of Francisco Julião must be placed, a fluidity which reflects the ideological competition between two styles of making revolutions, the liberalist and the socialist. To rest content with a demonstration of the communistic nature of Julião's peasant movement, and to make any serious options inoperative through intransigent opposition to confiscation and to revolution in general, do little but aggravate present tensions with Brazil.

Julião has much in common with Castro: revolutionary fervor with a heavy dosage of naïve romanticism; direct appeals to the peasantry coupled with patriotic and nationalistic gore. With Julião as with Castro we are faced with a revolutionary leader not of our choosing, and not limited to the United States-sponsored alliances for progress. In Brazil the social and political pressures arising from discontent with the large landholding pattern, with the system of latifundias, are reaching an explosive point. Once more the United States is in the position of either joining or struggling against the "rising tide of revolutionary expectations." The monumental size and importance of Brazil make the study of Julião and his Peasant Leagues of Pernambuco the first order of hemispheric business. To condemn Julião's movement as communistic is only to insure a Soviet victory where none need take place. Julião's "politics" are frightening and extreme. But conditions in Northeast Brazil are more frightening and more extreme.

The "writings" of Francisco Julião, directed as they are to Brazilians of the northeastern part of the country, can be considered of "provincial" interest only by those with an ethnocentric attachment to institutionalized politics. Indeed, Julião's style strongly reminds one of those peasant qualities—directness and bluntness—found in the poetry of the Frenchman, Charles Péguy, and in the early prose of John Steinbeck. Julião's prose bears the stamp of oratory. It is not the circumscribed and judicious statement of the scholar, nor the sifted economy of poetic love of language. For many it has a simple and broadly romantic appeal. Julião is frankly a propagandist, albeit a unique one: he is not really educating his audience or organizing a bureaucratic machine, so much as moving them to an articulation of their grievances and also to a commensurate form of action. His language is limited for the sake of the illiterate peasant, but perhaps there is an unconscious attempt to invoke the *mystique* of language, the repetition of words to build a genuinely religious sense of collective solidarity. In short, Julião is a speaker who is writing, and not a writer speaking. But the message Julião delivers to the *Camponesas* of Pernambuco has become the common, irreducible, and subversive demand of "underdeveloped" nations everywhere: land redistribution, an end to feudal social relations, mechanization of agriculture, a voice for the peasants in the councils of the mighty, and political and juridical equality. These are not jealous and selfish demands for "consumer affluence" but basic social demands by which we have come to differentiate the democratic from the totalitarian tradition.

One might imagine that the cry for agrarian reform through land redistribution has by this time become a commonplace, if not a platitude. However, in Brazil, where the intellectual tradition is a conservative one, the custom has been to celebrate the plantation system, or at least to present it as if it were the essence of Brazilian cultural achievement. Even an authority like Gilberto Freyre, in *The Masters and the Slaves*, tends to wax rhapsodic in discussing the plantation and the latifundia: in short, the feudal inheritance.

The social history of the plantation manor house is the intimate history of practically everything Brazilian: of its domestic, conjugal life, under a polygamous and slave-holding regime; of the life of the child; of its Christianity reduced to a family religion and influenced by the superstitions of the slave quarters. The study of the intimate history of a people contains something of a Proustian introspection. It is as if one were meeting oneself. . . . It is in the plantation manor house that Brazilian Character achieved its best expression down to our days: our social continuity is in its story. In this story the political and military part is minimized, and instead of the striking things it offers us, we are given the routine of life; but it is in routine that one can best feel the character of a people.

Against this sophistication of Proust's continuities of mind, Julião proposes the bluntness of Péguy's discontinuities of flesh. Against the Brazilian "character" Julião poses the Brazilian "catastrophe." Against the calm equanimity of reasoned intellect, we are offered the angry shouts of sensate empiricism.

Governments come and go, the Colonial epoch went, the Empire fell, the Republic came improving the condition of all, but only worsening the peasants' condition. So far the peasant knows as his companions hunger, misery, nakedness, slavery and death. Patriotism, loyalty to the country, is for him an immense sugar refinery where he moans like the slave. . . . Between himself and liberty, which is his dream, there is a dragon: the latifundia. That dragon kills hunger with its flesh and thirst with its blood. For him there is nothing. No shelter. No bread. No medicine. No schools. No happiness. No peace. Nothing.

Julião's *Nirvana* comes up against Freyre's *Utopia*. It is not that one is right and the other wrong. Both are "right," but for different people. And it is precisely the question of social privilege, of rank, of interests, that forms the hub and the thrust of Julião's peasant ideology. It will be remembered that once books were written about the Chinese as if they lived in a collective rose garden in which calm, serenity, and the capacity to suffer were universal characteristics. In this "China of the Western world," as Freyre describes Brazil, it is little wonder that the same stereotyped characterizations are made about the Portuguese penchant for compromise. But it would be foolish to expect such designations to survive the present nostalgia-dominated ideology of the Brazilian *pensadores*.

Julião undoubtedly shares Freyre's estimate of Brazil as a "tropical China." At least the persistent reports of the circulation of Chinese communist literature among the members of the *Ligas Camponesas* (Peasant Leagues) would indicate an ideological common ground. Mao Tse-tung's essay on guerrilla tactics receives wide circulation throughout the Northeast. The pamphlet, printed in China, in a Portuguese version, also includes instructions for agitation by rural populations led by peasant leaders. Conservative Recife newspapers attempted to establish a direct line between the ideologies of Mao and Julião. And while this elicited a denial by Julião that his *Ligas* were responsible for distributing the pamphlet, he made no attempt to dissociate himself from the ideas therein expressed. Clearly he could not. The ideological road from Yenan, where the Chinese Revolution began to take shape, to Recife is circuitous but continuous. Julião himself dates his movement back to the peasant leagues of fifteenth- and sixteenth-century Germany—or at least to Engels' vision of the German peasant wars.

Francisco "Junior" Julião and his Peasant Leagues have come to signify for a militant sector of the Brazilian peasantry what Ahmed Ben Bella is for Algeria, what Kwame Nkrumah is for Ghana, and, it must be flatly stated, what Fidel Castro is for Cuba and Mao is for China. He is the "third force." He represents the outsider to modern industrial society—the peasant. He is neither a captive of conventional "bourgeois" politics nor an agent of "proletarian" anti-politics. He is neither "capitalist" nor "communist" in his ideology. He is the marginal "transitional" man, a generation removed from feudal beliefs and obligations.

Julião, his poetic bombast aside, is nonetheless an authentic voice of an authentic agony. And for reasons of authenticity he is revolutionary in a more menacing way than conventional Latin American "radical" politicians. The latter have, it must be frankly admitted, found their niche in the paternalistic power spectrum. Whatever the historical reasons, radical parties (including communists and socialists) have been singularly impotent in their efforts to organize and recruit the Brazilian peasant to revolutionary causes. Conventional radical parties are linked to factory workers, are based in the cities, and often relate national policies to world-wide goals. Julião's successes are in considerable measure a consequence of turning each of these propositions upside down. His Leagues are linked to the poor peasants, are based in agricultural areas, and have no organic connection to international political movements. Precisely his success at a regional level may mitigate against his ever becoming a truly national leader of Brazil. However, his comments are not the rhetoric of revolution, but the reason for revolution.

As all geography textbooks remind us: Brazil is a nation of immense size, large-scale untapped resources, and big commercial cities. Brazil is also a country exhibiting certain classic features of development common to Latin America: extreme gaps between poverty and wealth, overdeveloped coastal areas and underdeveloped interior portions, a small governing elite and a huge *homo economicus* having nothing to do with or to say about politics. Julião comes from that part of Brazil usually described in these geography books as "full of potential." He comes from Recife, the capital city of the northeastern provinces. In this sector of Brazil Julião makes his home. Here, gaping poverty is a fact. Here, one out of two children is deprived of formal education. Here, earning power, the wages of the laborer, is *sixteen times less* than in the southern and central coastal regions of Brazil (none too high even in these "prosperous" sections when compared to United States earning standards). In the North the peasants live in mud huts called *mocambos* and scarcely dream of seeing, much less working, in the imposing administrative buildings of Brasília designed by the brilliant Oscar Niemeyer. In this area the illiteracy rate reaches 70% of the total population in contrast to the 15% of the southern regions of the country. Here, in Pernambuco and Piaui, infant mortality reaches the incredible rate of 50-60%. Here, tuberculosis, the poor man's disease, infects 31% of the population. The majority of Brazil's 70 million people, and nearly all of the peasants in the drought-stricken northeastern region, live on a subsistence diet. The nationwide average daily caloric intake is only 2,150 compared to the 3000-3800 recommended by nutritionists for active persons. Deficiencies of protein, calcium, vitamins, and other elements are serious. There is little variety in diet. There is simply not enough cultivated land in economic units to permit even independent small farmers to live any better than marginally. And with the resistance of latifundists to the cultivation of present unused land, such as *Campos Cerrados* in the Northeast, it is not an exaggeration to say that the alternative to radical social change is slow starvation or, for the fortunate peasant, migration. This is the dismal data which adds up to one word, "feudalism." And feudalism is a chronic social ailment in a nation striving to break the mold long established by latifundists and peasants.

These facts have a fascination and a drama all of their own, especially since they automatically become a basis for comparisons with other parts of the world. The illiteracy rate among the peasantry in Julião's world is estimated to be 90%. Needless to add, this means that the voting franchise is severely curtailed, confined in the main to the latifundists, civil servants, bureaucrats, and other professional groups of the area. Of the 42 million Brazilians connected to agricultural production, 150,000 own three-quarters of the arable land. And in the Northeast, 2% of the proprietors own 50% of the arable land. Every fact of life underscores the reality of extreme poverty and, no less, extreme wealth. This duality of wealth and power is the essence of underdevelopment. Out of this crucible the poverty of culture, no less than the culture of poverty, is formed.

The huge masses that work in the fields and constitute the major portion of the Brazilian population derive no appreciable benefit from industrial development. The peasantry see their standard of living reduced in comparison with that in sectors occupied in commerce and trade. The industrial force represents a kind of

middle class within Brazilian society. It grows numerically in relative terms, but does not appreciably improve the standard of living of the population in general. Industrialism has opened a still
wider gap between city workers and farm workers. As Celso
Furtado indicates in his study of *The Brazilian Pre-Revolution*:

> It is not only in the concentration of income that economic develop-
> ment has produced social results of an extremely negative character.
> Because of the anachronistic structure of Brazilian agriculture, it has
> led in many regions to a relative increase in the rent from land, thus
> rewarding parasitic groups. Similarly, in the absence of a conscious
> policy designed to further the social purposes of state action, a variety
> of subsidies have been improvised, which—in the name of development
> —have very often put a premium on investments which either were
> superfluous or fostered a still greater concentration of income in the
> hands of privileged groups. Through capital contributions, such as
> subsidized exchange and credit, large amounts of social wealth have
> been transferred to a few hands.

Historical models and explanations aside, what is ineluctably
clear is that the rural peasantry of northern Brazil is being subjected to an economic form of mass extinction. The importance
of the Peasant Leagues must be measured against this situation:
either semi-feudal relations will be erased peacefully or swept
away by violence, but a halt must be called. A people facing extinction cannot be asked to have patience while the nuances of
world geopolitics are explained to them. The rhetoric of democracy is less important than some concrete redefinition of democracy in terms of food consumed, money earned, land parceled,
justice rendered. The situation can hardly remain constant. Despite the Portuguese inheritance of moderation and the feudal
inheritance of service to the masters, the men who succeed Julião
will tend to have progressively less of the Gandhian element in
their movement and, correspondingly, will display a good deal
more violence in asserting their claims. Those who choose to
ignore the Peasant Leagues, or declare them to be part of an international communist conspiracy, shall only receive the bitter consequences of this sort of self-fulfilling prophecy. For precisely
through such pious declarations against the agrarian reform movement in Brazil will these Leagues become more insistent, more
demanding, and more strident in connecting the existence of

latifundias in Brazil to corporate interests abroad which seek to maintain a single-crop situation.

Francisco Julião is a short, wiry man of forty-seven, who is becoming a trifle stocky with age. He was born of a family of small tenant farmers, with an earning power that was slightly better than average. He went to the University of Recife, where he pursued a career in law. After graduating in 1940, he proceeded to serve peasant interests in legal cases involving land tenure and land distribution. It was during this maturation period in the forties that Julião arrived at the formulation of his basic political tenets: *there can be no transformation in the living standards of the Brazilian peasants without a corresponding political change-over.* And latterly, *there can be no authentic political transformation without the active pressure and participation of the Brazilian peasantry.*

Julião proceeded to act on both of these premises in his personal career. After World War II, with the downfall of Getulio Vargas' first regime, and the consequent multiplication of political parties and the re-establishment of parliamentary norms, Julião became affiliated with the Brazilian Socialist Party (PSB). Today, he represents his party in the legislative assembly, and also occupies a place as secretary-general of the Pernambuco section of the party. Julião also serves as a member of the national directorate of the party—that branch connected with the formulation of programs of political action. After electoral defeats in 1945 and again in 1950, he finally succeeded in 1954 and also in 1958 in gaining sufficient electoral support from the "literate elements" in Recife and the surrounding provinces to be elected to the Brazilian Congress. With the victory in 1962 of Julião's ally, Miguel Arrais, as governor of the State of Pernambuco, the political strength of Julião in the North increased considerably.

The other "side" of Julião—indeed, what stamps him as a unique political figure in Brazilian political history—is his direct activity among the peasantry of the region. He continues to spend all of his free time—holidays, weekends, periods in which Parliament is not in session—living among the peasantry. Learning their ways, their problems, and their limitations, he absorbed the traditional virtue of peasants everywhere—patience. He has adopted the customs and mores of the area's people, and he speaks in the simple language of the peasant. He has also learned to avoid the pitfalls of the would-be reformer in certain respects: the glad hand and the easy smile of most politicians, and the vague promises of reform that mean nothing in either the long or the short run. In brief, Julião became re-educated to the consciousness of peasant existence. In part, this has served to strengthen Julião's political position in Brasilia. He has created a political substratum which serves both as an electorate and as a shield for his own political future.

He works tirelessly among the suspicious peasants, defending them in court actions, curbing the violence of hired overseers, cutting the red tape of their indemnification procedure which makes land redistribution in Brazil virtually impossible. However, as legally oriented as Julião is, he has been forced to the opinion that juridical iniquity itself would have to be changed if any wholesale breakthrough in the situation were to be effected. Julião has increasingly redirected his energies to mass politics: working to convince the peasants that the law, however favorable to the latifundists, could indeed be changed in their favor; that, in fact, such change would have to be provoked if the peasant was to escape his "eternal fate." Julião had first to overcome the peasant's ingrained fear of the law, and this was a complicated struggle, not only in itself, but because higher authorities tended to reinforce passivity by assuring the peasant that salvation was a matter of faith and not law, of the next world and not this one. The threat of eternal damnation and mortal sin hung heavily over those peasants, deeply religious as they are, who sought to take a more positive attitude toward social and political change.

The first League of Peasants was formed by Julião in Vitória de Santo Antônio, near Recife, in 1954. The success of these Leagues is demonstrated by the fact that by May 1958 Julião's Leagues could claim 3000 hard-core followers, who represented perhaps 50,000 peasants. By 1960 the figure rose to between 8000–10,000 activists, who probably represent five to ten times their number. The political possibilities of these Leagues were shown in the presidential elections of 1960, in which the defeated candidate (supported by Julião because he promised the abolition of literacy tests) Marshal Teixeira Lott did as well in the Northeast as the victorious candidate Jânio Quadros, despite the basic disenfranchisement of the peasantry and the overwhelming popularity of

Jânio Quadros. The Leagues have become a potent pressure group, influencing wide sectors of public opinion in northern Brazil—whether or not this public is affiliated with the Leagues. It was at this time that Julião first came into national prominence.

The three forms of action instituted by Julião's Leagues are: (a) the unification and politicalization of the peasantry against the feudal system of land tenure; (b) the enactment of appropriate legislation to protect the peasantry; and (c) the most difficult of all, the development of an agrarian reform movement, involving the basic reorganization of economic power in the North—breaking the power of the landed oligarchy. Julião's Leagues are basically economic in content and intent. Politics is viewed simply as *one* possible agency of social change.

The differences between Julião's Peasant Leagues and the communist-sponsored Union of Agrarian Workers in Brazil (ULTAB) run deep on matters of both ideology and strategy, although it must be added that Julião has never repudiated assistance from any quarter—be it communist or nationalist. For Julião, sociological and political *development* is not equivalent to physical or chemical *law*. They do not have the same measure of universality. Under laboratory conditions, the same approach (socialism) and the same forms of political organization should result in the same consequences in Russia, China, Cuba, Algeria, and Brazil. But this has not been the case. The results have pointed toward a "polycentric" communism in China, a technological communism in Russia, reformist communism in Eastern Europe, etc. "The people are not laboratories. The road of each depends upon its unique national conditions," says Julião. An ideological orientation which asserts the "vanguard" role of the factory proletariat may be doctrine in Czechoslovakia but dogma in Brazil and in other underdeveloped regions of Latin America. The strategic difficulty of a dogma is that it generally immobilizes radical responses by strait-jacketing them into stereotypes. In Cuba, the *Fidelistas* were at first considered "revolutionary romantics" by communist officials. In China, Mao Tse-tung's revolution proceeded essentially without the support of the Soviet Union, and in Brazil, Julião's Peasant Leagues are termed "utopian" by the communists.

Although American journalism tends to consider almost all popular movements "communist" in inspiration and organization, a closer look reveals the sharpest sort of differences—at least in political origins. External pressures tend to have an effect of unifying polyglot socialist movements; but if left to operate without interference, their differences assert themselves. For Julião, the Leagues are open to all equally, as a matter of principle. Nonetheless, the core of the Leagues remains the peasants. And all propaganda is aimed at welding together this uneducated, unwieldy, and superstitious mass of Brazilian humanity. Julião is firmly convinced that the aims of the Leagues must be pursued through all available political channels—from extreme right to extreme left. In this way, the Leagues function in a manner not unlike an American-style trade union. Their immediate purpose is to exert pressure for concrete economic and political goals on a wide-ranging set of social issues.

The socialist-dominated Leagues of Julião, in addition to competing with the communist-dominated Leagues in ULTAB, face an even more bitter contest for peasant loyalties with the Catholic League. Among the last comments of Pope John was an exclamation "on the great work to be done in Latin America." And one of the initial public releases of the newly elected Pope Paul was to spell out the character of this work.

The memory comes to our mind of the greatest cities in Brazil—Rio de Janeiro and São Paulo—which we visited personally three years ago. It fills our heart with bitterness, with anxiety and with lively preoccupation and recalls the sweet lament of our Lord: "The harvest is great, but the laborers are few."

In a recent comment (1963) before a seminar at the Pontifical Catholic University, one of the most effective "laborers," Bishop José Távora of Aracaju, insists that Brazil must recognize the justice of demands by farm hands for an equitable wage which would permit a decent standard of living. He added that the time also had come when owners of the huge sugar plantations must cease exploiting the field workers by declaring their inability to pay the minimum wage required by law. Most interesting of all were the words which Bishop Távora reserved for his fellow clergymen.

It is not only the rich who must dispose of some of their luxuries, but also the clergy, which must adopt itself to the social and economic conditions of the country, using wooden crosses instead of golden crosses, with simple chains to hold them, and dressing modestly.

The Church, traditionally less influential in the lives of the Brazilians than anywhere else in Latin America (with the possible exception of Uruguay), is seeking to rectify this by playing an intensive role as the key agency of social justice in Northeastern Brazil. However, such Catholic spokesmen of the poor as Padre Mello in Cabo, Pernambuco, Bishop Eliseu Simões Mendes in the Paraná region, and others represent a form of organization which, however radical its present posture, holds out little hope of any immediate rapprochement with the Leagues of Julião. This helps to explain Julião's bitter denunciation of the "false Christianity" that has reinforced conventional modes of regional and national exploitation. The Christian mission is to seek some sort of "new deal" parity between the peasant and the latifundist. The collectivist mission is in search of nothing short of political victory of the peasant over his adversary.

Nonetheless, Julião's respect for Catholic organization and ideology, as well as his shrewd political sense, has led him to manipulate Christian symbols alongside the more profane slogans of the nationalist and socialist movements. It would be absurd on this ground to claim that Julião, in his bid for wider support, is simply a political careerist. Politics remains, in Brazil as anywhere else, the art of the possible—for Senator Francisco Julião no less than for Bishop José Távora. The fact that Julião has called attention to the plight of the Brazilian peasantry, and elicited a dynamic reaction on the part of communists, Catholics, and government experts, is ample proof, if any is needed, of the vital role being performed by Julião and his co-organizers. But it also calls attention to an apocalyptic and utopian dimension to his movement.

Important elements in the Julião movement are the millennial and messianic features characteristic of the history of the Brazilian Northeast. From the Tupi-Guarani Indians in the pre-Christian era, to Father Cicero's movement in the Christian era, the longing for utopia has been a powerful factor both in generating interest in political salvation and, through the "safety-valve" device, in draining off political strivings into religious or pseudo-religious channels. Thus, what René Ribeiro writes of *Brazilian Messianic*

Movements in general is particularly apt in explaining the utopistic character of Julião's Peasant Leagues.

Three hypotheses may be considered compatible with the Brazilian evidence. In the first place a traditional belief in an unstable world order and in a Land without Evil that can be reached by courageous mortals who will first purify themselves through ritual will tend to give rise to such movements. Secondly, a situation of social constraint forcing the collapse of cultural values may incite people to recall their legendary fantasies. Finally, social and cultural isolation and sluggishness may create an ideal climate for the reception of apocalyptic teaching. The fundamental motivations for the individual to join a messianic movement seem to derive from two kinds of dissatisfaction. He may be dissatisfied with the current social, economic, or political order, or with the rewards of institutionalized religion. In either case a desire for change may be aroused, and hope for the realization of familiar apocalyptic fantasies may then flare up.

Whatever the causal bases or historical antecedents for Julião's movement, it remains a fact that he is responding to very real, and not just imaginary, deficiencies in the feudal society of the Brazilian Northeast. The real question, and one which can scarcely be answered at the present juncture, is whether the solutions posited are truly political or apocalyptic. The ambivalence of themes in Julião's exhortations, the constant shifting about from economic to religious metaphors, suggests that Julião himself is not exactly clear as to the functional and ideological character of his movement.

A subtle but quite real difference between Julião's Leagues and the political parties of Brazil is that immediate gains registered by the peasantry are not viewed by Julião as part of a long-range blueprint for political revolution (or as a scheme for advancing the leader's career). Julião is essentially a political pragmatist, not a Marxist. He does not see the emancipation of the peasant as depending on a wider revolutionary movement. On the contrary, he sees the wider revolutionary movement as meaningful only insofar as it promotes the interests of the peasantry—and even his definition of the peasantry is pragmatic, that is, it includes all who own up to one hundred hectares of land no less than sharecroppers, peons, and tenant farmers. As such the "peasant revolution" exhibits a classical narrowness of intellectual vision and political organization that historically characterizes agricultural economies. There is, in addition to the pragmatic quality of Julião's thinking, a strong undercurrent of the politics of non-violent resistance, a tactical pacifism not far removed in tone or temper from Gandhism (despite the fact that Julião prefers to think of himself in terms of the Chinese Revolution rather than the Indian Revolution). Given the essential divisions among the Brazilian peasantry in relation to the land and hence in ideology, their organization against the latifundists, the state, and the law seeks as much as possible to operate within the confines of each: latifundists will be invited to Peasant League meetings; peasants will be told how important it is to participate in the activities of the state, and also instructed on how to use existing statutes to their own advantage or promote such statutes where none exists. The attitude of Julião toward "direct action" is now being framed in terms of non-violent resistance rather than pressing for armed rebellion. He tends to see violence as the exclusive weapon of the latifundists and their private police force. And he sees in their violence a boomerang effect. While striking fear and terror into the heart of the peasant, violence has the long-range effect of crystallizing more effective resistance. Strong proof of Julião's antipathy for maneuvering within major political party structures was demonstrated by his complete avoidance of entangling the Leagues in the civilian-military crisis that has plagued Brazil since the abdication of Quadros.

This combination of pragmatic shrewdness and pacifist strategy has not preserved either Julião or the Leagues from charges of being a communist front or, more damaging to his cause, of being anti-Christ and irreligious. In an area of intense religious loyalty, Julião has had to spend much of his time convincing the peasants that the Testaments are documents of social justice. The truth is that much religious opposition to his Leagues is politically inspired and is not founded on matters of faith. Julião's remarks strike a primitive note. His comments on religion are scarcely illustrative of higher Biblical criticism. Nonetheless, he is addressing himself to a situation in which his religious opponents are not exactly at the analytical level of a Karl Barth or a Reinhold Niebuhr, and some of whom, in the form of the Catholic Peasant Leagues, represent direct political competition to his leadership.

The appeal to social justice via religion and the economic aims of the Leagues are but two ingredients of the practical effort to keep the organization an independent and yet changing force. We must note that Julião's pacifism seems more a matter of strategy than of principles. He increasingly reveals a disillusionment with the ballot box, the latifundists' law, etc. Pressure for social change, coming as it must in devious or non-legal ways, may yield an ambivalence toward bearing arms. Feeling closer to Chinese communism than to Indian socialism on the one hand, and having to produce results like any self-appointed "people's leader" on the other, he may come to put increasing reliance on violent measures. To avoid this Julião would have to win a stupendous numerical force among the peasantry, which seems unlikely, or enter coalition politics, which up to now he has sought to avoid. His commitments are to agrarian reform, political enfranchisement of the peasantry, liquidation of illiteracy—but not to a doctrinal pacifism. The political climate around him, rather than philosophic principles within him, is likely to prove the ultimate determining factor in the question of continued non-violent action. Peasant weapons are indeed silent; but they do in fact exist.

Julião and the other Peasant Leagues confront Brazilian politics with an explosive force. The challenge is first to the traditional disparity between political rhetoric and economic fact in Brazil. Second, it is a challenge from the underdeveloped Brazilian countryside to the developed and relatively affluent urbanized portions of the country. Third, it is an open competition for power between the agricultural North and the industrial South. And lastly, the Julião movement compels the Brazilian middle and industrial classes to make a declaration of intentions with regard to the other main sectors: the landed oligarchy on top and the peasants of the lower depths.

The traditional "united front" of Brazil's ruling classes is being severely tried and tested by the new elites. The growing nationalism of the Brazilian middle classes and their declaration of independence from aristocratic domination contribute to the political maneuverability of the peasant agrarian movement. On the other hand, the entire political equilibrium of Brazil rests on the "great compromise" effected by the bourgeoisie and the latifundists after the collapse of the Vargas dictatorship. The risks are great. The Peasant Leagues may indeed turn out to be uncontrollable as a social force.

On further consideration, the peasant situation leaves few options. The Brazilian working classes and lower middle classes are in the grip of a seemingly endless inflationary spiral, which has seen the cruzeiro climb from 330 to the U.S. dollar in May 1962 to 840 to the U.S. dollar in December 1962. And inflation claims as its chief victims the lower sectors of an underdeveloped economy. The financial crisis has compounded the intense political instability. The compromise worked out between civilian and military leaders after Jânio Quadros' renunciation of presidential power has proved untenable. Goulart needs allies. Conservative politicians like Lacerda and others from the prosperous southern regions will not give him much aid and comfort. Nor can an intransigent Congress, heavily conservative, beholden to and representing landholding interests, be browbeaten into radical decisions. Thus, Goulart's power must increasingly come to rest on an industrial working-class base (which is relatively small) and the agricultural class (which is very large) if indeed it is to rest rather than tumble in the face of a right-wing *coup d'état.*

The position taken by the peasant leadership appears to be that the present Brazilian political trend toward "presidentialism" will redound to the benefit of the peasants if they can assert their economic demands effectively and gain cohesiveness as a social force. If the Leagues are stymied, if Goulart instead chooses to ignore the peasant question, the "golden opportunity" of the present crisis might well be missed once again. What Brazil needs is not the printing of more money but the redistribution of real wealth. It is for Goulart to calculate which approach carries the greatest risks: support for the urbanized middle sectors and the labor aristocracy, or for the landless and voteless peasant.

Whatever the outcome of the immediate crisis, Julião's political ideology represents a rise to consciousness of the huge peasant sector of Brazilian society. He has given to the peasantry a self-consciousness of both present misery and future destiny. It is unlikely that they will be willing to wait another three hundred years for social change. This consciousness of self which the vibrant Julião has helped to provide will increasingly prove to be a factor of major importance in the forging of the Brazilian nation.

A central problem faced by the various types of radical peasant organizations is the form of alignment, the kind of association they are to have in relation to the growing crisis in international communism. Has the peasant revolution the capacity to transform itself into a socialist revolution? How deeply involved should a "regional" political movement become in "national" (or even "international") affairs? Should a Latin American or a Brazilian posture be adopted in terms of policy questions? In the search for historic "models," should the Brazilian revolutionary movement be tied to China, to Russia, to India, or forge its own models? Up to now, peasant revolutionaries have not had to face such questions because of the parochial regionalism of Julião's movement. But with an expansion of power one can anticipate a widening of vision. They will obviously be required to come to grips with the internal effects of world communism, third-force politics, relations with the United States, attitudes toward nuclear armaments, etc., if any of the peasant groups hope for nationwide success. Furtado has put the matter clearly:

Let us now squarely face the Brazilian problem. In the light of historical experience it isn't difficult to explain because the peasant class in Brazil is much more susceptible to revolutionary techniques of the Marxist-Leninist type than the working class, although from the point of view of the orthodox Marxist it is ultimately required that one be in the vanguard of the revolutionary movement.

It is that ours is an open society for the working class but not for the peasant. Indeed, our political system allows the working class to organize to bring about, within the rules of the democratic game, its recovery. Nevertheless, the situation of the peasants is completely different. Since they possess no rights they cannot have legal recourse. If they organize it is assumed that has to do with subversive ends. The necessary conclusion that we must come to is that Brazilian society is in great part rigid: that part composed of the rural sector. And with respect to that portion the thesis is valid that Marxist-Leninist revolutionary techniques are effective.

We come thus to a conclusion of extraordinary importance for us: the existence of a duality in the Brazilian revolutionary process. To the degree that we live in an open society, the attainment of the highest social objectives tends to assume the form of successive approximations. To the degree that we live in a rigid society, those objectives will tend to be reached through a cataclysmic rupture.

A kindred problem is the posture to be taken in relation to the United States. Castro's approach was to make as complete and rapid a break as possible with traditional economic and geopolitical interests of the United States. The successes of the Cuban Revolution became measured in terms of the relative absence of American domination. Against the forces of the United States and its "allies" in Latin American governing elites, Castro posed the "needs" of the peoples of Latin America and their shared sentiments which favored the objectives of the Cuban Revolution over those of the traditional classes who maintained power by coercion and compromise. Thus, Castro has in the main pursued an "international" course, relying heavily on political movement throughout the hemisphere as well as upon Soviet might. Julião, for his part, gives every indication of steering a "nationalist" course, which can signal either a less bellicose attitude toward United States' area interests or a conviction that consideration of foreign interests is largely irrelevant.

Given the size and power of Brazil, and respecting its capacity for almost infinite development in both agricultural and industrial sectors, the likelihood is that national communism rather than international communism will be Julião's *modus operandi*. This is a highly tentative conclusion. It should be remembered that Castro has political power while Julião does not; that Castro is a self-declared Marxist while Julião is not. Nevertheless, the success of the peasant revolutions in China and in Cuba (whatever the post-revolutionary developments have turned out to be) provides an enormous impetus for Julião and other Peasant Leagues to try similar methods.

The Communist Party as such represents a fraction of Brazil's revolutionary potential. And it may even turn out to represent a *faction* of that revolution. The potential for revolutionary action should not be equated to the actual size (or lack of it) of the communist movement. It might well be that as the Soviet-oriented Communist Party of Brazil weakens, and as the schisms of the international communist movement become more apparent, revolutionary forces in Brazil will become stronger. It would be foolish and dangerous to dismiss the potential for revolution by Julião and his movement. In practice and in theory his forces are independent and untrammeled agencies for social revolution. It may well be that as the communists sat in Havana deriding the "revolutionary romanticism" of Castro and his military band, the communists may sit out the revolution in São Paulo and Rio de Janeiro deriding the "revolutionary romanticism" of the man from Recife. In short, present *ideological* divisions and splits within the world communist movement may prove an advantage and not a deficit to Julião's social revolutionary movement.

Julião's messages to the peasantry show a certain development, or at least a changing orientation. In 1960 Julião was still focusing his exclusive attention on the relationship between the peasantry and the latifundists of Northern Brazil. By 1961 this struggle was telescoped in the larger conflict between the Brazilian ruling classes and all other sections of the people—of which the peasantry was the most central force but, nonetheless, not the exclusive force. By 1962 Julião had enlarged the context of the dialogue to include the struggle between "imperialism" and "national interests." This is indicated by his choice of April 21, the Day of Tiradentes (hero of an abortive revolutionary independence movement), for a speech not specifically addressed to the Peasant Leagues. Whether this reflects Julião's increasing faith in orthodox Marxist formulas or is simply a response to his expanding sense of being a national rather than a sectional leader is hard to determine. All that can be asserted with any certainty is that Julião, in the process of awakening the consciousness of the peasantry of northeastern Brazil, has himself acquired a consciousness of national perspective and proportion.

What this signifies on the plane of political action is yet another matter. It is now clear that Julião sees his Peasant Leagues as one form among many. And again, while they prove a vital agency of change, he is undoubtedly rethinking his strategies before engaging in any precipitous actions. Should his Leagues be reconstituted, along with other Leagues, into a new political party? Should they be merged into existing political parties? Should "united front" tactics be adopted? Under what conditions should political coalitions be formed? Would coalition politics with an industrial proletariat have a boomerang effect? Would it estrange the peasantry from action? These are the sort of questions that must be raised, and in part settled, if Julião is to become a successful *national* figure and not simply a convenient tool for the Brazilian government to use for bludgeoning or blackmailing support from the Western-bloc nations.

The United States is once more presented with a choice: to support the general needs and drives of a legitimate social movement or face the wrath of a ravaged people. The necessity for such a choice is immediate. Whether the United States claims 42 million Brazilian peasants as "friends" or "enemies" is a decision we must make today. The postponement of an answer will be received as a categorical "no." The political consolidation of "Jango" Goulart's government, the rise of his personal power, and his moves in the direction of vast agricultural reform provide the United States with an immense opportunity to make the Alliance for Progress live up to its pledged support for land redistribution.

In the words of the former President of Brazil, Juscelino Kubitschek, the American response to Brazilian discontent has thus far been unrealistic. In a slashing attack before the Council of the Organization of American States made in June 1963, he noted that "there lies an almost frozen zone between President Kennedy's promises and the actual achievements of the Alliance . . ."

I am compelled to conclude, regretfully but firmly, that the Alliance for Progress during the first two years of its life has been far from meeting the ideals repeatedly proclaimed for it by the illustrious President Kennedy. I have observed that mistaken appraisals within certain circles of the North American administration with respect to other countries of the continent continue to make them shortsighted in vision and to influence their conduct. What is required is a revolution in the field of development.

In a sense, then, Julião is offering one type of response to this "frozen zone," one kind of impulse to "a revolution in the field of development." And through the innumerable, if thus far undisciplined and sporadic, series of peasant "invasions" of Brazil's latifundias and estates, the "message" of Julião is reaching policymaking echelons of Brazilian politics and economics.

III
THE PRACTICE AND
PREACHING OF REVOLUTION

. . . in which Francisco "Junior" Julião exhorts the peasants to
listen to the voice of revolution, explains the basic relationship
between latifundists and laborers, and hurls a challenge for true
Christians to join the revolution; this is followed by Celso Furtado's lecture before the students, examining the theoretical
dilemmas of European ideologies in solving the Brazilian land
problem, and calling for a revolutionary theory to match the
clear and present needs of the time.

Listen, Peasant
Francisco Julião *

I. LETTER FROM PERNAMBUCO (1960)

Peasant, I send you this communication. I have good news for
you. Your cruel enemy, the latifundia, is not in good health. And
I assure you that the disease is serious. It has no remedy. It will die
foaming at the mouth, like a dog carrying rabies. Or like an old
lion that lost his claws. It will die as it died in China, a country
very much like our Brazil. It will die as it was killed in Cuba,
where the great Fidel Castro gave every peasant a shotgun and
said: "Democracy is the government that arms the people." I was
there and I saw everything, peasants. In Cuba there is no more
cambão, nor *meia,* nor *têrça,* nor *vale-de-barracão,* nor *capanga.***

* Francisco Julião is the leader of Peasant Leagues in Pernambuco, and a
district leader of the Brazilian Socialist Party (PSB). For more information
see Chapter II.

** These terms are regional expressions of the Northeast. *Cambão* is the
day in the week that a peasant works for "free"; that is, his labor goes to
the landholder. *Meia* and *têrça* signify the amounts (one half and one third)
of the produce turned over by the peasant sharecropper to the landholder.
Vale-de-barracão is the privately issued "money" which is given by the latifundist and is good for purchase only at the "company-owned" stores. Thus,

On that liberated island nobody extracts profits from the plantation. Nor do they demolish peasant homes. Nor do they drive cattle into the tilled fields. Nor do they charge one hundred and fifty kilograms of cotton for a measure of land. There are no more ten- and twelve-hour working days like in Brazil. I was there and I saw everything clearly. The land now belongs to the man who works it and not to whoever makes use of it to enslave, the way things still happen here. Over there the fields that were old and sad are becoming new and gay. Everything has now become transformed into cooperatives. Every peasant owns a house made out of mortar and bricks. There is new furniture and even the statues of the saints are new. Women no longer give birth on straw mats or beds without mattresses but under sanitary conditions instead. The doctor lives in the countryside. They lack neither medicine nor schools nor seed for planting. Do you know, peasant, how this miracle came to pass?

This miracle was accomplished because of the unification of the peasant mass. They all united around Fidel Castro to break tyranny, injustice, the latifundia—with its private police force, its sharecropping system, meals of rotten sardines, migration, backwardness and misery. Hunger no longer sends children to the cemetery, nor the young girl to perdition, nor men to enslavement, nor the old to the door of the church or to railway stations, begging for God's mercy. It was unity which broke all of that in Cuba. And that is also the way it was in China. It will be that way too in Brazil. I tell you and repeat to you, peasant, as I have told you before: isolated you will be a drop of water; united you will be a waterfall. When you march alone your enemy mocks at your weakness, raises your rent, sends cattle into your food-growing areas, uproots your cultivated land, demolishes your hut, forces you to pay kickbacks or drives you from the land, crushes your rights and kills your liberty.

At the beginning of the voyage there were no roads. We had to open a pathway. Hard and painful. A soldier falling here; a little farther on another one running away. But today we can already speak of agrarian reform and of peasant organizations. Previously,

the landlords extract profits directly and also at the consumer end of the peasant life-cycle. A *capanga* is an armed bodyguard, privately hired. But in addition to guarding bodies, he performs directly terroristic acts on behalf of the landlords when such acts are called for. [ILH]

the latifundia did not tolerate this. The police prohibited associations. The Church was afraid. And reaction bellowed forth: "It is
communism." This word still frightens many people. It was used
against peace. And against petroleum nationalization. It is often
used, right now, against Fidel Castro and the Cuban people. I
remember well what a poor peasant told me four years ago. He
went to the home of a landowner, master of a great deal of land,
to invite him to be present at the founding of a new League of
Peasants. The landowner refused to go and told him: "That is
communism." The member of the association wanted to know
what kind of law that was. And the authority, rich with land,
gave this definition: "Communism is getting hold of what is not
yours, harming your own daughter, and prohibiting your own
religion." The member thought a little, and replied to the latifundist: "If that is so, that situation has existed ever since I have
become aware of myself as a person. See if I am right or not. The
poor man rents a piece of land, builds his home, fences himself in,
plants, takes ten, twenty, or thirty years taking care of the place,
paying rent and rendering *cambão*. All right. One day he discovers
that *cambão* is the remnant of slavery. Either he does not want to
pay the increase of rent because he can no longer tolerate conditions or he demands the wages due to starvation. Then the owner
of the land gets angry and expels him. The poor man resists. The
private army of the latifundist comes. The police come. Justice is
done. The poor man ends up losing everything. There is simply
no justice for the poor. The house is demolished. The plantation
is uprooted. The peasant is threatened with jail; that is, when he
is not murdered. He loses his job, his sweat, his peace, or even his
life. Could that be the rule of communism? If it is, we already
live under that rule for as long as I can remember. And it is against
that law that the peasant joins his brother and enters the League
of Peasants. Let us turn to another fact. The poor man has a beautiful daughter. The rich man likes her. He devours the hapless
creature. He throws her into perdition. He doesn't marry her because he is rich and she is poor. If the father turns to the authorities to ask for justice, he is expelled from the land. In the end he
always loses. Because he loses his temper he loses his daughter.
Apparently nobody takes charge of the matter. The trial, if there
is any, ends up in the archives, and the young girl in the street. If

that is the law of communism, the League of Peasants is against that law. We shall now look at the case of religion. A Protestant lives on the lands of a Catholic. It is enough that the Protestant tells the Catholic that he won't give him any more *cambão* for the Catholic to reply: 'I don't want you on my land any more.' From that moment on, it is the simplest thing to prevent a Protestant from practicing his faith. The opposite can happen too. The Protestant landowner can tell the Catholic: 'I do not want anyone here who worships graven images. Leave your parcel of land for a brother of my own faith.' Only because the Catholic refuses to pay the *cambão*. If that is the rule of communism then the League of Peasants is opposed to it. The League does not separate Catholic from Protestant. Both are brothers." So spoke the peasant who went to invite the latifundist to be present at the formation of a new League. This was four years ago.

Now the road is growing longer. Here, in Pernambuco, we have already won the battle of the Galilee Sugar Refinery. This was the work of the League. It was the fruit of unity. The League grows. Throughout Brazil, they are talking about our Peasant Leagues. And even outside of Brazil. When the League was born it was a candle. Now it is a star. In the past it was a drop. Today it is a river. It was a tree. Today it is a forest. The star is the guide of victory. The river is the road of liberty. The forest is the shelter of peace. Where the League plants its flag, hope is born and fear dies. Whoever thirsted for blood because of hatred begins to hunger for the land. It is hunger for the land and not bloodthirstiness that makes the League grow and gain in respect. While the League of Peasants grows, the latifundia loses its strength. And the agrarian reform movement takes shape. It is already in everyone's consciousness. You sleep thinking of it, peasant. And the latifundist does likewise. You know that it will come earlier if you join your brothers without delay. The latifundist also knows that it will come as it came to China, as it came to Cuba. It is best that it come without shedding blood. With churchbells ringing out joy. With a longer trail of flowers than that which accompanied the deputies when the law which ended slavery was approved in Brazil.

Agrarian reform can come through the ballot. But it is necessary that not only those who can read should be able to vote. The illiterate must also be enfranchised. In Brazil, almost all the peasants

are illiterate.* More than twenty million of them do not vote because they don't know how to read. But they pay taxes. And they
carry the country on their backs. Your battle, peasant, must be in
that context. You can be sure that the day the illiterate votes, enslavement of the land will end in this country. The latifundists will
lose their spurs. They will remain as tame as fat capons. Why?
Because the peasant being landless, the immense majority that does
not know how to read, that majority will only vote for candidates
who will engage in the fight for agrarian reform.

Do you know, peasant, that there already exists in Congress a
proposed constititutional amendment in favor of the vote for the
illiterate? Do you know that if you remain with your arms crossed
that this amendment will never be approved? It is an important
step to attain the vote for the illiterate. Go everywhere, peasant,
to convince your brother, your friend, and your countrymen that
they are in a position to vote and that they should vote. This
country shall never be a complete nation while there exists a peasant driven off the lands harvested by the usurer, who lends two
thousand for one hundred acres only, without land, without fertilizers, without seed, without agricultural machinery, without financial or technical assistance, and without price guarantees for
this production.

* The problem of illiteracy in Northeast Brazil is basic. The political consequences of disenfranchisement are matched by the economic consequences
of exploitation. Bernard L. Collier, in a series of articles entitled "Brazil—
Sick Giant," New York *Herald Tribune*, August 1963, reports on a sample
experiment in an average small town, Angicos (where water costs twenty
cents for five gallons, where dry spells may last for years, and where the illiteracy rate is over 80% of the population). The author, reporting on the
success of a small-scale literacy drive sponsored by the Alliance for Progress,
gives the following vivid picture: "The success of the education program is
not good news to everyone in Rio Grande do Norte. To the peasants who
can get better paying jobs it is a blessing, but to the landowners it is, as one
bluntly put it, 'a Communist curse.' Not long after the alphabetization team
left Angicos the town had its first strike on a public school construction job.
There was loud talk about 'subversion,' and the education program was
roundly accused of causing more trouble than good. When the government
investigated, however, it found that the workers had a legitimate complaint.
Wages long owed them had been embezzled by the construction boss. Said
one of the workers: 'Before we would never have had the nerve to complain.
We could never talk to any of the bosses because we felt so small. Now we
would talk to the President himself.'" Here we see illustrated the revolutionary potential of learning—its stimulus to social change. Although it
should be added that education does not produce any automatic radicalizing
effects. [ILH]

But even though the vote for the illiterate does not come, and agrarian reform is not achieved, you must avoid standing with folded arms. Miracles do not happen any more like in the age of Moses, who touched the rock and made water pour forth, or in the time of Jesus, who from one bread and one fish made many breads and many fish. Each one of us today has to win daily bread with the sweat of his own brow. This is how the Testament, which few people follow, commands us. If there are no longer any miracles because Moses passed on and, after him, Christ, you can, peasant, even crucified to the land like a slave, achieve anything you want, without depending on miracles. You can conquer liberty, have bread in abundance, live in peace and well-being, if you are able to join your landless brothers. No word has more strength than this: Unity. It is the mother of liberty. Learn how to defend your right at the side of your landless brother. Never stand alone. Always march with him, to the Court of Justice, since you are beside him at Church, at the party, at the funeral, at the market, and at work. Remember that if he is persecuted today and cannot count on your assistance, tomorrow, when misfortune befalls you through the latifundist's hatred, you will not be able to count on his help either. That has always been your downfall. To separate you, the latifundist always uses violence, cunning, and money. Let us consider violence. For this the *capanga* sends the police to your door. And justice. It is always better to deal with the law enforcement authorities. Once in a while a judge appears who rebels against the latifundists, even if he is a son, a son-in-law, or a friend of the landowner. He softens the rigors of the law because he sees in poverty an injustice. One cannot expect too much from justice when it says that there is no other path but compliance with the law. It is because the judge always accepts what is written. He does not rebel. He rests his conscience on the law. And he lives on that fact. What is the road? To change the law. And how can the law be changed? With the unity of all. With the movement of the mass. With pressure. That is why the League of Peasants exists. There must be unity for that. If the violence of the *capangas* and the oppression of the police do not vanquish you, if you have a ray of light in your conscience and are ready to die for your liberty, the latifundist will use the pretext of God. How? I will explain. The latifundist says the following: "God punishes whoever rebels against him. If one is rich and another is poor, if one owns land

and the other does not, if one must work with the spade in order to pay taxes and the other makes a living and enriches himself with the fruits of that tax, if one lives in a palace and the other in a hut, it is because God wills this. He who rebels against that rebels against God. He suffers punishment from the heavens above: pestilence, war, and hunger. And when he dies he goes to hell. The poor must be poor for the rich to be rich. The world was always that way. It is Providential Will." So speaks the latifundist, peasant. He uses the name of God to frighten you. Because you believe in God. But that God of the latifundists is not your God. Your God is as tame as a lamb. His name is Jesus Christ. He was born in a manger. He lived among the poor. He surrounded himself with fishermen, peasants, workers, and paupers. He wanted the liberation of all of them. He said that the land should belong to whoever works it. And that the fruit of it was common to all. These words are his: "It is easier for a camel to pass through the eye of a needle than for the rich man to get to heaven." Because he said this and other things he was crucified by the latifundists of his time; today he would be shot. If not locked away in an asylum for the insane or jailed as a communist. Listen well to what I tell you, peasant. If a priest or minister talks to you in the name of God who menaces you with pestilence, war, and hunger, lightning and thunder, and even with hell-fire, know that that priest or minister is a puppet of the latifundists. They are not ministers of God. The priest is false. That minister is no good. The real priest or the good minister is the one who rises up and says: "God made the earth for all. But the more brazen gained control of it. You will earn bread with the sweat of your brow and not with the sweat of another. No one should be enslaved by anyone else. Nor one people by another people. Nor one man by another man. Because men are all equal in the eyes of the law. And in the eyes of nature. And in the eyes of God. If this is communism then God is a communist. Because that is what the sacred texts say. Christ too. And all of his Apostles."

It is already time, peasant, that you should learn to utilize unity against your cruel enemy which is the latifundia. Follow the lesson of the worker. Of the student. What does the worker do to overcome the employer? What does the student do to defend liberties? He relies on the arm of the strike. The strike is the unity of all. It has the strength of the river's current. And the sound of the waterfall. The worker stops the factory and gains a better salary. The student closes the university and goes into the streets to proclaim liberty, peace, oil, free education. Use the strike like your arm. I will explain. There are many kinds of strikes which can be effected in the country. For instance: A latifundist demolishes a peasant's house and uproots his plantation. How should you proceed? It is simple. All the peasants must unite. One hundred, two hundred, one thousand, two thousand, three thousand. And march toward the city. Carrying the debris of the houses and uprooted plants. They go to the authorities. To the priest. To the judge. To the tax commissioner. To the police officer. To all they clamor for justice, together. And justice will be done. Why? Because those who are asking for it will be many. If it were one alone he would be sent to prison. Ten might not be heard. But one hundred will be. And one thousand even more so. The police officer becomes tame, the judge turns into silk. The priest receives them. Authority melts. Not to speak of the tax commissioner. It is not necessary to use the sickle. Nor the spade. It is the mass which makes the law. What governs is the unity of the people. I will show you another example. A police officer jails a peasant because he was pressured to leave his land and he did not want to obey. Then the League of Peasants calls for a meeting and tells everyone so that no one will go to the market in that city or town governed by that authority. The League erects barricades on every road to block the path of the peasants that might try to break the strike cordon. And the League becomes stronger. And the peasant respected. Without shedding even one drop of Christian blood. Learn how to use that powerful arm called the strike. The worker uses it already. So does the student. And our Constitution, which is called the Supreme Law, guarantees this right, without differentiating between the student and the worker, or between the worker and the peasant, because the Constitution itself says in one of its articles: "All are equal before the law." And what is the Constitution? It is the law that is born of the people. And the peasant is of the people, as is the worker, the student.

I do not want to end this communication, peasant, without an outcry in favor of your other brother, less fortunate than you who are a rentier, a sharecropper, or a farm laborer. I am talking about the peon, about the paid agricultural worker. It is he who endures the whole weight of the burden. He works from Sunday

to Sunday. He wears rags. His house has a roof made out of straw.
Walls made of mud. There is no front and there is no back. There
is no door. The table is the ground. The bed is made of sticks. He
does not save a penny because there is nothing left. When he sings
his song is sad. In the sugar refinery, the tea plantation, the rice
plantation, the cacao plantation, or the coffee plantation. In the
siringal. Like the song of the slave. If he falls sick he dies in hard-
ship, before his time. And if he reaches old age he becomes a
beggar. With an outstretched hand. And an empty bag. The hand
is full of "gold coins." They are the blisters of the spade's handle.
Governments come and go, the Colonial epoch went, the Empire
fell. The Republic came, improving the condition of all but only
worsening the peasants' lot. So far the peasant knows as his companions hunger, misery, nakedness, slavery, and death. Patriotism,
loyalty to the country is for him an immense sugar refinery where
he moans like the slave for whom Nabuco did his all to set free.
Between himself and liberty, which is his dream, there is a dragon
—latifundia. That dragon kills hunger with its flesh and thirst with
its blood. For him there is nothing. No shelter. No bread. No
medicine. No schools. No happiness. No peace. Nothing. None
listen to his moans of pain. The Church folds its arms and preaches
resignation. As in the days of slavery. If a priest cries out in favor
of him he is punished. If he is a layman, he is called a communist.
So it was in the times of the Colonial State, and in the Empire
when the Church remained silent because it had lands and slaves. I
am not the one who says this. It is Joaquim Nabuco,* who was
born a Catholic and died a Catholic. And what has the Protestant
done? And the spiritualist? And the atheist? The Catholic quarrels
with the Protestant and the spiritualist with the atheist. And while
they quarrel, the peasant's arm grows weaker, the spade grows

* Joaquim Nabuco was a leading late nineteenth-century Brazilian publicist,
statesman, and diplomat. Several aspects of his work were of particular significance. First, he was a leading spokesman, along with Ruy Barbosa and
Antônio de Castro Alves, for the immediate abolition of slavery. Indeed, he
actually succeeded in having legislation passed to this effect. Second, he represented that faction of liberal positivism which saw the military sector as a
non-partisan lever for the protection and promotion of national interests in
contrast to sectional or class interests. Third, Nabuco was himself a product
of the old plantation system, rather than an urban intellectual product. These
seem to be the main reasons why Julião invokes his name so frequently in his
exhortations to the peasantry. *See* Carolina Nabuco, *The Life of Joaquim
Nabuco,* trans. by Ronald Hilton (Stanford University Press, 1950). [ILH]

heavier, hunger increases and liberty diminishes. From which I must conclude that it is no use being a Catholic or a Protestant, a spiritualist or an atheist, to follow this or that religion, to adore God or to negate Him, if all of us are worried only about bettering our lives and crushing others. It is no use being a priest or a minister if one stays within the Church delivering sermons or in the Temple reading portions of the Bible, much less a spiritualist invoking the dead, and an atheist only denying the existence of God. All that is worth nothing while there are millions of peasants treated like beasts of burden by those who have a chapel in their homes, go to mass, to the Protestant meeting, or to the spiritualist center in search of salvation for their souls. Either the preacher rebels against the misery of the peasant and fights to liberate him or everything he preaches deserves no consideration or faith. Either the minister goes out to the country to fight for a piece of land and for a fair wage for the country brother or the sacred Bible will burn his conscience as the stones burned the hands of the guilty. Either the spiritualist joins the atheist to save the landless peasant from hunger, from degradation, and from misery in this country replete with wealth or it is no use clamoring to the dead much less to denounce God. Everything is in vain if nothing is done, not only with words, not only with hymns and religious canticles, but with acts and courageous deeds, to liberate that slave, that poor brother of ours, that humble and good peasant, from the dragon's claws, the latifundia. His misery should shame not only the priest, the minister, the spiritualist, or the atheist, but also the landowner, whoever lives off trade, whoever dominates business, whoever governs, and also the doctor, the judge, the tax collector, the lawyer, the engineer, the student, the worker, the housewife, the professor, the journalist, the militarist, the civil servant, in a word, the entire nation. Because it is the peasants who feed us and dress us, receiving in exchange the subjugation of the slave, the infamy of the *cambão*, the pistol of the *capanga*, the saber of the soldier, the ruined house, the destroyed plantation, the school-less son, without medicine and without food, migration, the floor of the hospital, the old and retired without shelter, and lastly, the unmarked grave in the cemetery where only bones arrive enveloped in tortured skin. That is all that remains of you, unhappy peon, robbed in the general store, cheated on invoices, in the wages of hunger, in working hours, be it North or South, at the seashore or in the confines of the Mato Grosso, throughout immense Brazil which you dig with your spade and water with your sweat and your slave's tears.

For the rentier and the tenant farmer, as for the small owner, there exists the League. And what exists for the peon, for the peasant who rents his arms, who lives on salary alone, in the generator plants, in the rice plantations, in the tobacco areas, in the cacao fields, in the rubber plantations, the coffee and tea plantations? The road is the labor unions. But who can speak of rural labor unions in this country? * How many are there? What do they do? How do they work? Everything exists only on paper. In the will of some. In the hope of others. The latifundist hates the labor unions with the same foaming hatred he bears against the League. When one is founded, the police harass it. Ministerial authorization should be the letter of emancipation of the peasant who hires out his arm. But it still is not. The landowner can have his society. The worker his labor union. The industrialist, his center. The student too. And the civil servant. They can all unite and defend themselves. Not the peasant. No League, no labor union. Because the day when each peasant will be in his League and in his labor union, at that point the country's direction will change. The latifundia will cease. And a new life will emerge. As it emerged in China which so closely resembles Brazil. As it has just emerged in Cuba with Fidel Castro at the forefront of the battle for agrarian reform.

There was a man, who many years ago broke the silence which weighed upon the peasant. He spoke of labor unions. And he provided the first steps. That man was Vargas. When he was preparing to take the decisive step, he was struck down. The whole weight of his memory fell upon another man. That man's name is "Jango" Goulart. Unable to carry it alone he divided the task with another comrade. That other man's name is Lott. Even together they will not be able to liberate the peasant from the latifundia. Nor Brazil from selling itself. One of them has Vargas' letter.**

---

* The growth of rural labor unions actually began in 1960. Presently there are peasant unions and landholder unions, both of which operate within the Brazilian corporative system. [ILH]

** The "letter" Julião refers to is the suicide note left by Getúlio Vargas in August 1954. Despite the fact that Vargas' suicide is a highly unusual act in Latin American politics, the note did have the effect of uniting his supporters.

The other has the sword of Floriano.* The letter is the road. The sword is liberty. So it was in 1955. So it will be in 1960. But without the unity of the peasant there is the risk that the letter might get lost and the sword broken. With the letter and the sword the trip will be shorter. At the side of the worker, of the student, of the intellectual, of the housewife. Of the *Candango*.** Of the nationalists. Of Brasília. Of *Três Marias*. Of *Furnas*. Of *Paulo Afonso*. Of *Volta Redonda*. Of *Petrobrás*. Carrying many glorious flags. One of them, in the hands of the "Laboristas" with Vargas' face smiling to the people. Another one in the hands of the Social Democrats with Juscelino's finger pointing to Brasília. Another one in the hands of the socialists, with old João Mangabeira fighting for liberty. Another one in the hands of the communists, with Luís Carlos Prestes calmly looking at the future. Another one with Bento Gonçalves' nationalists and this slogan: "There is no longer any room in Brazil for those who sell out."

And at the head of the whole immense column [Teixeira] Lott and Jango [Goulart]. Lott with the golden sword. Jango with Vargas' letter. The letter showing the way. The sword guaranteeing liberty. Come on, peasant. The dawn is rising. The sun is yours. For the latifundist nightfall begins. May darkness be everlasting for him. And for you, peasant, may the sun of liberty be eternal.

Come on, peasant. The sun has already broken through the clouds.

Vargas' brand of military "democracy" might well be compared with that of Juan Perón and the Peronism of Argentina. [ILH]

* The "sword" Julião has in mind is that wielded by Floriano Peixoto, who together with General Manoel Deodoro da Fonseca and Benjamin Constant led the army plot which finally led to the abdication of Pedro II in November 1889. It was this military *coup d'état* which created the First Brazilian Republic. It should be noted that Floriano's position can only be described as crudely authoritarian. The symbol of the sword was used by Lott in his political campaign, against the symbol of Quadros' brush. *See* Gilberto Freyre, *The Masters and the Slaves: A Study in the Development of Brazilian Civilization*, trans. by Samuel Putnam (New York: Alfred A. Knopf, 1946). [ILH]

** The workers who worked on the construction of Brasília. [ILH]

II. LETTER FROM RECIFE (1961)

From Recife, cradle of the Peasant Leagues, I send you this letter, peasant of Brazil, with the hope that it will reach your home. You and your brothers make up almost the whole of Brazil. It is you who satisfy our hunger. And you die of hunger. It is you who clothe us. And you live in rags. You provide the soldiers to defend the country. And the country forgets you. You provide the sheriffs for the latifundia. And the *capangas* crush you. You provide alms for the Church. And the Church asks for resignation in the name of Christ. But Christ was a rebel. And that is why he ascended to the cross. And like Christ, the good Saint Francis of Assisi of Italy was also with you. And those who are still alive, Mao Tse-tung of China and Fidel Castro of Cuba. All of them were successful because they were with you and because you were with them. You were and you are. You are and you shall be.

This letter, peasant of Brazil, will reach your hands. Even if you are lost in the jungles of the Amazon. Or under the *babaçus* of Maranhão. Or under the *carnaúbas* of Ceará. Or on the sugar-cane plantations of the Northeast. Or under the shade of the Bahian cacaos. Or on the Southern coffee plantations. Or in the rice fields of San Francisco. And in the tea-growing region. And in the Pampas. Or where there is only stone and thorns. With your brother dressed in leather. And your other brother with the ax and stoker in his hand, fighting against the jungle to win the land. Or with the rifle [*papo-amarelo*] fighting against the *grileiro* to defend the land. In the State of Rio de Janeiro. In Paraná. In Goiás. In Maranhão. Along the open roads over the heartlands of Brazil. In the places everywhere where you moan night and day, at the end of a spade, of a hatchet, of the sickle, the machete, the reaper.

This letter, peasant of Brazil, which I am writing you from Recife, the general headquarters of the League of Peasants, shows you the roads which you must follow in search of your liberty.

I am telling you that the trip is long and full of pitfalls, but your victory is as certain as the fact of the sun rising in the morning. The latifundia is cruel. It rests on the police. And on the *capanga*. It chooses your worst enemies. To win your vote it uses two recipes: violence and cunning. With violence it frightens you.

With cunning it deceives you. Violence is the *capanga*. It is the police. It is the threat of throwing you off the land. Of demolishing your house. Of uprooting your plantation. Of killing you with hunger. Of calling you a communist. That is to say that God punishes you. As though there could be a greater punishment than those conditions under which you live. Chained to the latifundia. In the name of liberty which is not your liberty. And of a God who is not your God.

Cunning consists in feigning equality. It consists in entering your home as tame as a lamb. With claws concealed. With poison kept under wraps. It is offering you a flask of medicine. And the jeep to take your wife to the hospital. Or lending you a little money. Or an order of credit at the general store. It is to catch you unawares when election time comes and you are told: "Countryman, prepare the credentials. If my candidate wins, things will change." And when the candidate does happen to win, things do not change. And if they do change, it is always for the worse. The latifundist fattens his holdings while you peasants swell with hunger. The years go by. The centuries go by. Listen to what I say: the one who has to change, peasant, is you. But you will only change if you destroy your fears. And there is only one remedy for eliminating fear. It is unity. With one finger you cannot hold the spade, the hatchet, the sickle, or the reaper. Nor with open hands—because the fingers are separated. You shall have to close the hand, because fingers unite. The League represents the closed hand, because it is the unity of all of your brothers. Alone you are a drop of water. Joined to your brother, you are a waterfall. Unity makes for strength. It is the bundle of sticks and not the individual twig that provides heat. It is the swelling tide. It is the marching people. It is the *capanga* running away. It is liberty rising. With the League in its arms. And with the labor union in its hands.

The roads which will carry you toward liberty are many. Liberty means land. It means bread. It means a home. It means medicine. It means schools. It means peace. I will show you those roads. But I tell you over and over again. It is of no use to travel if you travel alone. Invite your landless brother, or your brother with a little bit of land. And ask him in turn to invite others. At first there will be two. Then ten. Then one hundred. Then one thousand. And finally, there will be everyone. Marching united. United as you go to the market, to the party, to mass, to religious meeting, to the funeral, to the election. I tell you and repeat to you: unity is the mother of liberty. The roads over which you will be able to travel with your brothers are many. They start at different places but they all wind up at the same place. What are those roads? They are: (1) democracy for the peasant; (2) the labor union for the peasant; (3) the cooperative for the peasant; (4) humane and just legislation for the peasant; (5) the vote for the illiterate.

I shall explain all of this one point at a time. I have hopes of exciting your imagination. To drive away the vampire which dwells in your spirit, sucking away at your courage. That vampire is fear. Once the light that drives away fear shines, that light, tomorrow, will grow like a bonfire. And later, like an incendiary blaze.

Let us take the first road. What does democracy for the peasant mean? I will explain. It is to remove the soldier from your doorstep. It is to disarm the *capanga*. Because your business must be resolved by law, never by the police, much less by the sheriff. The police and the sheriff crush your liberty. It is to break with the regimen of the *cambão*. That *cambão* exists throughout Brazil —even in a state like São Paulo, that golden wagon which the other states push forward like a broken-down locomotive.

The *cambão* is the free day you give to the landowner besides paying him rent. This system has lived for many centuries. It was born with slavery. And it is still riding roughshod on your backs. Changing its name. And even without a name. Turning up in contracts. In bookkeeping records. It is to break with the regimen of the *meia* and the *têrça*. What is the *meia*? What is the *têrça*? The words reveal the answer. It is to give the landowner one half or one third the produce of what you plant, you work, and you pick, in payment of rent. There is no greater robbery of labor performed by others. It is to break with the credit system of the general store. What is this "system"? It is a little paper which circulates like money in the house of the "lord of the estates" and in the sugar refinery. Not for your benefit, but to subjugate you even more to the latifundia. Forcing you to buy more expensively the waste which the city does not want. It is to break with the ten- and twelve-hour working day. It is to fight against the increase of rent which from one year to another goes from two to four and doubles up annually. It is to break with any and every form of subjugation, of servitude, of enslavement. That is why the League of Peasants exists. And that is why you must enter and participate in the League. Fight for the League. Because the League is the waterfall. It is the bundle of sticks. It is unity. And union, I say and repeat, is the mother of liberty. Whoever is a rentier or a small landowner must enter the League. And march with it. Because it is the guide which shows him the road to liberty.

The other road is the rural labor union. What is the labor union? I will explain. When you are not a landowner, a sharecropper, or a tenant, you are a peon. You rent your labor power. Your life is even more difficult. You have a right to nothing. You have no permanent residence. You are a bird in continual flight. Today in the North. Tomorrow in the South. You work from sun up to sun down. And day in and day out. Without a day of rest. You die before your time. From hunger. Tired. Gnawed at by human parasites. Your "alphabet" is the spade. Your "rest" is the floor of the hospital ward. Your "school" is the jail. Your "retirement" is the cemetery. Governments come and go but your condition does not alter. You have no spare time for anything. The wages are never enough. And hunger is your constant companion. You are a slave by day and a slave by night. When you are awake you are a slave. And you are a slave in your sleep. Your son is hunger's feeding ground. And when he dies it does not even hurt you. Because your heart is no longer a heart. It is a blister in your breast. Your road is the labor union. The worker already has it. But you, not yet. And when you do have it, it is of no value. Because the latifundist does not recognize it, and the government does not allow it. When one is organized the latifundia shows its teeth. It sends the police. It frightens the priest. Because for the priest, the rural labor union is "communism." With few exceptions. For the priest only the Catholic Organization of Workers (COC) is of any use. But the organization does not fight for your liberty. If it lights a candle for you, it has a mace kept in store for the latifundist's exclusive use. Sometimes the police shrug their shoulders. And the priest loses his fear and allies himself with you. Then the greatest barrier emerges. The Ministry of Labor. There is always a deputy minister or a senator at the Ministry. He is a puppet of the latifundists. Chosen through your vote. Look, the empty talk lasts for hours. There are banquets. After that, the minister visits the deputy minister or the senator. More banquets. And the labor union does not come to pass. And if the labor union does not emerge, substandard salaries are not exposed, nor the extra hours worked without recompense, nor the absence of paid holidays. Everything is "explained." The labor union will emerge only if you join your brother. If you learn how to vote. Or if you conduct a strike. Letting go of the spade. Lowering the sickle. Leaving your work place. Marching to the city. One hundred. One thousand. Ten thousand. Everyone. Shouting at the judge, at the mayor, at the police commissioner, at the priest: "We want a labor union." This is the formula for getting a labor union. And the labor union is the guide which leads to the road of liberty.

I will show you now the third road. It is the cooperative. What does it mean? I will explain: Cooperative means one for all and all for one. What is its use? It is useful for the rentier. For the tenant and for the small landowner. And for the middle-range landowner. In the fight against the latifundia. Against the middleman. Against isolation. I will give you an example. In a village there are five hundred owners, possessing less than one hundred measures of land. They are the middle-range owners. There are one thousand landowners owning less than twenty acres of land. They are the small landholders. There are five thousand families who rent land. They all unite, the small and the middle-range landowners with those who rent the land. They create a cooperative. There is a law indicating how this should be done. With the cooperative you defend yourself against the latifundists who live with their eyes on your piece of land, your cotton crops, your rice, your bananas, or your coffee. As a member of the cooperative you pay a monthly fee which your pocket barely misses and that money can be used for many purposes. To free you from the claws of the moneylender and speculator who lends you one hundred *cruzeiros* for two thousand in return. To liberate you from the middleman who buys your produce for the price he wants and winds up enriching himself with the fruit of your labor. The cooperative can take your products to the city by truck for an inexpensive fee. And provide you with agricultural machinery, fertilizers, seed, insecticides, for a price which you will never find in the market. The cooperatives will have an agronomist to show you how to make the land produce more. And a doctor to cure you. And a lawyer to defend you. And a teacher to educate your children. The cooperative breaks your isolation. And offers you the possibility of a new life. The cooperative is unity. All for one and one for all. And unity, I say and repeat, is the mother of liberty. Therefore, the cooperative is a good path to take.

I will speak to you also of a humane and just law for the countryside. A civil law for you if you are a tenant farmer or a rentier. A labor law if you are a peon, if you sell your labor power. Everything remains yet to be done. For centuries things remain unchanged.

There has been too much screaming already. And all for nought. It is because the shouting came from too high up. From too few voices. It does not move the latifundia, which is death and has a heart of stone. It is necessary that the clamor come from below, from you. With all your brothers. Shouting and marching. "Down with the latifundia." "Down with tyranny." . . . "Long live agrarian reform." . . . "Long live liberty." All ears will listen to this clamor if it comes from the mass. And the stone-hearted latifundia will melt like ice. Because the clamor from below possesses the heat of fire. And the force of water. And the shattering roar of the waterfall. We need a law which will defend those who live on the land against the *grileiro*. Whoever got there first, who broke down the mountainside, who fought malaria, beri-beri, the poisonous cobras, solitude, hunger, and made his home where he did his planting, multiplied his children, has a sacred right to the land he conquered with his courage. Whoever comes later, with refined hands, with a ring on his finger, with a golden tooth, with fine clothing, with a deed crackling with newness, fabricated the Devil knows how, is no more than a thief, a robber. He is the *grileiro*.* Whoever protects him is even worse. Between the two, who should remain? It is you, the possessor, who conquered the land with your courage, watering it with your sweat, wetting it with your tears. And with your blood. Then the sheriff of the *grileiro* arrives or the police serving all the corrupt governors of Brazil, to expel you under the pretext that they are acting in accordance with the law. This blot should be erased once and for all. The tenant should remain forever on his land. Never the *grileiro*, even if his title of ownership is adorned with seals and signatures. Squatter! What kind of democracy is this which assists in your cold-

---

* Thugs who roam the countryside, either in the service of landowners or as "independent" operators. [ILH]

blooded assassination? That sees your blood moistening the earth which you conquered with your hatchet and does not come to your aid? That democracy is not yet truly yours. It is that of the *grileiro*. How many rivers of blood will yet run through this immense Brazil before democracy shall recognize that no *grileiro* title should prevail over your "title," which is your own life? The law depends on your unity, because democracy depends on your unity. It is therefore necessary that you should unite, squatter, like cement and steel for democracy to feel your strength and the law should be made over in your favor.

And you, rentier, sharecroppers, also do not yet have a law which will protect you from the profits of the landowner. The rent laws favor the city-dweller who lives in a house which is not his own. It has not yet come to help you. Because the majority of Parliament is compromised up to the neck with the latifundists. He who owns no land is like he who does.

No punishment exists for whoever, from one year to the next, doubles your rent. Or forces you to pay kickbacks. Or takes one half or one third of your crop. Or rents you one measure of land in exchange for one hundred and fifty kilograms of cotton. Or drives the cattle into your plantation, before harvesting the crops. And he still confronts you with the sheriff. And he demolishes your house. And he uproots your plantation. Or else he murders you for non-compliance. There is no punishment for the latifundist. He lives in freedom like a tiger. With his teeth sharpened for you. Ready to jump. Devouring your work. And what does Parliament do? It lets time pass. It ignores your condition of servitude. Look beyond and applaud other countries which have achieved agrarian reform. If someone rises in Parliament to clamor for the reform of agriculture, his voice is drowned in silence. There are many legal projects which have been introduced in your favor since 1945. More than two hundred bills and not one of them has been approved. Not even for the love of God. Why? Because you are not yet organized and united like the factory worker, like the student, like the military, like the public servants. Because you have not yet learned how to march from the countryside to the city. The way you do when the crops fail and hunger and thirst drive you from the land. Because you have not yet used the powerful weapon of the working class: the strike. Leaving the cities without food for their marketplaces, and stopping the work in the countryside. Not buying in the stores of the enemies of the Leagues and labor unions. And for you, peon, salaried farm workers, the situation is even more difficult. They don't even pay you a minimum wage. The money they give you is credit for the general store. The medicine you know is tea made from herbs or the drink made from pine disinfectant or from tree roots. When you have an accident and when blood is gushing your medicine is a little chicken crushed alive and eaten with feathers and intestines. You are exploited by fear, backwardness, ignorance, misery, and hunger. You have never heard about licenses. Labor legislation is for you a fairy tale. It does not exist. What does exist is work. From sunrise to sunset. Week in and week out. An armed robbery and the deceit of the pencil. And the rotten sardine and rancid oats. It is the *capanga* at your doorstep. It is running away from exhausted soil. It is the extended hand begging for alms. It is the soldier's saber, the hospital floor. It is the cemetery, your retirement. Your rest. So often asked for. So often found. And Parliament, what does it do? Parliament is afraid. Parliament ignores all of this. Parliament is Christian. That is why it waits for a miracle to happen. As it happened also in China and in Cuba.

I shall finally tell you about the vote for the illiterate. Brazil has 70 million inhabitants. And only 15 million are eligible to vote. If the illiterate should vote, the adult Brazilian population would then be able to vote. There would be 35 million voters. There is no greater injustice than denying the vote to the illiterate, who pays taxes and carries the country on his back. Why does the illiterate not have the power of the vote? Because the latifundists do not want this. It is in the Constitution. That is why our democracy is not the rule of the people and by the people. Because the people constitute the majority and the majority is not allowed to vote. It is necessary to amend the Constitution and obtain the vote for the illiterate. With the pressure of the mass. Of the peasants and workers. Out of every one hundred peasants only five can spell their names. Only one out of a great number can read. With the workers it is not so extreme. If the country does not have schools to teach you, peasant, it is not your fault. And if the fault is not yours the country cannot deny you your franchise. You must demand through the Leagues, through the labor unions everywhere, that the Constitution be reformed and that you be able to vote, even if you are unable to read and write. In other countries this is already happening. There are many ways in which your vote can be used. With that vote you could change the face of Parliament. And the reform bills that now exist only in theory can be approved. With your vote the latifundia would lose its spurs and from a fighting cock it would become a stuffed capon. With your vote you could force schools to emerge everywhere. To teach your children. And you would learn how to read. With your vote there would rise humane and just legislation for the countryside. Rural labor unions would be born throughout the whole of Brazil. And the expropriation of the lands would easily be accomplished. Paying indemnification not in money nor instantaneously, but in federally sponsored bonuses and in credit, as in other countries.

With your vote there would come a law to guarantee the tenants against the *grileiro* and the rentier against the latifundist. With your vote, the *cambão*, credit for the general store, the sharecropping system, the sheriff, the club, the subjugation, all these and other forms of robbing you of your sweat, of your peace, of your life, will disappear overnight.

With your vote the battle for agrarian reform would be won more rapidly and would cost much less blood. Because blood has been flowing for centuries. And it still will. With your vote you would be more respected because, being the majority, your voice would be louder in the regional Chamber of Deputies. In the legislative assembly of the State, in the National Parliament, in the governor's mansion and in the presidential palace as well. The vote for the illiterate depends upon your unity. You already are the majority. The non-voting majority. You must make up the voting majority. Because only in that way will you be the numerical majority and the parliamentary majority. But as long as you are not, conquer this right, learn your alphabet, find yourself a free hour, and go, tired and hungry, in rags, to your fellow worker who can read and learn through him how to spell your name and how to sign it properly.

Your sacrifice is great. But with that sacrifice you can achieve your franchise. That franchise is a step you are taking along the road to liberty. Tomorrow belongs to you. Go and meet your day. Do not greet the sunrise sleepy-eyed. Open your eyes wide to look at it as though it were your mother coming to greet you. And open your arms wide to receive the dawning. There is nothing more beautiful than the face of liberty. Only a mother's face resembles it. Go. And take your brothers along. Liberty awaits you. It is your mother.

III. LETTER FROM OURO PRETO (1962)

From the headlands of Queimada, from this rich town of Ouro Preto, heart of Minas Gerais, a portrait and synthesis of Brazil's poverty, I write to you, comrade and countryman, to you who live in the fields and the cities, awaiting the hour of your redemption. I am sure that you will hear me as I am no longer a voice lost in the immensity of the country.

From all corners of enormous Brazil, from the landless peasant of Paraná to the boatman of the Amazon, from the soldier to the general, from the worker of Volta Redonda to the industrialist of San Pablo, from the student of Goiás to the professor of Guanabara, from the *candango* of Brasília to the *maloqueiro* of Pôrto Alegre, from the employed public to the grocer, from doctors, lawyers, engineers, Catholics, Protestants, spiritualists, communists and non-communists, from the greatest variety of philosophic creeds, politically partisan affiliations, hundreds and hundreds of letters and telegrams have reached me, all in fervent support of the Peasant Leagues and of the struggle that I come from waging for many years against the latifundist and for agrarian reform.

From other countries, like Chile, Uruguay, Peru, Venezuela, Bolivia, to cite some from Latin America, I have received invitations and calls. What does all this mean? It means that the people of my country and neighboring peoples, the humble and the patriotic, sense that I bring a noble and lofty message for the exploited and downtrodden of the cities and the countryside, so noble and lofty that the mercenary press in the service of reaction, of the latifundia and the trusts, cannot contaminate it with the spittle of calumny, knavery, and hatred.

Let us consider Brazil. The picture that I am going to paint for you, comrade and fellow patriot, without laying the colors on thick, is more somber yet in the rest of the Latin American countries under the aegis of "Christian Democracy," all with the unique exception of Cuba.

We have seventy million inhabitants. Bear it in mind: we are the fifth country of the world in territorial expanse and eighth in population. And you will see to what we are reduced. Let us begin with the elections because through them we establish the government and parliament. Government and parliament in small letters. Do you know, comrade, that less than a fifth of our population voted in the last electoral meeting? And that because it was the greatest dispute in the entire life of the republic. Why is it so? Because the illiterate don't vote, in a country that is not ashamed of showing 90% illiteracy among the peasant mass and 70% of the total population. And those who vote, under what circumstances do they go to the ballot boxes? This minimal percentage of voters, from which the soldier and the sailor are also excluded, does not even have a right to choose its candidates. These emerge from prearranged agreement, an arrangement between connected persons and groups that work in their own interest. The connections are the parties. When by exception the candidate emerges from the masses, he has to filter through the fine sieve of the parties, adjust to their exigencies, obscure his ideals, deform his conscience, lie to the people. Once elected he leaves behind the program used for the campaign because he is compromised by the network of forces and interests that form these connections. Because behind the parties, the big parties, pulling the strings, are the forces that retain economic power. What are these forces? The latifundists, the big industrialists, the bankers, the intermediary bourgeoisie, and, above all, North American imperialism. They are precisely those forces that command in Parliament where the law is made. Their law. If our Constitution takes away the right to vote from the illiterate, the soldier and the sailor, if the electoral system establishes unequal treatment for parties and candidates, if they allow the buying of votes, the theft of conscience, the control of propaganda, falsification of will and general corruption, what is the result? It turns out that peasants with little or no land, the working class, the soldier, the sailor, the student, the petty bourgeoisie, that form the near totality of our population are not represented in Parliament nor in the assemblies. Therefore, in Brazil and in the other representative democracies of Latin America, there occurs this curious, grotesque, repugnant, cynical phenomena: the latifundist legislates on behalf of the peasant, the banker for the housewife, the loan shark for the student, the general for the soldier, and imperialism for our nation, a nation that it impiously ransacked, as in the Amapá with manganese and through the four hundred companies which run it from abroad, it created blood, drudgery, and the tears of millions of Brazilians. With this system, shot through with maneuvering and collusion, it is constructed, it is erected, it is balanced, it maintains itself, it rose up and exalted representative democracy, so very much more Christian when more Occidental.

Now you will see, my brother, my comrade, my countryman, some tragic, dreadful, cruel evidence that our representative democracy offers with Christian piety to the world, when people that are already themselves liberated from this plague, from this farce, from this crime, from this affliction, from this infamy, are building a new society, a new civilization, another humanity, with neither anxiety nor dishonesty, with land, the factory, the school, culture, bread, home, liberty, and the future within reach if not yet of everyone, then of the great majority.

Nothing less than 80% of arable lands and pastures of the country is in the hands of only 2% of the Brazilian population. I am speaking of the best lands, of those which have means of communication and access to big population centers. There are landowners with more than 200,000 hectares when dozens of millions of peasants do not have a hand-breadth of land. Those among our own brothers would lose no time in being buried alive, as if they were plants, in order to take over seven measures of land.

From these arable lands and pastures less than 10% are cultivated. There are those who say that if all the plantations of coffee, cane, cocoa, grass, millet, hay, rice, wheat, and other produce of the country were put together, they would not extend far enough to cover the State of Piauí. Going from Sergipe to Ceará, the Northeast has some 46,000 kilometers of humid strip. Of this fringe only 4000 kilometers are occupied by cane plantations and other cultivated produce. The remainder is unproductive or undeveloped latifundia valuable for real estate speculation or it serves as a tax for the fat loans that the Bank of Brazil and other credit institutions make to the latifundists. This happens in an area where the density of population tends to be thicker than many European countries and where poverty prevails in desperation. This is the motive that gave birth to the Peasant Leagues in the humid zone of the Northeast. But not only in the Northeast is there poverty. It is there throughout the whole country. Feudalism exists everywhere. In the State of São Paulo this means 1,400,000 landless peasants. According to the government's own calculations on that State, which elaborated a plan of agrarian revision considered the most audacious in the country—so much so that its author, the Secretary of Agriculture, José Bonifácio, rests on it for his candidacy—it would take exactly 2000 years for the whole peasant mass to have land. In the "miners' triangle" it is common for the poor peasant to say that his ten-year-old son has never eaten beef. In Rio Grande do Sul the small landholder hands over half the rice as payment for leasing the land. The civil code defends the partnership with tooth and claw and sanctions other iniquities. Our civil legislation is seriously diseased. And decrepit. And the Brazilian is still more diseased. It is sad. Hookworm, according to data gathered by Franklin de Oliviera, afflicts 23 million Brazilians; endemic neck tumor, 18.5 million; swamp diseases, 8 million; malaria, 4 million; tracoma, 1 million; Chagas disease, another million; syphilis, 600,000; leprosy, 64,000; and mental illness, 43,000. Not less than 100,000 people die annually of tuberculosis.

Every 42 seconds a child disappears, which corresponds to 85 per hour and 2040 per day. Every year 6 million Brazilian youths of 16 years of age are borne off to the cemetery. Of every 1000 children, 350 to 400 die before growing up. The average life span in the Northeast is 27. More than 30 million Brazilians do not wear shoes and hundreds of thousands live naked, in infested hovels like animals. More than 90% of the prostitutes are farm girls and illiterates. They bud like flowers on the putrid corruption of the latifundia. The worker also comes from the country. And the soldier. All bear the mark of servants. All are fleeing from the bludgeon, from graft, from "justice." But the latifundia too comes to the city. In the soul of the captain of industry feudalism is carried to the factory. In Brazil all industrialists are latifundists. And since the latifundist commands more than the industrialist because he lives here for a long time, something shocking happens: the indifference, the alienation, or the resistance of the industrialist in the face of agrarian reform, despite the fact that this is the only way to create a strong internal market capable of independence from external pressure. He prefers to allow himself to be devoured in silence by imperialism, like a pittance for an alligator, or to give it the lion's share, frightened that alliance with the humble might liquidate private property of the land and of the means of production and move toward socialism. For that reason they prefer the "Alliance for Progress."

Do you know, comrade, compatriot, that only half the child population of the country—that amounts to 18 million—attends school and scarcely one tenth completes the primary course? And that education is furnished to only 950,000 of the 14 million that form the population between seven and eighteen years of age? And finally that barely 5% of Brazilian youth have access to the university?

Perhaps I should tell you about the fabulous profits of the privileged minority who have come here today on this excursion to Ouro Preto, to weep their crocodile tears over this graveyard. These same men whose ancestors quartered Felipe dos Santos and hanged Tiradentes now celebrate this day as a national holiday. But I prefer to tell you of an oppressed mass almost as insecure and exploited as the city and country workers: the big middle-class sector without a right to a home, that urgently need agrarian reform. They are the millions of household heads and housewives tormented by scarcity that grows at an average of 3.5% monthly, by the difficulties of educating, attending, and guiding the family to a future, security, and decency. They are the small traders, the little industrialists and artisans that suffer the blood-letting of the exchequer and of national and foreign sharks.

This is a pale portrait of today's Brazil. This is the country of the much invoked Southern Cross that lights up silently every night, as it was already illumined before the arrival of the first ransacker and it will continue to shine after we turn the thief out, away from our wealth.

We want quite a different democracy for Brazil. It matters little what I label it provided that it serves the people. Whether it is called Christian, popular, or socialist, provided that it bears within itself radical agrarian reform as a first step. But I ask you, comrade and countryman, if it is possible to attain this reform within this system. The whole nation knows that a new farce is being prepared. They are already exploiting the anti-communist industry. To maintain it they make a little bundle of billions, they form an alliance of the small minority of the "big" against the great majority of the little fellows, they unite the sacred family, techniques of propaganda mystify the masses, they use the brashest language, run through rivers of money, the nation is stirred up, and finally the mountains bring forth a mouse. The farce is repeated. The Magnus changes style, gesture, words, but the little stick that used to be Portuguese colonialism is today in the hands of Uncle Sam. Pan-Americanism, Good Neighbor Policy, Monroe Doctrine, Truman Doctrine, Marshall Plan, Alliance for Progress, Food for Peace, words, panaceas, patches, all to cover up the sacking of wealth that is unending, luxurious payments that are ceaseless, changing government loans that don't industrialize but serve instead as compensation to indemnify the telephone companies and distributors of electrical energy, the quick dollar, real exchange without discounts, with previous agreement made in Washington amidst smiles, to the tune of millions, the applause of the dominant oligarchy, the stifled rebellion of the people and the pledge of the nation. They run to save the Northeast as if Brazil were only the Northeast, from hunger and poverty, from the "demagogy of evil Brasileiros" seeking to harass the Christian family, in instituting the rule of the firing squad, by inebriating the country, by violating its "glorious democratic traditions" with alien regimes contrary to our temperament as a pacific people. For these last-minute "saviors" the Christian family is that which lives in a palace, travels in a Cadillac convertible, and is owner of the land, of livestock, of the bank, of industry, of trade, of the public honor and the life of the people. Christian family is not what lives in a miserable hut, in ashes, in the *maloca* in a blind alley, or being vilified on the latifundia, under the *capanga* and the hired police ruffian. Christian family is the latifundist who arms to the teeth with rifle and machine gun, throughout the whole country, boasting a feudal regime, private property of the land.

Brazil, "Christian country," has surplus land, but no land to spare for millions of peasants. Brazil, "Christian country," has inexhaustible wealth but also hundreds of thousands of unemployed workers. Brazil, "Christian country," has property owners that live on the rent of one hundred, two hundred, five hundred, one thousand houses, while there are millions gathered in hovels, wretched as pigs. Brazil, "Christian country," has magnates that realize a profit of up to 9000% over and above capital that multiplies with the rapidity of plague bacilli, and like these assassins coldly assassinate those that make the miracle of multiplication possible. Brazil, "Christian country," boasts the sad privilege of possessing the highest rate of infant mortality in Latin America, despite industrialization and the development so publicly proclaimed under the most supine government in national history. Brazil, "Christian country," is undeveloped, underfed, unfree, because our nation is the country of "un." Everything here ends in pillage, deceit, theft, insolence. Now agrarian reform is stylish. It is the order of the day. The throbbing question for this electoral year. Therefore the young Minister of Agriculture runs, serving many miles of land, in a region where the peasant is the most miserable of all, and exhibits his project for agrarian reform, trumpeted to the four corners of the country as if it were a tablet of salvation for the regime. When the project is revised the evidence will show that a minister of the Imperial Epoch should present something less timid even with the support of the advocates of slavery. Education, the profitable industry of special secondary schools, which is cared for with such affection, is not open to debate, by virtue of which the number of illiterates grows and the possibilities of the youth, son of a worker or middle class, diminish for pursuing a course at school or dreams about the university. The salary that inflation leaves no sooner buys bread than it is expropriated by the wheat trust. Liberty in this "Christian country" consists of not touching the privileges of the dominant caste. The dignity of being human in this "Christian country" is measured by the bank account, the factory hearths, the big cargoes, and kneeling before Mister Kennedy.

I confess to you, brother, comrade, countryman, that I would pray, and with me millions and millions of Brazilians, to Our Father for the eternal repose of this democracy that fattens the shark and kills the people's hunger, pardons the oppression of the latifundia and denies land to the peasant, permits one business enterprise to earn up to 9000% but commands the pointing of machine guns at the breast of the worker who strikes to increase his wages, gives to foreign capital the broad freedom of monopolizing the nation's wealth and even facilitates its flow out of the country, for factory overseers, brigadiers, and admirals, but refuses security to the sergeant and the vote to the soldier and sailor. That alone fulfills the law which benefits the powerful, that is to say, the Christian family. Often social foresight is blackmail. Rural unionization doesn't exist; the thief of the popular economy doesn't go to prison. Not one piece of *trabalhista* legislation applies to the peasant. The right to register candidates is even denied to the Communist Party. This doesn't even happen in the Catholic Italy of the nice friendly peasant that is Pope John XXIII. This party exists in fact, has a press, participates in the political life of the country, and makes alliances with other parties. I do not believe that the redemption of my country will come from the ballot boxes. Nor from the elites. Nor from the Christian family. It will come, yes, and in that I firmly believe, from the anguished masses, from the landless peasant, from the unemployed or badly paid worker, from the student without a university, from the sick without a hospital, from the childhood without a future, from the aged without a past, from the illiterate, from the soldier and the sailor without franchise, from the unfortunate father, from the priest who gives no benediction to Uncle Sam, from the intellectual who neither sells his conscience nor hires out his pen, from the sergeant without security, from the artisan, from the grocer, from the housewife, from all who have a heart to feel and a mouth to sing the hymn of independence: "Be free, for we will die for Brazil."

IV. REFLECTIONS ON THE BRAZILIAN PRE-REVOLUTION
Celso Furtado *

In my contact with university youth all over Brazil in the course of this past year, I was able to observe what great anxiety dominates their spirit. The conscience of the country has been made keen, moving toward transformations of great scope; so that under our feet, like a deep current, unfathomable forces operate. All, or almost all, the young people want to understand what is going on, trying to participate conscientiously in these transformations, wanting to take an active part and contribute to molding a future *par excellence* that belongs to them. I know very well that though often indecisive and insecure, youth are confident. They are urging upon us all a clear definition of positions; so that

* Celso Furtado is director of the Banco Nacional de Desenvolvimento Econômico in Rio de Janeiro, formerly chief of the Development Division of the Economic Commission for Latin America. He is minister without portfolio for the João Goulart government.

we may know to choose with courage the objectives and methods that we will have to use in the struggle for the conquest of the future.

Allow me, then, to use this opportunity, to reflect on questions that are posed by young men and women, recently having left the universities of various regions of Brazil. I present these reflections like an open personal declaration, so that we may be able to continue the dialogue, often interrupted when scarcely had we touched upon the essential.

Brazilians are now widely conscious that their country is on the march toward transformations in its economic and social structure. They want to understand what is happening so that they can take intelligent positions on the issues involved. Those who must make decisions of major importance therefore owe it to the public to define their aims clearly and disclose the methods to be used in achieving them. What follows is an attempt to satisfy this requirement.

The first question often raised concerns the disproportionate social costs of the notable economic development that has been taking place in Brazil over the past several years. Economic analysis deals exclusively with the cold description of reality. We know that this development of which we are so proud has brought about no change at all in the living conditions of three-fourths of the country's population. Its main feature has been a growing concentration of income, both socially and geographically. The large mass of people who toil in the fields and constitute the majority of the Brazilian population have reaped no benefit. Worse than that, the masses have witnessed a relative decline in their standard of living as compared to those engaged in commerce and other services. As for the industrial workers, who represent a sort of middle class in the Brazilian social framework, they have grown both in absolute and relative terms, without having improved their standard of living to any large extent. They, too, have suffered a relative worsening of their economic position as compared to higher income groups employed in urban services.

It is not only in the concentration of income that economic development has produced social results of an extremely negative character. Because of the anachronistic structure of Brazilian agriculture, it has led in many regions to a relative increase in the rent from land, thus rewarding parasitic groups. Similarly, in the absence of a conscious policy designed to further the social purposes of state action, a variety of subsidies have been improvised, which —in the name of development—have very often put a premium on investments which either were superfluous or fostered a still greater concentration of income in the hands of privileged groups. Through capital contributions, such as subsidized exchange and credit, large amounts of social wealth have been transferred to a few hands.

In political and administrative fields the distortions are still more glaring. The expansion and diversification of state functions— both as cause and effect of the development—have not been followed up by the necessary basic reforms within the state structure, and as a result waste in public administration has enormously increased. This, combined with the state's increased role in the field of investments, has created ideal conditions for the illicit acquisition of capital at the people's expense. Big contracts for public works have become the current source for amassing fortunes both within and without the government.

The resulting popular indignation, especially among the young, is easily understood. People see their supposed representatives being elected through the influence of contract-mongers for public works; they see an alliance between operators of the feudal machine and those who make budgetary appropriations resulting in the election to Congress of legislators who know they will survive politically only if they remain docile stooges in the hands of their financial patrons.

Some might object that things were much worse before; elections then were a mere formality, since an oligarchy decided for itself what would be called the will of the people. But the objection is no longer valid. If we know where the failings of the system lie—and we do—then we are able to change them; if we do not try to do so, we will be conniving with them.

There is also the other side—the positive gains of development. It has provided the country with the instruments to make decisions, given it the ability to exercise choice and, by making the people conscious of their destiny, has made them responsible for their own failings. The root cause of the present state of uneasiness in Brazil is this simple truth: we know where the errors of our development lie, and we know that it is within our power to eradicate or minimize them.

The second point which I would like to elaborate is the need for a philosophy to guide our action. Many people both in Brazil and abroad have asked me why Marxism has permeated Brazilian youth so deeply. The reason is simple: Marxism, in any of its varieties, affords a diagnosis of the social reality and a guide to action. We must approach this subject with absolute frankness if we are to maintain an effective dialogue with the idealistic and active youth of our time. What does their Marxism consist of?

It may be summed up by describing a few of their attitudes. They maintain: (1) that the present social order is based to a great extent on the exploitation of man by man, which favors the well-being of a class sheltering many a parasite and idler and leaves the great majority in poverty; (2) that the social reality is *historical* and thus in permanent change; therefore the present order must be superseded by another; and (3) that it is possible to identify the strategic factors which affect the social process; this in turn opens the way to a conscious policy of social reconstruction.

If we go deep into the core of this philosophy, we shall find on the one hand the wish to liberate man from all chains that socially enslave him, allowing him to fulfill his potentialities; and on the other hand an optimistic attitude concerning the capacity of human communities for self-determination. In the last analysis, what we find is a higher stage of humanism, for while it places man in the center of its concerns, it recognizes that full individual development can be attained only through a rational guidance of social relations.

Whatever name we choose to give this conception, it is impossible to object to it openly, for it is inspired by the most profound longings of modern man. It has its roots in the humanism of the Renaissance, which taught man that he could affect his own destiny; and its inherent optimism emanates from the Industrial Revolution, which gave man the power to affect his own environment.

In our dialogue with the new generation we must reach agreement as to what is really fundamental. We should relegate to the background all things that are merely instrumental or subordinate to the ends pursued. For example, it would not be possible to ascribe more than an instrumental character to the private ownership of means of production—in short, to private enterprise. We are all agreed that private enterprise is merely a decentralized form of organizing production which must be ruled by social criteria. Whenever there is a conflict between the social aims of production and its organization as a private concern, measures have to be taken to preserve the social interest. On the other hand, as a greater abundance in the supply of goods is reached, that is to say, in the higher stages of development, the actual organization of production becomes less important while the control of political power increases in importance. It is the latter, finally, that dictates the patterns of distribution and utilization of social income, in the form of either public or private consumption.

We may well ask, therefore, what are the fundamental aims on which we can unite? Should these aims be considered as ends in themselves and related to our own conception of life? It is of the highest importance, I believe, that we define these objectives clearly. Otherwise we shall not distinguish means from ends and will risk treating what others consider merely means as though they were ends. We have the right to take a stand as to the ultimate ends we are trying to attain without reference to the issue of Russian or American pre-eminence on the world stage. To subordinate the future of our culture to the tactical conveniences of either of the two great centers of military power would mean to give up the struggle before it is joined. We must consider the Russian-American stalemate as a given fact of the present day. By doing this we admit that it is not in our power to change the balance of forces to any significant degree. Our very helplessness regarding the world conflict gives us a wider margin of liberty to establish our own aims. And, as often happens, greater freedom gives rise to greater awareness of responsibility.

It is against this background that we must establish irrevocable aims of political action. I believe that they can be described as humanism and optimism concerning the material development of society. Or, to use more current terms, liberty and economic development.

I have used the word humanism because liberty can also be understood in terms of nineteenth-century individualism, which often saw the individual as opposed to society. There is not the slightest doubt that aspirations of our present-day youth center about authentic humanism. What makes them angry is the inhuman aspect of our development—the growing contrast between wasteful wealth and abject poverty. They see peasants living in the country but unable to grow enough food and suffering hunger almost every day of the year. They see state capitals where 10% of the population are listed in hospital registries as suffering from tuberculosis. And we know that all this can be remedied, indeed has already disappeared from a large portion of the world. We can see then that what worries youth is man and his degradation, and the consciousness that we are also responsible for it.

Once we have defined our aims, the question is how to pull ourselves together to achieve them. How can we prevent the struggle for intermediate or secondary objectives from making us forget our authentic ends? It is an extremely difficult problem, especially as the historical experience of recent decades has suggested that the underdeveloped countries must make a choice between individual liberty and rapid material development. This false dilemma is posed both by the champions of liberty and by the promoters of mass welfare.

It is now clear that the rapid material development of the Soviet Union, until recently an underdeveloped country, was achieved partly by the use of inhuman methods. The requisitioning of agricultural surpluses in order to finance industrial development was accomplished by the use of armed force, through compulsory collectivization, and the violent suppression of all resistance. In order to justify these drastic methods, the "theory" was put forward that the peasant was fundamentally an individualist and that the only way to overcome such "individualism" was by enforced collectivization. This is the theory of salvation through punishment. To achieve administrative efficiency an enormous price was paid in human lives. But even if we put aside the painful Soviet experience, account must be taken of the evidence that the rapid economic development of the communist countries has been achieved under forms of socio-political organization in which individual liberty was restricted beyond the limits which we would consider tolerable.

It must be recognized, however, that the masses in the underdeveloped countries have not generally put the same high valuation on individual liberty that we do. Since they have not had access to the better things of life, they obviously cannot grasp the full meaning of the supposed dilemma between liberty and quick development. Also, if we were to assert that rapid economic development of socialist countries was achieved only at the price of restricting civil liberties, we must then accept the corollary that the liberty enjoyed by the minority in our society is paid for by a delay in general economic development, hence it is at the expense of the welfare of the great majority.

Even less effective with the peasant is the argument that the development of the socialist countries is being obtained at an enormous human cost, including forms of semi-slave labor. The fact is that the underdeveloped peoples are quite prepared to pay a price, even a very heavy one, for their development. They know by hard experience the extremely high price they pay for remaining underdeveloped. How many millions of lives are sacrificed every year in a country like Brazil by underdevelopment? How many millions of lives are lost through hunger and physical exhaustion? How many millions of human beings live without access to primary education, or any opportunity of sharing in secondary and higher education? Very few of us have sufficient awareness of these deeply inhuman characteristics of underdevelopment. When we do become fully aware, we understand why the masses are prepared for any sacrifice in order to overcome it. If the price of liberty for the few had to be the poverty of the many, we can be quite certain that the probability of preserving freedom would be practically nil.

Insistence on false alternatives nevertheless goes on, elaborated in different forms by opposing champions. The self-appointed defenders of liberty argue that the structural changes in the social order necessary for the rapid acceleration of economic development have always been associated with the suppression of fundamental human liberties. Those who take the opposite side argue from the historical fact that the only effective method for introducing the social changes necessary for rapid development has been a revolution of the Marxist-Leninist type, which by its own nature requires the setting up of a rigid dictatorship. So both sides acknowledge that social change is the effective instrument for accelerating material development in underdeveloped countries. The discussion of this very important point has been bedeviled by a great confusion of ideas, either unconscious or deliberate. We should not forget that the method of Marxism-Leninism was created and perfected in the struggle for the overthrow of an entirely rigid socio-political structure—that of tsarism. The historical experience of the last decades has shown that such a revolutionary technique applied against other rigid structures—Nationalist China, Japanese-occupied China, and Batista's Cuba are obvious examples—can be highly effective where accompanied by a Spartan discipline in the rank and file and the daring of an Alexander in the leadership.

The same does not apply, however, to "open" societies. The example of Western Europe seems conclusive: Huge party machines guided by Marxism-Leninism found themselves bewildered by an ever changing socio-political reality. This was because Marxism-Leninism sees in the state—which it defines as "a special repressive force"—the dictatorship of a class, the bourgeoisie. From the moment the state ceases to be the mere dictatorship of a class to become a composite system, though under the aegis of a certain class, the unity of revolutionary action is weakened by an inability any longer to define the party's aims. The need to discriminate between good and bad policies of the state requires a capacity for adaptation that a monolithic revolutionary party cannot have.

We cannot, then, ignore the historical fact that the Marxist-Leninist techniques have been proved ineffective in dealing with open societies. Nor can we escape the following conclusions: (1) that dictatorships were not created by the acceleration of development but preceded it; (2) that the acceleration took place only in structures which were previously rigid (dictatorships); and (3) that the techniques which have so far been used for the rapid transformation of social structures have been effective only in rigid societies (dictatorships).

So the fundamental problem we face is to develop techniques which will make rapid social transformations possible, while retaining the pattern of an open society.

Before turning to specifically Brazilian questions, I will indulge in one more observation on revolutionary methods: Since Marxism-Leninism is based on the substitution of the dictatorship of one class for that of another class, it would be politically retrogressive to apply it to societies which have attained more complex social forms—that is, modern open societies. It would mean, in the last resort, a sacrifice of the very objectives previously described as essential. While it is true that economic development means a fuller life for man, it is no less true that the pattern of social and political organization is the warp that sustains the woof of a fuller and richer life. Although it is probable that in the future materia. abundance will coexist with forms of socio-political organization which permit the full realization of authentic human values, that does not necessarily occur at the present historical stage. To have attained higher forms of social and political organization is at least as great an achievement as that of high standards of material development.

Historical experience has demonstrated that whenever a revolution of the Marxist-Leninist type has been imposed on a complex social structure—as in the case of certain European countries—socialism as a form of humanism becomes perverted. As there is no possibility of converting an open society into a dictatorship without creating a climate of frustration, there is a deterioration of social values. Since the dictatorial regime does not permit the individual to play his proper part in society, a series of social myths is put forward in order to replace genuine human values. Thus, material development can take place at the same time that the dictatorship is consolidating itself upon principles which are the antithesis of humanistic revolutionary ideals.

Let us now face up to the Brazilian problem. The fact is that our society is an "open" one to the industrial workers, but not to the peasants. It is therefore not hard to explain why the peasant is much more susceptible to revolutionary techniques of the Marxist-Leninist type than is the industrial working class, although from the orthodox Marxist point of view the latter should be the vanguard of the revolutionary movement. But our political system allows the urban workers to organize themselves in order to press their claims, within the rules of the democratic game, whereas the situation of the peasants is altogether different. Since they have no rights, they cannot have legal claims. If they organize themselves, the inference is that they do so for subversive purposes. The necessary conclusion we must draw is that Brazilian society is rigid at least in that large sector composed of agricultural laborers. As regards this sector, we have to accept the fact that the Marxist-Leninist revolutionary techniques are effective.

We come now to a conclusion of great importance in Brazil. To the extent that we live in an open society, the attainment of higher social aims tends to assume the form of gradualism. To the extent that we live in a rigid society, those objectives will tend to be attained by cataclysmic disruption. Thus there is a duality within the Brazilian revolutionary process.

What is the likelihood of an effective Brazilian revolution through Marxist-Leninist methods? I believe there are two ways in which this might occur. As suggested above, the first one is connected with the land problem. We must not forget that over half of the Brazilian population gets its living from the land. If this sector maintains its present rigidity, every peasant movement will tend rapidly to adopt revolutionary techniques of the Marxist-Leninist type. Thus we have an important segment of the population with a Marxist-Leninist bias which, given certain conditions, might be able to take the lead in the Brazilian revolutionary process. The practical results would be the predominance of the least developed sector of our society. The real objectives of our development, as previously defined in terms of humanism, would thus be partially frustrated at the very start.

The second way in which a revolution of the Marxist-Leninist type might be carried out would be as a result of social and political retrogression. We have observed that a revolution of this type is hardly likely in an open society, unless it is imposed from without, as happened in some countries of Central Europe. Nevertheless, the possibility of "putting the clock back" must not be excluded. The imposition of a right-wing dictatorship, making the whole political structure rigid, would create favorable conditions for an effective revolution of the Marxist-Leninist type. But even in this case, the agrarian sector would be likely to predominate. In the absence of conditions resulting from political retrogression, the only possibility of a Marxist-Leninist revolution lies in the persistence of an archaic agrarian structure.

In order to achieve a high rate of economic development, in accordance with truly social criteria, we shall have to bring about some important changes in our basic structures. Because we have not been prepared for such changes, anxiety has grown from day to day. We have come to live in what may properly be termed a prerevolutionary period, in which drastic change is a political necessity. Thus techniques of social transformation and revolutionary methods are in the forefront of present-day political concern. If we are to avoid dictatorial regimes, whether of a social class or ideological group or rigid party machine, we must: (a) prevent all forms of retrogression in our social and political systems; and (b) create conditions for fast and effective change in the country's archaic agrarian structure.

These general directives must be elaborated into specific lines of action. Political retrogression will not come haphazardly, but as a reflection of panic among some privileged groups confronted with growing social pressure. Where structures are rigid, preventing gradual adaptations, these pressures may create cataclysmic situations, leading to emergency solutions or preventive coups. Thus, the first task is to give more flexibility to the existing structures. We have to tread boldly the path of constitutional change which will permit agrarian reform and a radical change of government administration of the fiscal system and the banking structure. We have to subordinate state action to a clear definition of the aims of economic and social development. The Congress has the right to draw up directives, but local politicians must be deprived of the power to allocate public monies. We have to give the government effective means to punish those who embezzle public funds, to control extravagant consumption, and to dignify the function of civil servants. We must have legal statutes to subordinate the action of foreign capital to the aims of economic development and to the requirements of political independence. The recent law affecting the remittance of profits constitutes a clear indication that, even in a legislature where conservative views prevail, there is an awareness of a need for such discipline. Passed at a moment of serious political tension, the law contains ambiguities and, therefore, ought to be improved. It is taken for granted that the cooperation of foreign capital is indispensable for the development of any underdeveloped country; but in the absence of regulation, conflicts of economic interest may become conflicts of a political nature, harmful to international cooperation. Also, the government must have thorough knowledge of the sources of all investment in means of mass communications. And above all we must have a plan for economic and social development compatible with our own possibilities and in conformity with the aspirations of the people.

What must we do to translate into action all these objectives?

I believe that the most immediate task is to organize public opinion so that it can express itself. It is up to the students, workers, entrepreneurs, intellectuals, and perhaps even the peasants, through their incipient organizations, to start a frank debate about what they expect from their government. The more complex problems must be given systematic study by groups of specialists, and their conclusions must be publicly debated. Brazil is mature enough to start thinking about its own destiny. From general debates and from expressions of public opinion must emerge programs that will serve as a basis for the renewal of popular representation.

I am convinced that the youth have to be capable once more of containing the direction of this great mobilization of national public opinion on behalf of the authentic cause of the development of our country.

IV
CHARISMA, CONSTITUTIONS,
AND
BRAZIL'S MEN OF POWER

. . . in which the significance of Brazil as an emerging world power is analyzed in terms of continuities and discontinuities with Hispanic America: leadership strivings and the divorce of politics from parliamentary rule; how the "Giant of the South" has sought to escape the domination of the "Giant of the North"; Vargas' New State and the paradox of reactionary revolution; Bonapartist Democracy from Kubitschek to Quadros; the isolation of politics from economic and social realities.

WHAT BRAZIL does politically cannot be said to be of trivial moment. There are, to be sure, twenty Latin American Republics. But there is only one with the geographic dimensions and economic potential of Brazil. The fact that at the Punta del Este meetings of the Organization of American States, Brazil repeatedly urged caution in relation to Cuba, voted against sanctions and, again, against the move to expel Cuba from the OAS—which was supported by the United States—should make it clear that Brazil is determined to pursue an independent foreign policy. Its further ability to convince Argentina and Mexico to do likewise, to defy, in effect, the wishes of the United States, reveals how forceful a voice Brazil has in the councils of the more powerful states in Latin America. We should further note that whereas the shock of Argentina's unwillingness to declare itself openly against the Castro regime caused outraged cries that Frondizi was "soft on communism"—outbursts which contributed considerably to the *coup d'état* which replaced the Frondizi regime with a veiled military-sponsored government—the result in Brazil was only a further consolidation of a left-wing oriented government. The renunciation by Jânio Quadros of presidential power, and the subsequent rise to power of the labor socialist "Jango" Goulart, served only to further accelerate the pacification of Brazilian international policy. It must be noted that Brazil was the only Latin American nation to qualify its endorsement of the United States quarantine on arms shipments to Cuba in October 1962.

By the close of the twentieth century Brazil will claim 200 million inhabitants. By all accounts it will be, if it is not already, the most important country in the Latin American sphere from an economic point of view. Nor is Brazilian power solely a matter for future market considerations. Between 1956 and 1960, the Volta Redonda, Latin America's largest iron and steel complex, doubled its production capacity. Further, Brazil has reached the point where it refines nearly all of its petroleum products. It produces nearly all of its pharmaceuticals and is developing a heavy chemicals industry. Its electronics industry now provides a large portion of all household appliances sold in the country. It produces nearly all of its textile requirements. Brazil has one of the world's largest labor forces, whose productive capabilities are steadily being increased through technological improvements in working conditions (air-conditioned factories, automation, etc.) and through vocational training (the development of secondary trades schools, vocational colleges, etc.). The economics of self-sufficiency may not be the *sufficient* condition for political sovereignty, but it certainly is a *necessary* condition.

The Brazilian Leviathan can no longer be either humored or coaxed into making decisions against its better judgment. The American can no longer afford paternalism, a position which asserts that whatever happens, Brazil goes by its own rhythm. For not only has Brazil engaged in the general radicalization of Latin American political life, but threatens to assume quickly leadership in those policy measures aimed at increasing the independence of the hemisphere. A recent comment by Gilberto Freyre typifies this new attitude of area leadership in the Brazilians:

Brazil is the most Hispanic nation in the world, because it is of *both* Spanish and Portuguese formation. Due to this, it is both the heir of Portugal and yet sensitive to certain subtleties that are purely Spanish. This places Brazil in an ideal position to mediate the divergencies that still exist between nations of Spanish formation. It has understanding yet it also stands apart from the intimate rivalries between these Spanish nations.

To speak of politics in general is to deal in unrewarding ambiguities. Politics, following the Hobbesian and Hegelian traditions, consists in the defense of the integrity of the state from within, and the defense of sovereignty from external dangers. Put more directly, the two sides of politics are: foreign policy, and the relationship of authority to citizenry within the state. We shall discuss the politics of the emerging Brazilian Revolution from both of these perspectives.

Any Latin American country, particularly a nation such as Brazil, which exhibits strong strivings toward leadership, is faced by a monumental hurdle: the more influential it becomes in Latin American affairs, the more it must come up against the established hemispheric leadership of the United States. It is no accident that United States diplomatic relations with Brazil have become increasingly "touchy" as Brazil seeks to extend its influence beyond its geographical borders. "The Giant of the North" is first "among equals." It crowds and cramps the potential "Giant of the South." In one sense, this is a traditional hemispheric problem—faced by Mexico under the leadership of Juárez, by Argentina under the leadership of Perón, and by Brazil under the leadership of Vargas. Up to now, all efforts to create a countervailing political power in the Western hemisphere have failed, and failed miserably. The United States has remained the ultimate arbiter of the competing interests of its twenty "sister republics." In brute fact, there has been only one "big brother." And as in any extended family, it is hard for big brother to accept his declining influence with grace, and equally difficult for the would-be heirs to power to know just how to cope with new situations and new opportunities.

The informal "rules of the game" in the big Latin American countries entail a pragmatic recognition of United States sovereignty over the area, while nationally, for "home consumption," they create an image of resentment of such sovereignty. Latin American nations talk in terms of *Bolivarism* but act in terms of *Monroeism*. The pre-World War II efforts to unite the "ABC" countries (Argentina, Brazil, and Chile) into a united political-economic phalanx failed. The World War II neutralism of Perón's Argentina, and Vargas' procrastination in relation to the Axis Powers, also collapsed as a tactic. The United States came out of the war stronger than ever, while Germany's position as an international power was completely eliminated. The post-World War

II strategy of nations such as Mexico, Argentina, and Brazil was to create a distinct orbit of Latin American power as a whole. This too failed, as the big nations of Latin America were impotent to impose their designs on the smaller nations. With the "Giant of the North" carefully watching developments and curbing any pretenses toward a countervailing imperialism, the big nations of the South were once more frustrated in their attempts to change the inherited "rules of the game."

How does a sovereign nation escape the problem of being both large and insignificant? This problem was tackled anew by Jânio Quadros and by the present Brazilian President, João Goulart. For the "Jan-Jan" movement, that political force which elected both Quadros and Goulart in the 1960 elections, the way to political influence on a world scale is not through bloc arrangements with hemispheric neighbors, but through rendering the competition for leadership in the Inter-American system, first, inept and then, inoperative. This was to be achieved by focusing on the world at large rather than on hemispheric problems in particular.

Brazilian political leadership has decided to join the world. This sounds like a meaningless platitude. It is not. Nothing can be as constricting and as provincial as politics in South America. Traditionally, the world *is* Brazil. What goes on within the nation is politics; what goes on elsewhere is mythology. Judging by the Brazilian press, problems relevant to the building of Brasília clearly outweighed the Berlin crisis, nuclear test bans, East-West power struggles, etc. The problem thus facing the successors to Vargas and Kubitschek was how to break with this provincialism, an ethnocentrism more damaging to a "developing nation" than to one already fully developed, since it replaces the struggle for real power with shadowy images of power. This false nationalism provided Brazil in the past with prestige without power, a sense of bigness measured exclusively by the fractured mirror of other Latin American states.

Between 1930 and 1960, between Vargas and Kubitschek, the development of that shadowy phenomenon called "national pride" overtook Brazil. Vargas built upon the esteem of the Brazilian working classes and Kubitschek built upon the status-consciousness of the Brazilian industrial and managerial classes. In each case this pride was frustrated. First, there was frustration due to the failure of *both* the working classes and the business classes to develop styles of work and levels of production necessary to an advanced society. Vargas created a bureaucratic system which saw sectors of the working classes living off the state apparatus by having six-hour workdays, moonlighting among the civil service staff, and a general lack of interest in craftsmanship. Kubitschek did nothing to correct these aberrations and indeed contributed to them by converting Vargas' *Estado Novo* from a political ideology into a bureaucratic extravaganza. Pride unfulfilled turns quickly to prejudice. And the sorry fates of both men indicate as much. The fact remained that neither made Brazil a *world* power, although, in all fairness, it should be added that Vargas saw the problem as one which clearly required structural transformations in Brazilian society, and not just changes in political posture.

As José Honório Rodrigues noted, in his discussion of *The Foundations of Brazil's Foreign Policy*, that Brazil, from an historical view and despite the rise of new classes to positions of economic prominence, remained tied to traditional oligarchical and slave-holding views of its world position. Before Quadros, it supported colonialism and imperialism as if it were a recipient of the benefits rather than the deficits of the colonial system.

Brazilian foreign policy is neither a party policy nor does it represent the interests of a class; but since the country was formerly ruled by an oligarchy which represented landed interests, it has reflected this oligarchy's opinion and aspirations rather than those of the people, who were until a short time ago politically non-existent. The middle and working classes were not organized as a political force. The government of Getúlio Vargas, in spite of restricting the ruling power to a very limited circle including the armed forces, promoted national feeling and brought the working classes into the political arena. From 1930 on, new groups of the middle and working classes with their demands have become more influential in Brazilian politics without, however, affecting the policies and attitudes of the Ministry of Foreign Affairs.

Brazilian political leadership between 1960 and 1963 has attacked this problem in four distinct ways: (1) A new policy toward Africa, particularly toward the Portuguese colonies with which Brazil's considerable Negro population acts as a link, and which shares a common language. A policy of trade pacts and student exchanges has now been in effect for two years with substantial success. (2) A new policy of neutralism with respect to East-West struggles. This is reflected in Brazilian support for the seating of Communist China in the United Nations, and in the opening up of diplomatic relations with the Soviet Union and Soviet-bloc nations. While this neutralism is political policy, it is also clear that the loyalties of Brazil are with the Western democratic ideology —in this way avoiding the painful and perhaps unacceptable schism between revolutionary ideologies and capitalist realities. (3) A new policy toward the European mainland, especially toward Portugal and Spain. The discreet support given to more democratic elements in Portugal and to the idea of Iberian liberation suggests that Brazil would like to establish closer ties with Latin Europe—but on grounds determined by Brazil rather than by Portugal or Spain. Brazil is, in fact, now in a condition of political parity with the "mainland" nations. And in its attempts to redirect those nations with which it has had the richest of historical links, the prospects of Brazil emerging as a recognized world power are greatest. The positive reception given this approach by Brazilian political and economic leaders, and the equally forceful reception given by such stalwarts of a "Latin world on both sides of the Atlantic" as Charles de Gaulle, would indicate that the new course is a seed that has borne fruit. (4) A new policy toward the more distant Latin nations, such as Cuba, has also been instituted. If in the past Brazil has sought strength from nations with contiguous borders, it now sees itself large and independent enough to express itself on inter-American affairs as leader rather than as partner. As has already been mentioned, the Brazilian reticence to punish or censor Cuba was an independent decision, taken whether all other nations of the hemisphere agreed with its position or not. The fact that Argentina, Mexico, Bolivia, Chile, and Uruguay supported the Brazilian position against the United States position was an added bonus, and undoubtedly a welcome one—but it does not minimize the Brazilian initiative. By so doing, Brazil has become a more significant political factor in the hemisphere than any sort of power-bloc establishment could have made possible. Jânio Quadros, in a forthright statement on foreign affairs, made the new turn plain.

The still dramatically present question of Cuba convinced us, once and for all, of the nature of the continental crisis. In defending with intransigence the sovereignty of Cuba against interpretations of an historical fact which cannot be controlled *a posteriori*, we believe we are helping to awaken the continent to a true awareness of its responsibilities. We stand by our position on Cuba, with all its implications. Surely the Brazilian attitude has been understood by other governments, and as it gains ground, the entire regional system shows signs of a regeneration in the assessment of the responsibilities of each member nation. . . . As to Africa, we may say that today it represents a new dimension in Brazilian policy. We are linked to that continent by our ethnic and cultural roots and share in its desire to forge for itself an independent position in the world of today. The nations of Latin America that became politically independent in the course of the nineteenth century found the process of economic development delayed by historical circumstances, and Africa, which has only recently become politically free, joins us at this moment in the common struggle for freedom and well-being.

It cannot be said that the United States has met this new Brazilian posture either with calm or prudence. When the new Soviet Ambassador to Brazil arrived early in 1962 to present his credentials and to open the Soviet trade exhibit, many rumblings were heard in Washington and in the American press to the effect that the Goulart government was falling under "communist influence." The fact that other nations in South America had established diplomatic relations with the Soviet Union long before 1962, and had not capitulated to the red sirens, apparently did not halt the flow of verbal misgivings on Congressional Hill.

The fact is, of course, that the first sign of Brazil's emergence as a world power has emboldened its governing factions to propose or take steps which could only be interpreted as discontent with United States policies and interests in the area. In November of 1961 the Brazilian Chamber of Deputies passed a tough law penalizing foreign capital, a move calculated to please nationalists, socialists, and communists by minimizing the relative importance of the external sector in the process of capital formation. The proposal never reached the Brazilian Senate. The proposal did, however, serve sufficient notice upon the United States commercial interests that the least they could expect was a reapportionment of the profits extracted from Brazilian agricultural and industrial produce. Another event, perhaps even more explosive, took place in February 1962. Governor Leonel Brizola, of the State of Rio Grande do Sul, often described as a "free-wheeling left-wing nationalist" and a vastly ambitious politician, expropriated a tele-phone company which was a wholly owned subsidiary of the International Telephone and Telegraph Corporation of New York. Brizola's initial compensation offer amounted to 5% of the com-pany's value as assessed by its owners. It is difficult to imagine that this will be the last case of expropriation that will take place in Brazil.*

The effect of these moves and maneuvers on United States for-eign policy has been mixed and ambiguous. Resolutions were offered in the House of Representatives and in the Senate calling for a halt to all aid to Brazil, including a severance of Alliance for Progress aid; American business reports urged a reconsideration of further investments in Brazil. The Kennedy administration, however, moved to counter any extreme reaction, and indicated that nothing could be worse than a series of anti-Brazilian resolu-tions at a time when the "dialogue" was more important than ever before. Indeed, the likelihood is that whether an equitable settle-ment of the expropriation case will be forthcoming or not, United States assistance to Brazil, particularly to the restless Northeastern region, will be stepped up under the terms of the Alliance projects, if only to prevent outright disintegration of the "Inter-American" system.

At the present time, to deal with Brazil in terms of established European categories, e.g., political democracy, dictatorship, the rule of the masses, etc., is dangerously misleading. At the most, such phraseology indicates the need for rule-of-thumb conven-tions. The politics of revolution dictates a maximum of mobility in terms of the forms of political nomenclature. For this reason, the "opening to the left" and the various "appeals to nationalism" in Brazil must be understood as providing the mass support neces-

---

* While the American government has continued to provide financial support to the Brazilian economy, it has become increasingly clear that such support in the future will have as a minimal asking price an "austerity pro-gram"—the very reverse of President Goulart's lavish inflationary policies. Furthermore, it is dubious whether there will be a continuation of heavy private investment in Brazil with the threat of expropriation hanging heavy. Because of the financial and political atmosphere in the sixties, new private investment has virtually ceased and a process of economic disengagement of foreign capital has set in. What complicates the situation from a Brazilian point of view is that without fresh investment capital, many of the nation's plans for the modernization of industry and technology will be seriously impeded.

sary for the conduct of foreign policy. As long as the United States insists that Brazil should *always* act in terms of *principles*, while reserving for itself the entire realm of *tactics*, political relations between the two giants of the hemisphere will continue to be abrasive and unsatisfactory.

The sad truth is that political relations between the two nations have sunk to such a level that the United States could now more readily destroy the Goulart regime by embracing it than by sending threatening messages and menacing personal representatives.* Within many sectors of Brazilian society, notably those sectors which have the most delicate *political* sensitivities—students, intellectuals, urban labor—there exist majorities as prone toward an irrational anti-Americanism as we are toward an irrational anti-communism. The formalistic shell of the "American Way" may have been exportable in ages gone by. It is not so today. Although the Brazilian has developed a fine taste for the consumer and industrial products of American capitalism he recoils at the outward political features of the "free-enterprise" system as inappropriate to the area and insupportable by the population. Their image of us is a society of economic vitality directed by a policy of ingenuous conformism and mass hysteria. Our past impulse to support garrison states, to aid that which is dying in the Latin American world, also deepens the suspicion that our urgings toward democracy are rhetorical, and not to be taken too seriously.

It must also be pointed out that the Brazilian attitude regarding the United States is damned if you do and damned if you don't. Too often, the Brazilian spokesman will condemn United States intervention in the affairs of another sovereign state; at the same time he will condemn the United States for being impotent, manipulative, and without feeling if it does not so intervene. In the case of Cuba, the failure of the United States to take an early initiative in terms of economic sanctions led to widespread criticism that the United States was letting down its hemispheric neighbors, that it is ready at all times to "abandon" its friends—as it supposedly did its "friends" in Eastern Europe. On the other hand, firm United States action in the Caribbean, carrying with it the threat of invasion, was just as roundly condemned for being a

---

* The scandals exposed in June 1963 of a flow of United States corporate funds to bolster key reactionary legislative figures certainly have not handicapped Goulart in his struggles with Lacerda.

classic example of gunboat imperialism and aggressiveness. Were these contrary approaches to emanate from different quarters, one could say that they represent different sectors of Brazilian life. But too often the same spokesman will be urging caution and action, diplomacy and intervention.

This is not an effort at equalizing guilt or responsibility. There is no doubt that the major burden for political failures of the United States in relation to Brazil must be assumed by the former. However, it is also true that the political leadership of Brazil has been on a pendulum moving from opportunism (for example, refusal to give early support to the United States' call to join the democratic cause against Hitlerism in the hopes that a military stalemate would liberate it from American economic imperialism) to ambiguity (for example, refusal to support the United States stand for economic sanctions against Castro's Cuba in 1961, and then giving the United States a virtual blank check to blockade Cuba in 1962). The amorphous quality of Brazilian political relations is directly related to the political history of the Brazilian nation.

Characteristically, the newly developing nations have highly articulated and independent foreign policies, but poorly defined internal political structures. It is simpler for Brazil to develop a grid of differentiated political responses to the chief power blocs (including the Soviet bloc and the Third World nations) precisely because it avoids the necessity of a direct confrontation with United States foreign policies. The delicate balance of terror which prevails between the United States and the Soviet Union has made possible a degree of latitude in Latin American foreign policy that was unknown to previous generations. This is especially true in Brazil, where the nationalistic common denominator was previously frustrated by the overwhelming predominance of United States corporate investments. With the entrance of the Soviet Union into Latin affairs, first, through the political support rendered to the Castro revolution in Cuba and, second, through the economic trade agreements negotiated with several of the larger Latin American states, foreign policy in these areas has been in a position to acquire an independence that is not necessarily reflected in any appreciable strengthening of the political apparatus of the Latin nations as such.

Brazil thus presents us with a dichotomy: on the one hand it has a relatively well-delineated foreign policy; on the other, this policy is neither a cause nor a consequence of internal political stability. That this is a common condition in the newly emerging nation-states is shown by Egypt, which maintains a neutralist foreign policy and still leaves much power in the hands of the sheikdoms; by Ghana, which has a leading hand in the pacification of Africa in general, despite the continuation of tribal life and association. Thus while the political neutrality of Brazil might occasion displeasure in certain quarters, it should not come as a surprise. The plain fact is that Brazilian foreign policy under Quadros and now Goulart is increasingly neutralist. Such a "third-force" posture satisfies the nationalist aspirations of right, left, and center, and in so doing, removes a considerable amount of pressure for social and political reformation in the home country.

To deal with politics inside Brazil is to treat factors of power and men of power directly. This is so because the political party system is exceedingly clumsy, top-heavy, factionalized, and without local and regional supports characteristic of Anglo-American politics. The Brazilian political machinery exists under widespread depreciation and deprecation. Local State (*estadual*) governments have political organizations of their own. And given the power of the governors of important States, national politics is a badly compromised entity. This is one chief reason why "presidentialism" and "personalism" are such impressive factors in the political life history of Brazil despite the relative absence of violent *coups d'état.*

The Brazilian sociologist, Luís Pinto Ferreira, has pointed out that no political party has gained a clear-cut majority in the elections of 1945, 1958, or 1960. The three leading parties, *Partido Social Democrático* (PSD), *União Democrática Nacional* (UDN), and *Partido Trabalhista Brasileiro* (PTB), have divided approximately 70% of the vote, while ten other parties have carved up the remaining voting blocs. Furthermore, there is a relative stagnation of the size of the voting population. Fifteen million voted in the 1954 elections, and a trifle less voted in the 1960 presidential elections. What this leads to is a jockeying for an advantage through tenuous coalitions. But this is not the most serious defect in Brazilian political structure. The really major problem is that no political party can claim the adherence of its own leaders, much less any hard-core membership.

Take, for example, Jânio Quadros' acceptance of the support of the *União Democrática Nacional*. This was simply a necessary rubric for Quadros to appear on the ballot. It carried no significance beyond that. Ideologically, the UDN is far to the right of Quadros. Quadros, for his part, never intended to promote the party or become its "titular" leader. This was simply a marriage of convenience. The authentic leader of the party is Herbert Levy, member of the Chamber of Deputies from São Paulo. Quadros' unsuccessful opponent in the 1960 elections, Marshal Teixeira Lott, drew heavy support from the far left, from the forces of Prestes' Communist Party and Julião's Peasant Leagues. Lott, for his part, was probably campaigning on a less radical platform than Quadros. João Goulart's situation presents a similar paradox. His affiliation is with the *Partido Trabalhista Brasileiro* (PTB), the organization built by Getúlio Vargas. This party, far from providing actual support, contains the most violent anti-Janguista sector in the country, the *Grupo Compacto*. Indeed, for a time during Quadros' Presidency, this group actually succeeded in isolating its leading public figure (and then Vice President) from the party apparatus. And as if this compounding of confusions were not enough, a separatist movement called "Jan-Jan" emerged which urged support for both Quadros and Goulart, although they were from different parties and represented different ideologies. Most observers agree, in fact, that the "Jan-Jan" movement was a large-scale factor in the election of both men.

All of which should make clear that the cult of personalities which pervades the Brazilian scene occurs in a context of political chaos, not organizational terrorism. The depth of the schism between parties and personalities is made clear by the Communist Party. The "de-Stalinization" of the Party took place toward the close of 1960. The "old guard" of Maurício Grabois, João Amazonas, and Pedro Pomar were relegated to minor positions, while the "revisionists" led by Jacob Gorender and Mário Alves took control of the Party's executive commission. But this did not in the least upset the fiction that Luís Carlos Prestes was the leader, or the secretary-general, of the Party. His survival is guaranteed not by his voice in party councils, but by his public image, his caudillo-like eminence. The only distinction is that whereas, for the other parties, personalities reign supreme over the apparatus, the reverse holds true for the Communist Party. But not even they would dare to violate the collective mania for personality cults. In Brazil *charisma* is king.

For the North American this personalism is intolerable at the intellectual level, and probably incomprehensible at the practical level. Most North Americans are ethnocentric enough to believe that it is either indecent or useless to play by any set of rules which denies the premise of majority decision. This frustration with things Latin is well illustrated in Frank Tannenbaum's remarks on *The Political Dilemma in Latin America*.

There is no effective local self-government. The schools, the roads, the police, the tax-collector, the agents of *formal* government are in the central administration. The governors are appointed or are removed by the central administration. The intervenor in Argentina and Brazil, the authority to declare that a state has lost its constitutional powers in Mexico, are illustrative of the central government's control over the state even in countries where there is a constitutionally established federal system. . . . All of this follows from the traditional principle of authoritarian and centralized rule. The president must make every decision and he must provide for all needs. He must do this because there is no effective local government; and in the absence of that, there is no means of developing a political party that can provide the needed support to make the presidency independent of the army.

The Brazilian attitude shows a marked unconcern for these points. The view of Brazilian intellectuals, and that of most Latin Americans, is that the political party system is intrinsically conservative. A Brazilian definition of a party working efficiently is an apparatus working bureaucratically. Parties function only in terms of elections, in protection of their feudal "rights" to divide patronage in an equitable fashion. Brazilian political parties are devoid of activities designed to educate the population socially. They have no capacity to act as impersonal pressure elements. Consequently, they are parties in name only. They depend on national leaders for the simple reason that this personalization of power makes for responsibility of office. Gilberto Freyre in a recent interview with an American writer put this fact into a context of Brazilian social history.

In Brazil parliamentary democracy emptied itself of its messianic content by allying itself to a liberal democracy tied to the *coroneis* (the semi-feudal *fazendeiros*, the great landlords of Brazil) of the interior. In every municipality, there were two "colonels," each linked to one of the two parties. Both parties were ostensibly "democratic"; but these "colonels" were, in fact, merely successors to the imperial barons. This led to a devaluation of the word "democracy."

What appears so obvious to the Brazilian—the class character of politics—is difficult to understand for those raised in a North American world in which parties strive to overcome (if not obliterate) factors of social class. The plain fact is that parliamentarianism is an historically conservative and politically reactionary force in Brazil. Parties are sustained by the "sadism of command" disguised as the "principle of authority." The political party system combines demagogy and liberalism. It is operationally restrictive, if not restrictive in principle. As such, the struggle between personalism (whose faults have only too often been recited in textbooks on Latin American history) and parliamentarianism (whose virtues are shibboleths of every North American kindergarten student) is often presented as an example of hopeless immaturity and the undemocratic strains in the Brazilian temperament. In the light of real history, in terms of the wide and varied uses of parliamentary rule to frustrate political reform and social development, one can see that the bureaucratic machinery, so brilliantly highlighted in the Brazilian film, *Black Orpheus*, is no real friend to Brazilian democracy.

To cope with Brazil's politics is to deal with personalities. Indeed, it is customary to speak of political leaders by either first names or "nicknames." But this usage is in no way pejorative. To the better-known factors responsible for a continuation of personalism—(a) the maintenance of the feudal structure in rural areas and the consequent intimacy of contract between masters and serfs in the *casa grandes;* (b) a powerful but, in comparison to the Spanish Church, benevolent Catholic Church; and (c) the ruling-class character of the political parties which exist—must be added (d) the most powerful factor of all: personalism works unusually well in Brazil. This is why, no matter what the topic under discussion might be, conversation soon turns from policies to personalities.

During the Portuguese Empire period of 1822–31, Dom Pedro I, aided by his able Prime Minister, José Bonifácio de Andrade e Silva, successfully fought the economic and political institution of slavery, the destruction of which took place gradually and without bloodshed. It was at this point that a constitution was fashioned which enshrined personalism by making the Emperor "the mediative power." This gave to Dom Pedro the ability to nominate certain members of the upper house of Parliament for life terms. It further carried a proviso for a veto power over all legislation. After a brief interregnum which preserved the political and geographical integrity of Brazil at a time of intense separatism in the Spanish American nations, Brazil came under the rule of Dom Pedro II, a rule which lasted an incredible length of time when measured in South American terms—from 1841 to 1889.

While the rest of Latin America was declaring in favor of republican forms of government, Brazil continued its course of Empire. Benevolent despotism is a more likely political counterpart to feudalism than republicanism. At least it must be considered so in the context, if for no other reason than the relative stability of the regime in Brazil. Under Dom Pedro the idea of personalism continued to grow. The "mediative power" was neither law nor politics. It was men. More specifically, the ruling sector. What this meant in raw political terms was that the Emperor could claim powerful allies among the ruling classes—the court nobility, the *fazendeiros* or latifundists, the Church authorities, and of course, the armed forces. At the same time, the Dom successfully cultivated newer social forces in the nation: middle-class business and commercial interests, religious free-thinkers and Freemasons, and a small but articulate intelligentsia. As long as these forces were in a relative state of equilibrium, Dom Pedro II had little executive trouble. But "mediative" despotism, like neo-falangism in the twentieth century, suffers from one huge shortcoming. The "pillars of power" doctrine contained no provision for social change, for the emergence of new institutions and the circulation of elite membership.

The regime of Pedro II and the end of Empire came about through an international breakdown of support: the Catholic Church refused to aid an emperor who showed increasing and alarming respect for Protestants, Mormons, and Masons. The latifundists turned against the Empire for its vigorous pursuit of the abolition of slavery. And the army was mutinous and divided between nationalistic and Empire-oriented factions. Coupled with this breakdown of traditional sources of support were the unfulfilled but constantly rising expectations of the trading and commercial factors. Among the key items on the bill of particulars was the absolute failure of the Portuguese rationally to exploit the Brazilian interior; an educational system that could easily be counted among the worst in the world; banking, railroad, and mining interests that extracted profits and left nothing in the country; and the growing pressure on Brazil to relate itself to the Portuguese Empire first, while its true matrix of interests in Latin America remained utterly frustrated.

But the end of Empire did not eliminate the "scourge" of personalism. The very opposite took place. Between the First Republic and the First Dictatorship, between Deodoro da Fonseca in 1890 and the rise of Getúlio Vargas in 1930, a crystallization of power in the hands of the middle classes occurred. But this power was badly compromised by the continued dependence upon foreign economic might and on the entrenchment of the latifundia in the Northeast. The end of Empire did not mean the end of imperialism. The beginning of republicanism did not mean the beginning of mass democracy. The First Republic was a "great compromise." The bourgeoisie settled with the latifundists. The former took the cities while the latter kept the countryside. The feudal barons were converted into appointed governors and generals. Portuguese interests dealt with the domestic bourgeoisie, who immediately turned around and opened the floodgates to the Dutch, the English, and, last in time but not least in significance, the North Americans.

This abortive character of the Brazilian *fin de siècle* period has been excellently summed up by Florestan Fernandes in *Pattern and Rate of Development in Latin America*.

Following the abolition of slave labor attempts were made to extend to everyone the rights which were the prerogatives of the privileged classes under the "old regime." Brazil drew up a very advanced Constitution which adapted the Brazilian Republic to democratic molds of a liberal nature. However, no similar process has taken place in practical life. It would be impossible, without special provisions of a very complex and costly nature, to "leap" from the slave and seigneurial system to a democratic social order. . . . Thus the Republic developed into a precarious compromise between the "old regime" and the new social order, preserving, through the colonel system and other forms of local despotism, the traditional patterns of patrimonial domination. The parties became alliances protecting the interests of the dominant strata, without any specific ideology, honest political aims, or dynamic influence of their own which would have enabled them to coordinate and direct the presidential regime.

The classical age of European parliamentarianism had come and gone, hardly causing a ripple in Brazil. The crystallization of the middle classes in relatively favorable conditions, such as those prevailing in Europe and the United States in the early part of the nineteenth century, could not be imitated in Brazil. Indeed, the utopian and millennial qualities of Brazilian liberalism stemmed precisely from this effort to reproduce a parliamentary system on the model of the Western nations, but under conditions of Brazilian dependence upon foreign capital and imports. The urban bourgeoisie could not effectively do battle with the latifundists, since the mainsprings of Brazilian wealth were rubber, cacao, and coffee, the products of the latifundias and plantations. Agricultural products were exportable. Brazilian industrial products were expendable. Under such conditions the bourgeois-legalistic forms of politics necessarily remained more fictitious than real.

In addition, middle-class parliamentarianism faced a rising tide of expectations from the hitherto disenfranchised masses—in the form of the "history-less" peasant and the very history-minded proletariat. Confronted by the nostalgic presence of the feudal sectors on one side and the increasingly discontented impoverished sectors on the other, the bourgeoisie grew more dependent upon the military, upon generals like Hermes da Fonseca and later Arthur da Silva Bernardes, to impose liberalism from above. But the whole theory of bringing about democracy through executive fiat simply compounded the felony by making Brazilian politics more personalistic than it was even during slavery and the Empire.

This attempt fostered more resentment than resolution; it led to repeated attempts to establish a "Bonapartist democracy." First of all, the rule of the urban capitalists, shaky as it was in terms of problems of social class, was even more unstable in the realm of sectional interests. The economic predominance of São Paulo and Minas Gerais produced severe political repercussions. The bourgeois monopoly over national politics which followed the termination of World War I aggravated regional tensions. The non-industrial states were open to any proposals which would curb the Center-South alliance of States. The fact that industrialization and urbanization had not reached the point where they invited political alignments along urban-rural lines tended to encourage separatism and sectionalism in political life. And this sectionalism accentuated the troubles of Brazilian democracy by driving a wedge between opportunistic regional interests and national policy. The virtual impossibility of national politics along traditional parliamentary lines made three types of response possible: the fascist, the communist, and the Bonapartist, i.e., the direct political rule of the military or military-oriented leaders. It should be noted that all three had this much in common: they were alternatives to parliamentary government. True enough, the communism of Luís Carlos Prestes and the right-wing nationalism of Carlos Lacerda (himself a former leader of the Communist Party) make appeals to different sectors of society, but they are inspired and distinguished by their militaristic character. In the "long march of 1924," the revolutionaries were composed nearly entirely of army men—some of whom went on to perform significant roles in the Vargas government, and all of whom cleaved to the right or to the left. None had any confidence in the liberalism and positivism of the Brazilian bourgeoisie, because none had any confidence in the capacity of the middle classes for self-sacrifice as such.

This then was a perfect opportunity for a new Dom Pedro, for a new charismatic leader to play the "mediative role." In Getúlio Vargas, Brazil found its ideal type. Vargas had the support of the sectionalists, because his home state, Rio Grande do Sul, represented the epitome of regionalism in Brazil. His political beliefs offered no threat to either military or civilian interests and to accept him was to stave off if not eliminate a more powerful attack on oligarchical and bourgeois commercial interests. Vargas' "political renovation" simply brushed problems of social class under the political rug. Between 1930 and 1945 industry continued to expand, aided in considerable measure by the benefits of yet another world war. The industrial working class became increasingly organized into trade unions, while creating an articulate leadership capable of realizing labor interests. Vargas' policy of fostering education served to enlarge the scope of an intelligentsia which represented a dynamic new elite within the bureaucratic structure.

The most viable political formula was to adapt presidential aspirations to the Brazilian situation. What this meant was a political hodgepodge and eclecticism characteristic of Latin America. From the communists Vargas took over the slogan of working-class salvation. From the fascists he took over the slogans of supernationalism. From the militarists he took over the theory of the guardianship of the Republic. Vargas' eclecticism was his strength, and at the same time his ultimate undoing. For while he nationalized the railways he did nothing to improve the transportation system. While he encouraged making capital more easily available to the middle classes, he did not recoup this investment through taxation of the wealthy classes. While he placed the ownership of power and communications under state control and assisted in the monopolization of petroleum and electricity interests, he did not convert this positive step into a broad-based program for exploiting these natural and social resources scientifically and rationally. Instead of balance there was chaos at the end of the war. In addition, Vargas had no real political apparatus to withstand fresh winds of doctrine, and to offer new forms of organization.

With Vargas and the *Estado Novo*, the New State, social forces were to be balanced. Like Falangism in Spain, Corporativism in Italy, and Peronism in Argentina, the political commonweal was to come to a state of rest on the perfect Aristotelian balance which was presumed to exist between capital and labor, civilian and military, secular and clerical. The columnar theory or "sector approach" satisfied demands of the right wing for Integralism, satisfied Bonapartist impulses of the army bureaucracy and the leftist demands for greater voice in the popular bases of the regime. The Communist *Aliança Nacional Libertadora* was eliminated as a factor through the imprisonment of Prestes and the absorption into the government of the lesser officials of the Tenente movement, while the fascist *integralistas* in the *Partido de Representação Popular*, representing the "best" families and the bureaucracy, were similarly absorbed. In this technique Vargas remained true to the Brazilian political style: *absorb rather than crush.*

What then went wrong? Simply that social change was completely left out of the picture. The theory behind the New State was a sterile variant of equilibrium and pattern maintenance. In European fascism this dilemma of political immobility was somewhat compensated for by an adventurist foreign policy which had the capacity to maintain an internal stability through conquest and gain. But in the absence of this sort of geopolitics, the weaknesses of the *Estado Novo* became manifest. It is not so much the relative absence of middle sectors which accounted for the instability of Brazilian dictatorship, because as a matter of fact this sector grew considerably under Vargas, but the unrequited and unfulfilled demands of every other sector (labor in particular) which led to the demise of the Vargas era.

Two aspects of the Vargas era which deserve further attention, and which parenthetically may help to explain the weaknesses of his regime are: (a) Vargas' own *civilian* background; and (b) the increasing demand in Brazil's middle sectors for "modernism" in place of structural development. The first factor, Vargas' civilian status, tended to cut him off from a chief source of power in other Latin American reactionary revolutionary regimes—the military. To institute the sort of widespread structural reforms he proposed without firm military backing proved in the long run to be impossible. And while the Vargas regime was comparatively gentle with its opposition, precisely because of its civilian status, it was unable to realize the program of structural development without a considerably higher degree of coercive power than the dictator could muster.

This leads directly to the second factor mentioned above; namely, the growing consumer orientation which followed in the aftermath of World War II. Monies piled up, goods were scarce, and the middle classes were unable or unwilling to delay their consumer gratification for a longer period of time than was absolutely necessary. Vargas' fundamental belief in social development at the expense of modernism, at the expense of gratification of consumer wants, went directly against the aspirations of shopkeepers, white-collar workers, and the bureaucratic apparatus itself. Thus it was that Dutra, with a single stroke, "solved" two issues: the pivotal role of the military—putting them back into direct power channels; and the acceptance of modernism, affluence, and consumer orientation, as a Brazilian style of life. The period between 1945 and 1950 amply demonstrated the anti-democratic character of the *nouveaux riches* and, no less, their willingness to convert structural development (involving painful short-run sacrifices) into a form of modernism which simply brought to bear new pressures on Brazil from the colonial and imperial powers.

The proof, if any is required, that the middle sectors were not democratically motivated in their efforts to end the Vargas regime is the fact that power reverted directly to the military after 1945. General Eurico Gaspar Dutra, who inherited the Vargas mantle, ruled until 1950 through a coalition of rightist and centrist political elements. The swing to the left exhibited by Vargas was still too amorphous to register itself in rule. Dutra's New Brazil was a reversion to the coalition of latifundists and industrialists who had ruled prior to 1930—with a sop to the modernism of the urban wealthy. Despite its toleration of parliamentary forms, it served only to narrow the political base. And this was made possible by the decadence of the Brazilian party system and the unwillingness of the *nouveaux riches* to effect structural changes. The three main parties—excluding the Communist Party of Luís Prestes and the Fascist Party (PRP) of Plínio Salgado—were all polyglot affairs representing neither political nor economic realities within the country.

Just as the fall of Empire did not signify the end of personalism, so, too, the fall of dictatorship did not end the cult of presidentialism. Indeed, presidentialism is simply a secularized response to personalism—a personalism which attempts to rationalize charismatic authority. The Social Democratic Party, the National Democratic Union, and the Brazilian Labor Party still remain pawns of this cult of presidentialism. Vargas' return to power in 1950 was achieved through deals with all three parties (as have been all subsequent national elections). In exchange for this support, the parties were allowed to continue as feudal principalities, dispensing patronage and propagating the myth of constitutionalism.

The extent of the breakdown in political party processes is best observed in the election of yet another "strong leader" in the 1955 elections—Juscelino Kubitschek. In this election, the winning presidential candidate received a majority of the vote in only three of the twenty Brazilian States. Seen in this light, the 65% of the vote garnered by Jânio Quadros in the 1960 elections was a nearly unprecedented occurrence and opportunity. But as with Kubitschek before him, Quadros gained a personal victory rather than a party victory. This is clearly attested to, first by the extensive vote splitting, and second by the failure of the *União Democrática Nacional,* Quadros' party, to continue in power after his renunciation of the presidential post.

The postwar regimes of Vargas, Dutra, Kubitschek, Quadros, and now Goulart all serve to illustrate the primacy of President over party. But more significantly, they also exhibit the general separation of the nation's social and economic life from the political process as such. The rise of an articulate labor movement developed during Vargas' tenure in office continued on its course despite the more conservative moorings of later Presidents. The continued expansion of the Brazilian middle sectors continued under each of these regimes. The latifundists have shown a gradual decline in their power no matter who had office—since this decline was directly linked to the shrinking world agricultural market and not to political connections. Brazilian politics, precisely because of its charismatic, presidential character, operates in a fundamental vacuum, unable either to channelize or rationalize the course of social events. Indeed, the agony of Quadros was his frustrating effort to close the gap between polity and economy, and between decision-making and social life in general.

Fernando Ferrari, the candidate defeated for the Vice Presidency by João Goulart in the 1960 elections, gave succinct expression to this point in his article on the "Political Panorama of Brazil."

It is important to note that whoever cannot estimate what the opposition of the Brazilian people to the organized parties may be, ought not to judge their reactions to a phenomenon that does not exist. Indeed, we do not really have national, historical, or traditional parties. It is quite the contrary among other peoples rooted in European culture. We do not possess political groups with historical roots that impel the development of the nation. From the Empire to the Republic, with rare exceptions, parties have formed around the support of temporary causes to create occasional majorities, and not as organisms destined to defend great causes nor the management of programs. In this our party system imitates the panorama which exists in other similar collectivities, since the constant of Latin America is the existence of party alignments without profound ideological convictions. Only by examining the organized and active associations which hurl themselves upon the public bearing messages and programs do we have some basis for measuring the actual political tendencies of the Brazilian people.

Quadros' bureaucratic Bonapartism (in contrast to the earlier military Bonapartism) stemmed from an honest desire to make the communist appeal obsolete in Brazil by promoting a "businesslike" way of life and a social system that was responsive to the needs of a technological age and the nationalist sentiments alike. But in this very effort to curb inflation, establish an austerity budget, provide everyone with a minimum standard of living, and minimize the divisive influence of sectional interests, Quadros came a cropper of those very "pillars of society" which were frightened of any authentic change away from the status quo. To combat these imaginary forward-looking "middle sectors" Quadros once more took refuge in presidentialism, in rule by administrative fiat. Those who opposed Quadros were not, however, the "democratic" and "parliamentary" forces. They were indeed the famed "middle sectors" upon which many analysts from the United States pin so much hope. But why did these middle sectors oppose Quadros' Bonapartism? To promote democracy? Hardly. The plain fact is that these sectors remained basically unconvinced of the need to sacrifice consumer satisfaction and a stable federal budget for the purpose of generating a structural transformation in Brazilian economy, to get from a "mass society" to a "society of the masses." The clever Brazilian spokesman of these sectors, David Nasser, writing in Assìs Chateaubriand's famous Brazilian equivalent of *Life* magazine, *O Cruzeiro*, put the middle-class defense for maintaining incompetence and inefficiency directly:

Deep down in every Brazilian there is a Juscelino Kubitschek, laughing. That is the way we are: somewhat disorganized, somewhat inefficient, and madly Brazilian. We all approve Jânio's public health measures. We all want the guilty to be punished. We all want a clean government. But we do not want the Juscelino Kubitschek within ourselves to be killed, we don't want our rascality, that delightful "no good" side of our temperament which makes ours a happy country, to be destroyed by the Face of Wrath.

And to be sure, for men like Lacerda, Quadros represented the Face of Wrath. To bring Brazil into the modern world meant to connect politics to economic and social realities—an ambition notably begun under Vargas, but dropped by his successors, the Dutra and Kubitschek administrations. Structural development is precisely what the "middle sectors" want least of all. Fed on an ideological diet of consumer affluence, living off the proceeds of deals made with foreign entrepreneurs and domestic latifundists, the middle classes have proven to be least able to create the conditions for a middle-class solution to Brazilian political ailments. Quadros' "sin" was that he took bourgeois liberalist values at face value—without discounting their rhetoric. His shock of recognition translated itself into a dramatic renunciation of power. This was the dismal consequence of a man convinced by words—words championed by Quadros' own class in theory, but undermined by its social malpractices.

Nor can the present ruler of Brazil, João Goulart, disciple of Vargas and champion of the urban proletariat, hold out hope for transcending the problems bequeathed by his predecessors. In fact, it is doubtful whether Goulart has accepted the substance or the rhetoric of the classes whom he champions. The urbanized working classes of Brazil point up the terrible dilemmas for the political future. They are the guardians of nationalism, of *Petrobrás* and *Eletrobrás,* but they are often unwilling to make the sacrifices necessary to make nationalization of industry economically feasible. They decry the exploitation necessary to orient a society toward mass consumption of secondary goods, but they share with the petty bourgeoisie a desire to participate in the celebration of the tin-foil world of status without substance. In short, the "rascality" and "no-good side" of Brazilian temperament reveal themselves in the standards of living of the urban working class only to a less exaggerated extent than in the commercial classes—but it is there nonetheless. The Brazilian urban working class, like its counterpart in the United States, reveals economic strivings divested of political allegiances.

The opposition to Goulart succeeding Quadros was essentially short-lived, as was the later effort on the part of the business classes and the military to curb Goulart's presidential power by granting greater decision-making powers to parliamentary officials. Goulart spent the greater part of 1962 consolidating his hold over the military, curbing the opposition elements within his own Brazilian Labor Party, and accelerating the colossal inflationary spiral by granting year-end bonuses and huge wage increases to factory and office workers in the large cities. Presidentialism, the cult of personality, the triumph of charismatic rule over rationalized authority, has once more been affirmed in Brazil. The overwhelming mandate given to Goulart in the January 1963 plebiscite indicates (a) the ineffectual side of Brazilian parliamentary rule; (b) the personal prestige of Goulart; and above all (c) the steady radicalization of political opinion in Brazil, the realization that social reform entails the redistribution of real wealth.

Those sectors which fear fundamental changes in the structure of Brazilian society may or may not derive advantages from the return to presidentialism. Disorganization and inefficiency, corruption and inflation, the pride of the Brazilian "advanced" classes, have been temporarily preserved from the "face of wrath." Now that the absurdly principled "Slav" Jânio Quadros has been eliminated as a political factor, the political norms of corruption have been preserved. However, presidentialism also means a concentration of power that may permit widespread structural development. The anomaly is that corruption and change coexist so readily in Brazil.

The Brazilian political complex tragically points up the corruption of the "middle sectors" and not their potential grandeur. Politics remains a phenomenon performed by a small minority of Brazilians. It is a game played by "white men" against the "black men" of the country, contrary to the propaganda that maintains Brazil to be the most racially integrated nation in the world. Moreover, politics is a game played by the educated against the uneducated, contrary to the propaganda that Brazil's learned classes are the most responsible citizens in the world. Politics is a game performed by proletarians against peasants, contrary to the communist propaganda that Brazil's working class is in a "vanguard position." Above all, politics remains a game played by the landholders against the landless, contrary to the propaganda that Brazilian latifundists are amongst the most benevolent and easygoing tyrants in the world.

In such a political context, to argue the need for constitutional safeguards as a remedy for presidential power is to skirt the major definition of underdevelopment—the absence of integration between socio-economic processes and political structures; the uneven development of social sectors and social classes. For those concerned with a solution to problems of political rule, one must, paradoxically, turn to non-political avenues of expression. In the social and economic complex alone do we meet the people responsible for the real ferment in Brazilian life. And here we shall deal with the causes which make such ferment so dynamic and inevitable.

V
BRAZIL AND "THIRD-FORCE"
INTERNATIONAL POLITICS

... in which Jânio Quadros shows Brazilians a way out of United States domination and a way into worldliness; and in which Horácio Láfer relates the notion of Pan-Americanism to peaceful coexistence; this is followed by José Rodrigues' discourse upon the historical foundations of Brazilian foreign policy.

I. BRAZIL'S NEW FOREIGN POLICY
Jânio Quadros *

THE INTEREST shown in the position of Brazil in international affairs is in itself proof of the presence of a new force on the world stage. Obviously my country did not appear by magic, nor is it giving itself momentarily to a more or less felicitous exhibition of publicity-seeking. When I refer to a "new force," I am not alluding to a military one, but to the fact that a nation, heretofore almost unknown, is prepared to bring to bear on the play of world pressures the economic and human potential it represents, and the knowledge reaped from experience that we have a right to believe is of positive value.

We are a nation of continental proportions, occupying almost half of South America, relatively close to Africa and, ethnically, having indigenous, European and African roots. Within the next decade, our population will amount to close to 100,000,000 inhabitants, and the rapid industrialization of some regions of the country heralds our development into an economic power.

At present we are still beset by the evils of underdevelopment which make of the greater part of our country the scene for quasi-Asiatic dramas. We have poverty-stricken areas which are over-

* Jânio Quadros is the former President of Brazil, who resigned from office in 1961 and went into temporary exile. He has now returned to Brazil and re-entered politics.

populated, and we have vast regions—the largest in the world—still unconquered. And yet, great cities are becoming industrial and trade centers of major significance.

If Brazil is only now being heard of in international affairs, it is because on taking office I decided to reap the consequences of the position that we had achieved as a nation. We had been relegated unjustifiably to an obscure position, while—even in our own hemisphere—there were accumulating errors and problems in our way that jeopardized our very future. We gave up the subsidiary and innocuous diplomacy of a nation aligned with worthy though alien interests and, to protect our rights, placed ourselves in the fore-front, convinced as we were of our ability to contribute with our own means to the understanding of peoples.

Before I undertake an objective analysis of Brazil's foreign policy, the reader will, I hope, bear with me in a somewhat subjective statement of views. It will serve to clarify the underlying reasons why we have taken particular positions on world issues.

To be genuine, a nation's foreign policy, as such, must be the embodiment of the ideals and common interests that govern its existence. Idealistic aspirations are defined by the explicit or implicit establishment of the goals aimed at. They reflect the common interests and all those economic, social, historic, and political circumstances that at a given moment influence the choice of immediate aims and the selection of ways and means of action.

The ideals of the community are the backdrop against which the national drama unfolds, and are the constant source of inspiration of true leadership. They generally permeate the means and resources for the enforcement of political decisions. A national policy—as a tool for action—seems at times to turn against the fundamental impetus that gave it birth, in order the better to serve it; but in terms of the very essence of that policy, the truth of certain realities cannot be refuted. In order to ensure that the formulation of a national strategy is viable, popular desires and ideals cannot be ignored; but the truth of the matter is that very often the tactics must be neutralized and divested of idealistic or sentimental content in order to meet urgent interests and strengthen the ideals of the community itself.

There are two moments in the life of nations when complete freedom is permitted in the expression of what might be called a national ideology: when they are undergoing dire poverty, as the sole romantic consolation left to the people; and when they are thriving in abundance, as a duty imposed upon the nation by the multitude of interests asserted but never entirely satisfied.

A nation which no longer is so poor or unprotected as to be able to indulge in the luxury of dreamy consolations, yet is struggling against mighty odds to achieve the full possession of its wealth and to develop the potentialities of its own nature, must ever remain in the arena—alert, aware and vigilant. Such a nation cannot lose sight of its objectives, yet must avoid jeopardizing them by submitting to policies which—though in keeping with remote ideals—do not, at the moment, satisfy its true interests.

There can be no doubt that Brazil—thanks to a tremendous national effort—is making gigantic strides toward breaking the barrier of underdevelopment. The rate of national growth speaks for itself, and I am convinced that at the end of my term of office the country's rate of progress will be such as to make the population explosion no longer a somber prospect but rather an additional and deciding factor for advancement in the process of economic development.

We have no right to dream. Rather it is our duty to work—but at the same time to trust and hope—and work with our feet firmly on the ground.

In time, the foreign policy of Brazil will reflect the craving for developmental progress. Obviously, underlying the decisions which we are compelled to take in order to meet the problems of material growth inherent in the desire of the Brazilian people for economic, social, political and human freedom lies the interweaving of the country's material needs. Keeping our aims ever in mind, we must choose those of our country's sources of inspiration that can best be mobilized to assist the national effort.

Because of our historical, cultural and Christian background as well as our geographical situation, ours is a predominantly Western nation. Our national effort is directed toward the achievement of a democratic way of life, both politically and socially. It may not be idle to stress here that our dedication to democracy is greater than that of other nations of our same cultural sphere. We have thus become the most successful example of racial coexistence and integration known to history.

Common ideals of life and organization draw us close to the

major nations of the Western bloc, and on many issues Brazil can, in a leading position, associate itself with this bloc. This affinity is underlined by our participation in the Inter-American regional system, which entails specific political commitments.

However, at the present juncture, we cannot accept a set national position exclusively on the basis of the above premises. It is undeniable that we have other points in common with Latin America in particular, and with the recently emancipated peoples of Asia and Africa, which cannot be ignored since they lie at the root of the readjustment of our policy, and on them converge many of the main lines of the development of Brazilian civilization. If it be true that we cannot relegate our devotion to democracy to a secondary place, it is no less true that we cannot repudiate ties and contacts offering great possibilities for national realization.

The closeness of Brazil's relations with neighboring countries of the continent and with the Afro-Asian nations, though based on different reasons, tends to the selfsame end. Among these, in the majority of cases, are historical, geographic and cultural motives. Common to them all is the fact that our economic situation coincides with the duty of forming a single front in the battle against underdevelopment and all forms of oppression.

From all this, naturally, certain points stand out that may be deemed basic to the foreign policy of my government. One of these is the recognition of the legitimacy of the struggle for economic and political freedom. Development is an aim common to Brazil and to the nations with which we endeavor to have closer relations, and the rejection of colonialism is the inevitable and imperative corollary of that aim.

It is, furthermore, in the light of these political determinants that today we consider the future of the Inter-American regional system of first importance. The growth of Latin America as a whole and the safeguarding of the sovereignty of each nation of the hemisphere are the touchstones of a continental policy as the Brazilian government understands it.

The mistakes created by an erroneous equating of continental problems are only too well known. Insufficient or misdirected aid has increased regional disagreements. Nations at grips with grave problems in common—that is, all the countries of Latin America— must take stock of their needs and plan accordingly. Latin Americans are interested not in the prosperity of the small, leading groups, but in the national prosperity as a whole, which must be sought at all costs and regardless of the risks.

The United States must realize that today it confronts a challenge from the socialist world. The Western world must show and prove that it is not only Communist planning that promotes the prosperity of national economies. Democratic planning must also do so, with the assistance of those economically able, if the political system of a perplexed two-thirds of the Western world is to avoid the risk of bankruptcy.

We cannot too often stress the extent to which poverty separates us from North America and the leading European countries of the Western world. If by their success these represent, in the eyes of the underdeveloped peoples, the ideal of achievement of the elite of European cultural origin, there nevertheless is taking root in the minds of the masses the conviction that this ideal, for a country without resources and hamstrung in its aspirations for progress, is a mockery. What solidarity can there be between a prosperous nation and a wretched people? What common ideals can, in the course of time, withstand the comparison between the rich, cultivated areas of the United States and the famine-ridden zones of the Brazilian Northeast?

Thinking of this sort irrevocably creates in us a sense of solidarity with those poverty-stricken peoples who, on three continents, are struggling against imperialist interests which, under the umbrella of democratic institutions, mislead—if not destroy—attempts to organize popular economies. When nations competing with the democratic group make demonstrations of real or pretended and disinterested economic help, this problem seems more acute under the pressure of the conflict of interests.

At this point it might be appropriate to refer to the ideological prejudices of the capitalist democracies, ever ready to decry the idea of state intervention in countries where either the state controls and governs economic growth—which has become a question of sovereignty—or nothing at all is achieved. We are not in a position to allow the free play of economic forces in our territory, simply because those forces, controlled from outside, play their own game and not that of our country.

The Brazilian government is not prejudiced against foreign capital—far from it. We stand in dire need of its help. The sole condition is that the gradual nationalization of profits be accepted, for otherwise it no longer is an element of progress but becomes a mere leech feeding on our national effort. Let it be known that the state in Brazil will not relinquish those controls that will benefit our economy by channeling and ensuring the efficiency of our progress.

Economic imbalance is doubtless the most critical of all the adverse factors that beset the Inter-American regional system, and from it almost all others stem. My government is convinced that it is fighting for the recovery of Pan-Americanism and that this must start with the economic and social fields. Politically we are trying to give shape and content to the imperative principles of self-determination and non-intervention, and it is these principles that guide us in relation to the Americas as well as to the rest of the world.

The still dramatically present question of Cuba convinced us, once and for all, of the nature of the continental crisis. In defending with intransigence the sovereignty of Cuba against interpretation of an historical fact which cannot be controlled *a posteriori*, we believe we are helping to awaken the continent to a true awareness of its responsibilities. We stand by our position on Cuba, with all its implications. Surely the Brazilian attitude has been understood by other governments, and as it gains ground, the entire regional system shows signs of a regeneration in the assessment of the responsibilities of each member nation.

The government of the United States, through its recent aid programs, took an important step toward the revision of its classical and inoperative continental policy. We hope that President Kennedy, who is not lacking in the qualities of leadership, will carry the revision of his country's attitude to the very limit and will sweep away the considerable remaining obstacles on the road to a truly democratic, continental community.

As to Africa, we may say that today it represents a new dimension in Brazilian policy. We are linked to that continent by our ethnic and cultural roots and share in its desire to forge for itself an independent position in the world of today. The nations of Latin America that became politically independent in the course of the nineteenth century found the process of economic development delayed by historical circumstances, and Africa, which has only recently become politically free, joins us at this moment in the common struggle for freedom and well-being.

I believe that it is precisely in Africa that Brazil can render the best service to the concepts of Western life and political methods. Our country should become the link, the bridge, between Africa and the West, since we are so intimately bound to both peoples. In so far as we can give the nations of the Black continent an example of complete absence of racial prejudice, together with successful proof of progress without undermining the principles of freedom, we shall be decisively contributing to the effective integration of an entire continent in a system to which we are attached by our philosophy and historic tradition.

The attraction exerted by the Communist world, by Communist techniques and by the spirit of Communist organizations upon the countries but recently freed from the capitalist yoke is common knowledge. Generally speaking, all underdeveloped countries, including those of Latin America, are susceptible to that appeal. It must not be forgotten that whereas the independence of the Latin American nations was inspired by a liberation movement rooted in the French Revolution, the autonomy obtained by the new Asian and African nations was preceded by a wave of hope aroused by the socialist revolution in Russia among the oppressed classes and peoples all over the world. The Afro-Asian liberation movement arose against the domination by nations that compose —if not lead—the Western bloc.

These historical factors are of decisive importance and must be borne in mind when gauging the role that a country such as Brazil can play in the task of reappraising the dynamic forces that are at work in the new world of today in Asia and Africa.

For many years Brazil made the mistake of supporting European colonialism in the United Nations. This attitude—which is only now fading—gave rise to a justified mistrust of Brazilian policy. Misinformed circles, overly impressed with European patterns of behavior, contributed to a mistake which must be attributed more to a disregard of the deeper commitments of our country than to political malice. Our fraternal relationship with Portugal played its part in the complacency shown by the Ministry of Foreign Affairs of Brazil in this matter.

Therefore, everything points to a necessary change of position with regard to colonialism, which in all its guises—even the most tenuous—will from now on meet with the determined opposition of Brazil. This is our policy, not merely in the interests of Africa, nor for the sake of a platonic solidarity, but because it is in keeping with Brazilian national interests. These to a certain extent are still influenced by the most disguised forms of colonialist pressure, but call for a rapprochement with Africa.

I might add that the raising of the economic standards of the African peoples is of vital importance to the economy of Brazil. Even from a purely selfish standpoint, we are interested in seeing the social betterment and improvement in the production techniques of Africa. The exploitation of Africans by European capital is detrimental to the Brazilian economy, permitting as it does the fostering of commercial competition on the basis of low-salaried Negro workers. Competition on a civilized and human level must be found to replace that of enslavement by underpayment of an entire race. Here and now, the industrial growth of my country guarantees to the Africans a most important source of supply, which could even serve as the basis for arrangements for the linking together of our respective production systems.

We are setting up regular diplomatic and trade relations with several African countries and my government's emissaries have visited that continent to study concrete possibilities for cooperation and exchange. In time, the potentialities of this closer relationship, destined to be a milestone in the history of human affairs, will be fulfilled.

Here I must underscore another important aspect of the new Brazilian foreign policy. My country has few international obligations: we are bound only by pacts and treaties of continental assistance which commit us to solidarity with any member of the hemisphere that may become the victim of extra-continental aggression. We have not subscribed to treaties of the nature of NATO, and are in no way forced formally to intervene in the cold war between East and West. We are therefore in a position to follow our national inclination to act energetically in the cause of peace and the relaxation of international tension.

Not being members of any bloc, not even of the Neutralist bloc, we preserve our absolute freedom to make our own decisions in specific cases and in the light of peaceful suggestions at one with our nature and history. A group of nations, notably of Asia, is also careful to remain on the sidelines in any clash of interests which are invariably those of the great powers and not necessarily those of our country, let alone of world peace.

The first step in making full use of the possibilities of our position in the world consists in maintaining normal relations with all nations. Brazil, either through misinterpretation or distortion of its better political judgment, spent many years without regular contacts with the countries of the Communist bloc, even to the point of having only roundabout and insufficient trade relations with them. As a part of my government's program, I decided to examine the possibility of renewing relations with Russia, Hungary, Bulgaria and Albania; these have now been established. Negotiations for the reopening of relations with the Soviet Union are in progress and an official Brazilian mission is going to China to study exchange possibilities. Consistent with this revision of our foreign policy, my country, as is known, decided to vote in favor of including on the agenda of the U.N. General Assembly the question of the representation of China; this initial position will, in due course, have its logical consequences.

The possibilities of trade relations between Brazil and the Orient are practically *terra incognita*. Even in the case of Japan, to which we are bound by so many ties, our barter relations are far from complete. China, Korea, Indonesia, India, Ceylon and all of Southeast Asia provide room for the development of our production and commercial endeavors, which neither distance nor political problems can discourage.

The world must be made aware of the fact that Brazil is intensively increasing its production, looking not only to the domestic market, but specifically seeking to attract other nations. Economically speaking, my government's motto is "Produce everything, for everything produced is marketable." We shall go out to conquer these markets: at home, in Latin America, in Africa, in Asia, in Oceania, in countries under democracy, and in those that have joined the Communist system. Material interests know no doctrine and Brazil is undergoing a period where its very survival as a nation occupying one of the most extensive and privileged areas of the globe depends on the solution of its economic problems. Our very faithfulness to the democratic way of life is at stake in this struggle for development. A nation such as ours, with 70,000,000 inhabitants and with the world's highest rate of population growth, will not permit even a slowing down of its movement toward the full utilization of its own wealth.

Without fear of error I can say that the experiment in democratic progress being carried out in Brazil is decisive both for Latin America and for all the underdeveloped areas of the world. Therefore, this experiment is of deep interest to prosperous nations which are also proud of being free. They will remain so to the extent that success crowns the efforts for economic emancipation of the underdeveloped nations living under the same system. Freedom once again becomes the outgrowth of equality.

It must be pointed out that the idea behind the foreign policy of Brazil, and its implementation, has now become the instrument for a national development policy. As part and parcel of our national life, foreign policy has ceased to be an unrealistic academic exercise carried out by oblivious and spellbound elites; it has become the main topic of daily concern. With it we seek specific aims: at home, prosperity and well-being; elsewhere, to live together amicably and in world peace.

There is no need to spell out to Brazilians what we are in the world today. We are fully aware of the mission we must accomplish, and can accomplish.

II. THE SURVIVAL OF MANKIND:
UNITED NATIONS NOT A SUPER-STATE

Horácio Láfer *

Only a short time ago the American nations held in Costa Rica one of their most important conferences of Ministers of Foreign Relations. The most significant outcome of this conference is the affirmation of solidarity of the countries of this continent with regard to the principles and ideals that have formed the basis of our peoples' aspirations. Nineteen nations of this Hemisphere solemnly reaffirmed that the regime accepted by the American peoples as compatible with their traditions and collective aspirations is that regime characterized by the free expression of thought, by free elections, by the separation of powers, by the limitations upon the

* Horácio Láfer is the former chief of the Brazilian delegation to the United Nations.

terms of elective office, and by respect for civil liberties and human rights. At the same time, these nineteen nations declared that they attached quite as much importance to the need for economic development of their peoples as to these political aspirations. It was with this preoccupation in mind that the [former] President of Brazil, Juscelino Kubitschek, proposed the plan now known as Operation Pan America. Its basic aim is to lay the foundation of a close economic solidarity among the nations of the continent, so that, in the spirit of the ideals of peace, freedom, and democracy which characterize our political philosophy, it may be possible to foster the economic and social progress of Latin America as speedily as possible.

After the close of the Costa Rica conference, the American nations assembled in Bogotá, where the nineteen countries of the continent again accepted collectively a plan for social progress submitted by President Eisenhower, as well as measures to promote their economic development, within the objectives of Operation Pan America. Thus, the Latin American countries reaffirmed their desire to solve their dramatic problems of economic growth without sacrificing the ideals of freedom and respect for human dignity. Only two abstentions were recorded, and we hope that these will shortly disappear.

What is the real meaning of this consensus of opinion among the American countries in the United Nations? It means that America has its politico-social policy defined and adopted, and staunchly defends it. But this definition does not exclude respect for the ideas of others, particularly since intransigence is impossible today.

Indeed, peaceful coexistence of peoples is an imperative in our time. The development of nuclear weapons has ruled out war as an alternative instrument of policy. Faced with the inadmissibility of resorting to war as a solution, the world is confronted with the necessity of settling through negotiation those differences that separate nations. The only feasible path leading to a solution of our age's problems is that of permanent negotiation, the persistent determination to continue to negotiate. The United Nations is not a super-state, but is, rather, an affirmation that the world must live in a continuous, patient, constant state of negotiation. It is a mechanism that offers maximum opportunities for meetings and lines of compromise. Although it is true that this process of negotiation may always entail the risk of a stalemate, it is equally true that it is the only means for arriving at solutions that will assure the survival of mankind.

Nonetheless, to attain this state of peaceful coexistence that we are all seeking, a basic premise, a point of departure must be fixed. This premise is the acceptance by each one of the reality, just or unjust, of nations with regimes, ideologies, and organizations, not as we would wish them to be, but as they are today. This accept-ance must be accompanied by the pledge of non-intervention, direct or indirect, by one ideology in the sphere of another. How can we aspire to disarmament, cessation of the cold war and unrest, if there is fear that some countries wish to destroy or dominate others? So long as the principle of the *status quo* of the present political geography among the existing politico-ideo-logical organizations is not accepted, we shall waver between the cold war and the prospect of catastrophe. In this connection, a relevant role can be played, vis-à-vis the major protagonists in the current political scene, by the lesser, anti-war powers, which can become the impartial interpreters of the world's desire for peace. Attempts to modify the order existing today will merely delay the establishment of an understanding which is indispensable if the world is to look forward to disarmament, peaceful coexistence, and an end to the cold war. The stalemate in efforts to achieve disarmament stems from the lack of mutual confidence. Why not negotiate this point of departure now?

The problem has another aspect, which the President of Brazil has constantly stressed: only economic development can consoli-date peace among nations. The world spends at least 100 billion dollars per year on armaments, while the industrialized countries have in the last ten years spent about 40 billion dollars on aid, assistance, investments, etc., for the underdeveloped areas of the world. It is inconceivable that armaments, garrisons, and armies should be done away with; this Virgilian scene is chimerical. But the arms race can be brought to a halt, by applying the resources thus saved to economic development. Why, then, not adopt in a special conference a system whereby the powers would pool their savings effected by an arms reduction and turn them into a United Nations International Development Fund? It would be very diffi-cult to devote, in addition to the large sums turned over to the Fund, an equivalent sum to armaments as well. It would mean paying twice. Brazil supports the efforts to achieve international disarmament by realistic means in technically studied and effectively controlled stages. The accumulation of funds through decreases in expenditures for arms, linked with a percentage of resources that more highly developed countries could loan to this Fund, would instill life into the field abandoned and forgotten by the World Bank. The United Nations will win everyone's heart the day it enters upon the path of ample, generous programs of cooperation that will promote the social well-being and economic progress of nations.

In the United Nations' fifteen years of existence, we have not succeeded in creating genuinely effective instruments of economic cooperation, nor has international peace been consolidated. But the United Nations is, nonetheless, humanity's great hope today and constitutes, with all its serious limitations, the best instrument for diplomatic negotiations and the most perfect mechanism for maintaining the peace that we have been able to devise to date. The vigor, energy and speed with which the Security Council acted in the crisis involving the Congo, this crisis which so distresses and worries us, are proof of the organization's real possibilities. With the Council paralyzed by the veto, an emergency special session of the General Assembly was immediately called under the provision of the "Uniting for Peace" resolution. This session which ended two days ago approved, without a negative vote, the resolution which will make it possible for the United Nations to continue its activities in the Congo without disruption or delay. And it behooves me here to say a special word of praise and encouragement to the [deceased] Secretary General of the United Nations, Dag Hammarskjold, who with patience, courage, devotion and impartiality, has faithfully interpreted and forcefully expressed the yearning for peace which lies behind the anxiety with which the people of the world look upon the dangerous and delicate situation in the Congo.

Brazil, through officers of its Air Force, is participating in the effort being made by the United Nations to maintain law and order in the Republic of the Congo. Bound by cultural and historic ties to the peoples of Africa, conscious of the geographic affinities and the heritage of blood which link us with the nations of the Black Continent, the Brazilians follow with extreme interest the awakening of their African brothers. And here we extend our sincere and wholehearted welcome to the States newly admitted to the United Nations.

In Suez, also, with hundreds and hundreds of Brazilian soldiers, we are paying the price of peace in the hope that the Middle East may reach a peaceful solution of coexistence, in a spirit of mutual respect and self-determination.

If peace hinges upon the criterion, as we have pointed out, of a previous, preliminary, basic understanding, economic development has yet to find the means to attain it.

It is encouraging that one of the items to be considered by this General Assembly is that entitled Economic Development of Underdeveloped Countries, a problem that has been of concern to us since the establishment of the United Nations. Some important steps were taken with the creation of the Special Fund in the 1958 General Assembly, and that of the Commission of Industrialization in 1959. But there still remains on our agenda the question of establishing a Development Fund with resources for financing and expanding the economy of the underdeveloped countries where over a billion human beings await the social justice to which they are entitled. We are certain that the Development Fund will win full acceptance in this Assembly.

The Brazilian government, together with various other countries, has co-sponsored the request for the inclusion in the agenda of this session of the General Assembly the item referring to racial discrimination. Brazil has always supported all recommendations presented in the United Nations opposing the policies of segregation based upon differences of race, color, or religion, which are repugnant to the conscience of the Brazilian people and are clearly condemned by the Charter. Brazil submitted a draft resolution to the Council of the Organization of American States expressing repudiation of any and all forms of racial discrimination and segregation, a proposal which was passed unanimously by the American States. In this connection, I wish to recall that Brazil subscribed to and ratified the International Convention on Genocide approved in 1948 by the General Assembly of the United Nations. Racial persecution is contrary to the spirit and the purposes of the United Nations. Brazil, along with the civilized world, most vehemently condemns it.

This Assembly opens in an atmosphere of anxiety. Public opinion is fearful lest the men responsible for their governments may not find the formulas conducive to peace. Antagonisms are strong and deep-rooted. Allow me, gentlemen, to conclude this address with the earnest hopes of the President and the people of Brazil, and I trust of the entire world, that the wisdom of the statesmen present here may find the way, not to unify thought and action —an impossibility—but to allow each one in his sphere to respect his fellow man and make possible coexistence with a just peace.

III. THE FOUNDATIONS OF BRAZIL'S FOREIGN POLICY

José Honório Rodrigues *

Brazil adopted a foreign policy even before the proclamation of independence on 7 September 1822. The Prince Regent, D. Pedro, soon after the return of his father, D. João VI, to Portugal in 1821, fought the *Côrtes* (the Assembly of Estates) of Portugal, which tried to restrict his powers and to reduce Brazil to her former condition of colony after she had been for some years a kingdom and the seat of the monarchy. D. Pedro denounced the *Côrtes* to the principal nations of the world and asked them to recognize the Government of Brazil as the only legitimate organ of the monarchy, sending, for this purpose, four emissaries to Europe (to Great Britain, France, Vienna, and the Holy See), and others to Washington and Argentina. After 7 September these emissaries worked for the recognition of independence.

The negotiations were protracted and arduous, for the question was now that of a revolutionary movement comparable to those of the other South American colonies, and the Powers of the Holy Alliance wanted to re-establish the principle of the legitimacy of royal power which the French Revolution and Napoleon had denied. Recognition was all the more difficult to obtain because D. Pedro had proclaimed himself Emperor "by the unanimous acclamation of the people," ascribing the legitimacy of power not to hereditary law but to popular suffrage, thus violating the principles of the Holy Alliance. The title of Emperor was an additional impediment in the negotiations with Portgual for independence,

---

* José Honório Rodrigues is Director of the National Archives of Brazil and Professor of Economic History at the University of the State of Guanabara (Rio de Janeiro).

says Sir Charles Webster, for in it was implied the idea of superiority.[1]

What D. Pedro really wanted was the future reunion of the
Portuguese Empire, when he would be called to Portugal to reign
as D. Pedro IV. The United States was the first country to recognize Brazil's independence, on 16 May 1824, but the fate of Brazil
was linked to that of Europe, and chiefly to that of Great Britain.
The European Powers imposed stringent trade regulations as a
condition for their recognition, and this was achieved only
through British intervention. The price of recognition included
the sum of 2 million pounds sterling paid to Portugal and the renewal of the most favored nation privileges given to Great Britain,
as well as various special concessions that virtually made Brazil a
British protectorate until 1844, when she refused to renew the
agreements. For her part Brazil did not put an end to the slave
trade, as she had agreed to do, postponing this step until 1850.

The statesmen of the Empire (1822-89) were soon aware of
the difficulties created by independence, especially the fact that
Brazil's enormous territorial area was not being put to use and that
her natural and economic resources were not being developed.
With a population of almost 4 million people and a territorial area
of 8,511,965 sq. km., there were more than two sq. km. for each
person. Compared with the small Spanish States, Brazil, occupying
half of South America, was a unit singularly *sui generis*.

As a consequence of all these circumstances, the following principles guided Brazilian foreign policy, which was very troubled
in the first nine years and very timid until 1844.

(1) As a country potentially subject to attack on account of
her small population and her rich but unexploited resources, Brazil
adopted, *vis-à-vis* Europe and the United States, a pacifist ideology, favoring international arbitration. Brazilian foreign policy
has always preferred juridical to political solutions. Of Brazil's 167
Foreign Ministers, 145 graduated in law, although two of the
greatest distinguished themselves not by their legal knowledge but
by their political *savoir faire* and their historical and geographical
learning.

(2) In her relations with neighboring countries, most notably
over frontier problems inherited from the colonial era, the general

---

[1] *Britain and the Independence of Latin America, 1812-1830* (London:
Oxford University Press, 1938), vol. I, p. 57.

principle has always been to aim at a peaceful and legal solution. In the preservation of her frontiers against the territorial pretensions of some neighboring countries, Brazil, firmly supported by historical rights and by *uti possidetis*, has always sought a juridical compromise.

(3) In the defense of her territorial integrity, threatened by the possible re-creation of the Viceroyalty of the River Plate, Brazil's foreign policy was orientated not by legal but by political and military considerations. In her so-called interventionist policy, Brazil used the same methods that Europe and the United States applied in their differences with her. The policies of power and influence, of coercion and persuasion, of intervention and nonintervention, were variously applied in accordance with circumstances, aided by the political sagacity and the tactical skill of her statesmen.

Vis-à-vis the European Powers, especially Great Britain and France, and also in her relations with the United States, which used persuasion and force, Brazil's entire defense consisted in peaceful resistance and in eventual concessions. She always tried to keep intact her territorial patrimony and her national unity, two indispensable conditions of her future claim to respect and prestige in international life. She was forced to sign ignominious treaties from 1825 onwards, especially with Great Britain and France—for which the statesmen of the Empire who directed her foreign policy or discussed it in the Chamber of Deputies or in the Senate always expressed the greatest repugnance—paying exorbitant prices and granting special economic and legal privileges that were really equivalent to extra-territorial rights. Violence, insults, threats, pressures fill the pages of her diplomatic history of that time.

In the first twenty-eight years of Brazil's independent existence Great Britain was the focus of her international life, dominating her, harming her interests, threatening her, obtaining concessions and privileges that would be inconceivable today, but it was also on Great Britain that her independence and her sovereignty depended. The British demanded that she abolish the slave trade, for instance—a consequence of the policy of Castlereagh and Canning —which would have resulted in the ruin of her agricultural economy, damage to commerce and navigation, reduction of the income of the State, and an end to the importation of the slave labor she was not in a position to dispense with, could not be obeyed until 1850, when she began to prepare for the substitution of free for slave labor. The non-fulfillment of this obligation was the greatest obstacle to the recognition of *de facto* independence. It was thus necessary to find a compromise solution that would satisfy Brazil's aspirations to independence and sovereignty and at the same time not harm her agricultural interests, particularly the coffee and sugar plantations, which depended on slave labor. Torn between two quintessential interests, one permanent, the other of primary concern to the ruling classes, Brazil accepted the legal obligation of abolition without implementing it immediately.

Brazil's relations with Portuguese Africa were a keypoint in her diplomatic policy. These relations resulted in constant conflict with Great Britain, on account of Brazil's failure to fulfill her obligation to free the slaves, which she had assumed in a Convention and which Britain sought to enforce by considerable pressure and threats. "There are two things," Lord Aberdeen told Guizot, "on which my country is not tractable . . . the abolition of the slave trade and protestant propagandism"; and when Guizot asked him what might be the strength in the House of Commons of the abolitionist group called the Saints, he replied, "They are all Saints on such questions." [2] While the British demand may have been inspired by humanitarian motives or colored by economic interests and the desire to expand in Africa [3] and while Brazil's policy may have been to protect the needs of the landed class which ruled the country, the fact remains that Brazil never betrayed her interests except on paper. While resigning herself to stoic toleration of all forms of European coercion, she nevertheless continued the slave traffic and her commercial relations with Africa, especially with Angola which was practically a Brazilian colony and depended on these relations.

The struggle for freedom from British tutelage went on until 1844, when Brazil declared that the Treaty of 1827 had lapsed. [4] The Aberdeen Bill of 1845 and the assaults on Brazilian ships, the

[2] Sir Charles Webster, *The Art and Practice of Diplomacy* (London: Chatto and Windus, 1961), p. 43.

[3] *See* José Honório Rodrigues, *Brasil e África, Outro Horizonte* (Rio de Janeiro: Civilizacão Brasileira, 1961).

[4] *See* Alan K. Manchester, *British Pre-eminence in Brazil* (Chapel Hill: The University of North Carolina Press, 1933).

Christie question in 1862 with the reprisals of the British Navy at
the entrance to the harbor of Rio de Janeiro, the breaking of relations in 1864, all show the decisive role played by Great Britain
in Brazil's international life, leading perhaps to the point of forcing
her out of Africa.[5] The Aberdeen Bill was one of the greatest insults which a strong people ever offered to a weak one.[6]

Brazil's foreign policy was oriented not toward the American
continent but seaward. The River Plate was not at first, as some
have written, the dominant preoccupation of her Secretary of
Foreign Affairs, and, influenced by the British, she readily agreed
to the creation of Uruguay in 1828. Only after 1843 did events
in Argentina demand greater attention. Although the Secretary
of Foreign Affairs declared in 1831 that he intended to eliminate
some European missions in order to establish others in America,
by about 1833 Brazil had ten diplomatic missions in Europe and
only four in America; in 1859 these were increased to thirteen
and seven respectively; there were 157 consuls in Europe and only
37 in America.

The Treaty of 1827 between Brazil and France gave the latter
such extraordinary privileges, aggravated by the clause of perpetuity, that on several occasions Great Britain complained of not
being the most favored nation, especially in questions of succession
to property and intestacies. The articles of perpetuity that benefited France only were a source of conflict and bitter humiliation,[7]
forcing Brazil to conclude several very disadvantageous consular
agreements. But nothing would satisfy the ambition of the great
Powers, which demanded the exclusive jurisdiction of their consuls in all matters of succession, including those of Brazilian children of foreign parents, in flagrant contravention of Article 6 of
the Imperial Constitution of 1824. The consuls, especially the
French, considered that they had the right to conduct hearings,
to appoint guardians, to open wills, and to apply the law of their
own countries in Brazil.

The worst evils came, however, from the clause of perpetuity,

[5] In the recognition of independence D. Pedro accepted the clause prohibiting the adherence of the Portuguese colonies of Africa to Brazil, which
seems to have been a British condition. See Rodrigues, op. cit., pp. 142-44.
[6] R. Burton. The Highlands of Brazil (London, 1869), vol. I, p. 5.
[7] See Antônio Pereira Pinto, Apontamentos para o Direito Internacional
(Rio de Janeiro, 1865), vol. II, pp. 15ff.

with its pernicious effect on Brazilian interests. Every pretext was used by the British and French to make complaints and exert pressure, accompanied by threats of force, even in the simplest cases, as when Brazil used her sovereign right to increase tariffs on products imported from Britain and France.

Animosity against Europe and against the treaties, which inspired Brazil's statesmen and representatives in the first years of her independent life, was only natural. In 1847, after severely criticizing the obligations she had contracted in treaties greatly to the detriment of her development, the Barão de Cairu declared that such treaties were not the best way of strengthening ties between countries and that the Empire should proceed cautiously, agreeing to nothing that had not received the consent of all, and regulating everything else in accordance with the needs of the time and the economic and social interests of Brazil. In the Senate the conservative Bernardo Pereira de Vasconcelos, after declaring himself against the Holy Alliance and an admirer of Great Britain, confessed his indignation at the treaty with France and expressed the opinion that such treaties were hostile and hateful acts against Brazil.

The Empire did not renew the treaty with Great Britain which had lapsed in 1844, and in 1887 it refused a proposal to negotiate a Treaty of Commerce and Navigation. This proposal, wrote the Secretary of State, the Barão de Cotegipe, was contrary to the policy long followed by the Imperial Government of signing Treaties of Commerce and Navigation only with neighboring countries. And he added that experience had shown that special agreements were not necessary to protect British interests. "In fact, the Treaty of Friendship, Commerce, and Navigation of 17 August 1827 between Brazil and Great Britain lapsed in 1844, and since then, or for more than forty years, in spite of the nonexistence of another similar treaty, British maritime and commercial interests have constantly and progressively shown great improvement."

Brazilian foreign policy, therefore, without contracting obligations for unforeseen contingencies, or rather without negotiating agreements on bases proposed by other nations, did not create difficulties in the expansion of commercial relations with the European Powers or reduce British investments in Brazil. But the clause of perpetuity contained in the treaty with France remained and was not definitively denounced until 1907.

After 1843 Brazil's relations with the Republics of the River Plate (Argentina and Uruguay) became more complicated, but it was only in the period 1848–50 that they began to feature more prominently in her foreign policy. Even so this policy did not become regionalized or continentalized. Brazil endeavored to guarantee the territorial *status quo* and the balance of power, based on the principle of maintaining the independence of Uruguay and Paraguay, in order to avoid the dream of the Argentine dictator, Rosas, of re-creating the Viceroyalty of the Plate, which had dissolved during the struggle for independence. The maintenance of the *status quo* implied keeping these independent States divided and preventing their unification into a new group.

The policy of cautious neutrality pursued by Brazil in 1844 changed when the re-creation of the Viceroyalty, up to this time only a threat, appeared imminent. Before the Brazilian-Argentinian agreement, Domingo Sarmiento once asked if there was any impediment to the union of the Republics of Paraguay and Uruguay and the Argentine Confederation in a Confederation under the name of the United States of South America. Certainly Brazilian policy was opposed to it, for her statesmen saw in the efforts of General Rosas and his ally Oribe an attempt to separate the Rio Grande do Sul from Brazil and to renew the boundary Treaty of 1777 in order to recover the territory of the Missions. Furthermore, the *caudilhismo* that reigned there—in contrast to the Brazilian representative parliamentary system, however defective—was the source of continual incidents, violence, and extortions against Brazilian individuals and properties.

As a result Brazil and the Argentine Confederation were involved in several disputes. Argentina, once free from the last Anglo-French intervention (1849–50), increased her activity in Uruguay, in an effort to absorb the territory, and in 1849 decided to reincorporate Paraguay. Thanks to the skill of her statesmen Brazil concluded a defensive alliance with Paraguay, and shortly after that with the Provinces of Entre Rios and Corrientes; the war between Brazil and the Rosas dictatorship thus lost the character of a national struggle between Brazil and Argentina, thereby putting an end to the prejudices that had been generated during the colonial era.

The victory of Monte Caseros (3 February 1852) marked the beginning of Brazilian-Argentinian understanding and re-established a strict neutrality which was maintained during the struggles between Mitre's forces in Buenos Aires and those of General Urquiza, ending in the victory of the former in Pavón (17 September 1861). From then on friendly political and commercial relations between Brazil and Argentina were gradually consolidated, especially during the Paraguayan War (1864–70), which was, after the defeat of the Uruguayan intervention in 1864, the last step taken by Brazil to maintain the balance of power in the River Plate. In Uruguay and Paraguay, the resentments, hostilities, rivalries, and frustrations resulting from these military actions have still not disappeared altogether; indeed, certain groups still manifest a "victim complex" with respect to Brazil. In Argentina, Mitre, Sáenz, Peña, and Julio Roca were instrumental in dispelling feelings of hostility. Minority groups, however, are still unfriendly to Brazil. In the Brazilian military interventions in Uruguay, as well as in the Paraguayan War, the *status quo* with regard to the possessions of the two States was kept unchanged, based on the principle of *uti possidetis* and in violation of the boundary Treaty of 1777 between Spain and Portugal.

The policy of intervention was complementary to the policy of balance of power in the River Plate. It aimed at putting an end to the regime of *caudilhismo*, which threatened Brazil's frontiers, and at preventing the setting up of unstable governments. Brazil's statesmen at that time justified intervention by saying it was necessary to preserve her frontiers and the lives and properties of Brazilians. Ramón Carcano, one of Argentina's Ambassadors to Brazil and one of the best authorities on the subject of Argentinian-Brazilian relations, wrote that the Empire, by helping itself, also helped its neighbors.[8] The foreign policy of the Brazilian Empire *vis-à-vis* her neighbors was an intervention one, especially between 1851 and 1870, as was also that of Rosas, who tried to intervene in 1838 in the revolution of the Rio Grande do Sul.

Another aim of Brazilian diplomacy in the American continent has been the defense of the frontiers of the vast area that had been

[8] See *Guerra del Paraguay. Origines y Causas* (Buenos Aires: Domingo Viau, 1939), pp. 168, 169, 172, 190.

won and occupied by the Luso-Brazilians, their treaty definition, and boundary demarcation. More than 16,000 sq. km. were incorporated in Brazilian territory, without the loss of a single drop of blood, without a shot, based only on historical documents and maps and on the right of possession (*uti possidetis*). Here, as in her relations with Europe, Brazil's policy was dominated by peaceful methods and the principle of appeal to arbitration, precisely because the legal position served her national aspirations—the security and defense of her territory. Whether by direct negotiations or by arbitration, Brazil's frontier policy had only one aim: to defend the land she now possessed. Such was Brazil's integrity that after her victory in the Paraguayan War she agreed to the same frontier which she had previously demanded on the basis of *uti possidetis*, and when her claims on the frontier with British Guiana were not recognized by the arbiter she did not question the decision.

The definition of boundaries is practically completed today. Only a few doubts remain as to the sources of some rivers and the demarcation and definition of certain territorial limits. This task was not achieved by Rio Branco alone, though between 1893 and 1912 he successfully negotiated the most difficult frontier disputes, thereby incorporating in Brazilian territory about 430,621 sq. km., and purchased the Acre Territory (403,000 sq. km.). Rio Branco would not have achieved these victories without the preparatory studies of his predecessors, men such as his father, the Visconde do Rio Branco, Joaquim Caetano da Silva, and Paulino Soares de Sousa. Nor was this the achievement of a single regime or any single political party. It was the work of a whole nation, of foreign ministers, diplomats, historians, geographers, and pioneers.

With the establishment of the principle of the maintenance of the *status quo*, the fixing of frontiers, and the assurance that the balance of power would be maintained, continental harmony has been a permanent aim of Brazilian foreign policy since 1870. "With our neighbors, above all, we must be generous and avoid everything that may force us out of neutrality in all matters, without the sacrifice, however, of our national honor," D. Pedro II wrote in his political advice to Princess Isabel in 1871.[9] From then

---

[9] *See* Manuscript in the Archive of Palacio Grão Pará, residence of Prince D. Pedro, presumptive heir of the Crown. There is a limited (100 copies) facsimile edition.

on it became usual for the Emperor to declare in his Speeches to the Assembly that he was doing his utmost to maintain peace and cultivate cordial relations with all nations.

Whether Brazil's foreign policy tended to broaden or narrow her relations with other countries, she has always sought to keep her contacts with the United States cordial, and thereby to maintain an equilibrium among the eighteen Spanish American Republics. Another great country with which Brazil has always cultivated close relations is Chile, whose friendship contributed to an equilibrium in the South and Spanish American world. Brazil's relations with the United States began with the United States' recognition of her independence in 1824, and were strengthened by the Treaty of Friendship, Commerce, and Navigation of 1828. In 1846 Brazil's Foreign Minister observed that relations with the United States were growing more important every day, primarily because of the development of commercial interests between the two countries.

There was, of course, some friction with the United States and Brazil was subjected to affronts, threats, intimidations, protests, and discourteous language, such as she had experienced from Great Britain, but she never harbored the feelings of resentment experienced by other Spanish American States which had also suffered in the same way. The usefulness of the United States alliance has always been recognized as one of the foundations of Brazilian foreign policy, and her statesmen have maintained it in order that she should not remain isolated in the inter-American world or, rather, in order that she should remain a stabilizing factor in the American continent.

As the biggest buyer of Brazilian coffee, especially since 1865, the United States recognized in Brazil an important market, for which she had been competing with Great Britain since the lapse of the Anglo-Brazilian Treaty of 1844, when equal tariffs and privileges were accorded to both countries. In 1870, when the United States was already importing more than half the coffee exported from Rio de Janeiro, Minister Henry P. Blow offered some suggestions for the development of commercial relations and proposed to provide, in exchange for a reduction in the taxes on coffee and sugar, several other articles and manufactured goods at cheaper prices. These goods had until then been chiefly provided by Great Britain, which continued to be the principal exporter of products and capital to Brazil. He affirmed then, as Secretary Abel P. Upshur had previously done in 1843, that the Brazilian Empire had a future that must be looked upon with the utmost interest by the older nations of the world, but that none of them could be so completely sympathetic to her progress as his own nation.[10]

The frequent incidents between Brazil and the United States, especially as a result of Brazil's neutrality during the American Civil War and of United States' demands for the opening of the Amazon to foreign navigation—demands made from 1850 onwards and supported by Tavares Bastos, a Brazilian deputy and writer and a great admirer of the Anglo-Saxon world—did not affect the peaceful development of commercial and economic relations in general. Political relations between the two countries were greatly improved when the Barão do Rio Branco was Foreign Minister (1902–12). The greatest opponent of the United States shortly after the proclamation of the Republic (1889) was Eduardo Prado, who wrote a pamphlet entitled *The American Illusion*.[11]

From this epoch dates the tendency on the part of Brazil to draw away from her former European ties and to align herself as far as possible with United States' policies in the American hemisphere. It is certain, as we have said, that during the Empire Brazil had always recognized the advantages of this friendship and the disadvantages of any stand with the Spanish American States against the United States. Teixeira Macedo once wrote to the Marquês de Olinda, Foreign Minister: "We must be extremely careful to prevent the United States from thinking that because of our relations with the Spanish Americans this means that we are in a league against her. We must not sacrifice the friendship of an important power, whose commercial relations are advantageous to us, to gamble our welfare on future alliances of problematical importance." [12] The same thought was repeated by Rio Branco: "The

10 *See* W. R. Manning, *Diplomatic Correspondence of the United States* (Washington: Carnegie Endowment for International Peace, 1932), vol. II, pp. 122-26.

11 *See A Ilusão Americana* (São Paulo, 1893). This edition was confiscated and destroyed by order of the Brazilian Government. Several editions were published later.

12 *See* Sergio Teixeira Macedo to the Marquês de Olinda, Minister of Foreign Affairs. Washington, 26 April 1849. Arquivo Histórico do Ministério das Relações Exteriores, Ofícios Recebidos Reservado n.5.

so-called League of the Spanish American Republics to oppose the United States is impossible because of the lack of agreement among these States, and it is even ridiculous in view of the well-known weakness and poverty of resources of most of them. It is not with a policy of pinpricks and making nuisances of ourselves to the United States that we will be able to stalemate our opponents." [13]

It is also clear that this policy had been affirmed even before Rio Branco became Foreign Minister. An official Report of 1896 stated: "Without wanting to assume one iota of responsibility in international situations created and solved by the United States, Brazil is aware of and cannot escape the influence that the United States exerts in the destinies of South America." [14] Ever since she became independent, Brazil had always wanted to devote more attention to regional problems, but only at the end of the century was she able to attain this objective, although the two essentials of productivity, capital and labor, were still of European origin. As her commercial relations with the United States increased, her Foreign Ministers, and especially Rio Branco, sought to achieve that aim. The Americanism of Rio Branco signified a de-Europeanization of Brazilian foreign policy.

The two pillars of Rio Branco's foreign policy were friendship with the United States and with Chile; he had, however, inherited the colonial complexes of Spanish-Portuguese hostility and often felt the rivalries of Brazil's neighbors more than their friendships. He had also inherited many remnants of the Imperial interventionist policy in the River Plate. Not only Rio Branco but also his rivals, such as Estanislau Zeballos, proceeded along the same lines. It was for this reason that Rio Branco sought to cooperate with the United States and to create in Spanish America a friendlier and more understanding atmosphere for Washington. It is this policy of bringing the three Americas together around the axis of Brazil-United States friendship which Brazil has followed ever since, both on her own and in inter-American congresses.

Since the time of Rio Branco, Brazilian-American amity has been one of the principal aims of Brazil's foreign policy, even to

[13] See Dispatch of January 1905 to the Brazilian Legation in Washington. Arquivo Histórico do Ministério das Relações Exteriores.

[14] See Relatório do Ministério das Relações Exteriores, Rio de Janeiro, 1896, pp. 5-6.

the point of exaggeration, as in the case of Brazil's indifference toward the doctrine of non-intervention, when a man like John Barrett, Director of the Pan-American Union, warned his compatriots in the United States that it was time "to stop this careless talk of interference with the affairs of our neighbors" (*New York Herald,* 18 February 1912).

Although the Theodore Roosevelt Corollary of 1904 and American intervention in Nicaragua in 1911 had to a certain extent been counter-balanced by non-intervention in Mexico in 1913 (despite great United States pressure against her), the incidents of Tampico and Vera Cruz in 1914, which called for the mediation of the ABC countries (Argentina, Brazil, and Chile), the complex question of the Mexican boundaries in 1916, and the perpetuation of the Taft-Knox policy of 1916, known as "Dollar Diplomacy," spread the first seeds of Latin American revolt against the foreign policy of the United States. As a result, in spite of their general sympathy toward the Allies, only eight of the Latin American Republics declared war on Germany and only five of them broke off diplomatic relations with her.

Brazil, however, maintained her friendly relations with the United States. In 1917 the then Foreign Minister, Nilo Peçanha, quoted the opinion expressed by a former Brazilian Ambassador to France, namely that "Brazil's natural allies will always be the Americans from the North and from the South. It is in the United States and in Buenos Aires that Your Majesty must have Ambassadors or Ministers distinguished for their ability and their honor." [15] This suggestion has not always been followed, but from the time of Rio Branco up to the end of the Second World War, Brazil's international policy was directed more than ever to keeping the help and friendship of the United States.

The economic depression of the 1930's and the increased responsibilities of the United States, due to the war and to her growing world power, softened her old interventionist policy, and as a result coercion gave way to persuasion and domination to cooperation. The policy of non-intervention has never triumphed completely because great economic interests, as they become more and more powerful, do their utmost to influence the making of public policy and public opinion. Since the administrations of

[15] *See Relatório do Ministério das Relações Exteriores,* Rio de Janeiro, 1920, Anexo A, pp. 5-6.

President Hoover and especially of President Franklin D. Roosevelt, the Good Neighbor policy has become dominant in the American continent.

After the Second World War, when the Latin American States became conscious of their underdevelopment and expressed their hopes for rapid growth, Pan-Americanism was put to the test. The animosities in the Central American and some South American republics, the lack of United States' help to Latin America while help was given to Europe, the commercial loans offered as proofs of generosity, the fear of the sinister role that United States capitalists might play in internal affairs, the alarm caused by economic groups which manipulate colossal advertising sums to win over or intimidate public opinion, have all jeopardized the leadership of the United States and weakened the general loyalty to the Western community. The Latin American countries which the U.S. has tried to maintain in her political orbit, eager for progress, irritated by Western indifference to their problems, and fully aware that there are today some European countries more under United States influence than they, are promoting among themselves a unity hitherto inconceivable, and are broadening relations and alliances of which the United States in particular and the West in general are suspicious, and which may indeed come to constitute a threat to democracy in Latin America.

President Juscelino Kubitschek's Operation Pan-America (O.P.A.), which burgeoned into the Alliance for Progress of President John F. Kennedy, has sought to meet this challenge, and Brazil's foreign policy since then has been inspired by his consciousness of her being an underdeveloped country, or, to be more optimistic, of being a country in process of development. Operation Pan-America's aim is to utilize Brazil's resources to the full and to make this process as short as possible. As a policy of intensive development it seeks voluntary international cooperation where it can find it. With Operation Pan-America this cooperation has become regionalized and has moved in the direction of a Latin American Common Market, without other alliances and within the regional framework. However effective this policy may prove in the promotion of American or Latin American unity, the individual countries are separate cultural entities, with differing historical backgrounds, and have, besides their common future, an individual future which will call for individual action in their international relations. The common economic interests of the Latin American nations do not transcend their historical and cultural divisions and thus the limits imposed by political geography remain a pressing reality.

Brazil, for instance, because of her links and her geographical and ethnic similarity with Africa, and because of her practice of racial non-discrimination, has been and is conscious of the importance of the African continent in her future foreign policy. Brazil is also a continental nation which is beginning to think intercontinentally, not only in her relations with America but in her relations with the whole world.

With particular regard to relations between Brazil and Portugal, it must be stressed that in spite of the community of feeling that has for so long united the two countries, their national objectives do not coincide in the international field. The two form a sentimental, linguistic community, with an economic basis which exists today in name rather than in fact. The colonialism of Salazar has alienated Brazil still further, and if she is united to Portugal by blood the same is true in relation to Africa, which gave her 11% of her total population and a large proportion of her mestizo population (26% of the total). On the other hand, the number of Portuguese immigrants in Brazil has been diminishing (the Portuguese formed 0.92% of the total population in 1940 and 0.65% in 1950, with a very low index of naturalizations) while the number of immigrants from other countries has been rising. No country, with the exception of the United States, has received more Japanese than Brazil; no country has received so many Germans; very few have admitted so many Italians (the majority came between 1884 and 1930); and Brazil, with the exception of Mexico and Argentina, has the greatest number of Spanish immigrants, not to mention many other nationalities.

In a population of 70,700,000 inhabitants, only 3% are foreigners (the percentage in 1920 was 5.11%, in 1940 3.41%, and in 1950 2.34 %). For this reason foreign colonies do not exert an important influence on Brazilian policy and do not weaken the Luso-Brazilian cultural majority. It must be noted that only recently, for the first time in her political history, have Brazilians of the first and second generations of non-Portuguese descent won political leadership. The rate of growth of the Brazilian population, having increased from 2.5 % per annum in the 1950 census to 3.09% according to the 1960 census, implies a demand for greater economic development, and thus makes more urgent the broadening of her foreign relations.

For all the above reasons Brazil is essentially pacifist, but she is now more concerned with her own rights, opportunities, and interests. She recognizes that real independence signifies above all a foreign policy free from pressures and threats from other countries but subject to the fulfillment of international obligations, voluntarily agreed in treaties and conventions. Back in 1862 D. Pedro II spoke of the necessity of adopting a policy that was really appropriate for Brazil. This is what President Jânio Quadros sought to do when he defended an independent policy, a policy which, taking into account regional hemispheric interests, did not neglect inter-continental objectives, endeavored to broaden Brazilian commercial and political relations, refused exclusive commitments, and stood for peace and the defense of representative government.

The making of foreign policy has always been a function of the Executive power, sometimes debated in Congress, depending on the times and the issues. International problems have never been given a prominent place in the platform of Brazil's political parties. During the Empire the only aspiration was for peace. In 1870 the Republican Party accused the monarchy of keeping Brazil apart from America and the world. After the proclamation of the Republic and until fairly recently, party programs have expressed in a general way their concern for international cooperation, obedience to the principles adopted by the United Nations, and Brazilian integration in the inter-American community. The Brazilian Labor Party, going a step ahead, clearly champions the principle of non-intervention, which was upheld at Punta del Este by a Labor Minister. It was only after the Second World War that Brazilian political parties began to pay greater attention to international problems and to think of Brazil as an inseparable part of the world. Motions of approval or censure of the Foreign Minister have become more frequent as well as the demand that he explain his policy in the Chamber of Deputies.

Brazilian foreign policy is neither a party policy nor does it represent the interests of a class; but since the country was formerly ruled by an oligarchy which represented landed interests, it has reflected this oligarchy's opinion and aspirations rather than those of the people, who were until a short time ago politically non-existent. The middle and working classes were not organized as a political force. The government of Getúlio Vargas, in spite of restricting the ruling power to a very limited circle including the armed forces, promoted national feeling and brought the working classes into the political arena. From 1930 on, new groups of the middle and working classes with their own demands have become more influential in Brazilian politics without, however, affecting the policies and attitudes of the Ministry of Foreign Affairs.

This Ministry has undergone several changes in order to keep pace with its growth. Until a few years ago the recruitment of its personnel was dominated by the system of patronage. Public examinations for admittance, as well as the creation of the Rio Branco Institute for the professional training of diplomats, are recent innovations. The Ministry of Foreign Affairs is a closed institution, where all the departmental heads in all fields must be career diplomats. Up to now it has not sought for, or, if it has done so, only to a very limited degree, the advice and counsel of specialists in national or international affairs who could furnish information to policy-makers.

Economic groups in former times, such as the slave traders or the coffee planters, knew how to promote their interests in the making of foreign policy; today the new industrial and commercial groups compete with the agricultural classes for influence and advantage. Pressure groups such as the Catholic Church, the Military Club, and powerful economic interests also strive to exert influence, whether or not their interests coincide with the national interest. Regional and sectional influences, which are very important in domestic affairs, have little effect on foreign policy. The only exceptions are Rio Grande do Sul, which has always been sensitive to the problems of foreign policy due to its situation as a border state with consequent involvement in the international conflicts of the Empire, and the Northeast, where the Dutch occupation in the colonial era has left a significant mark.

Just as it is to Rio de Janeiro that, from the earliest days of her independence, Brazil owes her national unity, so it is Rio de Janeiro which has dominated Brazilian thinking in international matters. More than any others the newspapers of Rio de Janeiro, and, subsequently, the press of São Paulo—although they reflected the dominant interests of the great oligarchs, the landowners, and the coffee growers, as well as the prejudices of the middle and upper classes—have always felt a great responsibility in the analysis of Brazil's foreign policy. The reactions and behavior of the people of Brazil are superior to those of their leaders, and their instincts are more perceptive than the sophistries of the latter; there is no doubt, therefore, that their late but inevitable entrance into the arena of policy decision will mean progress, and will make of the optimism, which is a Brazilian characteristic, a philosophy of her historic hope for development.

VI
REVOLUTION FROM ABOVE

. . . in which Getúlio Vargas declares he will enter history by committing suicide for the people; and in which Fernando Ferrari discusses the separation of political leadership from the Brazilian masses and offers some proposals to overcome this bifurcation; this is followed by Hélio Jaguaribe's study of Quadros' Bonapartist Democracy and why it failed so quickly and dramatically; then the political sociology of uneven development in Brazil is carefully delineated by Gláucio Soares.

I. FAREWELL MESSAGE TO THE BRAZILIAN PEOPLE

Getúlio Vargas *

ONCE MORE the forces and interests against the people are newly coordinated and raised against me. They do not accuse me, they insult me; they do not fight me, they slander me and do not give me the right of defense. They need to drown my voice and halt my actions so that I no longer continue to defend, as I always have defended, the people and principally the humble.

I follow the destiny that is imposed on me. After years of domination and looting by international economic and financial groups, I made myself chief of an unconquerable revolution. I began the work of liberation and I instituted a regime of social liberty. I had to resign. I returned to govern on the arms of the people.

A subterranean campaign of international groups joined with national groups revolting against the regime of workers' guarantees. The law of excess profits was stopped in Congress. Hatreds were unchanged against the justice of a revision of minimum wages.

I wished to create national liberty by developing our riches

* Former President of Brazil and organizer of the New State, which saw the first stage in the modernization of the Brazilian social structure. He committed suicide in 1954.

through *Petrobrás* [government oil development company], and a wave of agitation clouded its beginnings. *Eletrobrás* [government hydroelectric development agency] was hindered almost to despair. They do not wish the workers to be free. They do not wish the people to be independent.

I assumed the government during an inflationary spiral that was destroying the value of work. Profits of foreign enterprises reached 500% yearly. In declarations of goods that we import there existed frauds of more than $100,000,000.

I saw the coffee crisis increase the value of our principal product. We attempted to defend its price and the reply was a violent pressure upon our economy to the point of being obliged to surrender.

I have fought month to month, day to day, hour to hour, resisting a constant aggression, unceasingly bearing it all in silence, forgetting all and renouncing myself to defend the people that now fall abandoned. I cannot give you more than my blood. If the birds of prey wish the blood of anybody, they wish to continue sucking that of the Brazilian people.

I offer my life in the holocaust. I choose this means to be with you always. When they humiliate you, you will feel my soul suffering at your side. When hunger beats at your door, you will feel in your chests the energy for the fight for yourselves and your children. When they humiliate you, you will feel in my grief the force for reaction.

My sacrifice will maintain you united, and my name will be your battle flag. Each drop of my blood will be an immortal call to your conscience and will maintain a holy vibration for resistance.

To hatred, I respond with pardon. And to those who think they have defeated me, I reply with my victory. I was the slave of the people and today I free myself for eternal life. But this people, to which I was a slave, no longer will be a slave to anyone. My sacrifice will remain forever in your soul and my blood will be the price of your ransom.

I fought against the looting of Brazil. I fought against the looting of the people. I have fought bare-breasted. The hatred, infamy, and calumny did not beat down my spirit. I gave you my life. Now I offer my death. Nothing remains. Serenely I take the first step on the road to eternity and I leave life to enter history.

II. POLITICAL PANORAMA OF BRAZIL

Fernando Ferrari *

The national elections of 1960, from which Jânio Quadros emerged victorious to assume the Presidency of the Republic, represent the fourth democratic contest for the election of the highest leaders of the land in a period of fifteen years, dating from the end of the New State of Getúlio Vargas.

Insofar as this is so, from the historical, social, economic, and political points of view, to that extent we can divide modern Brazilian life into two halves of fifteen years each. Taking as the point of reference the 1930 Revolution, the national elections of 1960 acquire an importance that will tend toward a reorientation of values partly as an expression of living experience and partly as an expression of the inmost desires of the people.

The victory of Jânio Quadros is characterized by the consecration of the political parties that came to power without compromises or circumscribed interests, and with an authority strengthened in an election won by majority vote, within an electoral system that regards, accepts, and disciplines the proportional majority.

It was a victory like the one that took place ten years earlier, when Getúlio Vargas returned to the head of the government by popular vote, beating the two major parties: the official PTB and the opposition UDN. Vargas had been a candidate for the PTB in 1950; but in that period, the PTB had not yet matured as a party, possessing neither density nor number to elect a President. Logically, the victory of Vargas grew out of his legendary stature, his bearing, his political acumen, and his historic achievement. This achievement is symbolized in Brazilian labor legislation, which assures a great number of rights and guarantees to workers, guarantees unheard of before 1930.

In four elections for the Brazilian Presidency it has been the case that the nominated candidates have not relied upon the political parties. As for the other two—General Eurico Gaspar Dutra

* Founder of the *Movimento Trabalhista Renovador* (MTR), the newest political party in Brazil. He was the defeated candidate for Vice President at the last general election. Before his recent death in an air accident he was a federal deputy in the national parliament.

in 1945 and Senhor Kubitschek in 1955—the nomination of the first arose from his position as soldier and Minister of War and his election is attributable to the direct recommendation and intervention of Getúlio Vargas. Moreover, at that time there could not have been party candidates, Brazil being a country where a tradition of stable political parties does not exist, the existent ones always being unstable and isolated from all organized activity since 1937.

If we dwell exclusively on the involvement of Juscelino Kubitschek with the PSD—Social Democratic Party, founded like the others in 1945—through which he had already been nominated in 1950, as governor of the State of Minas Gerais, we would have to assume that Kubitschek, in the period from 1945–60, had been the only President of the Republic who emerged from the background of the prevailing political parties. There is no doubt, however, that his personal ambition, his dynamism and imagination not only exceed but are opposed to any party perspectives, especially those of the indolent conservatives.

From another point of view, the candidacy of Juscelino Kubitschek was to some extent created by a reaction of the regime before the crisis that led to the tragedy of August 1954, when Vargas committed suicide. It was the reaction to an atmosphere of wavering authority which threatened Brazil with a *coup d'état*. Although through resolving this period of threats and instability an element of democracy was established—the result of the 1955 presidential elections—the solution of the regime's crisis did not come from the political parties but from the armed forces. Such a solution would influence the following presidential elections in 1960, through the petition for the nomination of Marshal Henrique Lott.

After the Kubitschek period, with Brasília already under way, the PSD did not have a suitable candidate for the presidential succession of its dynamic colleague. It appealed therefore to Kubitschek's Minister of War. The UDN, which raised the most heated opposition to Kubitschek's government, in the dispute between the political parties, found itself in the same situation and yet with a certain spirit of optimism. It neither had nor sought a candidate from the party for the presidential succession, turning to the device of concentrating on opposition to the candidacy of Jânio

Quadros, a non-party man turned into a supra-party man, with neither bilateral nor multilateral compromises.

Jânio thus rose to the Presidency strong and with a free hand to govern and reform according to his administrative style and political personality. This attempted retrospective analysis of the most recent years of Brazilian political life cannot, however, without grave distortion, lead to the idea that Brazilians reject parties on behalf of charismatic men. This would be admitting that Brazil seeks solutions tending toward personalist dictatorship. On the contrary, more than ever the democratic conscience is firm, absorbed in and defended by currents of opinion, influence, and authority in civil and military spheres.

The explanation of the phenomena lies in the fact that the victory of Quadros coincides, at all levels of Brazilian life, with a tide of great reform, in that what is being sought is the harmony and authenticity to confront the people and the problems intrinsic to national growth. The reform of political parties is thus an urgent stage in this period of basic reform, and concurrently the consolidation, living and perfected, of the representative democratic ideal is genuinely practiced by elections properly presided over by judicial power.

The astonishing resignation of Jânio Quadros showed up, in abundant detail, the cracks in the solid structure of the parties of Brazil and to the same extent the extraordinary inclination of the Brazilian to legality and the Constitution. Until there is an admission that the former President had been victimized by the vacuity of our party system and that he was abandoned at every turn, adequate political assessment is not complete.

How can we reconcile the historical constant of idealized men with the legalistic Brazilian spirit? In the first place, it is important to note that we cannot prove that the Brazilian people are opposed to the organized parties, since one ought not to judge their reactions to a phenomenon that doesn't exist as such. Indeed, we don't really have national, historical, or traditional parties. It is different with other peoples rooted in European culture. We do not have political groups with historical roots that impel national development. During the Empire period, with rare exceptions, the political parties had risen on behalf of temporary causes to create occasional majorities, not as organisms destined to defend great causes or impressive programs. That is to say that in this they reflect the spectrum of other collectivities of equal economic level. The constant of Latin America then is the existence of party alignments without profound ideological convictions. If we judge by organized and active associations which force themselves upon the public bearing messages and programs, we would surely have some basis for measuring the partisan tendency of Brazilians. And in such a case—undoubtedly—the test would prove positive. Then we would be a community historically adherent to Liberty and Democracy.

It is precisely this yearning for Liberty, inherent in the Brazilian people, that consolidates them around the law as the unique embodiment of their hopes. We saw it proven in the recent political crisis, when a small but active military group set up a constitutional substitute for the Presidency over the Vice President. Everyone, opponents and supporters of the Vice President-elect, united in the common cause of defending the Constitution, strengthening an outstanding popular victory, mature and capable of the exercise of governmental responsibility.

The critical hour in the historical evolutionary process of the Brazilian people has struck. Despite the surrounding turmoil, their political maturity and democratic tendencies are undeniable.

Observers of Brazilian life are agreed, for this very reason, that the time has come to adapt the party structure to national reality. Despite the lack of proper means, the representative-political consolidation emerges just when we are taking account of its effects, fulfilling also the claims of its extraordinary developmental impulse. This is the right goal in one of the most important periods of Brazilian life.

After a merciless fifteen-year struggle favoring the formation of an authentic labor party, which was to be transformed into a great national instrument for the advancement of the proletariat and social peace, the Reform Labor Movement (MTR) was founded and is recognized today as an autonomous political grouping. The new political movement surges forth like historical destiny amidst the industrialization and advancement of the rural masses. This is still what is unconsciously striven after since illiteracy in the rural areas is so widespread.

Labor reformism is embodied in the first great popular movement that breaks the traditional process of party politics. The parties, from the Empire period on, have moved from the "high to the low," that is, from the Ministries to the streets, paid for, calling for political power, calling for economic power. The MTR arises just when the people, by means of trade union and rural directives, firmly re-establish a new balance. From this, observers may ask if it will not be an agglomeration of republican "concretism." Indeed, if the parties grow artificially around political leaders or from the fires of economic failure, what is wrong with turning to the resources of the people?

The reformers—we are thus describing the members of the MTR —defend a sociopolitical system that sees in labor the prime source of productivity and considers it a moral foundation for ownership. Labor, as a creator of wealth, prevails over all that is in its domain. This point admirably approaches the ideas of Alberto Pasqualini and the struggles of Getúlio Vargas, one an ideological leader, the other a leader of the masses. The MTR is convinced that Brazil will only win the war against underdevelopment through labor, making the workers effective partners in national production. They emphasize this and consider it vital, because statistics show that only 10 million, in a population of 60 million, really live off their own labor. Labor forces are scarce in Brazil, where the privileged minority dominates and rules by caprice.

Inspired by the ideas of the American economist, Henry George, in referring to the superiority of labor among the justified factors for ownership, the MTR tends toward cooperativism and not toward socialism. This solidarism seeks to transform the solely human or political into an authentic cooperation of will and action. In a sermon on the dignity of man and the future of the nation, Henry George reflects on his people. The labor reformer is beginning to penetrate vast areas of the national conscience.

III. THE CRISIS IN BRAZILIAN POLITICS
Hélio Jaguaribe *

The strange personality of Jânio Quadros, erratically combining breadth of analytic comprehension with an unquestionable

* Hélio Jaguaribe is widely acknowledged to be the foremost political commentator in Brazil. He bridges journalism and scholarships with staggering ease. He is Professor of the Brazilian Institute for Higher Studies, Ministry of Education, Brazil.

emotional compulsiveness, evoked the interpretation that his resignation as President on August 25, 1961, was primarily explicable in
psychological terms.

The ex-President exercised power with such authority and detachment that public opinion had come to consider him the
supreme arbiter of events. Due to this, his resignation caused
amazement. It was a graphic episode in the country's general political process, one which tried to interpret Quadros' behavior
and motives in a purely functional way. Such an atmosphere consequently brought about the formation of two contrasting versions
as to why he resigned.

The first point of view maintains that Quadros resigned because
he frankly wanted to. He wanted power in order to exercise it his
way. Pressured by opposition in Congress, his authority defied by
Carlos Lacerda, the principal opponent in the electoral campaign,
Quadros understood that the conditions for rule no longer obtained. This version was first voiced by the governors that met in
Cumbica with the ex-President immediately after the resignation,
and was confirmed by immediate aides of Quadros, like Quinta-
nilha and Aparecido. This interpretation was divulged tentatively
prior to the resignation of Quadros.

When it was already clear that the *coup* planned by the military
was going to be frustrated, and when explanations were being
formulated in order to justify military intervention, another version began to circulate, explaining the resignation as the Machiavellian plan of Quadros to make himself dictator. Quadros would
win the campaign from Carlos Lacerda by testing the dramatic
gesture of resignation.

Weighing the threat of what transmission of power to Goulart
would mean to the right and what restoration of a military *junta*
would mean to the left, Quadros attempted by his resignation to
arouse in public opinion, the armed forces, and Congress itself a
queremismo * reaction. On the strength of this he would reassume
the Presidency with maximum powers.

The psychological interpretation of Quadros' resignation suffers from a two-fold inconsistency. As an explanation of an
historico-political event, it suffers from the incapacity of psychol-
ogism to grasp a process that goes beyond the motivation of

* *Queremismo* refers to the followers of Vargas. [ILH]

individuals and their interaction. On the other hand, the attempt to understand Quadros' resignation within the restricted range of its immediate causes, without taking into account the historic global process, is equally incapable of offering a valid causal explanation of events.

The neurotic interpretation, as much as the Machiavellian, had as its principal defect the presupposition of a serious emotional or intellectual failing in the make-up of Jânio Quadros.

It is evident that Quadros' personality contributes to heightening the extent of failure. Would this emotional instability be carried to the point of renouncing the Presidency through a purely voluntary neurotic act or through hysterical susceptibility to panic? Would his failures of insight reach the point of preventing him from recognizing that the powers of a constitutional President, though limited, are more solid than the supposed unlimited powers of a dictator? Does a *coup d'état*, since it is so uncertain, hold no possibilities for success if the main thrusts are entrusted to the unpredictable spontaneity of Congress, the armed forces, and public opinion?

In the strictest range of the immediate conditioning factors in the resignation of Quadros, the analysis of the available data leads to the conclusion that the ex-President was the victim of a *coup d'état*.

There is no doubt that the act of resignation in itself was made freely and deliberately by Jânio Quadros. From that one must not conclude that the resignation, in the broad political sense, was deliberately sought by the ex-President. Everything indicates, in fact, that Jânio Quadros had resigned with the understanding that his dramatic gesture was the only means still at his disposal to plan the recapture of power, a way of barely saving face when he was already deposed. This hypothesis emerges from the political analysis of events.

By August 24, when Lacerda unleashed a serious denunciation of the Ministry of Justice, through which he was effectively attacking Jânio Quadros, the military grouping on which Quadros' government rested had already transferred its solidarity and loyalty to Lacerda. In military terms, Quadros was therefore deposed because military loyalty to the President was transferred to the government of Guanabara, and the fact is that Quadros was not able to change the disposition of the military. Any alterations

in the military timetable and command would confirm the allega-
tion that they were being employed to prepare a *coup*.

The stratagem used by Lacerda had this merit: that to accuse
the President, in the form of the Ministry of Justice, of wanting
to strike at the state—what Lacerda himself was effectively doing
—deprived Quadros of the political conditions necessary to defend
himself from such a *coup*.

The President, in such a situation, had to depend not only on
regaining Congressional support, but also on his own discretionary
judgment. It is worth noting about the *pessedista* * majority that
its acceptance of Lacerda's denunciation implied its abandonment
of Quadros.

The deunciation was made, and seeing that Quadros had lost
military support, the *pessedista* majority in Congress planned immediately to take over the powers that the President had lost. It
was thus in a position to impose basic restrictions on the substance
of presidential power. Under the pressure of accepting Lacerda's
denunciation Congress spearheaded the symbolic disaffection from
Quadros.

In such circumstances Quadros decided to resign. And it is from
this point that plausible conjecture turns. Conjecture reveals his
resignation to be a stratagem meant to provoke a great furor to
compel Congress not to accept his resignation, thus allowing
Quadros to re-establish the government with all the prestige and
power of his office intact. Though Quadros was surprised at the
combination of his impending ruin, the deceit of the military, and
the alienation of Congress, his possible options included other alternatives aside from resignation.

There were two possible lines of action. One consisted of using
the weight of the state apparatus, still capable of acting against
the conspirators. The other consisted of calling on the public to
throw its weight against the state machinery.

The first alternative would have had the merit of relieving
Quadros from foreknowledge of what was already in progress—a
coup to depose him—shifting the burden of frankness concerning
their conspiratorial position to the plotters. Such an alternative
presupposed appreciable power reserves in fact or, better yet,
assumed the risk of feigning a power which Quadros no longer

* *Pessedista* refers to a member or follower of the Brazilian Social Democratic Party. [ILH]

commanded. With this line he sought to replace the military ministers and, in so doing, the military's devious commanders. He also sought to debate Congress on the accusations leveled by Lacerda.

The problem here is in evaluating the means still at Quadros' disposal in the state machinery. The immediate and solid adherence of General Pedro Geralso and others in the military cabinet of Quadros to Marshal Denys seems to indicate that the ex-President lost command of his own palace from the start, and lost control generally in Brasília. Up to what point did Quadros still have, before taking other preparatory measures, the liberty of moving to another State, such as São Paulo or Rio Grande do Sul, and from there reorganizing his forces for a counterattack?

If one considers the fact that the act of resignation profoundly surprised the military ministers, one is forced to believe that Quadros could have moved to a position where he might have been more confident; and from there he could have crushed the nascent military-*pessedista* rebellion. Considering the incredible rapidity with which the military-political forces of Marshal Denys assumed control of the country—Quadros becoming a virtual prisoner of that force on leaving Brasília—it should be concluded that the ex-President had no freedom of movement.

Nevertheless, Quadros always had a second alternative, that of denouncing the *coup* being prepared against him and mobilizing the public against the conspirators. This second alternative did not prevent him from planning to activate all the forces of the state apparatus that seemed sensitive to his call. The resignation itself, used like a tactical crutch, might have been compatible with such a line of action. It could have been sufficient for the resignation, instead of being put in irrevocable form, to have been presented as an imminent possibility. To explain his gesture, Quadros, instead of hurling vague accusations and courting the armed forces, might have clearly and vehemently denounced the persons and forces plotting to depose him.

Since there is little desire to penetrate the inscrutable sphere of subjective motivation it is acknowledged that the resignation of Jânio Quadros constituted a tentative compromise solution between the two alternatives examined above. Quadros did not want to run the risk of losing control, through replacement of his military ministers, to the *coup* which he assumed was already under way. He was frightened lest Congress approve an "impeachment," adding further to his ruin. He did not want, however, to denounce the *coup* to the people and mobilize the masses against conspiratorial sectors of the armed forces and Congress. He was fearful that such a denunciation would lead to a radicalization of positions, putting him more to the left than he cared to be or than he considered viable and, to compound the damage, uniting the armed forces against him and all the centrist and rightist forces in a presumably invincible conservative front. By using the strategy of renunciation, Quadros felt that, in principle, he would have the advantages of both alternatives without their respective disadvantages.

Fearing the rise of João Goulart, rightest forces would presumably return Quadros to power. The currents on the left, although still more favorable to João Goulart, would also have to accept Quadros' return to power, lest they be overcome by right-wing currents. Seen thus, the resignation would rally forces which move the state machinery, such as the broad masses. On the other hand, Jânio Quadros had to make it appear that the stratagem of resignation, in case it did not succeed, had the advantage of giving him a high moral posture of disinterest in power, a disinterest which would make possible a victorious retreat in the future.

This stratagem could succeed, however, only in theory. When concrete forces mobilized to strip him of power and eventually depose him, Jânio Quadros could not oppose them. He scarcely reckoned with the spontaneous reaction of interests. Perhaps, without a reasonable possibility for maneuvering of the state apparatus, he would have chosen the first alternative. Rather, deprived of the means to intervene in the state machinery, he ought to have chosen the second alternative, mobilizing the masses against the conspiratorial forces and reconquering the state apparatus through the people. Quadros, on presenting his formal resignation as President, allowed the PSD Parliament to grasp quickly at their own interests and adopt the ensuing measures.

The Quadros Presidency was doubly fatal for the PSD. In appearance detached from all forms of partisanship, Quadros did not give the PSD any clue as to what was happening, yet what was happening was vital to its survival as a party. The elections had drained it as an electoral machine able to promote access to the levels of power that would yield the rewards of affiliation. For a long time the Quadros government was deadly to the PSD because it mobilized and organized Brazilian society to function in terms of objectives and out of motives totally distinct from those which he could point to as political motives.

The alternative before the PSD prior to the resignation of President Quadros was either the preservation of a *status quo* insupportable to the party or the acceptance of the resignation as a unilateral and definitive act calling for constitutional successors. Due to the casual absence of Vice President Goulart, power returned to the head of the legislative houses. If no political or military complications emerged for Goulart, the presidential succession would then fall to him as leader of the PSD.

It would be difficult to determine the form and degree of connivance that caused the military-political union of Marshal Denys and his colleagues, Heck and Moss, with certain sectors of the PSD. The fact is indisputable that prior to the resignation the ex-Minister of Justice of the Kubitschek administration, Armando Falcao, and the *pessedista* groups most bound to him were formally aligned with Lacerda and with the military clique that supported the latter, the clique that later came to fill the power vacuum left by Quadros. It was certainly this alliance between the military and the *pessedistas* which led Quadros to believe that there was no path other than resignation. Finally, it is true that under the nominal Presidency of Mazilli and the effective occupation of power by the implicit military *junta*—formed by the Ministers of War, Navy, and Air Corps—Mazilli and some other higher-ups of the PSD carried out rigorously all that was prescribed by the military chiefs. If the *pessedista* command saw itself completely bound to the military clique of Marshal Denys, the truth is that the bulk of the party unequivocally repelled the traitorous conspirators.

Mazilli's connivance apportioned to Denys' group all the necessary facilities for total control of power. Mazilli's evil passion for the Presidency was evident from the time power fell into the hands of the military ministers and Marshal Denys was the real chief of the system.

At the airport at Cumbica in São Paulo, Jânio Quadros, personally expecting his return to power but objectively already a prisoner, could verify that the delay mechanism of his stratagem had been dismantled before it began to operate. Mazilli was irrevocably invested with titular power, the base of which was firmly set by the military clique of Denys.

Up to this point, then, the conspirators were triumphant. They had succeeded in wresting power from Jânio Quadros for themselves under the complacent Presidency of Mazilli, without paying the burdensome price of overt violence and violation of the law. One detail was missing: Congress determines the removal of a President. The rules governing impeachment, by requiring elections within sixty days, perpetuated a situation, in the name of the Constitution, that prolonged the vacancies in the offices of both President and Vice President. For these, with Quadros and Goulart out of the way, the conspiratorial forces considered themselves ready to choose their candidates. As an ultimate recourse and in the name of public salvation they would seat Carlos Lacerda, who since 1954, when the *coup* against Vargas was carried out by the same forces, had been designing a "state of emergency."

To Marshal Denys, who had resumed his leadership role in 1955 under Marshal Lott, it seemed simple to apply the same scheme in the new situation as then. Controlling power *de facto*, the military would solicit from Congress Goulart's removal from ascendancy to the Presidency, thereby giving Parliament the choice of either saving the nominal continuity of the regime or assuming responsibility for appeasing the military dictatorship, allowing the dissolution of Congress and illegitimate seizure of power by the plotters.

Despite the formal appearance of relations between the armed forces and Congress, there occurred in August 1961 a complete reversal from events of November 1955. At that time, the troops under the command of Marshal Lott, expressing the massive popular will and the view of the great majority of Congress, opposed the attempts of Carlos Luz to hold transitory power. The plotters were prevented from obstructing the assumption of political power on the part of President-elect Juscelino Kubitschek. In August 1961, Marshal Denys, violating the will of the people and of Congress, rose up against democratic legality, and tried to prevent Vice President João Goulart from assuming the Presidency. That profound difference of meaning between the events of November 1955 and August 1961 made the forces of Marshal Denys lose the most remote popular support. Nor could he succeed in maintaining unity internally.

The frustrated *coup* of Marshal Denys served to make clear that the Army is essentially a responsive organization, open to all influences that circulate about the nation, and representing prevailing trends of public opinion. In the case of the Air Force, dominated by the spirit of palace revolt, and to the displeasure and strenuous opposition of the armed forces as a whole, it revealed itself completely insensitive to public opinion and capable of resorting to schemes as implacable as those of a fascist militia, including the most unscrupulous psychological warfare. The Navy maintained the pose of an impartial observer. Divorced from the country by a splendid aristocratic isolation, the service did not lend itself to the conspiratorial designs. The Third Army, embracing practically half of the Army's forces under the command of General Machado Lopez, was decisively on the side of democratic loyalty.

The Second Army was less explicit. It adopted a position of passive resistance to the command of Marshal Denys. In the First and Fourth Armies, where the ruling officers maintained direct liaison with the Minister of War, opposition to legality was strongest. For that reason they had to be removed from command and, in large measure, were arrested. On the civilian level, resistance to the *coup* was widespread and tightly knit—except naturally those sections of the extreme right wing that grouped around Carlos Lacerda and some rare ambiguous cases like Governor Cid Sampario of Pernambuco.

The courageous attitude of Leonel Brizola, governor of Rio Grande do Sul, who opposed the *coup* from the first, was a decisive factor in the success of civil resistance. Santa Catarina and Paraná in the South, Espírito Santo and Goiás in the Central East, Piauí in the Northeast, and Amazonas in the North were officially bound to the defense of legality.

Clearly outstanding was the action developed by Mauro Borges, governor of Goiás, who besides consolidating resistance to the *coup* organized a popular militia for opposition to the military detachments of Brasília, to assure the national Congress armed protection for its free functioning. The military significance of this proposed action should not be overlooked due to the small size of his State. Also deserving mention is the noteworthy position taken by Carlos Lindemberg, governor of Espírito Santo, who was barely a few hours from the general conspiratorial command in the State of Guanabara, yet stood opposed to the imposition of censorship in Espírito Santo.

The firm repelling of the *coup* supported by public opinion, and the example of the State governors, strengthened the national Congress and encouraged them to confront the military drive. With the exception of the State of Guanabara, converted into a Holy See of the *coup* and where, under Lacerda's orders, the most reactionary forces of the extreme Brazilian right (and of Pernambuco) were concentrated and kept in a state of permanent readiness, the rest of the States aligned themselves against the *coup*. Celso Peçanha, governor of the State of Rio de Janeiro, promoted a meeting of governors to induce the military ministers to accept an honorable way out. And in all this, Congress almost unanimously rejected the ousting of João Goulart. Marshal Denys, revealing himself as the most judicious and moderate of the conspirators, agreed to Goulart taking over the Presidency under a parliamentary regime.

The crisis was ended with a compromise to avoid imminent civil war. Once again the national preference for solutions based on consensus asserted itself, to the detriment of those who might have been able to effect a profound disruption in the internal order. The *coup* had been frustrated. The people decisively asserted their political priorities and their determination to impose the sovereignty of civil power. It was clear that the armed forces could no longer try to set themselves up as guardians of the government nor manipulate the incitement of the public. As a compromise, civil law would have to tolerate the fact that the conspirators would go scot free, and what is more serious, that they would retain their strength and organization.

In view of what has been brought to light, the resignation of Jânio Quadros seems more or less rational since it loses that inexplicable quality it initially seemed to have. However, a lack of explanation persists in relation to the extraordinary military disorganization of his government.

The clash caused by the resignation and the tension created by the imminence of a *coup* by the ex-President's military ministers faded. The fact became known that for quite some time Jânio Quadros had been warned about the delicacy of his position with the military and the urgent need to improve his security position. From the way in which Quadros insisted on carrying out the political reforms that he proclaimed as a candidate, in that same way the incongruity and incompatibility between the politics of reform and the supporters of the government became patently clear.

In spite of Quadros' theatrical talent, in the course of his seven months in office his determination to carry out a program of great reform became undeniable. Some of those reforms went against the advice of economists, both Brazilian and foreign, and that is why, although the proposals were mild, they had a radical aspect. Others, like the new foreign policy, seemed dangerously revolutionary. Others still, although under study and preparation, like agrarian reform, threatened to assail a "multisecular" socio-economic structure, instilling panic in established interests committed to upholding the *status quo*.

The military arrangement on which Jânio Quadros had based the security of his government, meanwhile, was composed of the notorious extreme right of the military. Marshal Denys had shown in the last months of the Kubitschek government an attitude of barely constrained hostility toward his predecessor Marshal Lott, and frankly supported the extreme right-wing military. Admiral Heck had figured among the most open military chiefs of the abortive *coup* of Carlos Luz. Brigadier Moss was always partisan to the faction of Eduardo Gomes of the Air Force. Most radical and conscientiously rightist was the position of General Cordeiro de Farias (Chief of the Armed Forces), known to consider a third world war as inevitable and necessary for the survival of "Western Christian civilization" and to espouse the role of the Brazilian armed forces as the auxiliary body of the American armed forces. Under those military chiefs were placed officials who had taken part in the *coup* of August 24 of Jacarecanga and Aragarças.

The incompatibility between this military group and Quadros' policy of reform was painfully evident. Such incompatibility and its consequent risks were expressly pointed out to Quadros by Governor Brizola well before August. Other warnings in the same vein were sent to Quadros by nationalist leaders who had proposed approaching Quadros, Marshal Lott, and the legalist and progressive sectors of the armed forces.

Quadros always refused to admit the incompatibilities and risks of his policies. He refused to discuss relations with the military command in terms other than those of strictly disciplined obedience of the latter to the President, Commander-in-Chief of the armed forces. The course of the military break-up under Quadros, when the crisis that led to his resignation was over, could next be evaluated. It could be seen that, for the first time in the Republic, the President had not rested on the support of the military Establishment.

Quadros' strange trust in the security of his government probably derived from his strong petit-bourgeois conditioning and from the moralistic perspective peculiar to such a posture.

Petit-bourgeois reformer, deprived of a theoretical conception of historical process or of experience in practical promotion of social reform movements, Quadros in his short political career always behaved like a solitary non-conformist. Councilor to the President, he held to the prevailing norms without bothering about the underlying fundamentals of the prevalence of such norms. Provincial politician that he was, until his nomination for President, he thought more about things than about precepts, more about administrative tasks than about systems or programs. For him individual action was everything. It is the peculiar vision of the petit-bourgeoisie that they consider social events in the light of the qualities and individual intentions of the protagonists. The facts operate at the level of voluntary options and, consequently, in terms of good and evil.

This moralistic perspective led Quadros to adopt an interpretation of the facts and an attitude in regard to them that were not compatible with the reformist notions that had been growing within him at that time. Of such incompatibility Quadros took no notice, nor could he realize how he remained bound by his original petit-bourgeois and moralistic position. In reality, the currents of the right and extreme right could not deliver the promise of social reform. For social life is no longer based on custom. From its fear that educating the people is the root of all social evil stems the rightist imperative of granting power to men of influence, called agents of the good. From this rightist premise grew the campaign promoted by Lacerda and his stooges against the PSD and PTB alliance which, despite its tremendous limitations, expressed a progressive accord between the bourgeoisie and the proletariat through the ideology of economic development.

This alliance, which Lacerda called an association between

traders and the ragged, seemed suspect to Jânio Quadros. From this stemmed his sympathy toward the military that had been conspiring, from the Vargas to the Kubitschek governments, against a left-of-center orientation that tended to predominate in this period.

Out of his own moralism, the men of August 24, of *El Tamandaré* of Jacarecanga and Aragarças, seemed to Quadros to be (like himself) representatives of non-conformism in the prevailing order and of an ardent desire for reform. Quadros was never aware of the dialectical nature of reality. He didn't understand the difference between the non-conformism of the right, which resulted in the accentuation of class privileges (particularly military privileges) of the petit-bourgeoisie through economic and social modernization, and the real desire for social development which led to accelerating the extension of social equality and further increasing the rate of economic and social development.

The contradiction in Quadros between his reformist calling and his petit-bourgeois limitation made it possible for him to be elected President with a disconcerting accumulation of votes from both right and left. His histrionic capacity would have counted for little if the contradiction had not been in himself and in each sector of his constituency. Each sector saw in him a reflection of their own expectations. This same contradiction led him to depend on the military wing of the extreme right for his reform policy, a policy even more radical than others which military spokesmen had repeatedly undermined.

The Brazilian economy, over the great stages of its historical development from the colonial slave structure to the semi-colonial structure of the old Republic, experienced a growing expansion with the Revolution of 1930 and the Second World War. Accordingly, the economic process became endogenous, autonomous, and technically differentiated. The Brazilian people became stratified into classes, class sectors, regions, and States. This process of differentiation brought to the population a growing, more conscientious and deliberate participation in political events.

In the old Republic, the State oligarchies freely manipulated the electorate, whose franchise did not go beyond exchanging their vote for the candidate indicated by the local political chief for the protection or promise of jobs.

Vargas' election was a first indication of independence of the popular will representing a broad sector of the electorate. The process became increasingly accentuated as a break with the norm. Juscelino Kubitschek, to win the favor of the extremely powerful party machinery of the PSD and the also very powerful labor-union machinery of the PTB, had to make an immense personal effort to win votes. Quadros, in 1960, succeeded against these two machines on the basis of a campaign waged mainly outside the party system.

The Brazilian people became a "people for themselves," in which the political bearing of the citizen emerged from specific interests and values, as well as their complete penetration of the social system. The voting populace was no longer subject to maneuvers and pressures.

The formation and configuration of social classes in contemporary Brazil, resting upon economic development and the rise of new social strata as well as the decay of some of the old and the amalgamation of yet others, also led to a characteristic bi-polarization. By virtue of this bi-polarization, all social classes in Brazil subdivide into two sectors: one, archaic, established in the period preceding the semi-colonial economy that reacted against development; the other, modern, formed or differentiated by development and favorable to it.

For purposes of this essay it is sufficient to point out that among the bourgeoisie, merchant sectors of the urban group and manorial stratum of the rural group, there is hostility to development. Among the urban and rural middle classes and its technological managerial sectors, among the proletariat, the functional elements of the urban group and the salaried of the rural, there is support for development.

The polarization of Brazilian social classes into sectors for and against development makes for class conflict. However, it may be a less acute factor than the conflict between sectors over the effects of economic development. The fact is that economic development in contemporary Brazil unfolded differently from that of nineteenth-century Western Europe. In Western Europe, up to the First World War, development was a continuation of the bourgeois revolution against the aristocratic-feudal forces of the *ancien régime*. In Brazil, development is not a unanimous striving of the bourgeoisie nor is it under the leadership of sectors of the classes favorable to it. The leadership of development is just as often denounced by sectors favorable to it, such as the middle class and proletariat, as by sectors opposed. Because of this, the process of Brazilian development has an essentially open feeling. It is neither a question of a redistribution of rent nor of simple economic growth. It is a question of a growing modification of the social structure of Brazil, and no less, the establishment of higher forms of production and organization, a modification that directly or indirectly is constantly broadening the popular share in increased productivity and enjoyment of the highest standards of living.

A consequence of extreme sociopolitical importance comes from those characteristics; that is, the fact that Brazilian development has essentially a multi-class feeling. In Brazil, therefore, the positions of right and left neither in their European nor North American counterparts obtain. The political positions called right and left in Brazil are positions mostly referring to sectors opposing or favoring development, for or against public ownership of the means of production.

The fact that the semi-colonial state of Brazil's economy may barely have been superseded in our day resides in the failure of a major economic articulation of the country's diverse regions. Republican federalism lends institutional protection to the resultant tendencies of underdevelopment that have reached every region and each united federation. This is in accordance with the tendency that is imposed by the natural environment, to relate directly to foreign centers where raw materials are exported and from where manufactured products are imported.

Under such conditions, since they are inevitable, the political unity of the country is refracted horizontally, on two distinct planes: the higher plane of federal interests and the plane of regional interests.

Despite the acceleration of Brazilian development in the last decade, notably under the Kubitschek government, there persists the horizontal refraction of the political process between the federal and regional levels. Partially this is because the growing economic integration of the country affects the sociopolitical behavior of the rural voter and even of the urban voter outside of the great cities only gradually; partially, because administrative and political interests continue to be of local character. Therefore, the duality of the indicated planes will endure.

Similar causes to those already mentioned will lead to another form of refraction, vertical. Heteronomy, a primary characteristic of semi-colonial economies, prevailed in the country until recently, subject to a decision-making process that was external to the national interest. This was because decisions were made by leading foreign powers that operated in the country. The economic behavior of the country necessarily had to react in a way that reflected world economy, rather than national consensus.

Because of heteronomy, it was not until the present that Brazil crystallized relations clearly consistent with the four levels on which social life is divided, which are: the economic, social in a strict sense, cultural, and political levels.

The two-fold deficiency, horizontal and vertical, of the integration of the Brazilian political process led to a failure of unity in political representation. The horizontal duality of the federal and regional planes of political life affected the representativeness of the parties and public figures, especially in Congress, because whoever was elected tended rarely to have any relation to what was expected or what he would be called upon to do in Parliament.

From this stems the failure of the parties to have ideological and programmatic significance. The organized party men are national by virtue of law. But, in fact, they represent distinctly different interests. From this stems the incongruity that manifests itself in all the national parties, for example, their sectional orientations in such States as Pernambuco, Minas Gerais, and Goiás.

The deficient vertical integration of the Brazilian political process prevented establishment of consistent give-and-take politics between the four levels already cited. In politically integrated countries there is a reasonable accommodation for political exchange from one level to the other. At the base of the process, at the economic level, the class sectors demand organization and guarantees of protection and in return offer their contribution, financial or merely electoral, to political parties and their candidates for power. At the immediately higher level, in the strictly social sense, the trade unions and class associations demand ideological and programmatic orientation and offer possibilities of organization of interests, of prestige and protective guarantees. At the next level, cultural and political clubs, journals, and groups of the intelligentsia demand political-juridical sponsorship and offer programmatic and ideological formulation. At the highest level of the process, specifically political, political parties demand power and offer projects of politico-juridical sponsorship.

The existence of these correlates, in politically integrated countries, gives at the same time political-juridical protection to all economic interests of major social significance and offers representation and importance to the parties and to the government representing the prevailing party orientation. The debility and almost non-existence of such correlates in Brazil leave the most socially important interests unprotected, forcing them to resort frequently to underhanded tricks.

The three big Brazilian parties in operation, PSD, UDN, and PTB, based on the fall of Vargas' New State, are marked by two peculiar characteristics of the conditions of their formation. The first regards the composition of these parties, determined by the situation of the New State, from 1937 to 1945, in relation to the political currents of the country. The second regards the political function, such as aspiration for or exercise of power, felt in what has been petrified in these political alignments. These two characteristics, *mutatis mutandi*, affect the lesser parties.

The New State was marked by the transformation of its original position, essentially petit-bourgeois, to a trade-union orientation. In the last days of the regime it had a markedly proletarian character. Heir to the aspirations of the middle class as displayed in the 1930 Revolution and subsequent events, the New State was like a modified fascist bureaucracy managing the state apparatus to the advantage of the petit-bourgeoisie, broadening its possibilities of use, and harboring the inclemencies of free capitalism while keeping the proletarian masses under the discipline and vigilance of security detachments.

With the unfolding of international events, it became evident that the complete break-up of the Axis military and the ideological disintegration of fascism were inevitable, leaving the middle classes, especially in underdeveloped countries, confused between regressive and aggressive forms of imperialist capitalism and the frightening road toward the socialistic regimes supported by the proletarian masses.

The New State assumed a trade-union orientation through which Getúlio Vargas intended to win back supporters not yet in the middle class. For this task Vargas utilized the Ministry of Labor, which decided on an intense campaign of mobilization of the masses. The new orientation of the New State did not alter its structure. Jointly coexisting with the newly risen trade-union machinery was the outmoded representative politico-administrative apparatus of the original petit-bourgeois regime.

Decisive as an influence on the composition of the parties following the decline of the New State was the fact that the leaders of the outmoded politico-administrative apparatus of the New State organized themselves into the Social-Democratic apparatus. Those favorable to the new trade-union orientation, under the direction of the men who had managed the machinery of the Ministry of Labor, organized under the banner of the *Partido Trabalhista Brasileiro* (PTB). The coalescence of heterogeneous tendencies into a political leadership neither bound to the apparatus of the New State nor favorable to unionist orientation was concentrated in the *União Democrática Nacional* (UDN). The party structure in this way crystallized. This in turn was related to the feeling that the parties were now invested with a political function.

The regime which ostensibly aimed to cement the alliance of the middle classes to the working classes—the New State—in fact did so in a rhetorical and bureaucratic way which left the proletariat in a subordinate position. With the exception of occasional industrial initiative, like the National Iron and Steel Company, the New State did not try to modify the Brazilian socio-economic structure and did not formulate its own interpretation or at least a suitable one. The country remained subject to its semi-colonial and underdeveloped condition. The New State reunified into a centralized bureaucracy all the main features which the Republican regime had spread among the federal States and, concentrating power in the executive, proceeded to carry on with the same partisan politics that the old Republic had put into practice. This was possible because, despite the *divorcium aquarum* of the 1930 revolution, the persistence of the semi-colonial structure and underdevelopment of Brazil impeded the country's urgent need for movement toward real public services. It was this partisanship that indelibly marked the political parties that followed the New State and that in them acquired even greater stress, necessarily reinforced by the electoral struggle, to lead party politics to its ultimate consequences.

These two characteristics rendered the parties incapable of

adapting themselves to the new political exigencies that followed the change effected in socio-economic conditions of Brazil in the last decade. Based on the end of a period whose conditions no longer obtained and on the verge of the most profound and rapid structural transformation of Brazilian society, the political parties rapidly grew obsolete and were out of joint with a society whose political currents they were supposed to represent.

This disjointedness made itself felt precisely in the functioning of the above-mentioned characteristics. Maintaining a division between public figures, the parties were to be converted into simple electoral mechanisms. From this stems their peculiar stagnation. On the other hand, in keeping within the bounds of party politics, the parties lack true social representation and tend to distort that representation which for extra-party reasons eventually comes out in some political directive.

The Brazilian people, we have already said, became a people "for itself." Their political behavior really comes from interests and values inherent in the process of interaction in the social system. In such a situation what does it mean to vote for the PSD, for the UDN, or for their own PTB? The parties are frozen and non-representative. If it is certain that at the federal level they tend to acquire a gradual differentiation, the disparity in their State organizations increases their equivocal nature. In such conditions, present-day Brazilian parties are incapable of assuming agreed-upon political responsibilities because they lack true representation and internal consistency.

From the point of view of the electorate, the real political tendencies of the Brazilian public can no longer be channelized through the parties and for that reason they no longer move toward them, leaning instead toward extra-party movements such as nationalism, pro-development, etc.—or toward subversive movements, such as the conspiratorial theory, in opposition to which is formed the broadest of all extra-party movements, the "legal defense" movement.

Nevertheless, parties continue to be the only legal, authorized entity for registering candidates and for election debates, the most important and significant one for parliamentarian institutions being that over the Presidency. They have a two-fold context: party membership and ideological program.

Marshal Dutra, first President-elect after the New State, was also the last candidate whose election had no connection with his own ideological orientation. Even so, there is a vast difference between his election and that of the President of the old Republic. For behind Marshal Dutra, and a decisive factor in his victory, operated the *cle disse* of Vargas, attracting the popular hopes to the PSD candidate, thus setting him off in sharp contrast to Brigadier-General Edouard Gomes.

The path of the electorate in the last decade can be measured by the fact that Marshal Lott was not identified by the people with the role he assumed despite November 11 and the fact of his having been linked to the progressive forces of the labor and nationalist intelligentsia. It was in Quadros, despite the reactionary origin of his candidacy and the retrograde forces that encircled him, that the masses discovered their true image. Such an option, which seemed mistaken to all who did not believe in the sincerity of his reformist proposals, came to be fully confirmed, especially in the six months of his government.

The aforementioned double reference for the presidential election, party membership and ideology, evolved from Vargas in 1950 to Jânio Quadros in 1960 in the sense of the ideological reference becoming more and more accentuated, making the importance of party membership wane.

But in the election for the House of Representatives and in the Senate, the ideological-programmatic criteria of selection did not operate. The party system emerged dominant because of the proportional voting elections, and the oligarchies retained control of the parties as a result.

The consequence of this distinct form of selection of candidates, predominantly party-membership criteria for the National Congress and predominantly ideological criteria for the Presidency, was that the Presidents, up to the time of constitutional reform, found themselves in an oracular dilemma: either living up to their compromise with the masses, fearful of colliding with organized political forces, or skillfully adapting to the exigencies of those forces, betraying the essence of the mandate conferred upon them by the masses.

The election of Quadros was one of the most ambiguous events in the political history of Brazil. Comparable to that ambiguity, although to a lesser degree, we note that Getúlio Vargas was victimized at the end of his second term, when the proletariat lost consciousness of Vargas' political significance for the working classes and the middle class did not realize what immense effort Vargas exerted to attract it. In this way Vargas' government was deprived of support and was delivered up to the fury of the extreme right. The ambiguity of Quadros' election consisted in the disparity of interpretations regarding the meaning of his candidacy and prognostications on his future government, which brought contradictory forces casting votes that mutually excluded each other.

The masses had seen a message of renovation and social reform in Quadros and they believed in his sincerity and capacity to keep his promises. The elites, favorable or hostile, did not see such a message in his preaching and mistrusted his sincerity. It was because of their failure to find a new formulation (with the great exception of foreign policy) in the electoral message of Quadros that the intelligentsia turned to Marshal Lott. They hoped to compensate for Lott's limitations with a program they presented for him to follow in the historic march of socio-economic development. Also willing to support Lott was a still more intelligent sort who were distrustful of Quadros' sentiments for renovation and reform and were convinced that all his contact with the masses had the mark of a calculated maneuver. The forces of the extreme right wing, with Lacerda in the lead like a shining knight, rallied to the governor of São Paulo * and threw their weight behind his candidacy.

For the bulk of the middle class, the future government of Quadros looked like moral redemption. It was moralism in relation to administrative fulfillment of his proposals and the political stubbornness of his decisions. For the urban proletarian mass, whose support Quadros' preaching had failed to win, his candidacy seemed to be a typical example of the proletarianized petit-bourgeoisie, a man who possessed a superior knowledge of national problems and had already given proof, in the São Paulo government, of commanding the necessary determination to confront bureaucratic obstacles, which were an object of popular fear and hatred.

The government of President Kubitschek, favorable to development, gave the Brazilian people the practical evidence that the

* Jânio Quadros.

economic-technological contours of the country could be planned and rapidly modified. He gave them a feeling of national pride, which might have allowed Brazil to carry out such an enterprise successfully. On the other side of the ledger, the Kubitschek administration could never clearly establish the primacy of the Presidency in its confrontation with the other forces of the country, nor the independence and sovereignty of Brazil in its international relations. At the same time, economic development, so much desired and courted, had to be paid for by the masses through inflation. There was not even a faint glimmering of corresponding benefit in the level of social development. To the bourgeoisie, a new sector of the privileged that understood (apart from the new enterprisers, administrators, technicians, and a whole series of business intermediaries) that they were mingling their inheritance in politics and public administration with their participation in the new enterprises, the election of Quadros was critical. Quadros was just as much the candidate of the middle class as of the urban proletariat. He was considered a guaranteed radical with *Juscelinista* excesses, without being able to solve the problem of assuring continuity of the impulse to development. These excesses, real or imagined (in reality both real and imagined), were seen by each class or class sector in a reciprocally contradictory way. The distinctive mark of Quadros' campaign was the fact that he continued to couch his election preaching in terms that suited principal sectors of the electorate. The major slogans were: positively, in favor of economic and social development, of nationalism, of administrative morality, of the authority of the government, and of national independence in foreign policy; negatively, against scarcity, corruption, and big business parties.

For the elites, Quadros' election seemed to contain a quite different meaning. Adherents and adversaries shared a common disbelief in Quadros' sincerity. For the extreme right, Quadros was a genial impostor, capable of playing the role of popular hero defending maintenance of the *status quo* in the country's vast archaic and reactionary sectors. For the intelligentsia and for the forces of the left, Quadros was a dangerous farce who used ludicrous expedients to win the confidence of the masses and attract attention by promising a new foreign policy in order to gain left sympathy, but in reality was serving reaction and imperialism.

Which traits were genuine from among the diverse personalities displayed by Quadros or attributed to him? This Pirandellian question does not admit of an exact answer. Neither is it really important to undertake a profound and subtle examination of the most authentically representative personality among public figures of a many-sided character. What is important is the social significance, and this I conclude by defining. It was what happened to Quadros.

Despite the numerous and severe criticisms one could level at his government, the major one being his delay and vacillation in the preparation of a plan of development, it confirmed the intuition of the masses, confounded the suspicions of his opponents, and threw into paroxysms of frustration the forces of the extreme right.

As President-elect, Jânio Quadros revealed a personality as enigmatic and solitary as the one he displayed in his campaign. Affirming his position of independence in relation to the parties, he gave the UDN a discreet share in his government without converting it into a government party. Under the pretext of preserving the separation of powers, he withdrew the legislature completely from all contact with the administration. On the other hand, he converted the Ministers of State into executive secretaries of the President and intervened directly in the conduct of the affairs of each Ministry, prescribing to the respective heads the orientation they ought to follow, the tasks they ought to execute, and, frequently, the desired solutions in numerous particular cases, sometimes of extremely small importance, on which he demanded that the decisions he suggested be made.

Quadros' governing technique was a form of Bonapartism. Nevertheless, it is neither the Bonapartism of Louis Napoleon, who based power on the equilibrium of social classes, nor the Bonapartism of Bismarck, whose power rose out of the advancement of German development on the basis of an alliance between the bureaucratic military *junker* and the bourgeoisie. Quadros' Bonapartism shared the despotism illustrated by Pedro el Grande and Catalina. It was a tsarist Bonapartism, based on the apparatus of the state, that nevertheless gained a great deal of its power, like all Bonapartism, by practicing arbitration among classes, and he was less sure of his capacity for maintaining an equilibrium between conflicting social forces by the fact that each of them depended upon his authority to preserve its status and to pay attention to its new interests. This was his distinctive tsarist streak.

Brazilian social conditions still do not allow the practice of a pure Bonapartism, nor do they lend themselves to the realization of any form of the abovementioned despotism, especially the tsarist form.

I had occasion to analyze in another work the relations between economic development of a community and the political models most appropriate for the promotion of its development. I mentioned, then, neo-Bismarckism (contemporary-style and suited to the development of Bonapartism) as the most suitable regime for such an outcome in countries that may already have an appreciable degree of development, when they are subjected to the same conditions. Such is the case with Brazil. But the neo-Bismarckian model and the tsarist Bonapartism put into practice by Jânio Quadros are enormously different. The main distinction is that the neo-Bismarckian bases his authority on his rational functioning; tsarist Bonapartism bases its rational functioning in its authority.

Conscious of the lack of true representation on the part of our political parties, and wanting to defend himself from political pressures and the necessity of having to negotiate support for his bills and projects through Congress, Quadros didn't realize that the state in civil Brazilian society, and the President in the present chartist type of state, do not command enough power for feigning indifference to such a task.

Brazilian political parties, as we have already seen, are unchanging, non-representative, and equivocal. But for that same reason, they bring about consensus and conformity in the nation's social orientation, the Brazilian people being differentiated through classes, sectors, and regions and moving toward other organized forms of group division. It was not possible for Quadros to govern Brazil unacquainted with this. By abstaining from forming a system and an apparatus of mediation between his leadership and the social strata that were interested in the political orientation being adopted, Jânio Quadros was deprived of real support for the type of state that he was determined to lead.

Only in a traditional society, like old Russia, was it possible to base power of direction on the mystical-magic sense of the ruler's authority. And only in a society in which the class struggle is the core of social tension, such as France after the Revolution of 1848, would the simple promotion of equilibrium between classes through arbitration assure a sufficiently durable base for power.

In a contractualist society such as Brazil, in the process of rapid economic development, power is based on the capacity to apportion to each class the maximum benefits compatible with the general increase of productivity. The state can only exercise that function by relying on systems and instruments of mediation between classes. But this implies that power is seated in a genuine party of development. Deprived of real social support, the government of Jânio Quadros did not possess any firm evidence of popularly mobilized support at the time of his renunciation.

In keeping with the above, the misfiring of the resignation, like the counter-*coup*, was due in part to the special conditions of his isolation in Brasília. Nevertheless, even in those particular circumstances, if the popular support that Quadros counted on was with him instead of being distant, his resignation would have rallied a compactly solidified mass and would have barred the extreme right from preparing to depose him. Instead of an authentic party or political movement, Quadros counted on partial and wary support from a patronage party like the UDN, unlikely to give him real communication with the masses, and counted on the ambiguous favor of the Popular Movement for Jânio Quadros, which never had the characteristics of an electoral pressure group. The inevitable result was his abandonment.

Aside from not having intended to give real structure to the new type of state he tried to establish, Jânio Quadros committed the related error of not equipping himself with the necessary operative instruments to carry out his attempted reform of the state and assuring himself command of it. Product of the *partidista* policy, the Brazilian state is a Chartist state, one that neither financed nor was qualified to pay attention to genuine public services, but rather was uniquely destined and able to assure mediation of the party system. It maintained prestige by an infinite multiplication of jobs and bureaucratic prebends. With the end of the Chartist state in Brazil at the turn of the century, a chasm widened between what civil society demanded of the state and what it could offer. State reform became the most immediate and fundamental requirement for the socio-economic development of the country.

The Vargas government tried to attract little attention to its administrative reforms. Not noting, however, the intimate and necessary connection that exists between actual political parties and the Chartist state, Vargas committed the unpardonable error of confiding to the parties his deliberations on the administrative reform project prepared by the executive branch of the government. The result was that the project was filed away.

The Kubitschek government systematically avoided the question of trying to resolve this problem. Case by case, Kubitschek created new organs of economic planning (Council on Development), using the name BNDE profusely, giving new breadth to the Department of Highways, and departing from constant bureaucratic expansion, he entrusted to private initiative and to the trucking interests the task of assuring market distribution in the country.

This expedient solution of emergencies took some time before it started to reveal its deficiences; in fact, it lasted until the end of the Kubitschek government when, with the weakening of administrative commands that came as a consequence of the incomplete transfer of the federal administration to Brasília, the state apparatus went back to impasse and immobility. Administrative policies conflicted and no amount of pragmatic and opportunist decisions could balance the conflicts. The prescription of measures became more and more discordant with any control and sanction. The lack of discipline was general and distribution became independent of all higher coordination. Policies turned into payoffs for respective chiefs and dominant groups.

Having inherited this discordant state apparatus, Quadros intended to strengthen the administration, without entering into structural modifications, merely by his own will power and his personal capacity for direct intervention in the functioning of the administrative machinery.

In consequence of the unusual determination of the President and his personal intervention in the affairs of administrative routine, the state apparatus began to function. It operated, however, inefficiently, in an absurd way, without any correlation between the quasi-deluded energy that the President was developing in the management of the precarious and unconnected means of command and the almost powerless condition of the administrative gears.

A man of great intuition and extraordinary determination, Jânio Quadros did not show any talent for organization. Nor did he reveal any tactical sensibility. He failed to understand that without a structural and profound revision of the state apparatus, he could not carry out his policy. He failed to grasp that it was necessary to show control of some operative instruments that might assure him command of the state and thereby allow him effectively to pay attention to minimum necessities of public administration.

It is not important to go on to an analysis of the hiatus in which Quadros brought about some control of the state apparatus. We only note that it did not take any special insight to bring about the rapid materialization of statistical data to undergird his future programming. He didn't think about organizing a system that might control the degree and form of execution of the main administrative edicts that were so prolifically emitted.

He was not capable, except in the last days of his government, and even then in unsatisfactory manner, of resolving the impasse that sprang up in his Office of Technical Assessment for Planning, neutralizing its efficiency and fatally retarding its expansion. Finally, it never occurred to him to maintain a security detachment that might safeguard needed information on the state of the prevailing mood in strategic areas and give him defenses and initial means of action in case of attempts at sedition and *coups d'état*. The tsarist Bonapartism of Quadros, aside from joining the state to civil society, was exercised in a most timid and unknowing way in joining the Presidency with the state apparatus, costing him sudden and inevitable ruin.

IV. THE POLITICAL SOCIOLOGY OF UNEVEN DEVELOPMENT
IN BRAZIL

Gláucio Ary Dillon Soares *

The aim of this paper is to relate regional differences in Brazilian politics to underlying socio-economic differences. It is hoped that the conceptual development of this basic hypothesis, plus the accumulation of unsystematic descriptive data and organized statistical data will indicate the usefulness of the model. It is further

* Gláucio Soares is one of the promising crop of young Brazilian social scientists. He is presently engaged in research at the University of California, Berkeley.

hoped that this internally differentiated political model, based on varying socio-economic structures, is applicable to other Latin American countries undergoing fast and uneven economic and social change.

Some basic information on Brazilian political parties and electoral laws may be useful. In 1945, after the fall of Vargas, political parties were allowed to compete freely for the first time in years. Several parties presented candidates in the 1945 elections, and since then few basic changes have been introduced. The Brazilian Communist Party (PCB—*Partido Comunista Brasileiro*) was outlawed in 1947. Other parties disappeared. Some combined to form a new party and entirely new ones were created. In the 1962 elections there were thirteen competing parties.

Brazil uses proportional representation for Congressional, State, and municipal legislatures. The first is known as *Congresso* or *Camara Federal*. The second are the *Assembléias Legislativas Estaduais*, one for each State. The last are called *Câmaras Municipais*, one for each municipality—the political-administrative subdivisions of every State except Guanabara.

The number of representatives elected in each State to the Federal Congress is determined by its population, but subject to diminishing quotas (the inverse of the American income-tax system, for example). Thus the most populated States are inadequately represented and the least populated ones are "over-represented." This departs even further from the American single-member district system since each *município* does not have its own representative. Congressmen are elected in the State as a whole. Each State has an electoral quotient (*quociente electoral* —number of registered voters in the State divided by the number of State representatives). For instance, Sergipe in 1958 had 123,737 voters and seven representatives—therefore an electoral quotient of 17,677. The Brazilian Labor Party (PTB—*Partido Trabalhista Brasileiro*) received 13,203 votes and therefore did not elect a single representative. The National Democratic Union (UDN— *União Democrática Nacional*) and the Social Labor Party (PST —*Partido Social Trabalhista*) formed an alliance and received 58,434 votes. The alliance was then granted three representatives. But the remainders of both parties with no representatives and that of the other parties accumulate to form an over-all State remainder. That generally means one, two, or more representatives.

The first is assigned to the party with the largest remainder, considering those parties only with at least one representative. Each State has three representatives in the Senate and the President is elected by direct popular vote. A most important fact to bear in mind is that illiterates cannot legally vote in Brazil.

The standard way to correlate socio-economic and political variables is to develop censal measures of socio-economic variables on the one hand, and political ones on the other, and correlate these using the States or *municípios* as units. The assumption is implicit that these variables are continuous by nature, for at least theoretically there could be a State (or *município*) at any point between the two extreme values of the above continuous variables. For the sake of precision the *município* should be taken as the unit of analysis since there is considerable internal differentiation *within* each State.

Underdeveloped States will be considered as a group and opposed to and contrasted with a group of developed States. Obviously, a great deal of information will be lost as regards the interstate variance within each of the groupings as well as the intermunicipal variance within each State.

There are three basic reasons for this:

(1) The electoral data which seem most relevant to the hypothesis are given by State. That eliminates the possibility of using the *município* as a unit.

(2) My central purpose is to present a *comprehensive* description of the impact of uneven development on Brazilian politics, *not* to give a precise evaluation of its extent. This can best be done by comparing political data in two *areas* highly differentiated in socio-economic terms.

(3) Moreover, geographical continuity is necessary for developing the idea of political culture and for stressing its dependence on socio-economic variables.

Although acknowledging the usefulness of the information lost and the limitations inherent in the model, it is nevertheless suited to the purposes at hand. It will suffice here to present data so as to illustrate simply the great distance between the two areas, in terms of both economic and social development. The reader will become aware of the immense unevenness of Brazilian economic development, the extent of which is probably unparalleled in already industrialized countries. Attention will then focus on political differences. The following sections will suggest that these socio-economic differences have engendered not only differences in special political variables but two unique political cultures.

The extent of these differences is seldom, if ever, paralleled in stable, industrialized nations. Furthermore, *among* industrialized nations they are of a lesser magnitude. Average income per capita has a tremendous range among Brazilian States: 1955 estimates give Piauí Cr$2,319 and Guanabara (then *Distrito Federal*) Cr$28,-995 per capita. The latter has more than ten times the per capita income of Piauí. Among industrialized nations, there is much less than half the variation. These variations should be taken seriously by those who treat Latin American countries as if they were homogeneous units.

The two areas, which are distinct geo-economic regions, will be called Northeast and Southeast. They cover 75% of the Brazilian population. The former will include the following States: Maranhão, Piauí, Ceará, Rio Grande do Norte, Paraíba, Pernambuco, Alagôas, Sergipe, and Bahia; whereas the latter comprise Rio de Janeiro, Guanabara, São Paulo, Paraná, Santa Catarina, and Rio Grande do Sul. Other States, representing only 25% of the population, will be omitted due to intervening variables that would create serious classificatory problems.

With respect to most standard measures of social and economic development, the States composing the two areas do not overlap.[1] On the other hand, differences between regional *averages* do not reveal the full extent of inequality and unevenness. For even *within* regions there is great variation. Therefore, taking the two areas together, differences between top and bottom States can outstrip differences between regional averages many times over. In 1955, the then *Distrito Federal* (presently State of Guanabara), with less than three million inhabitants, had about the same gross product as the entire Northeast, with about six times the population. But differences are not only economic. In 1950, in the *Distrito Federal* 84% of the population aged ten years and over was literate; in Alagôas this was less than 24%. Urbanization rates range from 97% in the *Distrito Federal* to 5% in Maranhão, according to the census. Differences in average life span ran over ten

[1] The only exception would be urbanization, where Pernambuco stands higher than Paraná, Santa Catarina, and Rio Grande do Sul, in accordance with census showings.

years between top and bottom States. Therefore any description
of socio-economic differences based on regional averages is necessarily inaccurate and loses a great deal of information.

Many of these differences are continuously increasing. Recently
a long step was taken to cope with these problems by creating an
institution (SUDENE) with adequate financial support whose
function it is to accelerate economic development in the Northeast. Nevertheless, it is unlikely that this trend will be reversed
for the next ten years.

The first set of differences refers to what has been called the
urban-industrial syndrome. I believe that the unqualified use of
the word syndrome may be misleading in the sense that it exag-
gerates the consistency of the several dimensions involved. The
very incongruence between urbanization and industrialization is
extremely helpful in explaining *both* radical leftism and extreme
conservatism. When industrialization doesn't keep pace with urbanization there is a mass of unemployed and underemployed with
expectations heightened by urban living. With no possibility of
even minimally satisfying these aspirations, leftist radicalism finds
fertile soil.[2] In spite of the chronic shortage of urban industrial
jobs in the large Northeastern cities, miserable rural living conditions and periodic extreme droughts force these men to migrate.

According to the census, approximately 3,720,000 of the 17,-
970,000 Northeastern inhabitants were urban dwellers in 1950. No
less than approximately 9,680,000 of the 21,670,000 Southeastern-
ers lived in urban areas. This gives an urban population of
20.7% to the Northeast and 44.7% to the Southeast—more than
twice the Northeastern figure. Data for industrialization present
similar patterns: Table 1 shows that the percentage of the labor
force in the primary sector (agriculture, etc.) is 77% for the
Northeast and only 48% for the Southeast, thus showing the dependence of the Northern population on agriculture. On the
other hand, those employed in manufacturing represent only 6.9%
of the Northeastern labor force, but no less than 19.7% of the
Southeastern labor force.

[2] For an attempt to formulate a theory linking the *incongruency* of socio-
economic indicators with political radicalism, cf. G.A.D. Soares, "Desenvolvimento Econômico e Radicalismo Político: Notas para uma Teoria," in
Boletim de Centro Latino Americano de Pesquisas em Ciências Sociais (May
1961), pp. 117-57.

TABLE I. REGIONAL DIFFERENCES IN URBANIZATION AND INDUSTRIALIZATION, 1950
(per 1,000 inhabitants)

	a	b	b/a	c	d	d/c	e	e/c
Northeast	17,973	3,719	20.7%	4,843	3,730	77.0%	332	6.9%
Southeast	21,671	9,679	44.7%	6,319	3,031	48.0%	1,245	19.7%

a: total population; b: urban population; c: labor force, 10 years and over (not included: unclassified, housewives, and students); d: labor force in forestry, agriculture, and farming; and e: labor force in manufacturing.
Source: Anuário Estatístico do Brasil (Rio de Janeiro, IGBE, 1956)

Relatively *more* of those leaving the fields and agricultural activities in the Southeast go into secondary activities. This should be taken as an effective indicator of a meaningful difference in the degree of industrialization. The Southeast is *becoming* an industrial society. It should be kept in mind that these indicators are not fully consistent, allowing for a certain incongruency. Most data for economic development, mainly average income per capita (which, incidentally, was Cr$4,511 in the Northeast and Cr$18,382 in the Southeast, for 1955), tends to ignore this incongruency, thereby artificially emphasizing the degree of inconsistency. The Northeast lags in all aspects of the development syndrome, especially in industrialization. The next task is to see if there are concomitant variations in other, less strictly economic aspects of development.

One variable of great importance for political analysis is education. It has been found to correlate (negatively) with authoritarian traits,[3] political preferences,[4] and the like. In other articles I have attempted to demonstrate the usefulness of education as an indicator of social development.[5] What is important here is that education relates to ideology, interest, and participation.[6]

[3] Cf. Seymour M. Lipset, *Political Man* (New York: Doubleday and Co., 1961), Chapter IV; M. Janowitz and D. Marvick, "Authoritarianism and Political Behavior," in *Public Opinion Quarterly*, Vol. XVII (1953). Janowitz and Marvick suggest that education and authoritarianism are negatively correlated only in the middle class.

[4] Cf. Lipset, *op. cit.*; Berelson *et al.*, *Voting* (Chicago: University of Chicago Press, 1954); G.A.D. Soares, "Classes Sociais, Strata Sociais e as Eleições Presidenciais de 1960," in *Sociologia* (September 1961).

[5] Cf. Soares, "Desenvolvimento, etc." and "Desenvolvimento Econômico e Radicalismo Político: o Teste de uma Hipótese," in *América Latina* (1962).

[6] Cf. Berelson, *op. cit.*; Lipset, *op. cit.*, Part II; Lazarsfeld *et al.*, *The People's Choice* (New York: Duell, Sloan and Pearce, 1944); and Soares, "Interêsse Político, Conflito de Pressões e Indecisão Eleitoral," in *Síntese Política, Econômica e Social* (January 1960), pp. 5-34.

In *industrialized* societies the less educated tend more than the better educated to adopt radical ideologies. When one jumps from the personal level to larger units of analysis, seemingly contradictory facts may appear, such as the lack of leftist radicalism in less educated areas. Two explanations may be anticipated here: on the one hand, it is clear that *both* education and political radicalism correlate with other variables such as industrialization and urbanization. When the latter are constant, the relationship between the two former ones may weaken, disappear, or even reverse. Extremely low education—widespread illiteracy—may favor the permanence of a traditional culture, inhibit the development of an effective system of mass communications, and maintain a low degree of social change. Leftist radicalization in the early stages of rapid social change is therefore inhibited. Leftist ideologies not only face the obstacle of an aggressive traditional culture but are also inhibited by inefficient communication and very low participation.

TABLE 2. REGIONAL DIFFERENCES IN EDUCATION, 1950

	a	b	b/a	c	c/a	Literacy Range
Northeast	12,393	3,721	30.0%	18,585	0.15%	23.65%-33.63%
Southeast	15,669	10,269	65.5%	116,439	7.43%	52.47%-84.48%

a: total population, 10 years and over; *b*: literates, 10 years and over; *c*: college graduates; *a* and *b* are given per 1,000 inhabitants.
Source: as above.

Table 2 shows the educational gap between the Northeast and the Southeast. Whereas only 30% of the Northeastern population of ten years and over is literate, those who can read and write account for 65.5% of the equivalent Southeastern population. The low range of variation in the Northeast shows that this is a widespread and uniform phenomenon. Less than one out of a hundred has a college degree in the Northeast, a very low rate as compared with the Southeast, where more than seven in a hundred do.

When it is considered that the urban areas are included in the over-all Northeastern figures and that there is a tremendous urban-rural educational differential, then it follows that the Northeastern rural population is almost entirely illiterate.

Low education rates have always been incongruent with Brazil's stand on other development-associated variables. To a certain extent they are a deterrent to other aspects of economic development.[7]

Relevant to an analysis of political behavior is the pattern of land ownership. The latifundia are both cause and consequence of traditionalism, both general and political. If traditionalism breaks down before the land ownership system, then the heightening of aspirations in sharp contrast with the low standards of living will probably result in outbreaks of violence. The soporific effects of traditionalism will no longer be present. Looking at Table 3, it

TABLE 3. REGIONAL DIFFERENCES IN LAND DISTRIBUTION, 1950
(per 1,000 hectares)

	a	b	b/a	c	c/a	d	d/a
Northeast	58,341	11,675	20.0%	23,019	39.5%	6,123	10.5%
Southeast	57,647	16,525	28.7%	20,311	35.2%	3,199	5.5%

a: total area privately owned; b: area of holdings with less than 100 hectares; c: area of holdings with more than 1,000 hectares; d: area of holdings with more than 10,000 hectares.
Source: Mayer et al., Reforma Agrária, Questão de Consciência (São Paulo: Editora Vera Cruz, 1961; 3rd ed.), Anex II.

appears that the two areas are approximately equal in size of owned properties. But there are meaningful differences in the proportion occupied by small and large properties: whereas the smaller properties (less than 100 hectares) represent 20% of the total in the Northeast, they account for 28.7% of the total in the Southeast. The latifundia are more meaningful in the Northeast than in the Southeast, particularly the very large ones, with 10,000 hectares or more. This is even more important when it is considered that the fertile land is much more scarce in the Northeast and that the latifundia usually own the best land. It is interesting to note that the proportion of medium large properties (1,000 to 10,000 hectares) is slightly *higher* in the Southeast. This is probably due to coffee. Coffee farm workers are well paid but peasants working on the Northeastern latifundia have among the lowest standards of living on earth.

Though it is obvious that both areas exhibit extreme inequality in land ownership, differences between them are meaningful.

[7] For an analysis showing how low educational level has inhibited further economic development in Brazil, see R. Moreira, *Educação e Desenvolvimento no Brasil* (Rio de Janeiro: CLAPESCO, 1960).

These differences acquire new meaning when it is known that in the Northeast there are approximately fourteen million persons living in rural areas, two million more than in the Southeast. There are 3,700,000 members of the labor force engaged in agriculture and related affairs in the Northeast, against three million in the Southeast. Therefore, not only is land inequality more striking because the region is heavily dependent on agriculture in the Northeast, but the disparity is even more significant. As compared with the Southeast the rural population is larger and there are more members engaged in agricultural and related activity.

This is even more impressive given the fact that the percentage of used land is considerably lower in the Northeast. Not including Bahia and Sergipe, in the Northeast only 38% of all the privately owned land is in actual use for agriculture and pastures, whereas in the Southeast (excluding Rio de Janeiro and Guanabara) this is 66%. No less than 52% of the land in the former group of States is either unused (28%) or covered with forests (24%), whereas in the Southeastern group this is only 29% (13% unused and 16% set aside for forests).[8] For our purposes the most important finding is that the latifundia present a much higher percentage of unused land than the smaller properties.[9] Still another study shows that inequality in land distribution correlates *negatively* with indicators of *both* social and economic development and *positively* with illiteracy. The same study suggests that there is a general factor of economic development that is clearly bi-polar. The various indicators of inequality in land distribution, *together with illiteracy*, have a heavy negative stress on this factor.[10]

Inequality in land distribution is detrimental for economic development. It may be argued that differences in industrial development are perhaps more important and that rural-agricultural poverty is only a specific aspect of general underdevelopment which is to be explained in terms of lack of industrialization. Table

[8] Data from Mayer *et al.*, *op. cit.*, p. 267.

[9] *See*, for suggestions in this direction, S. Schattan, "Estrutura Econômica da Lavoura Paulista," in *Revista Brasiliense* (November 1959) and "Nota Sôbre a Estrutura Econômica da Lavoura Paulista," in *Revista de Ciências Econômicas* (June 1960).

[10] *See* Soares, "Nordeste: Latifundismo, Miséria e Morte," in *Síntese Política, Econômica e Social* (December 1962). These correlations can reach .70 as between the proportion of the privately owned land occupied by properties with 1,000 hectares and over, and the industrial income per capita.

TABLE 4. REGIONAL DIFFERENCES IN INCOME, 1955

| | PER CAPITA | | | PER HECTARE |
	General [a]	Industrial [b]	Agricultural [c]	Agricultural [d]
Northeast	Cr$ 4,511,00	Cr$30,111,00	Cr$ 8,989,00	Cr$ 575,00
Southeast	Cr$18,382,00	Cr$67,261,00	Cr$40,004,00	Cr$2,103,00

a: gross product/total population; *b*: industrial product/labor force in manufacturing; *c*: agricultural product/labor force in agriculture and related activities (primary sector); *d*: agricultural product/total area of privately owned properties. Population data for 1950.
Source: as above, pp. 45, 291.

4 shows that differences in agricultural income are *greater* than differences in industrial income, both on a per capita and a per hectare basis. Furthermore, agricultural produce is more important *both* in the Northeast and in the Southeast, though it is much more important in the Northeast.[11] In other words, agriculture is more important for the Northeastern economy than industry, as compared with the Southeast. Differences in per capita income are also more pronounced in agriculture than in industry between the two regions. Simply stated, the Northeast is the least productive, as compared with the Southeast, precisely in that sector which is more important for its economy.

One feature of extreme backwardness is its impact on social organization, including organization of an adequate system of communication.[12] This reveals itself not only in the lack of formal organization but informal organization as well. In a predominantly agricultural society, with the lack of capital and other severe problems that characterize the Northeast, cooperation would be the most elementary step to cope with these problems. Voluntary agricultural cooperatives are entitled to many privileges in Brazil and are the logical solution for many poor farms. It would be

[11] The Northeastern gross product in 1955 was Cr$80,915 million, of which Cr$33,530 million (41.4%) came from the primary and Cr$9,997 million (12.4%) from the secondary. Southeastern data show that gross income ran about Cr$398,361 million, with the primary contributing 30.4% (Cr$121,253 million) and the secondary contributing 21% (Cr$83,740 million). Therefore, the Northeast is much more dependent on agriculture and less on industry, as compared with the Southeast.

[12] E. Banfield, *The Moral Basis of a Backward Society* (Glencoe: The Free Press, 1958), gives a description of how extreme backwardness limited social organization in Southern Italian communities. Needless to say, Southern Italian communities look relatively well off by comparison with those of the Brazilian Northeast.

legitimate to expect farmers and landowners to join in business-type organizations and peasants to associate with agricultural trade unions that would protect their interests. However, this does not occur.

Family rivalries, an elitist conception of life, and ethnocentrism have prevented landowners from organizing to cope with common problems. In 1955 there were 1,170 registered cooperatives in the Northeast and 1,949 in the Southeast. This gives a ratio of 35 cooperatives per 100,000 members of the agricultural labor force in the Northeast, as against 64 in the Southeast. But the above data do not reveal the full extent of the real differences, for Southeastern cooperatives are often very large and the Northeastern ones are frequently very small. Thus differences in membership/population ratios are likely to be even more significant. If the tremendous problems referred to are not enough to stimulate cooperation, other factors must intervene. Two important ones are:

(1) the *latifundista* is oftentimes an absentee and his lands, being extensive, allow for a comfortable urban living for him and his family, in spite of low productivity per hectare, and
(2) the *latifundista* is not an entrepreneur. Property is taken for granted; land is a source of prestige and of a comfortable income. Expanding business, for purposes other than prestige and ownership satisfaction, and improving productivity are *not* his concern.

Extreme backwardness, extreme poverty caused at least partially by inequality in land distribution, and widespread illiteracy, which is associated with the previous factors, have inhibited the *peasants* from organizing around their own interests. The *latifundista*'s paternalistic attitudes toward the peasant have contributed to making him sentimentally attached to his master. The peasant cannot visualize his interests as *different* from the landowner's.

Widespread illiteracy is probably a very important variable in explaining the lack of class organization. Several studies show that both formal and informal participation is strongly associated with status—educational, occupational, or otherwise. Northeastern illiteracy rates cannot be properly understood outside their context. Land inequality implies income inequality, which in turn suggests the existence of a large population with very low incomes.

When income is at the subsistence level, child labor is needed and education becomes a luxury. This becomes a vicious circle: the prevailing structures imply widespread illiteracy; conservative politics help to preserve these structures; illiteracy favors apathy, an unquestioning acceptance of traditional values which immunizes the peasants against class organization and ideological rebellion.

Lack of cooperativism and class organization are presented here as illustrations only and should be seen as indicators of lack of social organization in general. For the purposes of political analysis, the important thing to notice is that the factors mentioned inhibit class organization.

It is logical that Northeastern politics are dominated by conservative parties. Qualitative inspection suggests that two of the four main parties, the Social Democrat Party (PSD—*Partido Social Democrático*) and the National Democratic Union (UDN—*União Democrática Nacional*) are conservative and rural-based although the UDN has tried to attract the urban middle classes with some success. The Brazilian Labor Party (PTB—*Partido Trabalhista Brasileiro*) is essentially labor oriented and the Social Progressive Party (PSP—*Partido Social Progressista*) in many areas is also working-class oriented, although ideologically less defined than the PTB. These parties do not enjoy equal acceptance in developed and underdeveloped regions, and they do not perform the same function in the different regions.

Party programs are generally nominal and no special attention will be paid to them. Outstanding exceptions may be the Brazilian Communist Party (*Partido Comunista Brasileiro*—PCB, outlawed in 1947), the far-right Popular Representation Party (PRP—*Partido de Representacão Popular*), the Brazilian Socialist Party (PSB—*Partido Socialista Brasileiro*), and the PTB. But, again, this varies regionally. In backward areas there is the widespread, non-ideological, instrumental use of parties. The politics of these areas is characterized by traditionalism and prolonged rule of dominant families, usually of landlords and small-town economic elites. Although highly symptomatic changes have recently been observed during the period analyzed, the model seems to be a working one. The politics of developing areas are characterized by a class basis and the increasing role of ideology in determining political behavior.

To an extent this model approached the one commonly used to describe politics in industrial areas.[13]

Northeastern politics is dominated by conservative parties but there are two qualifications to this:

(1) the pattern is not completely static; i.e., it allows for some change; and

(2) the pattern does not apply to the larger cities. These, living under chronic unemployment and underemployment, are indeed the most radical spots in the country.

Looking at Table 5 it becomes clear that the conservative parties have a strong position in the Northeast, where they account for almost 70% of all representatives elected to Congress. In the Southeast they account for only 45%.

TABLE 5. REGIONAL DIFFERENCES IN DISTRIBUTION OF CONGRESSIONAL SEATS, 1954

	PSD	UDN	PTB	PSP	Small Parties	Total
Northeast	39.8%	28.8%	9.3%	9.3%	12.7%	99.9% (118)
Southeast	26.2%	19.0%	26.2%	11.1%	17.5%	100.0% (126)

Source: Tribunal Superior Eleitoral, *Dados Estatísticos*, Vol. III, part 1a (Rio de Janeiro, no date), p. 99. In this and other tables percentages do not add up to 100% due to rounding.

There was a change from the 1945–47 to the 1950 elections, when conservative parties lost many seats throughout the country, mainly in the Southeast.[14] Since then changes have been moderate.

The appeal of the labor party (PTB) to the Southeast is perfectly clear. While retaining 26.2% of all seats in the Southwest, the PTB received only 9.3% in the Northeast. The PSP, which was said to be labor oriented, but less ideologically defined, appeals somewhat more to the developed areas. This last difference is not statistically significant, but it has repeatedly been confirmed in other elections.[15]

Another difference of the same kind is found when data is shifted to the State legislatures in 1950:

[13] Cf. Lipset, *op. cit.* An important difference, however, is the assumed increase in the importance of ideology. If anything, the role of ideology seems to be declining in industrial societies. Cf. Lipset, *op. cit.*, Chapter XIII; also Daniel Bell, *The End of Ideology* (Glencoe: The Free Press, 1960).

[14] Cf. Soares, "A Evolução dos Partidos Políticos Brasileiros, 1945–1958" in *Revista de Direito Público e Ciência Política* (1963).

[15] *Ibid.*

TABLE 6. REGIONAL DIFFERENCES IN THE DISTRIBUTION OF SEATS
IN STATE LEGISLATURES, 1950

	PSD	UDN	PTB	PSP	Small Parties	Total
Northeast	32.7%	30.9%	6.3%	7.4%	22.7%	100.1% (379)
Southeast	26.7%	18.6%	25.2%	10.4%	19.2%	100.1% (318)

Source: Same as above, Vol. II, p. 46.

The two conservative parties, PSD and UDN, held more than 63% of all seats in the Northeast and a little over 45% in the Southeast. This is not a phenomenon peculiar to any specific electoral level (Federal, State, etc.) nor was it a peculiarity of a given electoral year. It repeats itself every electoral year at all levels.

The PTB has proportionately four times more seats in the Southeast than in the Northeast, a striking difference. The PSP confirms the data presented previously: a milder tendency toward greater representation in the Southeast. The only important modifications refer to small parties, now with a slightly larger representation in the Northeast.

By and large, the picture remains the same: a large concentration of seats in the hands of the two largest conservative parties, this concentration being more pronounced in the Northeast; a labor preference in the Southeast, this preference being more pronounced for the main labor party, the PTB.

Any interpretation has to consider the class structure of both areas. The Southeast has a respectable industrial working class which supports labor-oriented parties, mainly the PTB. In the Northeast, the working class is much smaller and concentrated in the State capitals and a few other large cities. In terms of the total vote, the conservative parties dominate, for they receive urban support from the middle and upper classes and complete support in the upper-class-dominated rural areas, even though they often lose in municipal elections in large cities.

Party alliances and coalitions are another aspect of differential politics. Indeed they have an important meaning for developing the concept of differential political cultures. In a previous paper, I tried to develop two theories to explain why parties engage in electoral coalitions. For the sake of identification, these theories will be called (1) economic, and (2) cultural-ideological.[16] They

[16] Cf. Soares, "Aliancas e Coligações Partidárias: Notas para uma Teoria," in Revista Brasileira de Estudos Políticos (1963); Spanish version in Ciencias Políticas y Sociales (1963).

aim at presenting a comprehensive view of some factors which increase the likelihood that party alliances will occur. What is important is that a set of verifiable hypotheses was derived therefrom and tested with the available data. The results gave strong support to the theories which are *not* mutually exclusive.

The first theory was conceived after a hint derived from a careful reading of Duverger's *Political Parties* and MacRae's article on the differential behavior of representatives elected in "close" and "safe" elections.[17] The general principle could be crudely stated as follows:

It is always preferable to be elected without coalitions (subsidiary goal), but when being elected (primary goal) is endangered, then it is advisable to enter an alliance with another party for this will increase the likelihood of being elected.

Thus a few verifiable hypotheses could be derived:

(1) Smaller parties should elect relatively more representatives via alliances and coalitions.
(2) In majority elections (where, other things being equal, the probability of being elected is smaller than in proportional elections) there should be a higher percentage elected by alliances and coalitions than in proportional ones.
(3) In Federal elections there should be a higher percentage elected by alliances and coalitions as compared with State elections, for there are almost three times more seats in any State legislature than there are representatives of that State in Congress.

The data strongly suggested the soundness of these hypotheses. There is a second, more relevant theory. It was first elaborated as a result of integrating materials dealing with the uncompromising attitudes of both political and religious radicals,[18] combined with the observation of homogeneous bloc voting of radical parties in roll-call votes and the simple observation of the uncompromising attitude of persons committed to an ideology. Ideology is con-

[17] See M. Duverger, *Los Partidos Políticos* (Mexico: FCE, 1957), and D. MacRae, "The Relation Between Roll Call Votes and Constituencies," in Eulau *et al.*, *Legislative Behavior* (Glencoe: The Free Press, 1959).

[18] Cf. Adorno *et al.*, *The Authoritarian Personality* (New York: Harper & Bros., 1950); H. J. Eysenck, *The Psychology of Politics* (London: Routledge & Kegan Paul, 1954); M. Rokeach, *The Open and Closed Mind* (New York: Basic Books, 1960); S. Rydenfelt, *Kommunismen i Sverige* (Lund: Universitetsbokhandeln, 1954).

ceived here as a belief *system*, with two components—one an explanatory view of reality and the other an evaluation of reality and, sometimes, of an ideal state of affairs. An ideology is a cohesive and internally logical set of beliefs explaining reality and guiding action. These persons were mainly orthodox Marxists, orthodox Freudians, and extremely rigorous Catholics. This led to thinking of an ideological, uncompromising orientation toward life, as different from the non-ideological, open, *lack* of unitary orientation which is characterized by a less integrated belief system, or by a set of parallel, loosely related belief *systems*. The last case hypothesizes the existence of a person with various belief systems that are *not* dependent upon some central authority.

Impressionistic descriptions of rural-traditional politics pictured the prevailing ideology, a religious one, as pervading *all* classes and not characterized by ties with any specific political parties. Actually, party ties would be unnecessary, for Catholic ideology has the strong support of the ruling elite, which in turn dominates *all* parties, with the exception of the Communist Party. For various reasons, the more "political" ideologies did not pervade politics in these areas, having been prevented from reaching them. No class-based ideology developed in these areas, and political parties were ideologically empty, sheer *instruments* in the hands of the elites. Therefore, a nominal political party affiliation did not indicate a strong identification or ideological commitment, being indicative only of an accepted institutional coverage for electoral purposes. Thus, uncompromising attitudes raised by class-based political ideologies could not grow in these areas.

If these assumptions are correct, then the politics of traditional areas should be more likely to accept electoral alliances than the politics of developing areas. Alliances and coalitions *are* compromises with one's own ideological orientations and, other things being equal, the stronger one's commitment to a given ideology, the stronger the resistance to this kind of electoral and ideological "cooptation," to use Selznick's term.[19] Table 7 shows the striking differences between the two regions with regard to the proportion of Congressmen elected by party alliances and coalitions in the 1954 elections. In the Northeast no less than 61.9% of all Northeastern Congressmen were elected by party alliances and coali-

[19] Cf. Philip Selznick, *TVA and the Grass Roots* (Berkeley: The University of California Press, 1949).

TABLE 7. REGIONAL DIFFERENCES IN PARTY ALLIANCES AND COALITIONS,
FEDERAL CONGRESS, 1954, AND STATE LEGISLATURES, 1958

	CONGRESS			STATE LEGISLATURES		
	Seats	Alliances*		Seats	Alliances	
Northeast	118	73	61.9%	392	67	17.1%
Southeast	126	11	8.7%	336	8	2.4%

* Alliances in this table also include coalitions.
Sources: same as above and Vol. IV, p. 57.

tions; only 8.7% of the Southeastern Congressmen were so elected. The data refer to *elected* candidates, not to *all* candidates, but this is relatively unimportant in a proportional system. Table 7 shows that the same pattern existed in the 1958 elections for the State legislatures: 17.1% of those elected for State legislatures in the Northeast did so via inter-party alliances, whereas in the Southeast only 2.4% did so. In the Northeast and in the Southeast the proportion of men elected via alliances was smaller on the State level and higher on the Federal level. Due to lack of education and severe punitive upbringing, on the average, the Northeastern population is far more authoritarian than the Southeastern one. This does not affect politics and in particular party alliances and coalitions. It is possible that they have satisfied their need for "authority and structure" and a dogmatic belief system by means of intense religious activity. The vast majority of the population—the uneducated majority—does not participate in politics anyway. When it does, it does so submissively. It does not influence decision-making. In brief, Northeastern politics are entirely dominated by the ruling elites, and when the large rural population participates in politics, it does so under the guidance of the rulers. Parties have no meaning for the rulers, except as family property and electoral instruments providing institutional coverage at election time. Outstanding exceptions to this are the PCB and, to a lesser extent, the PTB. Also, it is necessary to emphasize that large cities are an exception to this pattern.

Southeastern politics are more ideological than Northeastern politics, and as such they display two factors operative against compromise in general and political compromise in particular:

(1) they are class-based and it is often hard to compromise when class interests are at stake, and

(2) they reveal a dogmatic *political* belief structure as a result of strong ideological commitment which is also opposed to compromise.

No direct evidence can be presented to demonstrate that these are the reasons why Southeastern political life is less characterized by coalitions and alliances.

Current theories hold that the Southeast has a more complex occupational structure and that this would, in accordance with interest-group theory in a proportional system,[20] lead toward a certain amount of electoral dispersion. Electoral dispersion is to be understood in terms of its two components: the number of parties competing and/or electing candidates, and the evenness of the vote distribution among the various competing parties. A study using a precise measure of this concept has shown that urbanization is related to electoral dispersion.[21]

New interests require political representation. Often this means a new party. Given the increased role of ideology, small ideological parties representing dissenting minorities should appear more consistently in "ideological" areas than in "non-ideological" ones. Current theories state that these small ideological parties are seldom backed by the less educated, for they represent only a long-term investment, without any possibility of immediate rewards through gaining power. Although in a proportional system this is less marked—it is easier for smaller parties to be represented —the fundamental fact that voting for small parties is a futile act persists. Therefore these parties depend upon a small, ideologically sophisticated minority. These minorities are likely to be found in the educated middle classes, which are much larger in the Southeast, as compared with the Northeast. If the above assumptions are correct, other things being constant, small parties are more likely to be supported in the Southeast. One way to check is to investigate how many parties elected at least one representative. Data suggests that in the Northeast there is a smaller number of States where five or six parties elected at least one candidate for both Congress and the State legislature. In both 1954 and 1958 five

[20] For a comprehensive exposition of interest-group theory, *see* David Truman, *The Governmental Process* (New York: Alfred A. Knopf, 1951).

[21] Cf. Soares and A. M. Noronha, "Urbanização e Dispersão Eleitoral," in *Revista de Direito Público e Ciência Política* (July-December 1960), pp. 258-70.

out of the nine Northeastern States had less than five parties represented in Congress, whereas only two out of six Southeastern States did so. In 1954 five of the nine Northeastern States had less than six parties represented in the State legislature, whereas all Southeastern States had at least six parties represented.

More parties elected at least one representative in Southeastern elections as compared with Northeastern ones. Another way of assessing dispersion is simply to measure the proportion of the total vote obtained by the two major parties. Looking at Table 8, it is seen that the two largest parties (which could be entirely different in any given State) consistently had a larger percentage of the total number of seats in the Northeast. Therefore, however inconclusive the data may be as an indicator of dispersion, it seems

TABLE 8. REGIONAL DIFFERENCES IN ELECTORAL DISPERSION,
STATE LEGISLATURES, 1950, FEDERAL CONGRESS, 1954 AND 1958
(% of the total number of seats obtained by the two largest parties
in each State)

	CONGRESS, 1954	CONGRESS, 1958	STATE LEGISLATURE, 1950
Northeast	67.8% (118)*	70.3% (118)	72.6% (379)
Southeast	62.7% (126)	58.7% (126)	58.5% (318)

* Total from which percentages were extracted.
Sources: same as above.

that the available indications are in the predicted direction. More important here is the problem of participation.

It is believed that widespread illiteracy affects participation not only electorally—recall that illiterates cannot vote in Brazil—but in other spheres. Available data refer mainly to electoral participation and reveal that not only does a higher proportion of the total population vote in the Southeast, but also that the relative difference is widening.

TABLE 9. REGIONAL DIFFERENCES IN ELECTORAL PARTICIPATION
1950, 1954, AND 1958
(per 1,000 persons)

	1950 †			1954 ††			1958 ††		
	a	b	b/a	a	b	b/a	a	b	b/a
Northeast	17,973	2,458	13.7%	19,655	2,774	14.1%	21,498	3,096	14.4%
Southeast	21,671	3,834	17.7%	24,248	4,773	19.7%	27,171	6,694	24.6%

† 1950 Census data   ††Population estimates
a: Total population; *b:* voters
Sources: same as above.

Voters in the Northeast amounted to 13.7% of the total population in 1954, and 14.4% in 1958—a very slow increase as compared with the Southeast, where the corresponding percentages are 17.7%, 19.7%, and 24.6%. One should consider that the Southeastern *population* is growing faster than the Northeastern one, due to both internal migration and much lower mortality rates—even though fertility rates are higher in the Northeast. Therefore, increasing percentage differences gain significance: in 1950 the ratio of Southeastern/Northeastern voters was 156; in 1954 it increased to 172, and in 1958 it reached 216. These drastic changes occurred in an eight-year period.

In all aspects the Southeast seems a more activated society, with a higher degree of participation. It is possible to construct two ideal models, one of an apathetic, non-participant society, where basic needs are continuously at stake and little or no time is left for *dilettanti* activities such as politics. This is linked with illiteracy and extreme poverty, which are in turn dependent in part on inequality, expressed in terms of land distribution. The Northeast approaches this model.[22] Nevertheless, the Southeast is far from approaching the "positive pole" model. It has appeared as an active, participant society only *by contrast* with the Northeast, and it would be naïve to believe that it appears as such when compared with other societies.

It may be the case that political participation on the one hand, and social mobilization and economic development on the other, are *not* linearly related. The existing body of evidence does relate economic development with social mobilization in a seemingly linear way. But it may also be suggested that *extreme political* participation is symptomatic of class conflict and political restlessness, which are likely to occur in rapidly *industrializing* societies and not in stable, industrialized ones.[23] In this sense, the Brazilian Southeast should present higher rates of electoral participation

[22] For a development of the social mobilization concept, *see* K. Deutsch, "Social Mobilization and Political Development," in *American Political Science Review*, LV (September 1961), pp. 493-514.

[23] This point has been made before by Lipset, *op. cit.;* H. Tingsten, *Political Behavior: Studies in Election Statistics* (London: P. S. King and Sons, 1937); W. H. M. Jones, "In Defense of Political Apathy," in *Political Studies* (February 1954), pp. 25-37; and Soares, "Participação Eleitoral e Separação de Poderes," in *Revista de Direito Público e Ciência Política* (January 1960), pp. 36-66.

than it actually does. First, Brazil has a high rate of population growth and that means a high proportion of the population is under voting age. These have not been considered in the above table, in the sense that they were not subtracted from the total. Second is the incongruent position of illiteracy with respect to other socio-economic indicators. Judging by the latter, Brazil should have much lower rates of illiteracy, and this applies to the Northeast and to the Southeast. In a recent study by the United Nations, Brazil is consistently placed fifth in a six-point scale in all but one indicator of socio-economic development—education —where Brazil is classified in the lowest category.[24] The same would apply to the Southeast, for its literacy rate is below what would normally be expected, judging by other socio-economic indicators. Added to the age composition of the population, that explains why electoral participation rates seem so low.

The traditionalism of the underdeveloped areas is here conceptualized as a broad value orientation, with heavy emphasis on its particularistic,[25] ascribed,[26] and sacred[27] dimensions, as opposed to universalistic, achieved, and secular. This value orientation is protected by the prevailing socio-economic conditions and in turn helps to maintain them. As such, they fit a specific pattern of social organization. For centuries this pattern remained the same in Brazilian rural areas: almost absolute illiteracy, lack of social and political participation, and almost complete submission on the part of the slaves and peripheral peasants, with a small sophisticated ruling aristocracy. Political power came from status and land ownership. It was, and to an extent still is, regarded as a natural inherited role of the ruling family members. Since the landowners never regarded the slaves as a political force, and

[24] Cf. Naciones Unidas, *Informe Sobre la Situación Social en el Mundo* (1960), pp. 52-53.

[25] The definition of particularism adopted here was given by Parsons: "The standards and criteria which are independent of the particular social relationship to a particular person may be called universalistic, those which apply by virtue of such a relationship on the other hand are particularistic," in "The Professions and Social Structure," in *Essays in Sociological Theory* (Glencoe: The Free Press, 1954; revised ed.), pp. 41-42.

[26] The adopted definition of ascription is also Parsonian: "the valued result(s) of the actions of individuals," in "An Analytic Approach to the Theory of Social Stratification," *loc. cit.*, p. 75.

[27] For a conceptual development of this idea, *see* H. Becker, "Sacred and Secular Societies Considered with Reference to Folk-State and Similar Classifications," in *Social Forces*, XXVIII (May 1950), pp. 361-76.

oftentimes don't regard the peasants as such, local politics is essentially a family business. The *município* more often than not includes more than one leading family, and when it doesn't, it frequently exhibits internal dissension within the leading family, with a common, two-wing split. Oftentimes one of these families affiliates with the UDN and the other with the PSD, but they sometimes are distressed with the party's State or national decisions and, consequently, simply choose from among the other parties a convenient label for continuing traditional family politics.

The political orientation is particularistic. It is deeply influenced by interpersonal relations as opposed to universalistic, *ideological* orientations. The peasant votes for the landowner's candidate (when the candidate is not the landowner himself or a close member of the family). The ruling elite takes political leadership for granted. It is a role attached to the well-bred male, not something to be achieved. This is also accepted by the peasants. This conception, coupled with a particularistic value orientation, helps to explain the non-ideological, *instrumental* use of political parties and public property.

Weber has defined traditional authority as follows:

Traditional authority rests on the belief in the sacredness of the social order and its prerogatives as existing of yore. Patriarchal authority represents its pure type. The body politic is based on communal relationships, the man in command is the "lord" ruling over the "subjects." People obey the lord personally since his dignity is hallowed by tradition; obedience rests on piety. Commands are substantively bound by tradition.[28]

The politics of backwardness resembles this ideal type. *Both* the social order and the undisputed landlords' right to authority and power testify to this. The Church does not endorse the existing order *per se*, but it contributes to its maintenance by strongly opposing those ideologies that might bring about revolutionary changes or any kind of radical change. It *implicitly* contributes to preserving the existing order. The landlord often has paternalistic functions. He baptizes the peasant's sons. He gives the peasant "extra" rewards. The peasant has such a low level of aspiration

[28] Max Weber, "The Three Types of Legitimate Rule" (trans. by Hans Gerth) in Amitai Etzioni (ed.), *Complex Organizations* (New York: Holt, Rinehart and Winston, 1961), p. 7.

that he is deeply gratified and feels indebted when the gift of a
doll is made to his daughter. He takes poverty for granted and has
no long-term aims. F.P.R., a peasant working on a farm in Minas
Gerais (a State not included in any of the two groups), said:
"Well, us has to work, because us will never be rich. All that is
left for us is to get old, if God helps. Don't you think so? Sometimes some folks make it in the lottery and then lose everything
again." [29] Referring to the possibility of fooling the boss, when
asked about his conception of a good worker, he stated: "To fool
the boss is to fool God. I live here fourteen years and I never pull
a trick on nobody. The poor has to help the boss, because he is the
one who is going to lose if he doesn't. My job is to grow the crop
and I know when one should do certain things using the time that
God give."

The Weberian definition of traditional authority is here applicable to a large extent. Hard life is taken for granted and inequality is uncontested. A note of fatalism is deductable.[30] Change and
continuation are explicitly attributed to God's will; by implication, so is the present state of affairs.

In such a stagnant system, change has to come from the outside.[31] This represents a long-term investment for a political party
and only recently did the first returns register. In most of these
instances, parallel changes in the municipal socio-economic structure facilitated the political returns. One study clearly exposed
the stagnant situation of a *município*, Barroso, Minas Gerais, where
for almost 250 years local politics were dominated by two opposed
leading families, who joined forces for the first time two years

[29] These interviews were collected in relatively developed rural areas, by
comparison with the Northeastern ones. The author is indebted to Professor
Joseph Kahl for the use of this and subsequent quotations.

[30] Joseph Kahl, in "Urbanização e Mudancas Ocupacionis no Brasil," study
published in *America Latina* (1963), came out with a traditional syndrome
of which fatalism is the dominant trait. Rural villagers usually had a much
higher score in the various component scales than urban ones of similar education. *Both* status and place of residence were good predictors. And, again,
Kahl's study was in a relatively well-developed rural area.

[31] *See*, for instance, O. Carvalho, *Ensaios de Sociologia Eleitoral* (Belo
Horizonte: Estudos Sociais e Políticos, 1958); Carvalho, "Os Partidos Polí-
ticos de Minas Gerais e as Eleições de 1958," N. S. Sampaio, "Eleições
Bahianas," and F. F. Castro "A Campanha Eleitoral de 1958 no Piaui," all
three published in *Revista Brasileira de Estudos Políticos*, VIII (April 1960).
Cf. also Sampaio, *O Diálogo Democrático na Bahia* (Belo Horizonte: Estudos
Sociais e Políticos, 1960).

after a factory had been installed in the *município*, and were defeated for the first time four years later.[32] The parties' history in this *município* is linked with the political wanderings of the families' leaders, and all seven parties functioning in 1958 had been created by members of one of the two families.[33] The instrumental use of political parties by these leading families is evident. Parties are created to mobilize support for a family member, being sheer instruments devoid of ideological content. Many exist during a campaign only. There is constant inter-party mobility and persons are often candidates for one party in one election, shift to another party in the following election, to a third party in the election after that, sometimes winding up with the original party.[34]

Some indication of change can be observed. In Barroso, even though other labor parties were used as electoral instruments by Geraldo Napoleao, one of the local family leaders, and the PTB came very close to this, the PTB is now a working-class party. It is class-based, has a selective recruitment and an ideology. Phenomena like the ones observed in Barroso are not exceptions. They occur in hundreds of Brazilian *municípios*. In the more deprived Northeastern areas, the peasants have been organized from the outside in radically oriented *Ligas Camponesas*. Traditionalism is still the main deterrent of this ideological rebellion. And yet, unless socio-economic conditions change drastically, this rebellion seems to be merely a matter of time. Barroso is a mild example. Perhaps a better one would be that poor peasant's daughter who, when referring to the landlord (the same one that her father respected as a god), stated: "I want to leave the country because in the country the farm worker and his family are slaves of the landowner; the time for slavery has already gone, but he who stays here stays as a slave."

If tradition characterizes the politics of backwardness, the politics of development are characterized by the increased role played by class and ideology. If socio-economic status and other class-associated variables are poor predictors of political behavior in rural backward areas, the opposite is true for developing areas.

[32] Cf. L. Silva, "Implicações Políticas do Desenvolvimento Industrial em Barroso-M.G.," in *Revista Brasileira de Estudos Políticos*, IX (July 1960).

[33] *Ibid.*, pp. 244-45.

[34] For an interesting description of Brazilian municipal politics, cf. V. N. Leal, *Coronelismo, Enxada e Voto, o Município e o Regime Representativo no Brasil* (Rio de Janeiro, 1948).

Both socio-economic status and social class identification, herein interpreted as a broad ideological orientation toward society, are useful predictors of party affiliations and other types of political behavior.

Studies have shown that status is associated with party preferences in several countries.[35] In a previous paper,[36] I have shown that socio-economic status, measured by education and occupation, was strongly correlated with preference for the presidential candidate in the 1960 elections. The present data pertain to the same survey, and Table 10 shows that the previous results are confirmed at the party level:

TABLE 10. SOCIO-ECONOMIC STRATA AND PARTY PREFERENCES

Party Preference	I	II	III	IV	V	VI	VII
UDN (conservative)	56.3%	54.5%	51.2%	38.2%	32.5%	20.2%	18.4%
PTB (labor)	11.1	10.9	17.2	28.8	28.5	39.9	42.3
Other Parties	9.6	13.9	13.5	11.8	17.1	14.2	14.8
None	9.6	8.9	9.0	10.6	13.8	12.0	12.2
DK's, no answer	13.4	11.8	9.1	10.6	8.1	13.7	12.3
Total	100.0%	100.0%	100.0%	100.0%	100.0%	100.0%	100.0%
Number	(135)	(101)	(244)	(510)	(123)	(401)	(196)

I, Professionals and High Administrative (10 or more persons under supervision); II, Middle Administrative (between 5 and 10 persons); III, Lower Administrative and Supervisory (less than 5 persons); IV, Routine Nonmanual; V, Manual Supervisory; VI, Skilled Manual, VII, Unskilled Manual.

Table 10 clearly shows an unbroken increase in the percentage of the total vote given to the conservative UDN as socio-economic status increases. Two breaks may be observed: one between categories III and IV and the other between categories V and VI. This can be interpreted as an indicator of a relatively small internal differentiation in the top three categories, relative proximity of white-collar workers and foremen, and a relatively small differentiation of workers' political attitudes following skill lines.

Contrary to the UDN, the PTB decreases with increasing status, but strata I and II and strata IV and V show no differences. Again the two breaks can be perceived: the percentage given to the PTB

---

[35] Lipset, in *Political Man*, analyzes in detail most of these studies.
[36] Cf. Soares, "Classes Sociais, etc.," *loc. cit.*

jumps eleven points from categories III to IV and from V to VI.

Both preferences given to other parties and lack of party preference show no definite pattern, but a manual/non-manual comparison shows that manual workers tend more toward other parties and also tend to have no party preference.

Class identification [37] shows a similar pattern. Qualitative interviews suggested that the categories used by the population at large to describe one's own class varied. The main alternatives were used to build a precoded question which included six classes: high or wealthy, upper-middle, lower-middle, working, poor, and operative. Whereas identification with the poor seems to be bereft of ideological connotations, identification with the working class and the industrial working class is symptomatic of ideological *cadres*. The PTB usually campaigns in terms of *both*, but communist propaganda is directed mainly toward *operários*, which means industrial workers. For now, these classes will be lumped together and called "working," as opposed to the merging of the upper or wealthy (which had only a few cases) and the two middle classes (upper and lower), which will be called "middle." At each occupational level, class identification helps to predict party preferences (*see* Table 11).

Table 11 indicated that for all six occupational strata, those identifying with the middle class give higher percentages of total preferences to the UDN, and lower to the PTB, than those identifying with the working class. Within each class, occupational status is still related to party preferences, although not in a strict linear way. Lack of party preference seems to be positively associated with working-class identification, but no clear relationship with socio-economic status can be observed.

Table 11 uses crude class-identification categories. The more refined categories would make a difference among skilled workers. For instance, the PTB receives 24.4% in the upper middle class (including a few cases of upper-class identification), 33% in both the lower middle class and the working class, 38% in the poor class, and 56% in the operative class. Thus, class identification with

[37] For an early work which developed the idea of class identification, cf. Richard Centers, *The Psychology of Social Classes* (Princeton: Princeton University Press, 1949).

TABLE 11. SOCIO-ECONOMIC STATUS AND CLASS IDENTIFICATION INFLUENCE PARTY PREFERENCES CUMULATIVELY

Socio-economic Strata

CLASS	I-II		III		IV		V		VI		VII	
	M	W	M	W	M	W	M	W	M	W	M	W
UDN	58.4%	47.8%	54.3%	28.6%	46.1%	28.2%	37.9%	24.5%	26.1%	18.3%	31.1%	14.0%
PTB	10.4	17.4	14.4	31.4	24.7	34.2	18.2	39.6	29.3	42.9	26.7	45.3
Other	11.9	4.4	11.5	25.7	10.5	12.9	21.2	13.2	17.4	16.3	24.4	12.0
None	7.9	17.4	9.6	5.7	9.5	13.4	9.1	15.1	9.8	12.6	6.6	16.0
DK's	11.4	13.0	10.1	8.6	9.2	11.4	13.6	7.5	17.4	10.0	11.1	12.7
Total	100.0%	100.0%	99.9%	100.0%	100.0%	100.0%	100.0%	99.9%	100.0%	100.0%	99.9%	100.0%
Number	(202)	(23)	(208)	(35)	(295)	(202)	(66)	(53)	(92)	(301)	(45)	(150)

M: Middle, W: Working

its more refined categories is a powerful instrument in the prediction of political behavior and attiitudes.[38]

This instrument can be used to understand the process of ideological conditioning of the rural population migrating to cities. Previous studies suggested that the rural migrant in Brazil changes some of his political views after urbanization.[39] Simão suggests that first he turns PTB and then communist.[40] The present study does not have data bearing directly upon this. By the time the survey was carried out, the Communist Party had been outlawed for thirteen years. But applying reference group theory [41] at the class level,[42] it is possible to say that due to the tremendous urban-rural inequality in wealth and general progress, the rural migrant thinks of himself as upwardly mobile. Comparison of his present economic status with that of his past gives him a feeling of relative reward. This may happen even though he is at the bottom of the urban stratification ladder.[43]

The urban middle and upper strata offer a different frame for comparison. Soon enough the migrant perceives that he is under-privileged, but he still retains some satisfaction derived from comparison with his past life. The realization that he is underprivileged and contact with the surrounding atmosphere lead many migrants to lean toward the PTB. The higher standards of living which they can observe probably tend to heighten the level of aspirations of many. To the extent that these aspirations are frustrated, they are open to extreme leftist indoctrination. Many never undergo such a process due to other variables, such as strong religious

[38] Data from the same survey have been utilized by the present author to show that social class identification influences party preferences even when *both* respondent's and father's occupation are held constant. Cf. Soares, "Mobilidade Ocupacional e Comportamento Político" (mimeographed).

[39] Cf. A. Simão, O Voto Operário em São Paulo," in *Revista Brasileira de Estudos Políticos*, I (1956), pp. 130-41.

[40] Ibid.

[41] For a theoretical development of this theory, cf. R. Merton and A. Kitt, "Contributions to the Theory of Reference Group Behavior," in R. K. Merton, *Social Theory and Social Structure* (Glencoe: The Free Press, 1957; rev. ed.).

[42] For an application of reference group theory at the class level, cf. E. Bott, "The Concept of Class as a Reference Group," in *Human Relations*, VII (1954), pp. 259-86.

[43] Rural migrants seem to be at a disadvantage in the urban stratification pyramid. Cf. Lipset and R. Bendix, *Social Mobility in Industrial Society* (Berkeley: University of California Press, 1959), and Soares, *Desenvolvimento*, pp. 128-32.

feeling. But others do, and these probably would vote, and express preference for the Communist Party, if the party were legal. The present data would possibly express this tendency along with an increase in PTB preferences as the period of urbanization lengthens among unskilled workers, but not necessarily among skilled ones, for the probability that their aspirations will be fulfilled is higher. An increase in industrial working-class identification, stronger among unskilled than among skilled workers, should be noted. Table 12 presents the data bearing upon these hypotheses.

TABLE 12. THE EFFECT OF URBANIZATION UPON CLASS IDENTIFICATION
AND PARTY PREFERENCES

	UNSKILLED		SKILLED	
Lived in Rio	Less than 20 years	20 years or more	Less than 20 years	20 years or more
IDENTIFICATION				
Operative Class	21%	31%	21%	27%
Poor Class	21%	10%	23%	17%
Working Class	37%	40%	29%	31%
% PTB	32%	50%	38%	37%
Number	(62)*	(42)	(92)	(72)

* Totals from which the percentages were extracted.
This table includes persons born outside of Rio only.

Identification with the operative (industrial working) class goes up in both cases, but more so among unskilled workers, even though the differential increase is statistically not significant. Identification with the poor goes down and identification with the working class rises in both cases. The percentage preferring the PTB goes up significantly with length of urban living among unskilled workers, but not among skilled workers.

Feelings of relative reward are replaced by feelings of relative deprivation as urban living makes socio-economic inequality more visible. The rewarding comparison with a rural life fades into the past, and gives way to a damaging comparison with higher standards of living. The level of aspirations is reactivated by those comparisons and is heightened. Upward mobility does not occur; there is an imbalance in favor of negative, deprivation feelings.

The urban workers, however involuntarily, engage in strike practices and collective bargaining.[44] Many of them follow na-

[44] Cf. J. R. B. Lopes, "O Ajustamento do Trabalhador à Indústria: Mobilidade Social e Motivação," in Hutchinson, *op. cit.*

tional news and some international news. The ideological jargon is everpresent in daily talk. This is entirely absent from the peasants' lives. The urban middle class is a regular consumer of political news, national or otherwise. Education and urban living bring heavy emphasis on universalistic and achievement values. Patronage is strongly fought. The national alliance between the PTB and the PSD has won several elections and these governments have been criticized by the middle class especially on grounds of corruption and patronage. *Moralismo* is the urban middle-class ideological issue and the *urban* UDN made it its banner. Economic liberalism and anti-communism are other ideological orientations of the urban middle class in Brazil.

The politics of development therefore is ideological politics. One party cannot enter into compromises in order to gain the support of a given class without losing part of its original following. Class polarization in cities like Rio de Janeiro and Recife is apparent. Political parties attract classes via their ideological program and then they are bound to their interests. As other parties compete for this support, the parties try to strengthen even further the existing links.

The politics of developing areas are not identical to the politics of developed areas. In the latter, interest politics prevail, with groups and classes competing for and aiming at larger portions of the national wealth. In the politics of development, present interests are oftentimes sacrificed in favor of ideological objectives. These ideologies have a strong differential class appeal. The politics of development are the politics of class and ideology.

In any country huge internal unevenness in economic development may be sufficient to provoke political differences to a similar extent. Furthermore, it has been suggested that these *quantitative* economic differences lead to *qualitative* political differences, in the sense that they lay the grounds for two entirely different political cultures.[45]

Rural economy is an agrarian economy and the class structure of rural areas is based on land ownership, tending toward a two-class system. The tremendous inequality which characterizes these areas provides for a close similarity to the Marxian model. Very

[45] An approach similar to the present one, where the author tries to explain a wide variety of dependent behavior, was undertaken by L. Lambert, *Os Dois Brasis* (Rio de Janeiro: CBPE, 1959).

low educational level and punitive upbringing probably contribute to create a peasant personality which is authoritarian and dogmatic. Why, then, are these areas politically conservative? A few suggestions that are not mutually exclusive can be made:

(a) High traditionalism inhibits ideological rebellion against the *status quo* by
   (1) preventing a perception of the class interests as different, to say nothing of preventing opposition;
   (2) providing strong legitimacy for both the class structure and elite politics; [46]
   (3) discouraging the organization of radical leftist parties, which receive faster and higher returns for the same investment by concentrating in the urban areas; [47]
   (4) preventing widespread political participation and creating an over-all atmosphere of complete apathy.
(b) Intense religious activity inhibits ideological rebellion against the *status quo* by
   (1) providing a dogmatic global ideology, which satisfies the hypothesized "need for dogma, authority and structure";
   (2) building a negative predisposition against radical leftist ideologies.

The politics of inequality and backwardness may be viewed as a highly explosive situation where revolutionary outbursts are inhibited by the above-mentioned factors. If these break down before the prevailing situation changes, the explosion is likely to occur.

In urban areas another race seems to take place. As aspirations are much higher, and traditionalism much lower than in rural areas, the race is between the growing aspirations of the working class and their satisfaction. Radicalization seems inevitable. Class organization is not inhibited and mass communications are available for the transmission of new ideologies. After the process of industrialization has been going on for a while, an existing working class transmits these values to incoming migrants. The latter

---

[46] For a development of the concept of political legitimacy, cf. Lipset, "Some Social Requisites of Democracy, Economic Development and Political Legitimacy," in *American Political Science Review* (1959), pp. 69-105.

[47] The Communist Party never developed a strong organizational network in the rural areas. During the past five years, however, intense activity aiming at the political mobilization and radicalization of the peasant has been developed, culminating with Julião's famous *Ligas Camponesas*.

bring built-in values which sometimes inhibit *extreme* radicalization and the acquisition of an ideological, class-conflict perspective. Probably the fact that the Church does not oppose the PTB but does oppose communism and socialism explains why most newcomers are readily indoctrinated by the labor parties, whereas those who go communist or socialist take much longer to do so.[48]

Labor parties may not provide a sufficient outlet for aggression when there are intense frustrations such as those provoked by the gap between high aspirations and lack of advancement or unemployment. The process of radicalization seems to be dependent upon the race between urbanization, which heightens the level of aspirations for increasing numbers of people, and industrialization, which satisfies them. In Brazil there are extreme cases where urbanization proceeds at a faster rate than industrialization. Recife and Rio de Janeiro (presently capitals of the States of Pernambuco and Guanabara) provide the illustration: in 1945 and 1947 the Communist Party had its greatest successes in these two cities.

The outlined regional differences may help to explain certain contradictions of Brazilian (and perhaps Latin American) politics where intellectuals, students, and the urban lower classes promote political agitation, whereas the most deprived areas remain strongly conservative. Parties are cut across by these regional differences, assuming completely different roles in different areas. The explanation lies in the fact that the country's politics cannot be analyzed in terms of one homogeneous unit. Socio-economic differentiation has engendered two distinctive political *cultures:* the politics of backwardness and the politics of development. When these are taken separately, their comparative analysis may contribute toward making the politics of uneven development more comprehensible.

[48] This process is probably faster when there is a large, institutionalized radical leftist party. Small leftist parties are uncertain, long-term investments for the voter, a condition which only the intellectual's ideological commitment is able to accept.

VII
FACT AND FOLKLORE IN ECONOMIC UNDERDEVELOPMENT

... in which the paradox of inflation and rapid growth is studied in terms of the clashing masters of nationalism and imperialism; the Brazilian class structure and the "pot of gold" investment philosophy; the rise and fall of the single-crop economy; Brazilian "prosperity" and two world wars; Brazilian "poverty" and the peacetime interludes; new trends and new friends, a diagnosis of the illness; from economic classes to social masses.

REASONS FOR Brazilian underdevelopment are sought in everything from climate to class structures. But these obstacles to Brazilian development are often rationalizations. They either forget or ignore that economic growth and consciousness of a world divided by affluence on one side and poverty on the other feed each other, stimulate the search for new and rapid solutions. At this level, the Brazilian problem is a common problem. C. P. Snow in *The Two Cultures and the Scientific Revolution* has put his finger squarely on both what ails and what irks the new Brazilian.

The main issue is that the people of the industrialized countries are getting richer, and those in the non-industrialized countries are, at best, standing still, so that the gap between the industrialized countries and the rest is widening every day. On the world wide scale this is the gap between the rich and the poor. In the rich countries people are living longer, eating better, working less. But in the poor countries people are not eating better than on the subsistence level. And they are working as people have always had to work, from Neolithic times until our own. Life for the overwhelming majority of mankind has always been nasty, brutish and short. It is so in the poor countries still. This disparity between the rich and poor has been noticed, most acutely and not unnaturally, by the poor. Just because they have noticed it, it won't last for long. Whatever else in the world we know survives to the year 2,000, that won't. Once the trick of getting rich is known, as it now is, the world can't survive half rich and half poor. It's just not on.

Revolutions can and obviously do take many forms. This is true within a nation as it is in a comparison between nations. A revolution proceeds at many levels and involves different human modalities. There is the organization and confiscation of land in Pernambuco. There is the expropriation of foreign-owned utilities in Rio Grande do Sul. There is the assumption to political leadership of left-wing forces in Brasília. There is the industrialization of São Paulo. And most subtle and perhaps most potent of all, there is the reformation and reformulation of economic policy in Rio de Janeiro. In short, the traditional equation of revolution with armed violence is hardly a necessary and sufficient description of the revolutionary process. The Brazilian revolution has for the most part been a "silent" revolution. Whether armed insurrection will be required depends on the outcome of the economic and sociological developments now under way. Here we shall restrict ourselves to the economic conditions of Brazil that demand immediate attention and solution.

On December 17, 1962, United States Attorney General Robert F. Kennedy went to Brazil to undertake a role long performed by Adolph A. Berle—that of "troubleshooter." The "Kennedy magic" was supposed to supply a genteel warning to Brazilian President João Goulart that the United States is serious when it says that Brazil must put its economic house in order, and restrain confiscation of American enterprises, before getting further financial aid. The problem as seen by the American government has two aspects: the first is a galloping inflation of 50% annually for the past five years, and the reluctance on the part of Brazilian leadership to adopt measures which would curb the inflationary spiral. The second is a supposed political drift toward communism. Press reports indicate that Robert F. Kennedy told President Goulart that the American taxpayers cannot be expected to approve heavy financial aid to Brazil, given its reluctance to take steps necessary to solve its chronic economic problems. The likelihood is that the Attorney General simply underlined the comments made by President Kennedy at a news conference earlier in December 1962. The late President stated at that time:

. . . there is nothing really, that the United States can do that can possibly benefit the people of Brazil if you have a situation which is so unstable as the financial and monetary situation within Brazil. . . . I think that the Brazilian government is aware of the strong concern that we have for this inflation which eats up our aid and which, of course, contributes to a flight of capital.

It is no secret that President Goulart was somewhat disturbed, and possibly angry, over the United States' position. And Goulart's perfunctory treatment of the Attorney General reflected a basic policy disagreement on the status of the Brazilian economy. A dramatic answer to the Kennedy visit took shape on December 18, just hours after Robert Kennedy left Brazil. A new committee including key Cabinet officials was formed to coordinate Brazil's expanding trade with the Soviet Union and the communist-bloc nations of Eastern Europe. The new trade committee, called COLESTE, initially operated under the direct supervision of Premier Hermes Lima. The Ministers of Foreign Affairs, Trade, and Commerce will take turns presiding at its meetings. Hermes Lima put the solution to Brazilian inflation in terms of an opening to the East, and not in conventional International Monetary Fund terms of "belt tightening" and "austerity." Lima declared:

The economic development of Brazil urgently requires the expansion of foreign trade, not only in traditional areas but through the opening or extension of new markets. The development of trade with the Socialist area in the past two years justifies the expectation of even greater expansion to come. The specific task of COLESTE in this is the coordination of trade between Brazil and the Socialist countries of Europe.

The critique and the rejoinder could scarcely be clearer. The timing of the two statements simply underscores the fact that Brazil refuses to follow the United States economic policy recommendation of reform through austerity. The policy of austerity has been a dreary failure in Argentina and Chile. The economic burdens on blue-collar, white-collar, and professional workers have only increased, while the political consequences in each case have been an unrest manifested in overt right-wing militaristic take-overs. It is apparent that Goulart and Lima viewed the alarums in the United States as premature and one-sided. For while it is true that the country has entered a period of extremely high inflation, it is no less a fact that Brazil has had a burgeoning economy with a 6%-7% annual growth rate over the past decade. Given Goulart's political base in the urban proletariat, a policy of austerity would be, politically speaking, suicidal. What remains is to increase the growth rate still further, institute a viable progressive tax structure, improve food supplies to the cities, and so reduce inflationary spirals through the acceleration of the industrial and technological complex.

It is sometimes forgotten that there is a large plus factor to some inflation (perhaps up to 20%) in developing regions. It is a struggle among groups for a redistribution of real income. The "negative interest" factor compels heavy investment, and no less is a factor making for commercial and banking instability. As Celso Furtado has indicated in his brilliant work on *The Economic Growth of Brazil*:

Inflation is a process whereby the economy tries to absorb a surplus of monetary demand. Such absorption takes place through a rise in the price level, and its main consequence is a redistribution in real income. Any study of the inflationary process concentrates on two aspects: the rise in the level of prices, and the redistribution of income. Yet it would be wrong to suppose that these are two separate elements. The very word "inflation" is inducive to such an error, because it stresses the monetary aspect of the process—that is, the expansion of monetary income. This expansion is, however, only the means whereby the system seeks to redistribute real income so as to reach a new position of equilibrium.

This is not to deny that Brazil is in a period of serious and perhaps damaging economic crisis. But just as the problems of Brazilian semi-feudalism are historical, so too must any proposed solutions take into account these historical, long-range features. Even a serious newspaper like *The New York Times* exhibits the kind of editorializing which calls attention only to the "ravages of inflation" and the "fall in the value of the cruzeiro," and pontificates about the United States "performing a bail out." This does a grave injustice to the actual role of monetary instability in Brazil. Let us therefore turn to these long-range features of the

Brazilian economy for a deeper appreciation of the total context of the revolution in Brazil.

A natural resource, red dye-wood, *pau-brasil*, gave Brazil its name. That the country should derive its name from a single economic source of wealth may be considered as an irony of its history, or simply as the shape of an underdeveloped economy under an underdeveloped colonial power. For whether it is red timber in the sixteenth century, sugar in the seventeenth century, tobacco and gold in the eighteenth century, cotton in the early nineteenth century and rubber later in the century, or coffee in the twentieth century, the Brazilian economy has been built upon the "Botosi Principle," the single-crop and get-rich-quick formulas so beloved by the Portuguese and Spanish *conquistadores*, which are not exactly frowned upon by latter-day enlightened colonialists either. From the point of view of Brazilian traders and exporters, the best economic approach is to focus energies on a single crop needed by the advanced buying nations of the world, and minimize the risks of diversification and competition, so that the inevitable quick profits for the few will automatically follow. The bankruptcy of this policy, fostered by latifundists and later by small-scale bankers and traders, each of whom were concerned with immediate profits which were then invested in foreign industries, deserves at least a brief historical recitation, if only for the light it sheds on present dilemmas in the Brazilian economy.

During the eighteenth century the Western world received its sugar supply largely from crops harvested by African slaves who worked the Brazilian plantations. Early in this century, Brazil's annual sugar exports amounted, in cash terms, to a volume which was greater than England's total exports for the same period. Today, sugar is produced in just enough quantity to satisfy the domestic Brazilian market. The rise of new forms of producing and refining sugar, and especially increased competition from the Dutch and British West Indies, brought an end to the pot-of-gold called sugar. But the demise of sugar production did not alter fundamental social relations; it did not end the master-slave aspect of Brazilian economic history. Cotton came. This proved an easy crop to cultivate. The slaves were ready at hand. And the latifundists saw their way to another fortune by keeping the cotton mills of Manchester and New Orleans busy. But cotton too passed away as a permanent panacea. Overproduction once again set in. The more cotton produced, the lower the prices on the world market. In addition, other fabrics such as wool were found to be superior to cotton for certain purposes; and there were textiles which could be produced even more cheaply by machinery than by slave labor.

But the lessons of the past centuries were not learned. The latifundists had become an enlarged social class with entrenched political interests. Brazilian raw wealth once more intervened to preserve the plantation system. Rural capitalists, land speculators, and latifundists found a gold mine in rubber. Brazil had a virtual monopoly in the Amazon basin region. Rubber came from the sap of the *Hevea brasiliensis*. A new "pot of gold" was located. At the turn of the century, Brazil supplied the world with 30,000 tons of natural rubber, while the rest of the world supplied the industrial nations with less than four tons. By the end of the twenties, Brazilian exports declined to half that amount, to 14,000 tons, while production in Asia had soared to over 800,000 tons. Fate dealt the latifundists' search for Eldorado another cruel hand. The rubber tree had been transplanted to areas of abundant and cheap labor. Once again the Brazilian economy had the choice of either making a decisive break with its past or continuing in search of yet another magic crop.

In the true spirit of economic backwardness and the corruption of the semi-feudal and semi-bourgeois strata, Brazil pursued the traditional search. The latifundists, their slaves "free" now to become serfs, turned to coffee. Here was the bonanza that would make all Brazil rich and famous. The taste for coffee spread in Europe and in North America. The "pot-of-gold" had arrived in the form of a hard bean. And then, the inevitable collapse came. Overproduction and the world economic crisis of the early thirties added to the woes of the coffee plantation owners, as did competition from Central America and Colombia, where more delicate types of coffee were being cultivated. Another crop had failed in its ostensible purpose of making every Brazilian wealthy.

Several aspects of this single-crop, pot-of-gold story deserve additional treatment. *First,* there is the extraordinary wealth in natural resources which Brazil possesses (although these resources are not particularly well located). This natural wealth, exploited in a feudalistic context, enabled the economy to ward off one disaster after another without suffering the disintegration which befell the feudal system in Europe. *Second*, there is the incapacity of the landholding and trading interests to adopt a truly national posture. The incredible greed and selfishness of traditional ruling classes of Brazil contrast markedly with their equally extraordinary nationalistic rhetoric. *Third*, the antagonism between the traditional oligarchy on one side and middle and working classes on the other is at its source a conflict between feudal and industrial social structures. *Fourth*, a distinction must be made between the rhetoric of nationalism and the reason for sincere nationalism. The force of the nationalism exhibited by Brazilian middle and working classes is not simply a reaction to foreign investment and investors (although it is that), but more significantly an irreducible belief that as long as plantation owners continue to maintain even their partial grip on the economic system, political sovereignty will be unattainable. And if the latifundists have now begun to show an interest in farm technology and crop diversification, one can only surmise that even they have come to understand that there are no longer any magic crops to make billions on. The age of miracles has passed. So too has the feudal age which fostered and in turn fed off the nightmarish illusion of single-crop economies.

The structure of the Brazilian land economy was, nonetheless, moulded by the single-crop concept. From the sixteenth century, agriculture was rationalized along strict class lines which reinforced the latifundia, but in plain truth these had nothing to do with authentic economic needs. The *capitanias* created in 1532 gave rise to the first latifundia in the country. These early latifundia were called the *sesmarias*, which were later divided into *fazendas*, within whose limits were set aside the *sítios*, from which in turn were derived the still more limited areas known as the *chácaras*. This system of land subdivision is matched by the various forms which exist among and between landholders and landworkers. Between renting land in its pure and simple form (which is the payment of money for the temporary use of the land) and sharecropping (the *parceria*, in which produce is divided between landowner and the cultivator) are a great variety of forms. It is precisely because of these multiple forms, or more properly speaking, sub-classes, that political unity was almost impossible to achieve. Special sub-class interests and ideologies prevailed over the general interests of the impoverished mass.

These sub-classes often had greater pulling power than general class interests because between serfs and sharecroppers, small land-holders and latifundists, there were and remain sufficient differences in standards of living to make class unity difficult to attain. But these differences have steadily diminished through a long process of obsolescence. The small landholders, comprising about half a million families or one-quarter the total of "landowners," own only .5% of all arable land. Few of them can live off their *miniplots*, especially since they lack the machines or the technical competence that intensive small-acreage farming requires. In addition they get the worst land, and little fertilizer. They are increasingly being compelled to work for hire, often giving up their plots of land altogether and sinking into the mass of impoverished agricultural laborers. Thus the localized differentiation of this sub-class is rapidly drawing to an end. The over-all competition between latifundists and farm laborers is assuming fully developed proportions. And with this development has come a sharpening of economic struggles in Brazil.

There are those who argue that the revolutionaries demanding agrarian reform are in pursuit of a false objective. It is claimed that the break-up of the *economic system of financial extortion*, advocated by SUDENE, does little to alter the feudal agricultural arrangement, comprised of *leguas* (four miles) and *alqueires* (six acres), which are rationalized to suit conventional crop production needs. The argument advanced by the technologists against the revolutionists is that agricultural reform must precede political reform. The difficulty with the technologists' position, aside from its obvious compatibility with the maintenance of power by the ruling elite, is that *a central problem in Brazilian agriculture is not adequate production but an adequate distribution of profits*. It must further be reiterated that the tradition of the single-crop economic unit strongly moves counter to any sort of technological land redevelopment. Thus, those political movements which place a central emphasis on land reform as class reform must be judged essentially correct. The problem of technology will not be solved without the destruction of the latifundia as the central agency of the land economy. Even if, contrary to the evidence, the latifundists initiated wide-scale technological reforms, this would only compound the sickness rather than cure the patient. It would produce the economic chaos and class warfare that was avoided in the past precisely because of feudal *noblesse oblige*. Those who wish to avoid a comparatively peaceful revolution now would thus be faced with a less manageable revolution later.

Too often, the concept of *agrarian reform* is seen exclusively in terms of *land redistribution*. While the two obviously intersect, it is important to appreciate the fact that agrarian reform is a social and economic policy, while land reform is a technical phase of such a policy. In addition to outright expropriation, there is the possibility of achieving agrarian reform through the revision of the tax structure with the aim of redistributing land as a consequence of eliminating economically unproductive farm areas.

Agrarian reform is a social reform, and not simply a "one-shot" dramatic act of turning out latifundists and installing uneducated and uninformed peasants in their place. The weakness of the *Ejido* program in Mexico illustrates the dangers and demagoguery in simple land-grant approaches. In any event, the need for social action is made mandatory by the absence of any impulse toward agricultural reform in either the sociological or technological sense of the term "reform" on the part of the Brazilian landholders. The task of agrarian reform is further complicated by the widespread feeling among the urban social sectors, business and labor interests alike, that any agricultural solutions must be part of the general industrial growth of a developing nation. What this means in practice is the postponement of the search for solutions to the land problem for an indefinite period of time. Those anxious for agrarian reform have a two-pronged battle, to defeat the latifundists and to convince the industrial classes of the need to balance national development.

The present bias against agriculture in the Brazilian economy is reflected in price policies designed to encourage industry and to hold down the cost of living of the urban working classes rather than stimulate agricultural development. This situation is further emphasized in the relative prestige of the various governmental agencies and ministries. The hostility is due in part to the differential rates of return to capital in industry and agriculture at the present stage of the general development of Brazil. The claim that peasant revolutionaries have placed social factors in the forefront and scientific factors in the rear must be seen as rhetoric against this combination of situations.

Confronted with a choice between agriculture and industry, Brazilian governments from Vargas to Quadros have put nearly all their investment capital into the industrial area. Whatever the blessings or shortcomings of such a policy approach, it has failed to modernize landholding practices. Under Goulart there has been a vast highway building project, which has the double purpose of opening up the interior to industrial produce, and developing a better system for bringing foodstuffs to the industrial markets. There can be no question as to the agonizing nature of this problem: the stage of rapid industrialization usually requires a large-scale sacrifice of and by the agricultural sector. In the Soviet Union and China, industrialization was made possible by a concomitant policy of collectivization of the land, sometimes by force. But the approach of Brazilian political leadership is basically remedial, to mitigate the harsh effect of land ownership and tenure while postponing a "showdown" with the latifundists. Since there is no proper economic "mix," since little is done to alleviate the traditional gap between rural and urban sectors, it is hardly a wonder that a revolutionary climate pervades the Brazilian countryside, where farm hands attempt land seizure in a sporadic form characteristic of medieval peasant revolts. Without an over-all policy decision, with the protracted continuation of the "double economy," tensions between the city and country will mount and not, as some politicians in Brasília apparently imagine, simply disappear.

The social infirmities of Portuguese colonialism, African slavery, and Indian nomadism, along with the poor topography and scattered locales of the mineral wealth, have combined to prevent Brazil from becoming an industrial power. Communications networks, transportation systems, and electrical and mechanical energy, the basis for industrial development, were hindered by these social and natural factors. On top of this sat the ideologies of Catholicism and Liberalism, each for its own reasons opposing industrialization. Brazil seemed destined to remain in the present century what it had been in past centuries: an important supplier of the world's food and raw materials.

The latifundiary nobility did not relish the prospect of losing out to the rising industrial classes. It marshaled the voices of a compromising political sector to praise the virtues of the land and condemn any remedial legislation. The nostalgic point of view was reinforced by the liberal-positivist spirit in political economy. The international division of labor was defended, and it was accepted as an indisputable truth that to Brazil fell the important position in the furnishing of food products and raw materials. It was affirmed that the national prosperity lay in agriculture. The favorable balance of trade Brazilian agriculture maintained throughout the nineteenth century lent weight to such ideas. With the monetary surplus, foreign exchange could be counted on for the purchase of desired industrial products in foreign markets.

The anti-capitalist spirit which motivated even liberal Catholic and positivist ideologists reflected an important economic truth: that Brazil came on the industrial scene long after industrialism had been achieved in Western Europe and North America. Most products of Brazilian industry still cost more than those of its more advanced competitors. Furthermore, Brazilian labor was essentially unskilled and uneducated, and therefore, from an industrial viewpoint, unproductive. The coupling of these various factors fortified a feeling that Brazilian industrial produce would be rejected on a world market, and that the sacrifice of the agricultural sector to industrialism would only result in calamitous consequences. The merchants and shopkeepers preferred to sell better quality imported goods (including a vast empire of contraband) instead of the national product. The latifundists, for their part, also preferred the agricultural idyl since they reaped the profits and purchased the consumer items. The peasantry was too ignorant and too unaware of the situation to make its voice known. Brazil entered the twentieth century as an almost exclusively agricultural nation, unequipped and unprepared for the industrial age.

A combination of internal and international factors finally led Brazil to enter the modern industrial era.

First, there was the end of slavery in 1888 and then the break-up of Empire in 1889 respectively. With the liberation of the slaves, rural proprietors, already undermined by republican propaganda, lost the human bondage that united them to the Empire. The nearly one million Negroes that were set free for the most part abandoned their former masters. No amount of "paternalism" could keep the former slaves at the hard work and low wages characteristic of life on the latifundias. With the exodus of the former slaves the entire system of agricultural exploitation was dramatically weakened. The blacks formed the nucleus of the new semiproletariat. But without industrial skills, education, or a way of life suited to urban development, they were necessarily limited to cruder secondary production, such as transportation and construction work.

Second, the end of Empire itself opened up new possibilities, as the form of Empire, patterned as it was after decadent Portuguese colonial models, had severely inhibited industrial growth. The initiation of strong protectionist tariffs, modeled on United States legislation, forced the Brazilians to rely upon native industry. In the last year of Empire, Brazil had only 636 industrial plants; six years later it boasted 1,088 plants, and showed an increase of 53% of plant capitalization within this same six-year period. With the end of Empire the decline of investment in industrial activities ceased. The market potential of a republican Brazil soon brought investments from the English, French, Portuguese, and the United States. A market of such size could hardly fail to attract foreign investment capital, especially since Brazil was a self-declared "open territory."

The stimulus supplied by foreign investors to Brazilian industrial development can not be underestimated. On the other hand, foreign firms also contributed to the uneven character of this development. The British, who were the prime investors in the nineteenth century, built the railroads. But they did so with the rapid extraction of mineral wealth in mind and not with general considerations of Brazilian development. Basically, secondary commodity goods were emphasized in the European-owned enterprises. The British built flour mills, match, tobacco, and shoe factories. The Germans developed breweries, cigar manufacture, and pencil and paper factories. French capital was invested in more basic enterprises, such as chemicals and pharmaceuticals, but turned these to the production of cosmetic products. The Dutch and Belgians became early investors in fuels for personal consumption. Often, mineral products were shipped abroad to extractive processing plants, and found their way back to Brazil in the form developed at a slower rate than was warranted by the size and resources of the country.

The figures supplied by the United States Chamber of Commerce point up the dramatic increase in American investments in the twentieth century—particularly after the First World War. In the period up to 1914, United States private investment in Brazil amounted to $28 million. By 1930, this figure rose fantastically to $577 million. The Vargas period of economic structural reform and ultra-nationalism resulted in a slight downward tendency in United States investments, but by 1950, the figure rose to $644 million. By the end of the Kubitschek regime in 1960, the figure of American investments reached the one-and-a-half-billion figure, or twice that of the previous decade. It only need be pointed out that foreign investment went, in the main, to the industrial and mining sector. This paralleled the investment procedures of Brazilian capital, which came increasingly to rely on light industry as a source of quick and certain profits.

Third, two world wars have been comparatively generous to Brazilian industrial development. Unscathed by the ravages of either war, Brazil's industrial products were in demand on the world market for the first time. Its consumer production was unimpaired by foreign competitors during the period 1914–18, and again, 1939–45. Industrial production in 1914 was $956 million; by 1917 it had risen to $2,424 million, an increase of 153%. Even taking into account, and adjusting for, the currency devaluation of the period, an increase of 109% in industrial production was recorded. During World War I, nearly 6,000 new industrial establishments came into existence. A similar phenomenon was registered during World War II, with the added advantage that for the first time Brazil was in a position not only to increase its output capacity of secondary goods, but to become a seller in the world market of finished commodities in such areas as rubber and textile products. Brazilian exports jumped from $278 million in 1939 to $445 million in 1943, and by 1945, the last war year, this figure leaped to $661 million. In short, the exceedingly high rate of exports, both in absolute terms and relative to the low rate of imports during the war years, gave Brazil a formidable trade balance at the close of the war.

Fourth, there are the changed sociological and technological factors of large-scale modern industry. (a) Educational opportunities were greatly increased during the first half of the twentieth century, providing an intellectual base for skilled work. (b) The dislocation of war and tyranny in Europe brought to Brazilian shores immigrants with badly needed industrial and commercial skills. (c) Technology produced vastly improved working conditions. Air-conditioning, that great equalizer of weather, is only one invention responsible for increasing the productivity of each laborer, and of labor collectively. (d) Finally, urbanism as a way of life is itself a proven stimulant to industrial and commercial activities. The chain between high productivity and urban standards of living is too well known to require amplification.

Given this combination of positive, growth-producing factors, the real question is what went wrong and where? By the inner logic of economic laws of development, Brazil should today be one of the leading industrial nations of the world. It is not. It should be a nation which has a favorable balance of trade. It is not. It should be a nation which combines a steady growth rate with a firm monetary situation. It is not. The uneven character of Brazil's economic development requires examination—if only as a lesson in the patterns of colonial inheritance and imperial conquest.

The limited successes of industrialization not only failed to silence the voices of nostalgia, but actually increased the crescendo of opposition to industrial solutions. The main problems created by industrialization point up the complex nature of the economics of nations developing under an imperial shroud—problems which tend to increase rather than decrease as the tempo of industrialization rises.

First, the focusing of energy on industrialism came at a cost of near total neglect of the agricultural sector. Mechanization of factories took precedence over farm mechanization, particularly as the value of industrial production increased. What contributes to the gravity and urgency of the situation is that this emphasis on industry is accompanied by internal migration, the flight from the countryside to the big cities. This created a "society of the masses," but also created a demographic and productive imbalance which has done more to disrupt than to build the Brazilian economy. One part overexpands to the detriment of the whole. Instead of the development of rural centers and middle-sized cities, there is the creation of an economic competition between town and country, between the big coastal cities and the big latifundias and estates. Another dimension to this bifurcation of town and country is a growing division of interests between proletariat and peasantry—a division which has had vast political repercussions in preventing the formation of any sound movement of "national redemption."

Second, the costs of Brazilian industrialization have often been dictated by nationalistic sentiments rather than intelligent use of foreign credits, investments, skills, and organization. This is particularly evidenced in the nationalized sectors of the economy such as *Petrobrás* (the petroleum monopoly). It functions as a symbol of popular political manipulation primarily, over and beyond its manifest function of providing Brazil with cheap fuel. The historic scarcity of fuel, without which industrial growth is impotent, has created intransigence toward a virginal and national exploitation of these resources. What this has meant in practice is the growth of a dual economy, with private and public sectors competing for the same natural resources. Thus, while the high-cost, small-profit exploration and exploitation phases of the petroleum industry are exclusively in the hands of the public sector, the lucrative distribution end remains in firm control of private capital and foreign capital. Efforts to remedy the situation are faced with nearly insurmountable hurdles.

Attempts to open up the complex tasks of exploration and exploitation of basic natural resources to private economic interests come upon a double intransigence: the unwillingness of domestic financial sectors to invest in low-profit and, for the short run, no-profit enterprises; and political demagogues who see in any private economic encroachments proof of anti-patriotic sentiments, a willingness to "sell out" the public sector to Shell Oil Company. Furthermore, efforts to meet the problem head-on, by taking distributive phases of the petroleum industry out of the hands of a small bourgeoisie and into the hands of a much-vaunted public sector, are also met with bitter opposition by the political elite. What one finds is a costly and unprofitable public economic sector (which the middle class is only too glad to avoid handling), and a lucrative and profitable private sector (which only further drains the Brazilian government of a potential source of wealth). This imbalance between public and private sectors is a significant element in the coexistence of high growth rates coupled with high inflationary rates.

Third, Brazilian industry remains almost exclusively limited to an internal buying market. Its overwhelming volume of commodities is geared to satisfy consumer demands for such goods as clothing and foodstuffs. What this means is that Brazilian industry does not produce the essential machinery and basic tools of production that would enable it to compete satisfactorily on the world market. Industry suffers from a mercantilist belief in protectionism. This keeps secondary goods of foreign manufacture out of the country, while encouraging further production in secondary commodity goods. At best, this approach satisfies the consumer demands of white-collar and blue-collar workers, as well as those of the middle sectors as such (bureaucrats, military, and professionals). At worst, this economic approach ensures the continuing impoverishment of those outside the money economy, such as the peasants and the disenfranchised of the cities (the unemployed, slum dwellers, domestics, etc.). Consumer goods production in a backward country makes the real growth of the country extremely difficult. Brazil exports less than 1% of the consumer articles it manufactures. Thus (unlike Japan) it has neither the profits derivable from large-scale export of secondary goods nor (unlike the United States) the possibilities of large-scale internal industrial production. The present per capita consumption of a Brazilian is 25 times less than that of his counterpart in the United States. This in itself contributes to keeping the Brazilian economy linked to satisfying the supposed needs of a limited sector of the Brazilian populace. Simple modernism is an approach without even the hope of a fundamental solution to an inflationary economic situation which is built on the exclusion of mass participation. Capitalism in Brazil has produced a "society of the masses" without the participation and intelligent employment of these masses.

The character of economic production is therefore shaped almost exclusively by the false alternatives of a latifundist sector, which seeks a return to a traditional role of Brazil as the great exporter and supplier of the needs of advanced countries, and the domestic capitalist sector, which seeks to convert Brazil into a vast dumping ground for consumer goods. In this situation the federal administrative apparatus has been severely limited in what it can do, because the support both these sectors give the state and the relative political disenfranchisement of those who might provide more potent and long-range solutions lead to a catering to sectional needs. This is not to minimize the *social* significance of the change-over from a feudal economy of scarcity to a capitalist economy of consumer abundance. But under present circumstances, the *economic* significance of this shift is minimal, particularly for those nation-states like Brazil, entering the modern world centuries after the European industrial revolution began.

Fourth, there is, of course, the inhibiting nature of foreign capital, which, once invested, might tolerate a certain amount of economic *development*, but will never admit the need for a corresponding change in the *structure* of Brazilian society. The economics of imperialism have become sophisticated: profit-sharing plans with domestic factory owners, cooperation with state-owned enterprises, new plant construction using domestic labor, circumventing the laws of minimum requirement of national ownership, production utilizing national resources to an ever-increasing extent. This, however, only flavors the onion with honey. It does not make the forms of foreign investment any more palatable. Profits must still be derived from these industries. The forms of production, as well as the goods produced, are still determined by foreign needs rather than by national needs. And the limits of national business competition are still determined by foreign investors. Paradoxically, despite the rhetoric of free enterprise, it is foreign capitalism which prevents Brazilian capitalism from reaching maturation. What this means specifically is a continuation of petit-bourgeois production, production which requires low-grade machinery, uses unskilled or semi-skilled employees, and satisfies short-range consumer demands. All of this signifies that the real industrial exploitation of Brazil is left in the hands of foreign investors whose orientation is determined by foreign demands.* Brazil's first priority is for tractors but only after the automobile market was entrenched are they now being manufactured. Brazil needs highways connecting the coastal cities and the interior re-

---

* It should not be thought that United States investors are unique in this maintenance of Brazil in a less-than-developed competitive condition. The Japanese, for example, have made tremendous headway recently into Brazil's small handicrafts industries. Over the past ten years, Japanese investors have accumulated 100 Brazilian subsidiaries, with products ranging from fountain pens to freighters. Investment opportunities are great, labor is cheap, and the exportation of capital equipment to build plants (under Japanese supervision) serves to provide Japan with export credits with which it can purchase the raw materials it needs for its home industry, and then to continue the process of profit-making by selling these products in Brazilian markets. One Japanese investor has aptly referred to Brazil as a "Volkswagen economy." But this is simply another way of saying that investment for profit does not necessarily serve to enhance the industrial or monetary position of the underdeveloped country.

gions, but until recently it got commercial jets. Brazil is rich in lime and clay so badly needed for construction purposes, but until 1957 it imported finished cement from abroad. Such are the economics of semi-colonial regions.

Fifth, the actual speculative character of foreign investment in Brazil should not be overlooked. Manufacturing firms will penetrate the Brazilian market "on margin." They will introduce 25% new capital, and recruit 75% domestic capital. Now while the infusion is considerable, the drain is much heavier and has a canceling effect. For a foreign concern can remit annually as profits an amount equal to 10% of its registered capital investment, which means 10% on the total investment. Thus, the basis of computation is not the real value of equipment and capital brought into Brazil, but the total declared value of the whole business. President Goulart has drawn attention to this in a memorandum to Finance Minister Carlos Carvalho Pinto, dated October 28, 1963. He pointed out that the balance-of-payments problem was largely attributable to excessive remittances for marginal investments. Thus, at the foundation of the balance-of-payments crisis is the conduct of the foreign corporations, not infrequently with the tacit support of the foreign political agencies operating within Brazil. The present pile-up of $100 million in unremitted, but accumulated profits represent a considerable factor in the present financial instability of Brazil. And not until a more rational definition of "just profit" is accepted by foreign corporations can any long-term settlement of the financial spiral be realized. An additional factor in the speculative character of foreign investment is the enormous borrowing power of large corporations with local banks and particularly with local branches of foreign banks.

If the United States is to avoid a catering, paternal attitude to Brazilian economic woes, it must squarely face the problems created *for* Brazil *by* a foreign enterpreneurial element. To do otherwise is simply to postpone the treatment of the ailment. Worse still, it is to demand that the patient get well, while simultaneously injecting the virus which contributes to (if not directly causes) the illness.

American misconceptions of foreign aid to Brazil aggravate the situation. The American public is given to understand that Brazil is a vast sponge which chaotically soaks up the American taxpayers' money. The facts are quite different. *First*, the magnitude of the resources actually made available to the Brazilian economy is much smaller than generally believed. Often figures relating to commitments or authorizations rather than to actual disbursements are used. Furthermore, the reverse flow of amortization and interest payments should be deducted from gross figures on aid in order to measure the net transfer of resources from the United States to Brazil. *Second,* about half of the disbursements are in the form of Eximbank loans, whose funds are derived from the sale of Treasury bills to investors. Such loans have consistently realized a profit for American investors. *Third,* 35% of the disbursements represent shipment of surplus commodities. The tax burden was incurred as part of United States agricultural price-support programs. Foreign aid was never the primary motivation of the tax effort, but simply a meaningful method of utilizing commodities for constructive efforts abroad, commodities which would otherwise remain idle and subject to storage and deterioration costs. *Fourth,* United States taxpayers have in the last few years (1955–61) benefited from a substantial decline in prices paid for Brazilian import products, while wholesale prices of United States exports to Brazil have risen roughly 10% during this same period. The effect of this price decline has been greater than the total U.S. aid for the entire postwar period. *Fifth,* nearly all of United States foreign aid to Brazil has been linked to the purchase of American goods and services. The long and the short of the matter is that the American taxpayer has gained considerably more than he has given in his government's transactions with Brazil.

It might be wondered how the two clashing masters of domestic nationalism and foreign profiteering can be served at the same time. The middle-class answer in Brazil is to make of nationalism a political shadow lacking economic substance, to endow nationalist phraseology with the mystique of Brazilian hegemony while leaving the nation in control of robust foreign interests working with an ingenuous middle class. Foreign products are found everywhere in Brazil. But as a palliative to national pride the most prominent feature on the product is often the phrase "made in Brazil." The most developed example of this process is that "pride and joy of every Brazilian," the automobile industry. A great propaganda achievement of the Kubitschek administration is that under his reign Brazil achieved a national automobile industry. Indeed, it is true that 98% of all necessary manufacturing processes do take place in Brazil. But what is left out of account is the fact that (a) these factories are almost wholly owned subsidiaries of foreign automobile producers; and (b) profits from the sale of automobiles and auto products (outrageously priced to begin with) do not generally remain in Brazil for reinvestment purposes, but go to the parent firm. The magic phrase, *do Brasil*, covers a multitude of economic sins. Thus we have the spectacle of *Ford Motor Company do Brasil, Willys do Brasil*, etc. Nationalist passions are satisfied, while foreign profits remain intact. Foreign profit-making has widened the investment network to include domestic capital—while turning blushingly modest, the better to extract profits. Conservative nationalism has turned sentimental by seeking to redefine social development as simple modernization of consumer services.

But for all of its halting and even hypocritical qualities, the industrialization of Brazil has registered solid *social* gains. (a) The latifundists are on the decline as a prime policy-determining element. (b) The military are being integrated into a civil bureaucratic form of government, instead of playing an openly reactionary role. (c) The Church is accommodating itself to the social revolution, to the society of the masses, and to the elites in the cities. Perhaps above all else, industrialization, however partial and fragmented, has given the Brazilian a sense of social and political solidarity with the modern world, and whetted the appetite for more industrialization.

The United States must face the fact that as the essential "outsider" inside, as the biggest single investor nation, it absorbs the pent-up criticisms of centuries of colonial exploitation. If a good deal of the criticism of the United States' investment policy is hypocritical and intended to cover up the extent of internal exploitation, it is nonetheless true that, for different reasons, there remain powerful industrial elements in Brazilian life which are solidly aligned against United States investment policies. The United States, for its part, has contributed to and reinforced these sentiments and images by linking its national prestige to parochial industrial investments. Thus, if a deficient portion of the International Telephone and Telegraph system is nationalized, the United States government feels it must protect I.T. and T., that American prestige depends on salvaging the private investor. Of course, this simply reinforces the common belief that the United States too often behaves as if it is servant rather than master of American corporate power.

It is difficult for most Americans to comprehend the resentment of Brazilians and other Latin Americans, for United States foreign investments represent a very small fraction of the national wealth of the United States, while these same investments represent a sizable portion of the economies of nations such as Brazil. As Charles Wagley recently noted in his contributions to *Social Change in Latin America Today:*

Foreign investments are flowing into Brazil at a volume that is increasing rapidly. According to the Brazilian Ministry of External Affairs, the inflow of direct foreign investment rose from $51.3 million in 1955, to $55.7 million in 1956, and over $108 million in 1957. Roughly two-thirds of this went into basic industry, according to the ministry's classification. The estimated value of foreign investment is over $3 billion. Of this, United States investments were $1.3 billion at the end of 1957, half in manufacturing enterprises and the remainder in petroleum marketing, public utilities, trade, and mining.

Although the rate of United States investment has slowed considerably since this was written, two conclusions can be drawn from the above information. First, that United States foreign investments are in basic industries, a fact which stands in notable contrast to the secondary consumer orientation of Brazilian capital. Second, that although the total profits received from Brazilian industry by North American entrepreneurs and merchants is but a fraction of 1% in terms of the gross national income in the United States, it represents considerably more than that for Brazil. Foreign investment, particularly United States investment, contributes considerably to the industrial sector of the Brazilian economy. These investments are in heavy industries: three-fifths in the extractive industries such as agriculture, mining, and petroleum; one-fifth in manufacturing; and the final fifth in services. Foreign investments therefore are limited agencies for Brazilian capital formation and internal development, for they are basically concentrated in the primary commodity export industries.

American private corporations play an important part in the internal policies of Brazil through the size of their wage payments, the revenues they pay to the Brazilian government through taxes (United States firms are undoubtedly the best taxpayers in

Brazil), and their part in the processes of production and capital investment. They also carry a great weight in view of the protection afforded to them by the United States government, and their central place in an over-all United States policy for the Latin American region.

Given these complex circumstances it is little wonder that the United States is hardly the beloved benefactor most Americans are led to believe in. More important from a policy-making point of view, this makes the Brazilian willingness to trade with the Soviet bloc understandable from an economic no less than from a political perspective. If United States interests cannot be expropriated, they can at least be neutralized in their effects by introducing a counterbalancing economic agent.

Brazil's trade with the communist-bloc nations is increasing at a rapid pace. Among the more ambitious projects are plans to have a Polish state enterprise construct a 200,000-kilowatt thermoelectric power plant in Rio Grande do Sul. This represents the first industrial project let with direct financing. The Polish enterprise, *Copek*, will provide a $26-million credit for seven years at 3% interest. The installation will operate within the Rio Grande do Sul State power system. This carries an added significance since it was this same system which took over the expropriated power plant of American and Foreign Power Company of New York when it was seized by Leonel Brizola in 1959. Also under consideration is the installation in Minas Gerais of an aluminum refining plant with Polish equipment and design. Up to now trade relations between Brazil and the Soviet bloc have been largely on the basis of traditional raw materials and foodstuffs. The stepped-up trade relations thus represent an intricate and involved set of relations with the socialist bloc—relations formerly reserved for Western-bloc nations.

Earlier, in 1960, Brazil signed a five-year treaty with Czechoslovakia providing for the construction of a Czech tractor plant in Brazil. The Czechoslovakian government would provide the equipment and technical aid to produce 2000 tractors yearly. The agreement anticipated $70 million in trade both ways in the first year. Brazilian economists explained that their objective was to make a foreign-exchange saving by diverting trade from hard-currency countries (the Western powers) to those with which Brazil had bilateral agreements (the East European bloc). A year later, in 1961, Brazil negotiated an agreement with Yugoslavia to barter goods worth $500 million over a five-year period. Yugoslavia also agreed to extend Brazil $120 million in credits. At the same time, Yugoslav freighters were acquired in exchange for an equivalent sum in Brazilian products. Finally, it should be mentioned that trade arrangements between Brazil and the Soviet Union have reached the $40-million level, and the new agreements, which include industrial projects (particularly electric and petroleum refining), should raise that figure to $100 million annually by 1965.

These trade agreements and negotiations, while they represent a considerable increase over the past, still remain more symbolic than effective deterrents to the current economic and financial crisis faced by Brazil. They point up Brazil's growing desire to gain a higher measure of political sovereignty through the mechanism of an economic "balance of terror." This was clearly implicit in Jânio Quadros' strategy of turning to Europe, Africa, and Asia for trade pacts. And it has become evident that this aspect of Quadros' policy is being seriously pursued by the Goulart government. Brazil's neutralist posture in political matters has been made increasingly feasible and even necessary by the growth of economic arrangements with the Soviet-bloc nations. At the least, Brazil gains the advantage in bilaterial barter arrangements of not having to pay out—as it does to the United States—hard currency, of which it has precious little. At the most, Brazil can reap the bargainer's gain: a more favorable financial arrangement with private investors from the Western bloc, as well as wider latitude in repayment of credits on loans negotiated with the United States, England, and the other European nations.

Foreign investors form a vortex of power which must be evaluated along with the domestic economic classes, such as the bureaucracy, the military, and the Church. Investment groups are influential in the loans and commercial policies of the United States, and thus occupy a decision-making position both as economic investor and political formulator.

The opposition of wide sectors of Brazilian public opinion to United States foreign aid should not be seen as a paranoid effort to recapture national virginity, even though from a strictly economic point of view such extreme nationalism may indeed at times prove to be highly irrational. The fact is that while the economics of nationalism might be wasteful and misdirected, Brazil is in a situation where economic investors from abroad are not simply monetary agencies, but political agencies as well. It is only when the political dimension of foreign aid and investment is taken account of that an accurate appraisal of Brazilian nationalism can be made.

Efforts to change the basic structure of the Brazilian economy are not subject to easy solutions such as "massive" dosages of American aid. One of the major problems confronting accelerated economic growth is inflation. Brazil has reaped both the positive and negative aspects of inflation. The Brazilian government has resorted to deficit spending to raise funds. It is far easier to reroute wealth by printing more paper money than to raise taxes. In addition to conscious inflationary policies, Brazilians are faced with excess demands by the consumer sector, which further tend to spiral prices by the absence of savings. Excess aggregate demand, imbalances between demand and available supply, rising import prices and money wages, as well as the absence of anti-trust legislation to rationalize competition, all aggravate the growth economy of Brazil. The primary commodity-export nature of the Brazilian economy has been beset by some very real monetary and fiscal problems. The recent price trends in commodities have slowed Brazil's economic progress by draining potential investment capital into secondary consumer purchasing.

The extent of this commodity imbalance is made plain by Luís Cabral de Meneses, vice president of the Rio de Janeiro Commercial Association, who indicates that the volume of consumer purchases in 1962 was three to four times as large as they were only several years ago. There is a wild dash to buy on credit. Commercial credit establishments are offering 36% annual interest to lenders. Prices have risen more than 50% in 1962 alone. Some idea of the extent of inflation can be gathered by the fact that Brazil's largest unit of currency in circulation, the 1000-cruzeiro note, is worth only $1.30 (at the close of 1962) on the free market. Any important cash transactions already involve carrying more cruzeiro notes than a man's pockets can hold. In areas of the interior there is a crippling shortage of bills, particularly of the smaller denominations. Yet everyone with cash or credit available continues to buy: refrigerators, airplane tickets, television sets, real estate, jewelry, or a hard foreign currency. The thing to do is to spend the constantly depreciating cruzeiros that keep pouring out of the treasury.

Inflation cuts into the productive processes by placing a great strain on the availability of credit and by depleting liquid funds. Manufacturers and merchants are hard pressed for cash, and now promise delivery only if they get full cash in advance. The price increases extend also to basic foodstuffs. Price controls have broken down as a result of the refusal of food merchants to deliver at government prices. The "solution" has been for the Bank of Brazil to print more paper money to meet the merchants' demands, which, of course, only further drains the economy. Former Finance Minister Miguel Calmón has told the Brazilian Congress that without additional tax revenues and borrowing power for the government, the federal budget *deficit* next year will be more than a billion dollars. João Goulart, for his part, has been reluctant to take effective measures either on subsidies, taxes, or decreasing the federal bureaucracy, since the bureaucracy, in combination with the organized railroad, maritime, and port workers, forms the basis of his political organization, and benefits from the redistribution of wealth that comes through inflation.

Each political faction and social sector is attempting to manipulate the situation for separate advantages. Business leaders for their part are accusing the Goulart regime of raising taxes and declaring bonuses without taking such indispensable measures as reducing the spending of the public sector. Landowners, through their parliamentary agents, are bottlenecking social legislation. Labor unions are discontented by their continued sacrifices for the Goulart regime in the name of political solidarity. In this context, the International Monetary Fund and the International Bank for Reconstruction and Development have devised a scheme for the reduction of the Brazilian trade deficit to nearly half of its staggering total of two and three-quarter billions by sales of American agricultural products for Brazilian currency. But they demand a "stabilization" program (including austerity) that would only slow the rate of industrial growth. Private investors from the United States, for their part, could considerably aid the Brazilian economy by fresh investments. But they insist on guarantees that no further expropriation or nationalization be attempted. Since

United States investments in the past have not guaranteed any higher living standards for the Brazilians, there is a great deal of agitation for further nationalization and expropriation rather than less, even if it entails short-run inflationary spirals.

The most negative aspect of inflation is that it prevents any extension of the money economy to all portions of the population, particularly to the peasantry. Inflation saddles Brazil with a dual economy. It lowers the standards of living, absolutely in terms of real income, and relatively in the relation of classes. Merchants, bureaucrats, and even organized workers have the means to pass along the cost of inflation to the unorganized masses of city workers and to the much abused peasant.

There is, however, a directly political consequence of inflation which tends to offset its negative economic features. Inflation reinforces support for the Goulart regime among the working classes by increasing their share of the national economy. By the same token, austerity programs designed to curb inflationary spending have the reverse effect. They weaken the working-class position at the expense of the stability of middle-sector investors abroad. Seen in this light, the May 1963 decision to increase civil service and military wages by 60%, and to return to a system of subsidizing petroleum and agricultural products, is not only a willingness to risk financial instability but, more profoundly, a belief that supports for the national economy (which admittedly stimulate inflationary trends by underwriting non-profit or low-profit industries) are more vital than satisfying the conservative policies of the International Monetary Fund. It also means that Brazilian economists share the faith of their politicians that the nation can continue to show a growth pattern even under conditions of a relative retrenchment in foreign private investments.

What this means from a long-term position is that, however serious the imbalance between differing economic sectors may be, however high the inflationary spiral, and however widespread the dislocation in credit standards, Brazil is ready to pay the social costs of rapid economic development. It is a *developing* economy rather than an *underdeveloped* economy. That means that certain sectors are outside the money economy, others thrive on intermediary and non-productive enterprises, and still others become fabulously wealthy. But the over-all Brazilian economy shows a very high average annual growth rate of 5.7% between 1950–60, as measured by the types and degrees of investments.* The social tendencies toward urbanization and basic tool production only further increase the possibilities for longe-range growth.

Superficially, Brazil shares in the dilemmas of other nations of Latin America. But there exists an acute difference: Brazil reveals a tendency toward structural development in its economic growth, while such countries as Argentina, Uruguay, and Venezuela simply move toward modernism, toward consumer affluence for a small portion of their society. As Brazil's dependence upon foreign imports of consumer items declines, as its general orientation toward the postponement of personal gratification becomes structurally reinforced, the other countries of Latin America, showing little tendency toward structural reform, only become more deeply enmeshed in the economics of consumption, and in the foreign and political commitments such consumption invariably entails.

The chief problem remains the dual economy. It is conservatively estimated that of Brazil's 75 million people about 32 million are under fifteen. Of the 43 million of working age, 23 million people, more than half, are for all practical purposes outside the money economy in that they are deprived of regular jobs. They live on produce and occasional barter, meaning that they simply do not participate in the "consumer revolution." Here we see that inflation, when combined with enormous labor surpluses, causes the lower strata of society extreme deprivation. It becomes not simply a fiscal problem, involving sums of hard currency, but far worse, it results in mass impoverishment of the poor. This is the risk factor in inflation that as yet has found no resolution.

The structure of economic development leads not only to the exclusion of the "masses" from the political life of Brazil, but more significantly from its economic life as well. To chart the course from politics through economics and finally to society itself is thus to chart the course from "classes" to "masses," from the

* It must be pointed out that this growth rate dipped from 7% in 1960 to 4½% in 1961. This might be a by-product of the exodus of foreign capital investors and a response of domestic capitalists reinvesting in foreign enterprises—both as a response to the inflationary exaggeration. How permanent this downward trend is remains to be seen. In the meantime absolute production output continues to rise in most sectors of the economy.

"whites" to the "blacks," from the rich to the poor, from the society of classes to mass society.

The economics of a developing nation makes possible the political integration of the working classes. Sharply contributing to the rising tide of revolutionary force is the inability of the Brazilian urban proletariat to share any longer in the industrial wealth of the nation without pushing for even more radical economic reforms. During the Vargas period one could speak of the "bourgeoisification" of the working classes. They shared in the easygoing, rising economy that characterized the wartime prosperity of Brazil. Except for the prosperous Paulistas, the present extended inflation has "proletarianized" the lower white-collar and blue-collar worker; that is, it has linked class consciousness to class membership. This, for no other reason than the material decline of the private economic sector: the increasing havoc of inflation on the urban proletariat; the workers' increasing reliance on slum dwellings (*favelas*); the liquidation of private savings; and the actual lowering of standards of living among most workers. These have contributed to a sharpening of political as well as economic demands. The potential combination of peasants and proletarians is what now makes Brazil, for the first time, the most likely candidate for a broad-based social revolution. The fusion and mobilization of "have-nots" and "former-haves" will clearly prove to be a potent force for radical change. Those who do not have cannot be asked to preserve. The Brazilian masses do not have. We can do no better than repeat C. P. Snow's comments which opened the chapter: "The world can't survive half rich and half poor. It's just not on." The agenda listing social changes can no longer be ignored. The Brazilian is becoming an "economic man" with a vengeance.

VIII
SOCIAL STRUCTURE AND
ECONOMIC CHANGE

. . . in which L.A. Costa Pinto and Waldemiro Bazzanella treat the connection between social change and economic development; this is followed by L.C. Bresser Pereira's examination of the class structure and the industrial "take-off" period; and Neuma Aguiar Walker discusses the role of labor in this process; Luis Suárez then examines the base of Brazil's economic plight, finding it in the connection between industrialization and undercapitalization; Josué de Castro reveals the "tragic expression" of economic backwardness by showing the relationship between colonialism and hunger on one side, and industrialism and affluence on the other.

I. ECONOMIC DEVELOPMENT, SOCIAL CHANGE,
AND POPULATION PROBLEMS IN BRAZIL

L.A. Costa Pinto and Waldemiro Bazzanella *

BRAZIL'S SOCIETY is changing, old patterns persist, but do not prevail; new patterns are present, but are not dominant. The social change is the result of the transition from an agrarian to an industrial economy, from a rural to an urban society, and from a parochial to a more secular way of life. Emerging social classes include an urban proletariat, a middle class, and a bourgeoisie of merchants and industrialists. The government is exercising great efforts to accelerate the rate of economic development of the country. An important feature of Brazil's demography is the high rate of natural increase in the population due mainly to the high

* L.A. Costa Pinto, Rio de Janeiro, is Professor of Sociology, University of Brazil, and Director, Latin American Center for Research in the Social Sciences. His latest work is *On Economic Development and Social Mobility* (1957). W. Bazzanella is Instructor in Sociology, University of Brazil, and Research Assistant, Latin American Center for Research in the Social Sciences. He is the author of *Estratificação e Mobilidade Social no Brasil: Fontes Bibliográficas* (1957).

birth rate and declining death rate, particularly in infant mortality.

Brazil is today the laboratory of a great historical experience in which we can observe, with almost classic purity, the process of economic development with its profound implications for all spheres of social life. The forces of social change that have made of Brazil a "modern nation" in the last fifty years are so clearly operative in all aspects of our national life that both national and foreign students of Brazilian society find themselves discussing the factors, conditions, and perspectives of that basic process regardless of the original focus of their studies. Anthropologists, folklorists, politicians, jurists, journalists, tourists, and even demagogues are fascinated by the theme, although most of them are not equipped to handle the subject. The basic transformations that Brazil is undergoing today are the subject of much talk but little study.

Our purpose here is only to present a tentative approach to some of the more significant aspects of social change in modern Brazil, particularly the main demographic implications. We hope that our remarks will be enough to show that Brazil, whose frontiers contain more than half of the population of Latin America, is a huge laboratory full of variety and possibilities for research where a movement in space may lead one back in time, and where one can find not only the fastest growing city in the world but extensive areas where, as a picturesque Indian expression goes, "the white man's hand never put her foot."

To study contemporary Brazilian society, we should start with the fundamental notion that we are observing a changing society at the very moment when the old pattern persists, but no longer prevails, and the new one, though present, is not yet dominant. Undoubtedly this structural imbalance and diversity in Brazilian society are an historical product. Without going into details, we may note that the present turn is the climax of the great transformation which began at the end of the last century—the transition from an agrarian to an industrial economy; from a predominantly rural to a predominantly urban society; from an archaic, parochial, and personal style of life to another more modern, more contractual, and more secular style.

In this process which has brought a growing integration to our national community, the sphere of economic development is the one in which the political authority exerts its main effort to ac-

celerate deliberately the rhythm of change. In this way change has
been stimulated in many ways through the displacement of traditional economic patterns by new ones geared to industrialization.
The more spontaneous economic changes are less and less numerous while the intentional promotion of planned change tends to
increase. As a result of the inevitable priority that is given to the
economic sphere by policy-makers concerned with the modernization of Brazilian life, the changes in the social structure seem to
be even less intentional or desired, even more spontaneous, not
planned, almost anarchical; consequently the total configuration
is asymmetrical, the rhythm of change of the various parts being
extremely unequal.

The fundamental problems in Brazilian society take shape
and emerge precisely at these points of cleavage, contradiction,
and discontinuity. The demographic questions that particularly
interest us in this paper are an excellent thermometer of the over-
all situation; they facilitate statistical analyses of social processes
and problems that in other spheres appear more imponderable,
less capable of objective record and study.[1]

The main feature of the Brazilian demographic situation is the
exceptionally high rate of natural increase of the population. In
1890 the Brazilian population amounted to 14.3 million while in
1940 it was around 41.2 million—a multiplication by three within
a 50-year period. In 1950 the number was 51.9 million, a 26%
increase over the figure for 1940. The annual geometric rate of
growth was 21.5 per thousand between 1890 and 1940 and 23.8
per thousand between 1940 and 1950. This extraordinary rhythm
of growth is mainly due to a very high birth rate which hovers
around 42 to 44 per thousand while the death rate is around 18 to
20 per thousand per year. Apparently this rate of growth is far
from declining. It is true that the annual average of live births per
thousand women from 15 to 49 years of age dropped slightly from
178.7 in the period 1930–40 to 177.3 in 1940–50; but this decline

---

[1] We should say, incidentally, that both the earlier absence and then the
later neglect of demographic material are among the reasons a recent generation of Brazilian sociologists have tried to compensate for lack of data and
scientific concepts by resorting to temperamental interpretations of Brazil's
social situation. Because of their literary flavor and spectacular setting, such
interpretations have gained wide circulation both within the country and
abroad out of proportion to their scant scientific validity.

in fertility was sufficiently compensated by a parallel decline in the death rate, particularly in infant mortality. We lack reliable mortality data on the total population, but we may well use as an illustration the reported rates of infant mortality for the State of São Paulo and some State capitals during the years around 1940 and 1950. In the period of 1939–41 the rate of infant mortality in the State of São Paulo was 162.7 per thousand; in 1949–51 it had dropped to 111.2 per thousand. For the same two periods the rates of infant mortality declined from 159.3 to 97.2 in the Federal District and from 137.8 to 93.4 within the municipal limits of São Paulo, the capital of the State. Even in the economically less developed areas it seems that infant mortality has declined steadily. In the municipality of Recife, the capital of the State of Pernambuco, the rates of infant mortality were 272.3 in 1939–41 and 243.6 in 1949–51; for the municipality of Salvador, the capital of the State of Bahia, the figures were, respectively, 206.3 and 162.6.

We can then say that whereas the birth rate in Brazil is among the highest in the world, its death rate has gradually declined as a result of new methods of fighting endemic diseases and of economic development with the consequent betterment of life conditions.

It is estimated that the Brazilian population will exceed 66 million by 1960. Although population forecasts are hazardous when referring to lengthy periods, we may expect that by 1980 Brazil will have about 100 million people.

With a high rate of fertility and a still quite high mortality rate, Brazil has a very young population. In 1950, 52.4% of its total population were less than 20 years old, 43.2% were in the 20-to-59 age bracket, and only 4.2% were older than 60. Although an advantage so far as the future development of the Brazilian population is concerned, this age structure creates problems at present because the proportion of inactive people is quite high in relation to the size of the active population. According to the life tables for the period 1940–50, the average life expectancy was 39.3 years for men, 45.5 years for women.

For an adequate picture of the demographic situation of modern Brazil it is not enough to note the rapid growth of her population. Its ecologic distribution and its composition, which are undergoing great changes, should also be pointed out. Those changes are mainly a result of the over-all process of economic development, whose impact marks so conspicuously the present social situation of Brazil. Following the creation of a free-labor market after the abolition of slavery in 1888, industrialization became possible; it really started at the beginning of the twentieth century, took a firm impulse after World War I, and has considerably accelerated since World War II.

In 1920 the number of industrial workers in Brazil was 275,512; it was 781,185 in 1940 and 1,256,807 in 1950—an increase of 4.5 times in 30 years. Between 1940 and 1950 the number of firms operating in manufacturing increased from 40,983 to 78,434 establishments. In the same period the people employed by those concerns rose from 1,400,000 to 2,230,000, an increase of 59.3%. The percentage of people employed in manufacture among the total active population of the country was 4.8% in 1940 but 6.1% in 1950. On the other hand the percentage of the active population employed in agriculture and cattle-raising declined during the same period from 32.5% to 27.0%. These data show clearly that an urban proletariat is in the course of formation, and although it is still relatively small, it has a decisive influence in Brazil today, particularly in the political sphere.

The highest percentage increase, 134.2% between 1940 and 1950, was in the number of people employed in services and social activities. Among the total active population 3.1% were employed in services in 1940, but 5.8% in 1950. These indices illustrate the expansion of tertiary activities, a clear indication of urbanization, since the supply of services is a predominantly urban activity.

The clear change in the occupational pyramid of Brazil becomes even more evident if we consider that from 1940 to 1950 the active population occupied in agriculture and cattle-raising increased by only 4.6%, while the rise for people employed in manufacturing was about 59.4%; in the same period the rate of increase in the labor force for the supply of services was 134.2% and 38.9% for commerce, transportation, and communications.

An important aspect of the changes in the labor force is the increasing participation of women, especially in the field of services, where the number of female workers rose 2.6 times—from 438,000 in 1940 to 1,160,000 in 1950. Apparently this considerable increase in female participation in the labor force is related to the growing bureaucracy of Brazilian society.

The process of industrialization, which depends upon the formation of an extensive internal market and consequent development of transportation and communications, has greatly contributed to social integration in Brazil. In the past, Brazil has been an economic archipelago whose units were more closely connected to their external markets than with each other; it is now becoming a completely integrated economic continent. This integrative tendency, however, is offset by the unequal development of the different regions. Industrialization is concentrated in eastern and southern Brazil, mainly in the metropolitan areas of Rio de Janeiro and São Paulo city; these two cities alone are responsible for 50% of the total value of Brazilian industrial production. Here again the structural diversity of Brazilian society is reflected in regional contrasts. There are areas where an archaic, traditional, and backward type of economy still prevails, firmly rooted in huge estates under extensive cultivation by primitive techniques. There are other areas which are characterized by industrialism, a mass market, and modern metropolises, or by an increasingly rationalized agriculture.

In Brazil, urbanization is rapidly progressing and is closely related, as elsewhere, to the process of industrialization. In 1940, 68.8% of our population was classified as rural and in 1950, 63.8%. Marked differences in the rural proportion reflect a diversity of industrialization among the different regions of the country. In southern Brazil the rural population dropped from 63.2% to 58.1% between 1940 and 1950. In the eastern region, where the Federal District is located, the change was from 66.9% in 1940 to 61.0% in 1950. In 1950, São Paulo, the most industrialized State of the Federation, for the first time in the history of Brazil reached a situation in which the urban population—52.6%—exceeded the rural population—47.4%. The population of São Paulo city multiplied 70 times in 80 years! The proportion of the population of the State of São Paulo living in São Paulo city was 3.7% in 1872 but around 25% in 1950.

For the whole country the rural population increased by 16.9% from 1940 to 1950 while the urban and suburban population increased by 45.8% during the same period. The high rate of increase of the suburban population indicates that urbanization is progressing not only through the formation of new cities, but also through the expansion of metropolitan centers such as the capitals of several States, especially the cities of Rio de Janeiro and São Paulo. Since the population of the suburbs in Brazil is composed mainly of lower middle-class people and industrial workers, the growth of suburbia suggests that a lower middle class is in the course of formation and also that a considerable part of the Brazilian population is entering the situation of the proletarian.

During the period 1940–50 the total Brazilian population increased by 26.0%—from 41 to 52 million—while the urban and suburban population increased by 45.8%—from 12.9 to 18.8 million.

The principal source of this urbanization is the current of rural-urban migration. The attraction of the big cities and of pioneer areas now being cleared mainly for the cultivation of coffee appeals to the people of economically stagnant regions; as a result Brazil is one of the countries with a very high degree of spatial mobility.

We do not have data for a direct appraisal of these internal migratory movements. However, we can gauge their magnitude by the indirect method of counting the people who are now living in other regions than the one in which they were born. In 1940, 3,451,000 people were living in a State other than their native one; for 1950 the corresponding number was 5,206,000. We should note that these figures refer to the net internal migration between the States; they overlook seasonal internal migrations and other cases of return of migrants to their State of origin; they also overlook movements occurring within the boundaries of each State. The number of migrants who died between these two census years are also not represented here. At any rate, it is extremely significant that the percentage of the Brazilian population living in other than their State of birth increased from 8.3% in 1940 to about 10% in 1950.

The main direction of rural-urban migration is toward the cities of Rio de Janeiro and São Paulo. The destination of most of the rural-rural migrants is the pioneer areas of northern Paraná, western São Paulo, or southern Mato Grosso, where the economic frontier is being widened, above all, by the clearance of wild land for coffee-raising. In 1950, 930,000 people living in the Federal District—that is, 40% of its 2.3 million population—had been born in other units of the Federation. The actual contribution of internal migration to the population growth of Rio de Janeiro city is even greater than these figures indicate if we consider that a relatively high fertility prevails among the migrants.

The great volume of internal migration is also reflected in the sex composition of the population of different regions already established. The generalization that the longer the distance between the centers of attraction and the area of origin, the larger the percentage of male migrants, is valid in the case of Brazil. The Northeast region, very far from the centers of attraction in the South, is a good illustration; in 1950 it had, among its population of 15 to 39 years of age, 2,531,000 women and 2,277,000 men—that is a proportion of 90 men per 100 women. In addition to the higher mortality of males, the excess of male migrants is certainly an important factor in producing this result. The excess of the number of women over the number of men decreases as we approach the centers of migratory attraction until we reach the extreme contrary case of the State of Rio de Janeiro. Here there are more men than women mainly because of the great demand for female labor in the nearby Federal District.

The emergence of new social classes is one of the social changes seen particularly in the more developed areas of Brazil. In addition to the formation of an urban proletariat and of a middle class, a bourgeoisie of merchants and industrialists is now present and seeks to conquer the dominant place previously held by the traditional agrarian elite of the great landlords. In this transfer of elites, of definition and redefinition of their social role, the values associated with the two often antagonistic styles of life are marked by considerable ambivalence. The current expression, "crisis of the elites," is justified if it means that the industrial and commercial elites have not yet quite taken the position of dominance that the agrarian elites are gradually losing. The structural diversification of Brazilian society can be clearly seen in what is happening to the elites. Brazil no longer has a single cohesive elite with one system of values and one style of life and thought. Two blocks of approximately the same strength compete for power and prestige —one struggling to keep a previous position of dominance and the other to conquer a new position.

II. THE RISE OF THE MIDDLE CLASS IN BRAZIL

L.C. Bresser Pereira *

Brazil, during the past thirty years, has undergone extensive social and economic change, amounting to a Brazilian "Industrial Revolution." It is always somewhat arbitrary to assign dates to broad historical events, but if establishment of a starting point for the Industrial Revolution would aid in its understanding, the best date is probably 1930. In the economic field, it is true, World War I represented a first step; in the cultural field, the Week of Modern Art (1922 in São Paulo) was the first significant manifestation of a really Brazilian culture. But in both cultural and economic fields, and especially in the political field, the Revolution of 1930 (when Getúlio Vargas came to power), and the world depression beginning in 1929, are the most important events. The phase that many sociologists, economists, and historians call either the National Revolution or the Industrial Revolution, the stage that W. W. Rostow prefers to call the take-off period, began at that time in Brazil.[1]

The take-off period is decisive in the development of a particular country, and once entered, economic growth becomes almost automatic. After 1930, the feudal forces that had dominated Brazil began to lose strength. It is in this period that Brazil changes from object to subject of history and becomes master of her own destiny. Until that moment, only in a legal sense could Brazil be considered a nation. Her economy was oriented toward Europe and the United States; she was a complementary economic unit of the industrialized countries. Her great role was to export agricultural products in exchange for industrial goods to be consumed by the richer part of the population. It was a subsistence economy typical of underdeveloped and semi-feudal countries. The internal market, one of the main characteristics of a well-developed economy, became important only after 1930.

Culturally, Brazil was also a complement, or imitation, of the industrialized countries. Brazil, trying to analyze its problems and

* L.C. Bresser Pereira is Assistant Professor of Business Administration at the Escola de Administração de Emprêsas de São Paulo.

[1] W. W. Rostow, *The Stages of Economic Growth—A Non-Communist Manifesto* (Cambridge: Cambridge University Press, 1961).

to formulate economic, political, and educational change, adopted indiscriminately concepts from abroad. European culture, European experience, was merely transplanted. There was no critical consciousness able to understand Brazilian problems and to adapt foreign culture to the Brazilian environment. It was generally assumed that what had been successful in Europe or the United States would also succeed in Brazil. The result was a culture without strength, without national vitality.

The industrialization process that has occurred in Brazil during the past thirty years has changed this picture radically. During this period, Brazil achieved her National Revolution, whose causes and paths we can now study. A complete analysis of this subject, however, is not the aim of this paper. In relation to this problem it is sufficient to point out the decisive factor behind Brazilian industrialization: the impossibility of importing manufactured goods in the desired amount.

Three external stimuli are the key to understanding Brazil's take-off. World War I; the depression of the thirties, which by a curious contradiction helped the Brazilian economy, causing a drop in coffee prices from 22.5 cents a pound in 1929, to 8 cents a pound in 1931, and a consequent decrease of 64% in the value of coffee exports, which fell from 805.8 million pounds in the twenties to 337 million pounds in the thirties; and finally, World War II, were the accidental external stimuli to Brazil's industrialization. After World War II, the government took planned measures to avoid importation of manufactured goods at low prices, through the Carteira de Exportação e Importação (CEXIM), Instruction 70 of the Superintendência da Moeda e do Crédito (SUMOC), and the Customs Tax Law. Responding to such protection and support, Brazilian industry developed rapidly. By the mid-1950's, Brazil had built its consumer goods industry, with the exception of the automotive industry. The emphasis at present is upon the development of heavy industry, including automotive and tool industries, whose growth began during the forties.[2]

* * *

[2] From 1949 to 1960, the rate of growth of the national income was between 5% and 6% a year. From 1945 to 1954, it was exactly 6.2%; income per capita increased at the rate of 3.8% during this period. While the participation of agriculture in the gross national product decreased, the participation of industry increased from 13% in 1939 to about 20% in recent years. (Source: Equipe da Renda Nacional da Fundação Getúlio Vargas.)

As a peripheral, agricultural, and thoroughly underdeveloped country, Brazil's social structure was very simple before the National Revolution. The Declaration of Independence (1822) did not transform Brazil into a truly independent nation. The Imperial Constitution of 1824 and the Republican Constitution of 1891 also did not change Brazil into a real democracy. Elections were controlled. During the first Republic, for instance, one of the parties always won the elections, while the opposition party received exactly one-third of the seats in Congress. A semi-colonial and almost feudal society, with an economy based on the exploitation of land owned by a small number of great planters, Brazil was dominated by a small and powerful upper class. The landowners were traditionally allied to the merchants (exporters of coffee, sugar, rubber, and importers of manufactured goods), and, after the Declaration of Independence, to foreign capitalism, particularly British. As the people had not yet achieved real participation in public affairs, the power of the nation was concentrated in a few hands, an oligarchy.

Before the National Revolution, the great majority of members of the Brazilian lower class were (and still are) employed in agriculture. Some had been slaves, while others had come to Brazil as immigrants to work on the coffee plantations. As a whole, they constituted a large group of impoverished, illiterate persons, living under miserable conditions. They were typical representatives of a subsistence economy working at the lowest level of productivity.

Between these two classes was a silent but growing middle class. This class appeared for the first time with a certain importance after the Declaration of Independence. With the withdrawal of the Portuguese, it was necessary to organize the state, to perform judiciary, legislative, and executive functions, to build the Army. It was the middle class, often connected by kinship relations with the upper class, that performed these functions. The first colleges of law (Brazil did not have a colonial university) were then opened to train members of this class. With the end of the slave traffic and the boom in coffee exports, which permitted the formation of a free-labor market, the coastal cities and their environs began to develop. The middle class developed as well. "The role fulfilled by the middle class was considerably enlarged: the more diverse urban activities, the infant commerce, new professions, the

Army, the Church, the bureaucracy. . . ." [3] But, in general, the middle classes "were formed and grown in the framework of our underdevelopment, as by-products of the urbanization of a country which remained agricultural and did not offer conditions for the participation of the middle classes in the productive process. . . . Their resulting unavoidably marginal position made them direct parasites of the government." [4]

Such, in brief, was the social structure of Brazil: on the one hand, an oligarchy of planters and merchants; on the other, a great number of impoverished peasants; and in between, a small but growing middle class.

The National Revolution brought vast change. Industrialization modified the Brazilian way of life, upset traditional economic relations, and originated great social, cultural, and political change. New classes arose, Brazil developed, and lost most of its feudal features.

In the upper class, the industrialists appeared to take their place beside the planters and merchants. Originating primarily in the middle class—particularly from Italian, German, Jewish, and Lebanese immigrants—and in the old upper class, their power and prestige increased rapidly with the industrialization process. Today, they may be considered the dominant group in Brazil. Their rise, however, was not easy. For years and years they waged political and ideological battle against the planters and the old merchants, who represent the traditional and non-progressive sector of the Brazilian economic and social system. Today, this conflict is ending. The position of industry in the Brazilian economy is now an established and definite fact.

In the lower class, transformation was also definite. As the industrialists were a whole new sector in the upper class, so in the lower class did the industrial workers become important enough to be singled out as a new sector. Most of them came from rural areas; they were peasants or sons of peasants who left their homes, attracted by the higher wages of industry. In agriculture, disguised unemployment was (and still is in many areas) dominant, and

[3] Nelson Werneck Sodré, *A Revolução Brasileira* (Rio de Janeiro: Livraria José Olímpio, 1958), p. 46.
[4] Hélio Jaguaribe, *O Nacionalismo na Atualidade Brasileira* (Rio de Janeiro: Instituto Superior de Estudos Brasileiros, 1958), p. 41.

consequently productivity and wages were extremely low. Therefore, when the peasant went to the city and took a job in industry,
his standard of living improved markedly. This is the urbanization
process common to all countries which have undergone an industrial revolution. From 1940 to 1950, the rural population increased
18%, while the urban population increased 45%. Brazil's population continues to be predominantly rural (about 60%), but in the
state of São Paulo more than half of the population (52.6%) is
already urban.[5] Today, the Brazilian lower classes as a whole,
peasants and especially industrial workers, receive better education and can afford better food than before. As the planter begins
to disappear or to lose power, society begins to become more
democratic.[6]

During the past thirty years, the middle class has undergone
change. Perhaps it is not proper to speak of the appearance of
entirely new sectors within the middle class, as occurred in the upper and lower classes, but the transformation is significant. At present, the middle class is probably the social class that is undergoing
the greatest internal change. Structural changes in the upper and
lower classes took place primarily in the thirties and forties, but
the most important changes in the middle class are occurring now.

Three fundamental trends characterize the development of the
middle class since the National Revolution: progressive integration of its members into the productive process; rapid growth;
and diversification.

Integration: The middle class was basically a marginal group,
primarily composed of public officials and employees who were
not supposed to work hard since they did not have much to do.
Now, they begin to participate efficiently in productive activities.
The industrial sector itself demands a large number of persons to

[5] Census of 1940 and 1950.
[6] These social and economic changes occurred throughout Brazil, but they
varied very much in intensity, depending upon the region. The center-west
and the north continued to be nearly deserted. Brasília, among other things,
is an attempt to solve this problem. The Industrial Revolution occurred in
the South, particularly in the triangle formed by the cities of São Paulo,
Rio de Janeiro, and Belo Horizonte. The Northeast, which presents a relatively high density of population, did not industrialize; it has remained basically agricultural and semi-feudal. According to the Equipe da Renda Nacional da Fundação Getúlio Vargas, in 1956 the per capita income in the
South was 18,431.60 *cruzeiros* against 5,132.60 *cruzeiros* in the Northeast.

serve as middle-level employees. But service industries that develop with industrialization and the formation of an internal market—commerce, banks, transportation, utilities, advertising agencies, real estate companies, fiscal and legal organizations, brokerage offices, the professions, and an infinite number of other small organizations—also offer employment opportunities to the growing middle class. Even the public service itself is involved in this transformation. During the colonial and semi-colonial period, the government had three functions: to maintain order, to administer justice, and to give employment to the old middle class, whose members were frequently distant relatives of members of the upper class. Now, the government is an active participant in the development process. Several companies owned by the Federal or State governments have been created, such as the Companhia Siderúrgica Nacional, Petrobrás, the Fábrica Nacional de Motores, the Usinas Elétricas do Paranapanema (USELPA), etc., in which the need and the struggle for efficiency is obvious. In the departments of Federal, State, and municipal governments, there is observed an increasing comprehension of the urgency of better organization, and strong desire for political morality. Examinations for admission into the public services become established practice, at least for the lower positions. The middle class as a whole—the "old" middle class, which was in existence before 1930, as well as and particularly the "new" middle class, which grew as a product of industrialization—becomes more and more integrated into the productive process.

Growth: Rapid growth is the second trend observed in the recent development of the middle class. Integration into the productive process results necessarily in growth. The middle class becomes a significant sector of the Brazilian social structure.

It is mainly the rise of the middle classes that makes the new Brazil basically different from the old, which had no place for such classes. The descendants of ambitious immigrants, the too-numerous sons of aristocratic families (families which had not yet employed birth control), all join the liberal profession, the public services, commercial business, the Army, industry, forming an individualistic society. . . .[7]

In the great cities, especially in São Paulo and Rio de Janeiro, this phenomenon is evident, but even in the small cities of the hinter-

[7] Jacques Lambert, *Le Brésil, structure sociale et institutions politiques* (Paris: Colin, 1953).

land, in the South, the middle class has emerged as a modern capitalistic system replaces the social system of the plantation.

There are no statistical data concerning this growth. Social research in Brazil is only beginning. In spite of its lack of accuracy, however, the testimony of Tobias Barreto, in his *Discurso em Mangas de Camisa*, a speech delivered at Escada in 1877, is illuminating. He declared that:

> With respect to these three thousand souls, or rather, with respect to these three thousand bellies, the following estimate is fairly reliable:
> 90% are impoverished persons, living almost in indigence
> 8% survive only with difficulty
> 1.5% live well
> 0.5% are relatively rich.[8]

In this estimate, the absence of a middle class is striking. Today, the picture is radically different. A study of the distribution of the Brazilian population was undertaken by the journal, *Desenvolvimento e Conjuntura*, based upon the Census of 1950. The study divides the population into five classes (lower, lower-middle, middle, upper-middle, and upper) and distributes the labor force among these five classes using only one criterion, that of occupation. The first task was to classify the labor force according to occupation (Table 1). From this table was derived a tentative

TABLE 1. BREAKDOWN OF LABOR FORCE ACCORDING TO OCCUPATION

OCCUPATION	THOUSANDS
I — Domestic employees	795
II — Unskilled workers and employees	10,692
III — Privates (in the armed forces) and similar individuals	151
IV — Office and commercial employees with a minimum of skill	792
V — Skilled workers and employees (and semi-skilled workers)	2,194
VI — Soldiers and middle-level employees, with functions of direction or supervision, and rural and urban artisans	665
VII — Liberal professions, intellectuals, and officers of the armed forces	276
VIII — Business managers	152
XI — Enterprise owners	779

Source: *Desenvolvimento e Conjuntura* (Rio de Janeiro: Confederação Nacional da Indústria, October 1958), p. 99.

[8] Quoted by Guerreiro Ramos, *A Redução Sociológica* (Rio de Janeiro: ISEB, Ministério da Educação, 1958), p. 38.

breakdown of the Brazilian population into the different social classes (Table 2).

TABLE 2. SOCIAL CLASSES IN BRAZIL *(tentative breakdown)*

SOCIAL CLASS	THOUSANDS	%
Lower (groups I/III)	11,638	70
Lower-middle (groups IV/V)	2,986	18
Middle (group VI)	926	6
Upper-middle (groups VII/VIII)	428	2
Upper (group IX)	729	4*

Source: Ibid.
* Not representative of the upper class.

The inaccuracy of the breakdown presented in Table 2 is obvious. Occupation is certainly one of the criteria for measurement of the social structure of a society, but it is certainly not the only one. Yet, since a better classification is not available, this one will aid in understanding the Brazilian social structure. It is necessary to underscore its many inaccuracies, for in this classification one inaccuracy exceeds all others. Group IX does not represent by any means the upper class. Actually, most enterprise-owners should be considered as members of the upper-middle or even the middle classes, since their businesses are frequently very small: 80% of Brazilian industrial units employ less than ten persons.[9] Probably less than 1% of the population should be considered as belonging to the upper class of Brazil.

Analyzing the data above, it is possible to observe that the middle class, even if the lower-middle were not included, already constitutes a significant part of the population. But there is no reason not to consider the lower-middle as part of the middle class. It is exactly that part of the population that is now entering the middle class. This is especially true of the skilled workers, whose standard of living has recently improved so much (part of Group V). It is also worthwhile to observe the Brazilian social pyramid, very large at its base (*see* Table 3). This is a characteristic typical of underdeveloped countries. The growth of the middle class in Brazil has not yet changed significantly the shape of her social pyramid. The lower class and not the middle class is still numerically dominant in Brazil.

The growth of the middle class, however, does not mean that

[9] *Source:* 1950 census.

the industrialization process has not had unfavorable effects upon the middle class. Representatives of the old middle class—many of whom have fixed incomes (generally from house rentals)—have been hurt by the process of industrialization, which has occurred during a highly inflationary period. These persons were forced to adapt themselves to quite a different way of life. And for them, as for many representatives of the old upper class (São Paulo's coffee planters, for instance, who used to call themselves "*Paulistas* of four hundred years*"*), this adaptation has not been easy.

TABLE 3. BRAZILIAN SOCIAL PYRAMID

Upper.	1%*
Upper-middle	2
Middle	6
Lower-middle	18
Lower.	70

* Assuming 1% for the upper class and leaving 3% undistributed.

Diversification: The third trend observed in the middle class is that of diversification. Specialization and division of work are much more highly developed in an industrial society than in an agricultural one. New professions, new types of activities appear, offering opportunities to the middle class (and to members of the lower class who wish to rise to middle-class positions). In a modern industrial corporation, for instance, a large number of new positions, positions of middle level or those between top management and the workers, are created. This middle group, and particularly staff and line middle management (we include in the definition of middle management the supervisory group also), that is now developing rapidly in Brazil, is probably the most representative part of a new middle class in an industrial society. This point will be made clearer when we take up the so-called second Industrial Revolution. There, the middle class and particularly middle management have their greatest opportunity to develop as a result of the formation of large-scale organizations.

The first Industrial Revolution marked the passage from mercantilism to industrial capitalism. In addition, it represented a definite blow to the feudal system, which lost its reason for being. In its place, so-called Manchesterian capitalism appeared. In the economic field, low productivity (compared with that of today); in the social field, urbanization; and in the political field, the ideology of liberalism—these were its essential characteristics. "This picture of capitalism, which was known to Marx and remained . . . an abstract model to which socialist criticism was directed, experienced, after the end of the nineteenth century, and particularly after World War I, very great transformations." [10] This was the second Industrial Revolution, which had its center in the United States.

If analysis of the first Industrial Revolution provides basic data for understanding the Brazilian Industrial Revolution, the second Industrial Revolution aids in comprehension of Brazil's present phase of development and its trends. The use of electricity for commercial purposes, the internal combustion engine, electromagnetic waves, physico-chemical discoveries, and the resulting mass-production techniques mark the start of the second Industrial Revolution. The development of large corporations, the rise in standards of living, middle-class growth, increase in social mobility, and the trend toward more equality of opportunity are among its basic consequences. "The change has been so great that, in retrospect, the typical factory of 1910 seems to have been closer to its great-grandfather, the artisan's workshop of pre-steam engine days, than to its own son, the modern mass production plant." [11] The emergence and tremendous growth of the "new" middle class represent the great social change brought about by the second Industrial Revolution. The "old" middle class in the industrialized countries—formed basically of small entrepreneurs (contrary to what happened in Brazil), farmers, and the so-called petty bourgeoisie—began to decline, while a new class of employees of middle level, serving directly or indirectly the large organizations, emerged. "Negatively, the transformation of the middle class is a shift from property to non-property; positively, it is a shift from property to a new axis of stratification: occupation." [12]

[10] Hélio Jaguaribe, op. cit., p. 83.
[11] Peter F. Drucker, The New Society (New York: Harper & Bros., 1949), p. 2.
[12] C. Wright Mills, White Collar (New York: Oxford University Press, 1953), p. 65.

III. THE ORGANIZATION AND IDEOLOGY OF BRAZILIAN LABOR [*]
Neuma Aguiar Walker [**]

Brazilian labor organization is considerably different from labor organization in the United States. In Brazil, labor unions were created by the state to serve as a primary source of support for the government and institutions of Getúlio Vargas; and the unions still function, with increasing unwillingness, under the supervision, direction, and control of the federal government.

In the United States, the creation and initial development of unions was in spite of, rather than because of, the government. Although they were frequently indebted to the government during the Roosevelt administration, they have achieved and preserved a basic autonomy from government control.

To understand Brazilian labor unions one must appreciate their formal structure. Unions are formed only with government permission. Possible membership is defined by the government. The individual unions—*sindicatos*—may only federate in legally prescribed and governmentally approved federations—*federações*. The federations may only join in similarly prescribed and approved confederations—*confederações*—which represent workers in different sectors of the economy. No organization may legally represent all unions; this is done by the Ministry of Labor, i.e., the government itself. Not only is the existence of Brazilian labor unions defined by a complex structure of law, but in many of their actions they must deal with the large, powerful, and bureaucratic organization of the Ministry of Labor.

The forms of Brazilian unionism are changing under the impact of national development and political crisis. Labor legislation, originally addressed to urban occupations, had been fully extended to rural occupations by 1962. As a consequence, many rural labor unions have recently been organized. Urban workers have also succeeded in creating an independent central union organization, although the law specifically forbids this.

*   *   *

[*] I would like to thank my husband Roger Walker and Irving Louis Horowitz for their many fruitful suggestions and criticisms, hopefully embodied in this essay. [NAW]

[**] Neuma Aguiar Walker is a graduate of Catholic University in Rio de Janeiro, and is now doing postgraduate work at Washington University, Department of Sociology and Anthropology.

There are Brazilian labor unions for workers, employers, and independent professionals. To form a union in Brazil the organizer must petition the Ministry of Labor with at least one third of the names of the members of an occupation in a given area. For the employers he must secure the names of at least one third of the owners of a given type of enterprise in a given area. Among other duties, a union is required to furnish legal assistance to its members, solve disputes between employers and employees, and cooperate with the "public powers" in the development of "social solidarity." [1]

Brazilians working in the money economy—employers, employees, and professionals—pay a union tax. Part of this tax goes to the union of their respective occupational category. However, union taxpayers are not necessarily union members. Many pay the union tax all their lives and ignore the union. The employee does not pay tax to his union directly. Employers discount the tax from wages and deposit it directly in the Bank of Brazil. In Brazil a migrant from the countryside may take some time to discover that unions exist. He may only find out about the union if he needs a lawyer in a dispute with his employer, if he needs a physician, if he wants to join a union-sponsored recreational club, or if he becomes involved in a strike.

Let us look at the financing of Brazilian unions. Money is crucial to union strength. Without funds a union can never engage in an extended strike. Several Brazilian unions have collapsed for insufficient funds to meet their minimum and routine obligations.

The union tax collected from each employee equals one day's earnings each year. (Employers pay according to their capital.) This is little enough to begin with, and the union receives only 54% of this amount. The remainder is divided between a Union Fund administered by the Ministry of Labor (20%), the Federation of Unions (20%), and the Bank of Brazil (6%). Not only does the state collect and distribute each union's income from the tax, but it also has some control over how the money is spent, thus effectively curbing strike funds.

Payments from the labor tax are not the union's only possible source of funds. It can also collect monthly contributions directly from members. But this process is also supervised and audited by

[1] Calheiros Bonfim and Silvério dos Santos (eds.), *Consolidação das Leis do Trabalho* (Rio de Janeiro: Edições Trabalhistas, 1963), Art. 514a, p. 94.

the state, which may cancel the license of a union if it finds that it is not in good financial standing, further increasing the union's dependence on the state. To compound this financial dependence, the high rate of inflation makes saving almost impossible. If a union does have funds and tries to strike, the government can freeze the union's accounts in the Bank of Brazil.

But a union is not likely to have enough money for a long strike in any event. For example at the end of 1960 the Printing Industry Union of Guanabara (the State encompassing the city and environs of Rio de Janeiro) had enough money to pay its 6,912 members the minimum wage for less than one third of a day; and an estimated 86% of the union members earned more than the minimum wage at that time. The union had had no unusual expenses during the previous year.

Yet this extended and constraining structure of law and regulation is part of a larger system of labor legislation and institutions which have greatly improved the lot of the Brazilian worker. Although the union financing is generally inadequate for independent contests of strength with employers, it does provide a minimum of funds for legal aid (usually suing the employer), medical expenses, and other worthwhile union welfare activities. The basic problems of settling disputes with employers are generally handled through a system of labor tribunals.

Before the time of Getúlio Vargas, employers usually handled their labor problems by calling the police or by simply dismissing some workers. As Vargas' presidential predecessor, Washington Luís, once remarked: "The problem of labor is a case for the police." Vargas' system of labor tribunals has three levels: the lower handles individual grievances; the intermediate handles collective disputes; and the higher handles cases beyond the jurisdiction of the lower two, such as constitutional problems, and appeals and deadlocks from the lower courts. Each tribunal consists of a Labor Judge appointed by the government, and a representative from both the employees' unions and the employers' unions. The union representatives are selected by the government from a group of candidates elected by each union.[2]

The tribunals gave a great deal to the workers. For the first time they had a right to present their grievances and hope to receive

---

[2] José Albertino R. Rodrigues, "Estrutura Sindical Brasileira," *Revista de Estudos Sócio-Econômicos*, XII (January-February, 1963), pp. 9-10.

just consideration. The tribunals imposed restraints on the employers, which were resented. (Vargas' policies, however, also allowed the employers to earn substantial profits.) [3] The employers have never regarded the labor tribunals as entirely legitimate, and, in general, their lawyers try to obstruct and delay the proceedings of the tribunals. In turn the workers' lawyers bring pressure to hasten the procedures and at times the workers strike toward this same end. In an inflationary situation, time is very much to the advantage of the creditor.

The labor tribunals, which have so greatly increased justice in the situation of the Brazilian workers, and which, in part, continue to do so, also act to restrain the workers' acquisition of greater political power, certain to yield more of the benefits but less of the burdens of national development. The system of representation in the tribunals is one of the few channels through which union leadership is taken over by the lower echelons of government. The system of directing labor disputes through an agent of the government, when combined with the near elimination of strike funds, also greatly reduces both the incentives and the resources necessary for the union to develop as an independent and powerful agent of class action.

The government exercises direct control over the leadership of each union. The law states that each union may have from three to seven formal leaders, elected by the members (usually with a high proportion voting in shop elections) and approved by the Ministry of Labor, but the government may substitute its own appointees for positions of union leadership. In 1947 most union leaders were appointed representatives of the Ministry of Labor.

Another factor leading to government control of the unions and union leaders is the system of Federations and Confederations. Five or more unions may constitute a Federation. Three or more Federations may constitute a Confederation. The total number of Confederations is regulated by law. The Union of the Workers in the Printing Industry, for instance, belongs to the National Federation of Workers in the Printing Industry and to the National Confederation of Industrial Workers. When the union elects its leaders, it also elects representatives to the Federation. The Federation, in turn, sends representatives to the Confederation. As

[3] *Ibid.*

occurs with the labor representatives in the tribunals, union leaders are generally selected as representatives to the Federation. There, they may be promoted in the union structure and be elected as union presidents. They may also be selected as representatives to the Confederation. The positions in the Confederation are significant. Generally they lead to important political appointments either in the Ministry of Labor or in Social Security Institutes.

Union membership in international associations is allowed only by permission of the Ministry of Labor. Although some grouping of unions is permitted, unions cannot have a central coordinating body. The center is the government itself. Despite this law, union leaders have succeeded in creating a Central Command of Workers—the C.G.T., *Comando Geral dos Trabalhadores*. There are now and have previously been other attempts to create central groups, but C.G.T. played a key role in the recent restoration of presidential government and has emerged as the most important.

Another important feature of Brazilian unionism derives from the definitions of occupational categories used by the Ministry of Labor. These usually define the unions on an industrial or commercial rather than craft basis. Those occupational categories which, in a given area, have too few members to support a union are grouped by the Ministry of Labor. Within any category only one union is allowed.

Each union is a grouping of several occupations, made necessary by the grouping of occupational categories, and the combined effect of low union income per member and obligatory union services which are very costly for small numbers of people. This has an important consequence for leadership: there generally are status differences between the occupations, and leaders tend to be recruited from the higher-status occupations. In the writer's study of the printing industry union in Guanabara State the linotypists were high status (better paid, better educated, higher prestige) and the pressmen were a medium-status occupation within the union. Proportional to their members, there were almost three times as many linotypists as pressmen elected to the union leadership.

The short duration of strikes in Brazil is at first surprising to the outside observer. Data are scarce for the whole country, but we have figures for the State of São Paulo in 1960 and 1961: [4] in 1960 there were 180 strikes stopping work in 954 enterprises. More than one quarter million workers participated at a loss of more than three and one quarter million man-hours, a mean of twelve hours per man, and an estimated mean strike duration of one and one-half days. In 1961 there were 154 strikes stopping work in 980 enterprises. Nearly one hundred and sixty thousand workers participated at a loss of more than three million man-hours: a mean of eighteen hours per man, and an estimated mean strike duration of two and one-quarter days.

The main reason for such short strikes is that there is little money in either the unions' or the workers' savings. Small salaries and the high cost of living make it hard for workers and their families to pay for a strike. Short strikes are an illegal but tolerated practice of pressuring the labor tribunals for early and favorable decisions.

Although short strikes are the rule, long strikes do occur. The improvised cooperatives set up to supply food and essentials to the money-less strikers are described in the following examples:

. . . In the strike of the workers in the Meatpacking industry of Nilópolis [Rio de Janeiro State] in August 1961, that lasted for 26 days, commissions were constituted to collect emergency funds. The 85 days' strike of the workers in the Santo André textile factory [State of São Paulo], in 1959, organized "collecting commands"—as they were called. These commands made propaganda in the city justifying the strike, and collected money and other donations: food, clothes, and other necessities. They also held a "meeting for collecting." In the last days of the strike they had already raised more than fifteen hundred thousand cruzeiros, having organized a store for supplying the strikers.[5]

Jover Telles writes [6] about the strike among the textile workers, in Recife, Pernambuco (1952). The labor tribunal had decided that the employers should give the workers a raise of 30%. But they refused to accept this, indicating that they would appeal to the higher court. The union, then, decided to strike. Thirty-seven thousand workers in the textile industry from Recife and sur-

---

[4] *Revista de Estudos Sócio-Econômicos*, V (January 1962), p. 23.

[5] Jorge Miglioli, *Como são feitas as Greves no Brasil?* (Rio de Janeiro: Editôra Civilização Brasileira, 1963), p. 56.

[6] Jover Telles, *O Movimento Sindical no Brasil* (Rio de Janeiro: Vitória, 1962), pp. 59-61.

rounding areas struck for one week. Commissions of finances collected money from the people in Recife, and workers and peasants gave contributions. The dockworkers gave more than one thousand cruzeiros, porters gave ten thousand, and the Peasant League of Iputinga brought supplies. The employers agreed to pay the raise and pay for the days of strike.

Brazilian union leaders are learning the fundamentals of class conflict: organization and solidarity. They are beginning to measure their potential strength and to grope for a line of action independent of the web of government supports and controls.

Brazil's long-delayed industrialization was given unexpected aid by World War I. An increased demand for raw materials and reductions in the supply of manufactured goods greatly stimulated investment in local industry.[7] By 1920 there were 13,500 industrial establishments in Brazil employing 293,600 workers. That same year there were more than 1.5 million immigrants. Among them were industrial workers and craftsmen of Italian, Portuguese, Spanish, and German origin; many established themselves in the growing industries of Rio and São Paulo.

They brought with them European working-class ideologies and formed the first militant groups in the national proletariat. Their main ideology was anarchism,[8] and the anarchists were active in Rio and São Paulo. They organized many strikes, distributed publications, and held meetings, but their anti-organization ideology prevented them from building effective working-class organizations. They had also to contend with harsh suppression from the government. Government attitudes toward labor were contemptuous. In 1922 the Brazilian Communist Party was created.

During this period the country was governed by an aristocratic establishment, dominated by the coffee planters of São Paulo. The electoral process was completely under their control, with a public ballot.

Of that epoch Vargas said:

Brazilians in their own land did not have the right to govern themselves. The workers had no rights: neither as workers nor as Brazil-

7 "O Brasil em Números," Appendix to *Anuário Estatístico do Brasil—1960* (IBGE—Conselho Nacional de Estatística), pp. 8, 42.

8 Everardo Dias, *História das Lutas Sociais no Brasil* (São Paulo: Edaglit, 1962), pp. 41, 209.

ians. Brazil lived as a colony, her wealth flowing out of the country. Under the banner of liberalism the government was always an oligarchy. Power was transferred by family succession, and governments had no knowledge of public life. . . . The examination of this half century of the republic may offer the casual observer a picture of stagnation, so shocking was the gap between social reality and its legal expression. But reality was quite different. We passed from monoculture to industrialism. Populations multiplied and developed a natural complexity reflecting the division of labor and the growing variety of social groups. The institutions remained apathetic and closed to the influences of general progress. There was constant maladjustment between political organization and socio-economic life.[9]

In 1930 Vargas ran for President against the government's chosen candidate. He was declared the loser. He declared the election fraudulent, which it probably was, and started a revolt. His success was certainly helped by the New York stock market crash, which had dropped the price of coffee and disorganized and demoralized the coffee barons.

The victorious revolt brought Vargas to an unsteady pinnacle of power, facing revolts from the displaced coffee barons, the fascist right, and the communist left. He derived his power from the army, the urban capitalists, and especially the urban working class —the laborers of Brazil. His famous *"Trabalhadores do Brasil!"* became a rallying cry in every city throughout the land.

To gain the support of labor he had to compete with anarchism and communism. In this he succeeded, with his complex union legislation. As a nationalist he restricted foreign participation in union leadership. Favoring class and national solidarity he opposed communism as an "exotic ideology" and a "non-Brazilian doctrine." [10] The communist union influence was restricted by requirements of certificates of political health for all union leaders. The certificate was issued by the police. Controls tightened mainly after the unsuccessful communist revolt of 1935.

Vargas also increased and centralized the power of the federal government over that of the States. He believed that the previous regime erred seriously by failing to do this. His labor legislation and administration were a product of his drives both

[9] Hans Klinghoffer, *La Pensée Politique du Président Getulio Vargas* (Rio de Janeiro: Impresa Nacional, 1942), pp. 41, 48.
[10] Hans Klinghoffer, *op. cit.*, pp. 495-508.

for labor support and for centralized control. He introduced a wide range of labor welfare legislation, where almost none existed before. The capitalists did not complain much, for he made sure that they had opportunities for tremendous profits. He encouraged both capital and labor to unite their efforts in building the country.

His labor legislation included: annual paid vacations of two weeks, pregnancy and childbirth leave of absence with half pay, forty-eight-hour maximum work week, 10% to 25% higher wages, better working conditions in unhealthy industries, no child labor below fourteen years of age, retirement and disability pensions.[11]

This partial list is impressive by any standards. His achievements for urban workers compare very favorably with Roosevelt's New Deal legislation in this area. Germani well describes what these new rights meant to the workers:

... The affirmation of certain rights in his immediate workplace, in the same environment he had considered humiliating, meant a partial liberation of his feelings of inferiority and affirmation as an equal human being.[12]

Vargas' *Trabalhismo* brought mass democracy to workers who were previously marginal. They began participating in national life as a major social force. But we should view it in historical perspective. The many benefits were given to the workers through institutions which bound them to the central government. Now, thirty years later, after a generation of participation in industrial life, the workers and their leaders are demanding autonomy to solve their own problems, independent of the government and its slow-moving bureaucracy.

Brazilian labor's role in politics sharply contrasts with labor's role in the United States. In the United States the prevailing labor ideology has been described as "economism," the pursuit of economic security and welfare goals, and dealing with non-aligned political organizations as a means to these ends. There are exceptions, but the expressed ideology and visible activity of the present leadership of the AFL-CIO seem to fall within this description.

11 Karl Lowenstein, *Brazil Under Vargas* (New York: The Macmillan Co., 1942), pp. 341-51.
12 Gino Germani, *Política y Sociedad en una Epoca de Transición* (Buenos Aires: Paidos, 1962), p. 244.

At the top of the hierarchy in which every legal Brazilian union is embedded is the Minister of Labor. This is a high-ranking cabinet post and a political appointment. It is as subject to the uncertainties of tenure as is any cabinet post. President Goulart became a central figure in national politics as Vargas' most dedicated and controversial Labor Minister. In the past the labor unions generally accepted their role within governmental structure. The few attempts at independent action may have reduced government support, but did not gain labor its freedom. The change came at a moment of acute national crisis—Jânio Quadros' resignation in August 1961. Since then some independent labor organizations have gained some power and momentum of their own, and politicians of both left and right vie to keep pace with, and control, the rising force.

In August 1961 there was the first attempt at a general strike. About this event Jorge Miglioli writes:

. . . The first [political strike] happened in the final days of that year (1961), during the occasion of President Jânio Quadros' resignation and aimed at opposing the possible military pressure that may have caused the resignation, and, after, the effective military pressure that attempted to impose on the country a military dictatorship of the right. . . . There was not really a general strike, but several uncoordinated strikes, of some occupational categories in some States. In fact the appearance of an unexpected crisis in national politics and the lack of a central command of workers made it impossible for these strikes to be more organized and to involve more people. . . .[13]

In that crisis the government, insofar as it existed, was in no position to act, in addition to being unfriendly to the constitutional successor, Vice President João Goulart—the unions' natural choice.

In June 1962, after Goulart had ascended to a Presidency shorn of its power and largely controlled by a conservative Congress, union leaders made a series of declarations on the national situation. They insisted upon a more active voice in politics. They demanded basic reforms. The conservative Congress elected a conservative prime minister and refused the candidate that had the most progressive program at that time. The powerless President gave his support to the workers, which constituted a general

[13] Miglioli, *op. cit.*, pp. 115-16.

command to strike. This group was composed mostly of transport workers. They called for a one-day general strike to demonstrate to Congress that the workers were alert to the dangerous political situation.

This strike laid the groundwork and organization for the longer general strike made eighty days later. Jover Telles describes the response to the call to strike in the key State of Guanabara. He cites total adherence from transport workers, metal workers, shoemakers, bank workers, and partial adherence of textile workers, workers in the printing industry, construction workers, employees in the light and gas companies, woodworkers, and garment workers.[14]

The second general strike was made in September 1962. Among other demands it required an immediate plebiscite on the return to presidential government for Brazil. This time the strike lasted three days and from north to south the work of the country came to a halt. It was victorious. Until the strike, Congress had decided that the plebiscite would be made only in 1965, when President Goulart would finish his term. The plebiscite was made in January 7, 1963. The transport workers, the core of C.G.T. *(Comando Geral dos Trabalhadores)* * were guaranteed payment during the strike days (the government was able to do this through its control of transport). President Goulart remained in control.

After these successes labor, for the first time organized for independent action, became more conscious of its power. Previously it had directly depended on government. During those months the President had directly depended on labor. From this time dates the struggle of the C.G.T. leaders to become legally independent of presidential power. While President Goulart had to keep the balance between left and right in the country, C.G.T. leadership pressured him more to the left as its leadership is composed mostly of communists and socialists. The President had always been sympathetic to labor, but the leaders were not willing to give up the power they had won and to return to the previous submission to the state. The Sorelian formula of independence through the gen-

<hr/>

[14] Telles, *op. cit.,* p. 179.

* C.G.T. has been the symbol used by several Latin American countries to identify their central labor organization. The model for this has been the French trade unions, which set the style for labor organization and struggle in many countries of Latin America.

eral strike was resurrected. The workers demanded basic reforms: land reform, the vote for illiterates and soldiers, approval of a law giving workers more freedom to strike.

Government moved to regain control of the situation. The leadership of the National Confederation of Industrial Workers was given to a man sympathetic to the President.[15] Oswaldo Peralva reports that after that there was a more moderate tone to the threats of the Comando Geral dos Trabalhadores (C.G.T.) for a general political strike. At the same time there was a movement to organize a União Sindical Trabalhista (U.S.T.) whose major ideology is trabalhismo (Vargas' ideology of labor). The Revista Trabalhista [16] calls it a third union force, or an independent force from communists or right-wing movements in labor. However, some of their leaders are from Vargas' time and represent the old labor dependence. Adherence to União Sindical Trabalhista or to Comando Geral dos Trabalhadores largely depends on ideological preferences; the latter, however, has a more active record.[17] Both organizations have a common demand for more striking power and freedom from labor tribunals, although U.S.T. also admits the legitimacy of government arbitration of disputes.

The Comando Geral dos Trabalhadores continues its orientation toward general strikes for independence and other gains. One event was the strike of the bank workers, when C.G.T. threatened a general strike if their wage raise was not granted. Another was a strike in São Paulo of 700,000 workers for a wage raise. It is reported that the Minister of Labor urged the workers not to strike. But his plea failed. The general strike seems to be becoming established as a means of collective class action for both political and economic ends.

The strikes remain short but effective because of the numbers who participate. In cities where a mass of poor immigrants pours in from the countryside, factories can easily recruit new workers, and men fear for their jobs. When the strike is massive, the strikers have less to fear.

While the trabalhismo of União Sindical dos Trabalhadores

---

[15] Oswaldo Peralva, "A Esquerda Positiva nos Sindicatos," Caderno Especial do Jornal do Brasil, August 18, 1963, p. 6.

[16] C. A. Monteiro, "Terceira Força Sindical," Revista Trabalhista, XIV (1963), p. 19.

[17] Peralva, op. cit., p. 6.

(that comprises mainly the federation of metalworkers of São Paulo) and the socialism of the *Comando Geral dos Trabalhadores* (comprising mostly the transport workers of the country whose main support is in Guanabara) are not irreconcilable ideologies, there is a third independent labor group, the *Movimento Sindical Democrático* (comprising the Confederation of Workers in Commerce) whose ideology is conservative.* They are unofficially under the influence of Carlos Lacerda. He seems to have exploited their preferences for paternalism to catch their support.

The rest of the labor movement is pushing for basic social reforms. For this reason they have been intolerant of any move of the President to compromise with the right.

As was mentioned, skilled, semi-skilled, and unskilled workers all belong to the same union. The skilled workers tend to have higher education, incomes, and job prestige. For this reason they tend to be elected to leadership positions more frequently. (We cited earlier a case where the skilled were about three times more likely to be elected than the semi-skilled.)

In contradiction to the commonly held proposition that higher-status workers tend to abandon working-class interests and identifications, several studies of class identification in Brazil suggest that:

(1) More skilled workers sometimes identify with higher classes, but more frequently they identify with the working class even more strongly than lower-status workers.

(2) The higher-status workers tend to be more active in class (particularly union) activities.

In the following table it will be noticed that the highest skilled groups more frequently identify with the *working class (classe operária)*, and the semi-skilled and unskilled workers more frequently identify with the *labor class (classe trabalhadora)*.

Identification with the labor class is identification with the class to which Vargas appealed. Vargas did not address the workers as *operários*. He spoke to them as *trabalhadores*. Unions carry the name *trabalhadores* in their titles, while the party of Vargas' followers is called *trabalhista*, and *trabalhismo* is its ideology.

* The fact that a federation is affiliated with any of the three central labor organizations does not necessarily entail a commitment on the part of any specific union to the political policies of the federation to which it is affiliated.

TABLE: SKILL AND CLASS IDENTIFICATION AMONG WORKERS IN
THE PRINTING INDUSTRY OF THE STATE OF GUANABARA

Class Identification	Skilled	Semi-skilled	Unskilled	Others *	
Middle and	22.0%	16.2%	7.8%	22.2%	
Upper	(27)	(13)	(5)	(6)	
Labor	24.4%	52.5%	51.6%	44.4%	
	(30)	(42)	(33)	(12)	
Working	36.6%	25.0%	32.8%	22.2%	
	(45)	(20)	(21)	(6)	
Poor	12.2%	6.2%	7.8%		
	(15)	(5)	(5)	11.1%	
No Answer	4.8%	—	—		(3)
	(6)				

* Others include both white-collars and janitors.

Operário, although it also refers to a worker, implies a higher degree of urban sophistication. It is more often used by radical groups. Before the establishment of Vargas' *trabalhismo,* militant left-wing groups always used the word *operário* in their titles. Nowadays militant groups are more likely to use the word *operário,* than the thoroughly established, and slightly conservative-tinged, word *trabalhador.*

In the study, the greater use of the self-identification of *trabalhador* by the lower status groups reflects a more conservative, straightforward acceptance of the established definitions of the urban worker.

Other studies support these results. Soares' analysis of 457 interviews collected in Rio de Janeiro contained the same association between occupational status and class identification.[18]

Asis Simão made a study of working-class districts in São Paulo. He notes that recent rural migrants tend to prefer the Brazilian Labor Party, which is *trabalhista;* but that long-time residents of the city tend to prefer the Communist Party, which is *operário.*[19]

Lowy and Chucid, in their study of the metalworkers' congress, state that the higher the status among the metalworkers' leaders, the more radical they were. They also reported that the metal-

[18] G. A. D. Soares, "Community of Orientation, Aspirations, and Value Differentials." Unpublished paper.
[19] Asis Simão, "O voto Operário em São Paulo," *Anais do Primeiro Congresso Brasileiro de Sociologia* (São Paulo, 1955), p. 211.

workers' leaders named communists and socialists as the best leaders. The majority of the leaders stated the opinion that the strike is the workers' best weapon, and that the labor tribunals tend to favor the employers over the employees.[20] Highly skilled urban workers with high incomes and education characterize labor union leaders. They are generally highly radical, and identify with the workers and illiterate masses.

Lower skill, lower education, lower income, and rural origin are generally negatively correlated with union leadership and positively correlated with *trabalhismo*.

These findings may be interpreted in terms of Marx's theory where the recent migrants constitute the *lumpenproletariat* who are less class-conscious than the urban industrial workers who have lived in the area a long time, and through interaction with other workers (we should also add through literacy and education) acquire class-consciousness.[21]

The leaders' status and ideology help us to understand why they formed the *Comando Geral dos Trabalhadores*, why they oppose labor tribunals, and why they are fighting for more freedom to strike. Not only does their tendency to identify themselves as *operários* indicate that they are more radical; it also indicates that they are likely to identify with the uneducated urban and rural masses who have not even risen to the bottom of the industrial class structure. In fact, to be a worker in Brazil is already a privilege if one compares the situation of the urban labor force with the situation of the agricultural labor force. In the urban labor force about 20% are unionized.[22] From these, a smaller proportion constitutes the leadership. Highly skilled men are relatively scarce and there is high demand for them. In this sense the leaders are the most privileged of their class. But their relative positions also create the conditions by which they see more of the system and want to change it.

[20] M. Lowy and S. Chucid, "Opiniões e Atitudes de Líderes Sindicais Metalúrgicos," *Revista Brasileira de Estudos Políticos*, XIII (1962), pp. 132-69.

[21] Karl Marx, "The Class Struggles in France, 1848 to 1850," in L. S. Feuer (ed.), *Marx and Engels, Basic Writings on Politics and Philosophy* (Garden City, N.Y.: Doubleday & Co., 1959), p. 298.

[22] *Cadastro Sindical Brasileiro 1961*, Serviço de Estatística da Previdência e Trabalho, Ministério do Trabalho e Previdência Social.

IV. THE CRISIS IN BRAZILIAN SOCIETY AND ECONOMY

Luis Suárez *

A symbol of old Brazil is *Jeca-Tatú. Jeca* is a man who philosophizes meditatively. *Tatú* is an insect. The *Jeca-Tatú* is the condensation of both into a man of yellowish pallor and pointed chin who was always seated in his doorway. Malaria and listlessness kept him inactive, bent close to the ground, idle. This symbolic little man said sharp, penetrating things but he never stood erect. He listened to the cuckoos when they told him: "You have nothing planted." And he answered the cuckoos ambiguously: "The land is good. It yields fruit." He planted no more.

Present-day Brazil, risen over a dearth of dormant resources, also has its symbol. It is the *Candango*, builder of the country. *Candango* is a man who knows what he has and wants to make good use of it. *Candango* is the antithesis of *Jeca-Tatú*. I believe that nature and the different spheres of Brazilian development still support conditions for the *Jeca-Tatú*, but everywhere one observes the *Candango* spirit.

The shift in temper is also found in government circles. It points up the two types of Republic that emerge in twentieth-century Brazil. From 1900 to 1940, Brazil is a Republic of lawyers, that is to say, men imbued with a French-style cultural humanism, men who made, or were capable of making, wise laws which were inoperative in relation to material transformation. From 1940 on, the Republic gives birth to engineers and economists; that is, planners.

One frequently hears, however, from governors and planners: "In Brazil one uses the device of a *coup* or nothing gets done." They get busy on the spot or the bureaucracy consigns achievement to oblivion. And the bureaucracy can be menacing when it is drawing up plans slowly. Here the builder-*Candangos* throw themselves into action, a little surprised at the weight and antiquity of the bureaucratic machinery. Here, too, such realizations may become splintered into factions in marked contrast to general

* Luis Suárez was born and educated in Sevilla, Spain. He migrated to Mexico after the Spanish Civil War in 1939. He works as a journalist, and has contributed to many of the leading scholarly as well as popular journals. His contact with Brazil has been long and intimate, and he must be ranked a foremost commentator on Brazil in Hispanic America.

development; slow and complex, the split between bureaucrats and activists accentuates what is considered the existence of two or more Brazils.

Contemporary dreams of Brazilian development entail a conscious effort to conquer old Brazil by reaching beyond the flat lands into the immense Amazon basin. But on occasion, and conforming to the fatalistic conception that things are done by a *coup* or they aren't done, this force is not measurable in the general contingencies. It is a question of doing at any price . . . even if the cost is ignored.

The old eagerness for a new capital reflects this approach. Brasília is a marvelous illustration of the *Candango*. Located in the high table lands, 1,200 kilometers of highway and 900 by air from Rio de Janeiro, Brasília is not only a passionately conceived urban, architectural, and plastic assemblage; for those who are its enthusiastic defenders it shows Brazil's desire to conquer its own territory. Brasília poses the central question of how to convert a dynamic economic-administrative economy into an agrarian-industrial economy.

Brasília answers the desire to create a new Brazilian civilization of the Central-West, the desire to get Brazil out of its coastal orientation, thereby displacing what is known as the Atlantic civilization which is reflective of Europe. Brasília is a spearhead thrust into the interior. Of the 8.5 million kilometers of Brazil, 5 million are uninhabited. With Brasília a path is beaten toward these 5 million. But what the cost of this force is, in the primary stages of the whole design, no one knows. The impassioned defenders of Brasília answer their detractors: "This is like a war. Neither was the cost of 'D-Day' known when the Allies landed in Europe during World War II."

This development bears consequences in which all Brazil shares. Next to other determining factors, such as the character of industrialization and capitalization that brings about unrestricted foreign investment, the construction of Brasília, while it has revived certain half-dead areas, has contributed to the inflation that imprisons the country in a net from which it will only escape by a radical breakthrough.

Aside from idealistic symbolism and more or less literary definitions, a contradictory reality is imposed on Brazil, contradictions due to the continued gap between its physical possibilities and its social limitations, contradictions which are apparent from the equator to the southern tip of the nation. Within a single State several countries coexist, and it cannot be repeated often enough that Brazil sees itself as a continent. Yet considering Brazil as a unique national state, we can make many observations on the political parceling and the different governments of the States that form the union.

Its vast distances, the isolation, and unequal development of various regions should suggest that there are at least two Brazils: one from Rio de Janeiro to the South; the other, the North with its immense Amazon region and feudal Northeast. Of course, there are some areas toward the Central North, like Minas Gerais, that from the point of view of development may be considered part of southern Brazil, but then socio-economic generalizations create necessary distortions of geographic division.

Perhaps it should be recalled that Brazil has a surface of 8,511,-965 kilometers with a population density of 8.39 inhabitants per kilometer. This mean does not rest on any calculation that suggests an even distribution over all of Brazil, and despite it being minimal, it still gives a false picture, since the contrasts between the empty zones and those areas with great population concentrations are enormous. It would be valuable to get the mean of each of these two Brazils and then it would be understood what a spacious expanse is still unpopulated in Brazil. For the arithmetic mean of southern Brazil we would find cities like Rio de Janeiro with 3.5 million inhabitants and São Paulo with 4 million in a State totaling 13 million inhabitants, or 53.34 per kilometer.

In the North, at first sight, we find the most completely uninhabited regions. One State, Amazonas, has 1,558,987 kilometers and only 721,215 inhabitants; in other words, it has more than two-thirds of the surface area of Mexico and a population no larger than one of Mexico's cities, e.g., Guadalajara or Monterrey. Its demographic density is .46 inhabitants per kilometer. The region known as Amazonia comprises the Amazon States. Part of the States of Mato Grosso and Maranhão, with a total surface of 3,579,-991 kilometers and a population that in 1950 was 1,844,655 inhabitants and that at the present time does not reach 3 million, have the same population density as the Territories of Río Blanco, Amapú, and Rondonia.

In the Northeast, where the principal States are Ceará, Rio

Grande del Norte, Paraíba, and Pernambuco, the four great property expanses of the latifundists are concentrated. On these estates there dwells, in 1,220,000 kilometers, 20% of the population of that part of the country. The peasants live in desperate and explosive wretchedness. Not without reason has the Brazilian Northeast become famous, although this is due more to North American fears of revolutionary uprising than to its intrinsic significance. For example, in order to ship cement and iron into the States of the Amazon, it is necessary to carry it for thousands of kilometers by a vessel that sails the mouth of the Amazon River in Belém and travels for several days to Manaus, the State capital. I have heard it said to Governor Gilberto Mestrinho that "there is much talk of foreign colonialism, but in Brazil there is a Brazilian colonialism reaching from the South [into the North]."

The rough sketch of these contrasts can give an idea of the profound gravity of the problems: national ones from the point of view of the State; continental ones from the geographic limits and different degree of economic and social development.

No one can deny Brazil's industrial advancement. But this development finds itself strung together by an unending skein that is twisted by foreign investment, with its characteristic of receiving capital dividends and selling utilities for fabulous profits. Industrialization sets off an inflationary spiral. Inflation is one of the great evils recognized by the men of state. To control inflation S.U.M.O.C. (Superintendence of Money and Credit) has been created. It assumes 40% liability in interests in order to insure continued public works. It also limits the opportunity for profit through speculation on the part of particular banks. But Brazil is nonetheless one country where banks proliferate like trees in lush forests.

The state finds itself in the contradiction of either bridling or diminishing public works that, like Brasília, attract labor from regions of hunger, or contribute to inflation. Neither can it resist the workers' pressure for increased salaries. Since the workers are one hundred times better friends of the nationalist politician, who wants to set President Goulart "right" on social reform, than big capitalists and landholders, whose power limits the carrying out of necessary changes in the economic structure, inflation is used as a weapon for change. The state, if it enters a period of austerity, can thus bring on a major social upheaval.

Goulart, in his message to Congress in March 1962, called inflation "one of the most serious illnesses of the economic physique of Brazil." He recognized that because of the growing inflation, the general level of prices registered from December 1960 to December 1961 was higher by 7%. In 1961, Brazilian exports rose by 10% over 1960. The deficit of the commercial balance, which in 1960 had been $193 million, had been reduced to $57 million in 1961. For the same periods, the balance of payments deficit was $405 million and $130 million respectively. The President himself calculated that the financial deficit for 1962 would exceed the 1961 figure by as much as 250 million *cruzeiros*.

Brazil imports coal from England and the United States, and wheat from the United States, Argentina, and the U.S.S.R. She tries to increase foreign trade. From this stems the tendency in the most responsible government circles to step up all types of relations with the countries in the socialist camp. The European Common Market is seen as a threat which restricts the possibilities of Latin American trade, especially that of Brazil. Brazil already has pretensions common to more than a few Ibero-American countries (like Mexico) of conquering African and Asian markets, more because it cannot cope with competition from the advanced nations, than out of loyalty to these newer markets. Brazil, however, is in a position to sell certain manufactured goods, such as fabrics and electrical appliances. It is in the same situation in which Mexico finds itself regarding African-Asian markets.

Among other things, 20% of the duties are going to defray the deficit of operating the state-owned railway system. The state takes measures to cut down on railway lines and open highways. But to open highways in Brazil turns out to be a gigantic task since it is necessary to link centers that are thousands of kilometers apart. The construction of new highways at the highest inflationary price will face firm limitation during the financial austerity period announced by the government.

According to my source of information, the writer and economist of São Paulo, Caio Prado Junior (one of the editors responsible for the important *Revista Brasiliense* of the left), Brazilian export reaches up to 14 million dollars, but of this, 20% is spent on freight. Here is born the urgent need of a shipping industry, which in the opinion of Prado Junior ought to have preference over the automobile industry. This same economist estimates that the government deficit in 1962 will be 400 billion. When he made this calculation the *cruzeiro* was at least 400 to the U.S. dollar. On October 1, 1962, the exchange rate rose to 600 *cruzeiros* to the dollar.

The United States comprises approximately half of Brazil's foreign market. Rui Facó, author of *Brasil século XX*, tells us that in 1959, out of a total estimated at $1,310 million in export, the United States would absorb $600 million. Although imports have been diversified, $530 million out of the total $1,290 million in imported goods comes from the United States. The decline in international prices of coffee, which are set in New York, has been a loss to Brazil, as to all coffee-producing countries; but more so in Brazil where the export of coffee is the chief line of business.

Foreign capital, especially North American, has strengthened its position in Brazil amidst the great nationalistic ferment. Some industries defended and some nationalists opposed the invasion of foreign capital. To impede the development of national capital, and to control the trade, which has been encouraged by Goulart's policy, of certain industries with socialist countries, the North American monopolies have acted with cruel haste, anxious to curb this trade before it expanded. Associated with Brazilian straw men, state-sponsored capital investors try to buy small factories and plants. If they don't obtain them, Americans come to their aid with fine proclamations of helping to industrialize the country, while in fact hindering the development process through crippling rivalries.

Prado Junior, interpreting the contents of official statistics, said when I interviewed him *that in 1960, $400 million more left Brazil than came in in investments, and in 1961, $200 million more left than came into the country. That is to say, as confirmed by Franklin de Oliveira, and by one of the principal advisers of the opposition nationalist governments of Rio Grande do Sul, Leonel Brizola, foreign investments reap dividends in a country without capital.*

Of twenty enterprises with an annual gross income of more than *10 billion cruzeiros*, twelve are affiliated with or subsidiaries of great imperialist trusts, six belong to the state, and only two are national private enterprises. The draining out of the country of national material resources is considered one of the main causes of economic disturbance in Brazilian economic life, along with the constant devaluation of money, inflation, and rise of prices.

The expansion occasioned by increased shipments abroad of utilities has favored the speculations of foreign capital. The law against excess profits approved by the House of Deputies, and enforced by the Senate thus far only in the anxious situation of August and September (1961), limits the shipment of monies outside the country to 10% of applied capital. This percentage, in any case, is large enough to prevent foreign enterprises from going abroad.

The automobile industry, manufacturing 98% of all parts necessary to a whole car, is the broadest expression of Brazilian industrialization. But the penetration of foreign capital here also brings its sequence of negative consequences. The door was opened to it in 1955, under the Kubitschek government. The accessories for automobiles are considered capital investments, and encouraged by official preference. São Paulo is surrounded by factories, whose foreign names, addended with these magic words: *do Brasil*, mollify the nationalistic spirit, e.g., Ford Motors *do Brasil*, General Motors *do Brasil*, Willys *do Brasil*, etc.

In five years the automobile industry of Brazil has grown to the point where in 1961 it manufactured 130,000 vehicles. It employs some 120,000 persons. At first, automobile production developed on the basis of national capital. This was invested in the production of auto parts, particularly small repair parts easily manufactured. This alone engaged about 90,000 people. In this government-sponsored private-sector undertaking, the participation of the Bank of National Development figured prominently. This bank set aside money for the creation of the automobile industry, but only for the purpose of underwriting the establishment of foreign firms. Willys sold stock to Brazilian capitalists. Ford and General Motors, which owned outlets in Brazil, were in the country as manufacturers. Volkswagen brought West German capital. Mercedes-Benz is associated with Brazilian capital, but manufactures only a type of bus. The Japanese trademark Toyoda is also in Brazil.

Despite the positive aspects of these activities, the negative side of the auto industry weighs down the Brazilian economy. Caio Prado told me that the vehicles are now more expensive to consumers than if they were imported without the obstacle of exchange or custom rates; that they are more expensive to the Brazilian consumer than to their foreign consumers; and that this industry engenders a bleeding of foreign currency which might be avoided if the state would impel the development of a National Motor Industry, whose products might be as good as or better than those of the foreign firms lodged in Brazil. For Rui Facó, "the automobile industry established in Brazil is delivered up to the international monopoly powers. . . . The factories are theirs; the utilities are theirs; the domestic market is theirs. . . ."

The nationalist current, from outside and from within some sectors of the official apparatus, presses for high-powered action against these obstacles. But foreign monopolies try to adapt themselves to such exigencies. And they *nationalize* through the prompt and deceptive procedure of establishing their Holy See in Brazil. Thus they are not foreign enterprises but rather Brazilian ones. Their search for proper indemnification or sale of ancient obsolete public service enterprises, in return for keeping the money in the country for investment capital in a more productive branch, is another of the roads of national concessions to foreign business.

Among the most outspoken nationalist leaders, one finds Brizola, brother-in-law of Goulart. The government of Rio Grande do Sul has confronted this situation. Former Governor Brizola expropriated the Riograndense Electric Company, subsidiary of Bond and Share, and the National Telephone Company, subsidiary of International Telephone and Telegraph Company. In seizing the first, in 1959, the government deposited one *cruzeiro* before the judge as indemnification. The governor said that the foreigners had already extracted many times their investment from our country and that we did not want to pay for an outmoded service. For the expropriation of the telephone company, the government deposited $400,000, but before that it tried to keep the enterprise from leaving the country by allowing it to keep 25% of the stock. The corporation did not accept this offer, the refusal of which even provoked some comment from the Secretary of State of the United States, Dean Rusk. "All that's missing is that they may lead the triangle to defend the company," commented Brizola. This is the way Brizola expressed himself in front of me. "Before this, there was an iron fist over the exploitive process. Brazil is like a pierced tin can. It is useless to cover the top of it if one doesn't cover the bottom. An iron fist is needed, top and bottom, against the ransackers and international corporations and against the groups and classes that collaborate in this plundering process." President Goulart did not avoid this problem of the basis of Brazilian progress. Answering the question on the main problem of Brazil, among others, he extended it from foreign capital to the thing common to all Latin American countries: "All of them," he said, "need, like Brazil, to liberate their economies from the domination of foreign interests that oppress them and they also need to improve the social distribution of wealth with the aim of benefiting all social classes and not only a determined, privileged group."

The importance of the political crisis which took place in Brazil after Quadros' resignation is difficult to estimate. An optimistic civil servant, Carlos Mauro Cabral, coordinator of the Technical Assessment Committee of the President, told me that "Brazil grows independently of the political and financial facts," and added by way of explanation, "This is because Brazil is a country without certain rules, and in it surprising things may happen."

Although recognizing the inescapable mess of the inflationary spiral, Cabral saw that it is not the ruin of Brazil. Certainly in Brazil there are natural and social forces capable of preventing decline toward unbridgeable chasms; but it will not succeed without urgent social reforms. These are in the forefront of the national conscience: reform of banking procedures, a new fiscal policy, agrarian reform. The need for these is seen in the general consensus. But there are those who use the consensus demogogically and in reality resist facing facts. This is particularly so with representatives of big business and the latifundists in conjunction with their straw men of foreign companies. These groups represent a majority in Congress which should have been defeated in the last October 7 elections. These are the men that made it as difficult as they could for a democratic national government to develop. They were clearly committed to ruinous vested interests and privileges in a country of such immense wealth.

Nonetheless, these vested-interest forces find themselves limited in their actions by virtue of the development of state-sponsored enterprises like Petrobrás, or Eletrobrás, whose success depends in good measure on their independence of private control. They were first formed from electrical works like Furnas and Tres Marias, and from the Volta Redonda iron and steel works, all symbols of the defense of nationalist forces in the struggle against domination by foreign capital.

The pressure for agrarian reform is a consequence not only of the general principles of revolt which guide it, or of economic rationalization, but must be seen in the specific context of the Brazilian Northeast. Taking the data of Franklin de Oliveira, we can say that 70% of the Brazilian population live in rural areas and that 18% still live in a completely primitive state. Of 10 million people employed in agrarian activities in Brazil, only 18% are property owners. The poverty bred by this situation is most extreme in the Northeast. Using reliable testimony we can cite the information given on May 22, 1962, in the House of Deputies by a Commission made up of members of all the parties:

Of all we've seen and noted, of all we know about every sector of the nation, one truth is evident: the problem of hunger in the countryside of Brazil is simply explosive, in turmoil, offensive to human dignity. The phenomenon is explained: the last census taken in 1960 shows the country's population of the rural area approaches 40 million Brazilians. And what is the living standard for that immense population? Unfortunately the lowest in the world in its level of poverty, chronic hunger, social waste, chronic illness, illiteracy. . . . In the Northeast, the average life span is 27 years. In Brazil a child dies every 42 seconds, 85 per hour, 2,040 per day. . . . Forty million Brazilians live in our agricultural fields like pariahs, vegetating. And scarcely 4% own land.

The Deputies called upon the House in this manner: "We are going to make our revolution legally, Mister Deputies. Pay attention to the demands of the Brazilian people before it is too late. . . ." But in this very legislative group, which has already ended its session, there are already 51 projects for agrarian reform pending. President Goulart ended the session, still a prisoner of the constitutional changes that were imposed upon him in replacing Jânio Quadros, with a discourse on why everyone must accept the urgent demand for reform. At the leadership level, there exists the awareness that agrarian reform must be brought into being to avoid violent revolution. As the newspaper *Journal do Brasil* has said, it is better to lose the rings than the fingers of one's hand. The slogan of Congress was "agrarian reform through law or by force."

Everyone speaks of agrarian reform in Brazil: bishops, priests, professional politicians, and leaders of the disinherited mass. But there is a radical difference between types of agrarian reform. For some, only cultivated lands ought to be expropriated. That would leave a great degree of power with the cultivated latifundias. For others, the reform should be mediating payment for proper indemnification. Where would the state, entangled in its financial difficulties, be able to extract all the money required for such a chivalrous procedure? The real partisans of an effective reform request the nullification of article 141 of the Constitution, which accepts the expropriation of the land, but calls for the indemnification of the landowners. And the Congress that has just expired, with a majority representing landowners and capitalists, felt sympathy for the hunger and death of the peasants of the Northeast, but was not willing to take either this step or others more timid.

Many professional politicians, encrusted in the shell of party politics already traditional in Brazilian life, live off what in the Northeast is called the industry of drought, the cultivation of sugar cane. But drought severely ravages these lands, making diversification difficult. It has become habitual to speak of a solution based on public works and dam building, pump-priming remedies for poverty, without attacking the foundation of the problem which is the unjust distribution of property and its concentration of ownership in the hands of the latifundists. In the industry of the dry lands, credit is issued on the basis of what benefits the latifundists at the expense of the state.

Indicative of wealth as an irritant was the behavior of the Federal Deputy, Northeasterner Ademar Carvalho de Souza, who according to the *Diário de Pernambuco* of May 9, 1961, cited by Franklin de Olivereira, spent 20 million on a wedding and 4 million *cruzeiros* on only one meal.

I have held back some data on workers' earnings in order to drive home the contrast with the agrarian regions. The minimum salaries in the industrial regions are around 14,000 *cruzeiros* monthly in São Paulo, industrial center *par excellence*. There are some workers who earn up to 20,000 *cruzeiros* and skilled workers like the typographers can receive up to 40,000 a month. In general, the minimum salaries in the main population centers waver around 10,000 *cruzeiros*. In Recife, capital of Pernambuco and heart of the Northeast, the minimum salary is 10,080 *cruzeiros*.

These incomes are still low but infinitely higher than those of the peasant who, idle and landless, supports population centers such as Recife, a city that with 800,000 inhabitants has 250,000 unemployed. The peasants in Pernambuco, in Paraíba, and in other agricultural regions earn 50 or 100 or somewhat more *cruzeiros* a day, when one kilo of tapioca flour costs 150 *cruzeiros*. Forms of precapitalist labor exist in the *sertão*, or inland regions. There are some landowners who still pay workers in merchandise. The landowners who continue to operate in the style of the *white guard* in Mexico, seek only to punish the leaders of the Peasant Leagues.

The Peasant Leagues owe their name to their enemies in the press, who gave this name to the Agricultural and Cattle Breeding Society of the Pernambuco Planters, formed by the peasants of Galilea farm, who were later to be defended by the lawyer Julião, now internationally famous as the leader of these agrarian struggle groups in the State of Pernambuco and with influence in other regions of the country. Near Recife, in the city of Cabo, lives the priest Antônio Mello, who has become a kind of Julião of the cloth, although of course he does not go as far as the leader of the Peasant Leagues, who more than anyone insists on the necessity for reform. Mello minimizes the scope of the problem, although he too uses violent language at times. For the priest, the problem is not land reform, but the absence of technical assistance on the part of the government to the landholders. His aim is greater rationalization of land grants, and other guarantees to the peasants. He wants to bring to the country a type of paternalistic syndicalism without affecting the latifundias. There are other priests more openly on the side of change in the country, who strive for the needed agrarian reform in the only manner possible: the division of the latifundias.

The Brazilian government heeds the problem of the Northeast with an integral conception. The plans for its transformation for a long time will depend on a special organization: S.U.D.E.N.E. (Supervision of the Northeast), at the head of which is a brilliant economist, Celso Furtado, one of the men most fought by extremist opponents of all reform and who has been named minister without portfolio in the finance ministry, headed by Hermes Lima. But I doubt that fundamental agrarian reform involving the distribution of land can be postponed or delayed while "integral plans" are made. It is an immediate need for the peasant to become a true agricultural producer.

Almost all Brazilian political parties live under the effects of a general loss of prestige. There is an unimaginable number of parties on the national and State levels (or *estadual* as the Brazilians say in referring to the division of the country into States). This in turn reinforces personalism, the extra-party nature of certain political leaders. It helps to explain the career of Jânio Quadros up to the Presidency. Quadros, like all aspirants to a post based on public support, needed to register his candidacy under the banner of a political party. But his success consisted of his symbol, the broom, for a clean sweep, especially of the politicians entrenched in the infinite catalogue of organizations and groups called parties. This also explains the personal prestige of João Goulart, although in his case, it is a question of the Labor Party under Getúlio Vargas' record in the second nationalist epoch. Out of all the other party men, Goulart had the most widespread base.

By the number of deputies in the last Congress, the Social Democratic Party is the majority. No one ought to look at that party as an aggregate that resembles any of the variations of European social democracy. It is followed in strength by the National Democratic Union and the Brazilian Labor Party. The P.S.D. and the U.D.N. are both conservative parties. But they bear out the general rule for all in the sense that none can be considered an organization of national scope and clear-cut structure since these parties group around members of diverse tendencies. In making policy at the State level, they reach alliances which turn out to be directly antithetical to their national party platforms.

The reactionary character of their national direction does not prevent them, for example, from skillfully managing local forces of various kinds in order to succeed in getting a governor or deputy elected. It is public knowledge that in the parliamentary factions of the three parties mentioned there are people much more progressive than those directing their respective party lines, communists included. "In Brazil there is no more genuine political party than the Communist Party; the rest are shells and coteries." I have heard this said in São Paulo to one of the closer collaborators of Jânio Quadros. The Communist Party is not legal but neither can it be said that it is absolutely illegal. Its leaders are neither imprisoned nor persecuted, and can act and speak in the name of their party. Luís Carlos Prestes has just presented a petition for registration before the Supreme Court of the country. The petition was not approved by Chancelor Santiago Dantas; however, he did not deny registry to the Communist Party nor did he fear its presence in the democratic midst. This was consonant with his ardent defense of an independent foreign policy. Yet his position of non-interference attracted a whole battery of reactionary forces struggling to make Dantas' nomination for President impossible, at least for then, although these same critics proposed President Goulart.

The substantive reforms, as the immediately pressing essentials are called, involve a reform policy for the political parties, with the aim of making them more fully and frequently responsive to the social forces and political tendencies that they represent or say they represent.

But the most often waged campaign, next to social reform, in Brazil is bound up with the return of presidentialism. Fearing political coteries of popular and nationalist tendencies around João Goulart, precipitous constitutional reforms were effected to limit his presidential powers, on his rising from Vice President to become President—thus imitating the Europeans and resulting in a hybrid formula which crippled the governing of the country. Parliament, with its conservative majority, bridles Goulart's every progressive impulse.

The President, for his part, persevered in his position on a number of major issues. Had he retreated there would be no executive power left in Brazil today.

The constitutional "reforms" did not calculate that Goulart would demand a referendum to determine whether or not he was to be given presidential power to go along with the title. Goulart was "assured" that he would not be able to govern with full power. Goulart had known how to manipulate skillfully in order to eliminate the danger of new military pressure from the right-wing chiefs. As Commander-in-Chief of the military he went warily about disengaging and reordering military authority. And today the generals of the *coup* are in virtual retirement. Once at the head of the Army and military matters, they now found themselves *mílites* who attacked constitutionality represented by Goulart. The strikes and demonstrations had taken on a two-fold character of pressure on the government and support for liberalization of the Presidency. One of Goulart's chief enemies, the ultra-rightist governor of the State of Guanabara, Carlos Lacerda (Rio de Janeiro has become its State capital since the national capital was moved to Brasília), is geographically near to the commander of the First Army, General Alvinos. The latter has already issued orders to the troops on various occasions, warning of the danger that the vaunted anti-communism of Lacerda and others might entail, that it could bring a fascistic and reactionary regime to the country.

But when to ask for the plebiscite? The most radical forces insisted on its being held the same time as the legislative elections of October 7, 1962. Goulart could not impose such a date on an unprepared public. Choosing January 1963 frustrated many of the plans of those who wanted to prolong the condition of an almost handcuffed President, for Goulart had by then "cleansed" his administration. In Brazil, with the trade unions, enthusiastic students, and restless peasant organizations, there is new ground for political understanding, in a solid democratic and nationalist front against the intervention of foreign imperialist elements and the insupportable survival of feudal structures. Of course, the attitude on the Cuban problem is: no intervention with the right of the Cuban people to set up the kind of regime they want—an independent foreign policy. These are the substantive questions of the day.

V. COLONIALISM, HUNGER, AND PROGRESS
Josué de Castro *

Hunger, the most tragic expression of the economic complex of backwardness, is the most terrible and the most widespread disease in our world. It takes an enormous toll of human lives. Hunger is the reason for the demographic differences between the poor and rich countries, differences so pronounced that I would describe the highly developed countries as a world in which people are born to live upon the earth, whereas the poor countries are the kingdom of starvation and misery, a world in which people

* Josué de Castro is past President of the Executive Council of the United Nations Commission on Nutrition and Agriculture. He is a professor at the University of Brazil. He is perhaps best known for his book, *The Geography of Hunger*.

are born only to ascend to the heavens like the angels. Over half the population in these countries dies in childhood. This mortality rate creates a new geography, a geography in which not the earth feeds man but man feeds the earth with his body.

Why is it that in the world of today two-thirds of mankind go hungry? And why is it that hunger reigns in those parts of the world which we refer to as underdeveloped? In my view the main reason for the hunger in the world is colonialism. Here I would like to make an explanation. Someone may say that people went hungry long before the colonialist era was opened by the voyages of Vasco da Gama in 1498. Yes, hunger has raged at all times in history. But judge for yourselves. In the past people went hungry because they didn't have the technical and scientific means with which to combat it. In the non-colonial countries, in countries which are highly developed and where the achievements of science and technology find practical application, mass starvation has been abolished. It continues to reign in the underdeveloped countries precisely because the colonialist economic structure there has not permitted the use of scientific and technical achievements to solve the problem of hunger.

Only 20% of the land which could be cultivated by man, considering the present level of technical development, is being tilled in the world today. Why is this so? Because agriculture is viewed through the prism of possible profit. Agriculture is frowned upon because its raw materials and foodstuffs are much cheaper than manufactured goods. This is the first consequence of colonialism. It was colonialism that led to the gap between industrial and agricultural prices and, consequently, damped down the interest in agricultural advancement and rational utilization of the land. Second, surely it is possible to enlarge agricultural production even if all the crop areas have already been tilled and the soil exhausted. Yes, this can be done. Provided the necessary capital, machinery, and labor are concentrated on a definite area of land, yields can be increased five- to six-fold.

So it is a lie to say that the land and the resources needed to ensure the food are lacking. Given the present level of technology it would be possible to feed a population ten times larger than that inhabiting our planet today. And with the advance of technology it will be possible to feed 100 times as many people because right now we can foresee the discovery of an artificial synthesis of organic substances. No longer shall we be bound by the biological world which makes us wait until the fruits have ripened. In the future we shall obtain them through synthesis in a brief space of time. And even without making any utopian plans, and by sticking to reality, we can affirm, on the basis of the latest scientific achievements, that Malthus was wrong.

The Malthus doctrine appeared at the time of the Industrial Revolution when the British ruling class, then pursuing a brutal policy in India, badly needed a salve for its conscience, that is, if it had such a thing. Its aim was either to conquer or destroy the Indians, do away with their textile industry and, consequently, condemn them to starvation. At the same time it wanted to find justification for its actions, to demonstrate that it was not the British who were to blame but the Indians who "were multiplying at a rate beyond control." Malthus rendered a good service to the colonialists. His name was given to the pessimistic theory which has proved so useful to the rulers of this world and which is as old as social injustice. Malthus was generously rewarded for his service: he was given a professorship in the East India Company's college.

It is now customary to say that colonialism is in its death agony; but I think that as yet it would be more correct to say that it is not in its agony but that it is suffering from a grave illness. The fact that forty countries have gained political independence does not yet signify the death agony of colonialism. Political independence has existed for over a century in Latin America, but economically these countries still are colonies. Fortunately, we are living now in the atomic age when progress in all spheres is proceeding at a rapid rate, and I hope that in Africa the agony of colonialism will be of shorter duration.

The colonialists have the means with which to cause a state of hunger and maintain it; they can do this by means of a mechanism which I shall try to explain by the example of India. When the British first came to India that country was emerging from the medieval phase of its history. The Middle Ages in Europe also witnessed considerable outbreaks of famine because the economic life of those days was based on autarchy, while means of communication were poorly developed. In the eighteenth century when India was emerging from her medieval stage, her handicraft industry was highly developed and attracted the rural population. What we now know as agrarian overpopulation was non-existent. The foundations of a modern economy were beginning to take shape, in which agriculture used only the labor power needed for production. But it was exactly at this moment that the British arrived and disrupted everything. They destroyed the handicraft industry, strangled industry at its birth, and forced the Indian to return to his village, which was now overpopulated in relation to technique and capital.

Then, as was the case in all colonies, a colonial type of agriculture was introduced in India, an agriculture based on crops for export, i.e., not the crops the country needed but crops that were profitable for the colonialists. Thus it was that production of these "colonial goods" became the occupation of the inhabitants of the tropical countries; occupation was simply the hypocritical covering for their subjugation and enslavement. The colonial peoples, forced to produce for the enrichment of the metropolitan countries, could hardly be enthusiastic. And then it began to be said of them, especially of the Indians in Latin America, that they did not like agricultural work, and that rather than engage in it they would prefer death. There is some logic in this statement. For in substance they were faced with the choice: either slow death from starvation or a quick death of their own free will. And not infrequently they chose the latter. It was more practical to do so than to die for the sake of work. Such kinds of economic activity as growing sugar, cotton, rubber, and coffee for export are destructive rather than productive—and all for the sake of exporting goods at cheap prices, with the receipts going into the pockets of a tiny minority.

To this day there are tribes in Black Africa for whom agriculture is the sole occupation. And while it cannot be said that they live in affluence, they at least vary their diet. This safeguards them against a shortage of vitamins, and meager though their diet is, it keeps life going. But the moment Africans migrate to the towns and begin to work in industry, they begin to suffer from malnutrition. What is the reason for this? The reason is that in the towns they are used as machines which are given only the fuel needed to keep them going—rice and manioc. But they are denied the fresh victuals containing vitamins and proteins. And as we know, the essential thing for metabolism is that the intake of vitamins should

correspond to the intake of carbohydrates. And the human organism quickly becomes run down, like a machine abundantly
provided with fuel to make it work at high speed but never re-
paired. And just as the hog is fed with corn to turn the latter into
pork, the worker is fed with manioc and beans in order to turn
them into sugar and coffee. The process is exactly the same as that
of raising pigs: if the most profitable way of marketing corn is
to sell it in a bag of pigskin, the most profitable way of marketing
manioc is to sell it in the form of sugar in the skin of a Negro or,
to be more precise, distilled from his sweat. This, then, was the
mechanism which upset and worsened the food balance of various
peoples.

But even with this kind of agriculture things could be improved
if the growers were paid more for the raw materials. But here major powers resort to another method by means of which the
nations dependent on them are kept in poverty. The prices paid
for the raw materials are steadily falling. Latin America is now
exporting three times more raw materials than it did before the
war, but is getting much less money for them. In 1958, for example, Brazil exported millions of sacks of coffee more than in 1948,
but received a million dollars less. So what is the use of working?
The more you work the less you get. Here, then, you have the
explanation for the "laziness" of the tropical peoples.

One of the profit-making mechanisms used by the Americans is
payment for not producing. In an indirect way this device is used
also in Latin America. The only difference is that in the United
States the farmers are generously compensated for not growing
crops, whereas in Latin America they are not. But in either case
money is paid for not producing, and here we have a contradiction of capitalism expressed in a glaring colonialist form and
providing no incentive for progress, for real economic development.

The United States concentrates in its hands 70% of the raw
materials of the Western world. This enables it to dictate prices
for raw materials. And because of this the other countries find it
impossible really to develop their economies. Long-term planning
is essential if there is to be any economic and social progress; but,
it may be asked, how is it possible to plan for five or ten years
when even in the course of a single year the prices of your prod-

ucts and your raw materials are likely to change in terms ranging between 50% and 200%? Maybe it's only the top politicians who can foresee these price oscillations: when they find out that a particular country is determined to vote in the U.N. in accordance with its own interests and not at the whim of its creditors, then the prices paid for the country's products fall. See what happened to Cuba. The United States bought her sugar, "generously" paying her more than she could get on the world market; the result was that Cuba became a country with a monoculture economy. Sugar filled everything there, just as in Venezuela where the unwholesome smell of oil has penetrated into every pore of her entire culture; one is conscious of it in the streets and even in the houses. Cuba was turned into a "sugar island" suffering from diabetes in exactly the same way as people suffer from it. The United States used to say to the Cubans: We will guarantee you a high export quota, so please be obedient and accommodating.

But there are always patriots who yearn for freedom and for its sake are prepared to sacrifice the sugar. For example, in 1932 Cuba made some efforts to free herself from foreign domination, and so the U.S.A., which prior to this annually bought 5 million bags of Cuban sugar, reduced the quota for the following year to 2 million. As a result, a crisis broke out in the country and its economy was disorganized. Sugar made up two-thirds of Cuba's exports; in Bolivia it was tin, in Venezuela oil, in Brazil coffee; this kind of economic specialization is the second melancholy consequence of colonialism. The concentration on a single product makes the country's economy unstable and dependent. And so long as this is the case, it will never get rid of hunger.

But this state of affairs can be changed. And the example of the selfsame Cuba is proof of this. In 1948 Cuba produced only sugar and imported $140 million worth of beans and rice. One should not overlook the "noble" gesture of the United States in this respect. In 1958 it paid Cuba $60 million more for her sugar than it would have paid had it bought the sugar at world prices. But then with the same "noble" gesture it sold Cuba $140 million worth of beans and rice. In effect, what the Americans paid Cuba was not the price of the sugar but the price of the beans and rice paid to the American farmers. Two years later, after the revolution, Cuba grew on her own soil beans and rice to the value of $40 million and $50 million respectively. She is now gaining for herself economic liberation. But the land is the same land, and she has the same tropical climate. There has been no change in her natural conditions. What has changed is the economic structure, and she has liberated herself from colonialism.

A few words about the International Monetary Fund. This organization is "international" in the sense that it represents various countries, but the seats on the Board and the votes are distributed in proportion to the contribution made by each country. Each vote signifies $100,000. But since the United States makes the biggest contribution, the Fund, from the standpoint of its decisions, is 100% a United States organization. For this reason there is always a certain amount of mistrust of the reports which the Fund submits to the United Nations. So that this, too, is a form of colonial oppression. My own country, Brazil, has been one of the victims of this oppression. On various pretexts it has been forced to halve the prices of its products. This kind of action deprives the underdeveloped countries of the possibility of buying industrial plants. Being exporters of raw materials, these exports are the only means with which they can buy the machines and develop their industry. But while raw material prices have been falling steadily, prices for the equipment purchased by the Latin American countries have doubled, in the same way as the purchasing power of the dollar has doubled at the behest of the International Monetary Fund. This safeguards U.S. industry against possible competition. Money is available for expanding agriculture and the production of raw materials for export, but it is never found for industrial expansion.

An obsolete economic structure is artificially maintained in the colonial countries. Their population is denied access to education and to health services, because both education and medical service are commodities, and access to them depends wholly on purchasing power, and purchasing power is extremely low. In each of these countries there is a tiny privileged group, the elite; this elite, associated with the big international trusts and the colonialists, cares nothing for the national interests. It makes no demands, and merely bends the knee in obedience.

The economic development which one can observe in these countries is but a fig leaf. Take, for example, Latin America. The per-capita income in Venezuela is $700, i.e., the same as in France.

But can Venezuela's cultural standards and social welfare be likened to those in France? By no means, because account should be taken not of *per capita* income, which is an abstraction, but the distribution of income. The $700 per head in Venezuela, an abstract figure, is the mean obtained by adding up the $700 million of the seven families and the poverty of the hungry masses.

The major powers have never been interested in including the economy of the colonies in the world economic system on an equal footing. Yet economic integration is a necessity. All the plans worked out for the colonies will remain a fiction unless they provide for equal economic cooperation.

Industrialization is the only way to end poverty and hunger. It is only in industrial countries that people eat well; in the purely agrarian countries starvation is greatest. But what kind of industrialization will it be? There is a colonial type of industrialization which creates an industry, national in the geographic sense but international in the economic sense, i.e., it does not belong to the country. But there is also the genuine kind of economic development, one that unites the masses. The colonial type of industrialization enriches only the "elite" and makes the bulk of the population poorer than ever. In point of fact there always has been in the underdeveloped countries an insignificant segment of the population with a very high standard of living, whereas the overwhelming majority live under pre-capitalist, feudal, and even pre-feudal conditions. That is why the peoples of Latin America, Africa, and Asia know that their hunger and poverty are not engendered by Nature but are the products of social injustice.

The hunger of the poor and the fear of the rich *vis-à-vis* the hungry must be abolished, and for this there is needed a revolutionary change in the existing system. Financial and technical aid alone to the countries with backward economic and social systems will be of little avail in this respect. All men of good will, all who are anxious to step out along the one road on the earth that belongs to all, should ponder over the problem of hunger.

IX
BOSSA NOVA IN BRAZILIAN SOCIETY

... in which the exodus from rural areas to the big cities is shown to be a costly, and sometimes tragic, form of progress; technocratic versus socialistic solutions to the land problem; democratic versus bureaucratic solutions to the city problem; the racial problem: the world of whites, blacks, and browns, its link to the class problem; paternalism moves from the "big house" to the presidential mansion; paternalism and revolution from above, the role and function of the Brazilian militarists; social redemption as social revolution.

THERE SEEMS to be current in the United States the soothing parochial fiction that 400 Peace Corps volunteers can set aright the problems which have been brewing in Brazil these past 400 years. We thus confuse self-therapy with social assistance. A tradition of malfunctioning, of maladministration, demands treatment at the root and branch. Simple increases in foreign-aid dosages only prolong the death agony of the old regime. Underdevelopment means many things. But it means, above all, inertia, an incapacity to move forward socially, an inability to keep pace with changes elsewhere in the world. The causes of inertia are complex. But they can usually be traced back to archaic and invidious social institutions: corrupt social classes that survive through parasitical claims on the poor; dysfunctional status groups displaying a collective egotism and ostentation characteristic of those who sense that there is no tomorrow; power elements who disguise their elitist contempt for democratic processes behind noble phrases of national redemption and regional grandeur; racial supremacists who disguise discriminatory practices behind a veil of integrationist preachments. Underdeveloped regions display a vast terrain of disintegration no less than inertia: the progressive deterioration of rural and urban life alike; material impoverishment of once prosperous and well-fed people; insecurity and contempt for professional and intellectual sectors. In brief, underdevelopment requires bold measures, revolutionary measures, because it is a synonym for structural deficiencies in a society, and not simply shortcomings which can be considered the result of a technical or cultural lag.

Modern social revolution emanates from certain common features. First and foremost is a large peasantry unabsorbed by the urban middle classes and uncontrolled by the rural feudal classes. Second is the existence of a large colored population living outside the dominant mores of the white ruling class and subordinated to a secondary role in both the economy and in the political decision-making processes. Third is a "military-mindedness," either on the part of established military chiefs or insurgent, peasant-based "anti-army" armies. These are what might be termed the positive variables in the modern revolutionary context. There exist negative aspects as well: the instability of political regimes, their inability to maintain the security and well-being of the citizens. This may be inspired either by confusion and dissension in the ranks of the ruling elites, or by a general internal corruption of official society, or by both. While Brazil exhibits such negative features in awe-inspiring abundance, we shall here concentrate on the positive variables in the revolutionary syndrome.

Let us begin by considering the Brazilian Revolution not as any apocalyptic set of events, but as a continuing social process. And let us examine this social process in terms of three sets of antipathetic relations: urbanism versus ruralism; segregation versus integration; and command versus consensus structures. Admittedly, these forces intersect and cross over into the others. Furthermore, there is no "metaphysical" demonstration that ruralism and urbanism are by definition necessarily clashing social forces. Like the other two, they are *in fact* the polarities of Brazilian life.

In examining the sociology of revolutionary movements we here exclude typologies based on the "natural history of revolutions"—which are simply doctrines of *ricorso* dressed up in contemporary social science garb. We are not concerned with the outer shell of revolution, with the imagined sameness of revolutions irrespective of space and time. We are concerned with the contents of revolution, a single Brazilian revolution, quite clearly defined both in space and in time. We eschew any dogmatic presupposition which ordains one and only one social sector to "lead" the revolution, as if revolutions either pursue blueprints laid out in advance or must be designated by such normative terms as "abortive," "partial," or "incomplete." The observable sociological facts are as follows: (a) Brazil is in the initial developing stage of a vast social transformation; (b) the Brazilian Revolution has a great deal in common with revolutions taking place in other parts of the underdeveloped world because it shares a common economic morphology and political physiology; (c) the expansion or attrition of a large world socialist movement is relevant to the rate and tempo of change in Brazil, but largely irrelevant in terms of the direction and contents of such change; (d) socialism, defined simply as the predominance of the public economic sector over the private economic sector, is the basic form of the Brazilian Revolution, although the specific features of this socialism are as yet largely undetermined and can only be settled by an inventory of continuities in Brazilian society and economy.

Brazil is undergoing a process of urbanization characteristic of developing societies the world over. Provincial nineteenth-century centers like São Paulo and Rio de Janeiro have grown in size to where each is now a major world city of more than 3.5 million inhabitants. In 1900, Rio had 744,998 inhabitants; by 1955 it had grown to 3,625,000 (or 6.2% of the national population). In 1900, São Paulo had only 239,820 inhabitants; by 1955 this figure had reached 3,325,000 (or 5.7% of the national population). Together these cities contain 11.9% of the Brazilian population. And with an additional 20.2% of the population living in cities having more than 20,000 people, one can say that the urban population is better than 30% and, what is more important, sharply rising. The clear transformation in population is readily observed in the occupational pyramid. From 1940 to 1950, the active population occupied with agriculture and cattle-raising increased by only 4.6%, while the rise for people employed in manufacturing was about 59.4%. To this must be added a rate of increase in the labor force for the supply of services which is 134.2% (indicative of the huge increase in the use of household electrical appliances, televisions, washing machines, etc.) and 38.9% for commerce, transportation, and communication. Such rises reflect the intensification of the urbanization process—one which places a heavy premium on light industrial production and consumer satisfaction. And in the "affluent" world of Rio de Janeiro and São Paulo, what is most required are just such service enterprises.

Urbanization of such a variety has produced huge pressure for imported consumer products. This in turn has served to drain the economy, since ever-growing deficits had to be covered by foreign credits. What this also reflects is that increase in production is small compared to the increase in consumption—for example, petroleum. The big increase in personal and public transportation has led Brazil, an oil-producing nation, to import more petroleum products than in the past. On the other side of the ledger, coffee, cocoa, and cotton exports have either remained stable or declined. Until mixed exports can be made the rule and not the exception, the process of urbanization will place greater strain on Brazilian society than any offsetting advantages urbanism may have brought in newly established economic bases and new standards of living.

Despite the heavy costs of urbanization, the short-run pressures must be absorbed if Brazil is to escape the long-run consequences of being a "have-not" nation. The Brazilian rural economy affords neither security nor stability. Nor does it provide a dynamic base for growth. If the process of political revolution is under way in Northeast Brazil, it is precisely to liberate the area from the fetters preventing the industrialization and mechanization of countryside and city alike. It is in the large cities, in the numerous smaller cities, and in the towns servicing the farmlands that fermentation and agitation for radical change are basically taking place. Therefore, urbanization, far from being a revolution-preventing panacea, is, in fact, a central aspect of the revolutionary process.

Urban expansion in Brazil has three distinct derivations: natural increase in population, immigration, and internal migration. Taking these factors individually, it should be said that the first is the least significant, since the national population increase tends to be lower in the large cities than in the rural sectors. In any event, such natural increase would not of itself account for the disproportionate growth of the urban centers *vis à vis* the rest of the country. The second factor, that of immigration, is a real key to the fabulous growth of Rio de Janeiro and, to an even greater degree, of São Paulo. The proportion of foreign immigrants settling in São Paulo averages more than 60% of all immigrants who settle in Brazil. With an additional 30% going to Rio de Janeiro, it can be seen that the influx of Italians, Portuguese, Spaniards, Poles, Russians, etc., has made a great difference in the life of the cities, while having relatively little influence on rural patterns of life. In addition to the technical skills they bring, immigrants to under-developed areas tend to preserve their former national and ethnic allegiances. The tendency to resist assimilation, to accept only a minimal formal integration, is particularly acute in the first generation and, to a lesser degree, in the second generation.

The foreign immigration population forms the basic core of the middle classes of large Brazilian cities. They come primarily from Europe. They bring various skills and attitudes: a high degree of labor and manufacturing technology and an advanced conception of proper and adequate living standards. They are thus quickly absorbed into the high-paying industries; and they can usually count on initial support from the separatist national and ethnic institutions which abound in the big cities. Thus, while the immigrants are not easily absorbed into Brazil's cultural-linguistic milieus, they do readily accommodate themselves to the economic opportunities available to the skilled and semi-skilled.

The European immigrants, in the main, tend to be a conservative social and political force (although this force is minimized by an absence of their primary participation in the organs of politics: the parties, the armed forces, labor organizations, etc.). But a huge ideological shift sets in by the third generation. Portuguese becomes the first language of the immigrant offspring, often to the dismay of the elders. And the young generation becomes deeply involved in the social and political problems which beset the nation, often with standards of political conduct imbibed impressionistically from the European scene. Retaining the "know-how" of their elders, imbued with the practical reform spirit of education, the progeny of immigrant families absorb the Brazilian national spirit and become involved with the social and political problems connected to the *Geist*. This offspring generation often forms the backbone of the revolutionary intelligentsia, supplying both the "brains" for industrial life and the strategies needed for political life.

The factor of internal migration is increasingly becoming the number-one reason for the growth of the cities. The movement from the farming villages to the capital cities is direct. Once migratory channels are established, they make the subsequent flow of people much easier. The obvious disparity in living standards between town and country, coupled with the increasing transportation and communication networks, makes internal migration a progressively increasing factor in Brazilian society.

Internal migration from the latifundias to the cities can only be described as a tragic example of a society without planning. Involved is a basic contradiction between twentieth-century work patterns and nineteenth-century living patterns. As to why the movement away from the rural areas has grown so sharply, perhaps the best "explanation" is that offered by Claude Lévi-Strauss in *Tristes Tropiques*: "The gulf between excess of luxury and excess of misery shatters the human dimension. There remains only a society in which those who are capable of nothing survive by hoping for everything, and those who demand everything offer nothing." The tragic fact is that the misery and oppression which drive the peasantry to seek refuge in the big cities often result in other "higher" forms of degradation and exploitation. Unwilling or incapable of resolving the problems of urban growth, the local governments of Rio de Janeiro, Minas Gerais, and Santos (among others) have simply allowed conditions to deteriorate to a point where these cities invite comparison with Bombay and Delhi in India.

In the process of eliminating proletarian dwellings, the *cortiços*, from the center of Rio in the name of slum clearance, laborers were driven from the center of the city (where land speculation combined with aristocratic sensibilities to increase realty values) into the outskirts of the city and along the railroad tracks leading to and from the city. But these areas are already crowded with newly arrived peasants from the countryside. The growth of peasant slums, *favelas*, is initially linked to several factors: a general flight from the countryside, a high rate of demographic growth, an excessive concentration of industry and commerce in the major port cities, and, finally, a nearly total absence of serious concern with the process of urban growth among bureaucratic officials. The careless elimination of working-class districts, which, however run down, maintained an organic way of life, has accentuated the social problem. At the same time, it should be noted that this "carelessness" of officialdom may have a boomerang effect, since the *favelas* provide a basic meeting ground between peasant and proletariat, black and white, the industrial poor and rural poverty-stricken. They have thus made "transitional sub-societies" a *permanent* feature of life.

In the face of the enormous need for urban planning, for the elimination of a *favela* population which is on the minus side of every standard index of social organization, the present regional rulers can only come up with bureaucratic solutions. Under Kubitschek, the country nearly went into bankruptcy in order to build a new capital city, Brasília, at a cost which was easily twice that necessary to clear up all the slum districts in every major Brazilian city. It is axiomatic that bureaucracy in an underdeveloped area is dysfunctional. The "creation" of Brasília has all the earmarks of the medieval emphasis on building magnificent churches in the midst of surrounding poverty and iniquity. And it is dubious if the administrative buildings of Brasília will have even the aesthetic permanence of the medieval cathedrals. Ironically, the *real* Brasília is growing up around the bureaucratic hub. This is where people live—while politicians fly back to the coastal regions weekly.

The brilliant Italian architect, Bruno Zevi, has described Brasília as "a Kafka nightmare." The perfect architectural expression of bureaucracy is monumentalism. This has the initial capacity to veil the eclectic qualities of Brasília but, in essence, simply invalidates its architectural structure.

Zevi's analysis has a pointed sociological conclusion which deserves a full citation. "What purpose does it serve?" Zevi asks.

Suppose we concede that Brazil's development must turn toward the interior, must the political and military center be established there? Did the Americans transfer their capital in order to found Chicago or Los Angeles? The Brazilians reply that in their case economic and political forces are so interrelated that government initiative is indispensable. If this is correct, many of the artificial aspects of the city are explainable. But the cost of the operation is high. Brazil's economic crisis may not be wholly attributable to the construction of Brasília, but certainly this is a noteworthy factor in the crisis. . . . Only a handful of intellectuals without following have objected *sotto voce:* "With just half the money spent here, the agrarian reform could become a reality." . . . The square of the Three Powers has a closed, classicist scheme dominated by the two towers of the parliamentary offices, by the cupola of the Senate, and by the saucer of the Chamber. To the left is the Hall of Justice; to the right the seat of government. There is even a hustings, and it seems especially ridiculous in an era in which electoral battles are waged on television. Behind the square along a rather rhetorical avenue is the parade of ministeries. It is a Kafka city, a paradise for bureaucrats.

The deeper tragedy of bureaucratic lack of planning in Brazilian urban life is the cynicism which underscores all criticism of present plans. It is asserted that if Brasília were not built, the monies would only have been squandered in a less visible way. Against such cynicism there is no reply. On the other hand, the magnificent growth of São Paulo offers a perfect reply to cynics and squanderers alike. One need only consider the words of Paul Johnson, in *The Plundered Continent*, to understand the duality in Brazilian social planning.

Unlike all other Latin American cities, São Paulo is not an artificial creation, an ant-hill refuge for men beaten by the land. It has sprung up as a natural process of economic growth: efficient farming led to the creation of agricultural surpluses; these in turn have produced capital; capital was invested in industry, selling its products to rich farmers and salaried labourers. Suddenly, in the last quarter of the 19th century, the process began to reach maturity, and São Paulo exploded. From a population of 25,000 in 1875, it has expanded to nearly four million, and is growing at the rate of 150,000 a year. It spreads over 700 square miles, virtually without slums. The center is a vast canyon of roads, lipped by the biggest skyscrapers in the southern hemisphere; around stretch pleasant residential suburbs, occupied—and in Latin America this is a miracle—by ordinary bank clerks and industrial workers. For, if São Paulo boasts of its 100 millionaires, it also has something which is economically far more significant: a million and a half regular wage earners—the vital atoms of a modern consumer economy.

And while even São Paulo has in recent years been deeply affected by an over-all economy of backwardness, it remains a beacon light which attracts people throughout the nation. Unfortunately, São Paulo also contributes heavily to a specious sectionalism inherited from the last century. A combination of high material and intellectual skills, natural wealth and wealth acquired through trade and commerce, excellent geographic and climatic conditions, have all contributed to a form of parochialism and regionalism that envisions São Paulo as a "worldly" city first and a Brazilian city only a poor second. The very recent transformation of the wage earners into conscious members of a wage-earning *class* might yet make São Paulo a center of revolution, no less than of commerce.

What gives an air of urgency to the Brazilian Revolution is the utter helplessness of bureaucratic feudalism. Bureaucracy is dysfunctional with a vengeance. *There is an acute difference between a bureaucratic apparatus established to resolve already existing complexities in the social order, and a bureaucracy which predates an industrial nation.* In the latter case, the Brazilian case, bureaucracy actually prevents orderly industrial growth, drowning material progress in the corruption of papers and procedures, a corruption which has become an art form in the centers of Brazilian administration. Hélio Jaguaribe has indicated a major source for this administrative breakdown.

The Brazilian state is a Chartist state. It is a product of *partidista* [coalition] policy, that neither financed nor was qualified to pay attention to genuine public services. Rather, it was destined and was in a position to uniquely assure the mediation of the party structure. Whatever the infinite multiplication of jobs and bureaucratic prebends, the maintenance of the regime was considered primary. With the crisis of the Chartist state, an abyss appeared between what civil society demanded from the state and what it could deliver. State reform became the most immediate and fundamental development of the social and economic evolution of the country.

Given the fact that all post-Soviet revolutions have been best described as peasant revolutions, and given the additional fact that Brazil must still be defined as a rural nation, the potentialities for complete revolution are very high. The position of the peasant requires vast agrarian reforms which the bureaucratic state has not been able to provide. Revolutionary solutions would have the double effect of gaining land reform and political reform at the same time.

The very phenomenon which was counted on to prevent a peasant revolution from occurring, urbanization, now enhances just such a possibility. The cities are incredibly overcrowded. The working classes have increasingly become proletarianized; the immigrant population is slowly diminishing, leaving in its wake offspring who form the backbone of the revolutionary intelligentsia and student movement. In Brazil, as in China, the vast cities on the coastal plains provide no real "buffer" against radical social change. In Brazil, as in China, bureaucratic solutions fail to come to terms with even the rudiments of social discontent. In Brazil, as in China, the cities provide the essential intellectual cement for the peasant "ramrod"—an intellectual force which is in the process of converting itself into the organizational-technological "know-how" which makes revolutions successful.

Arguing by analogy has always been frowned upon as the weakest form of evidence, and properly so. Yet comparisons do not necessarily have to be considered symmetrical. There are differences, vast differences, between China and Brazil. Geographical proximities differ, climatic conditions are not the same, the backgrounds of foreign exploitation are radically different. However, the shared geography of hunger joins hands with the demography of growth to convert broad proximities into deadly parallels.

We have earlier pointed out that nearly half of the Brazilian population is outside the money economy, that in effect feudal barter and direct exchange of labor power for goods and services characterize a large part of the Brazilian economy. Anisio Teixeira, in his *Revolution and Education*, indicates that approximately 60% of the Brazilians are within the monetary structure, and that these same people are in the power structure as well. The *classes* represent columns of stability: agricultural interests, military and civil servants, personnel of the social service agencies, railway and port workers, merchant marine, highway builders, heavy and light industrial interests, bank officials, and sections of labor officialdom. The higher stratum within each of these groups represents the elites; the strata themselves represent the classes.

This leaves a population "residue" of 40%—the "masses." They are composed basically of the peasantry and the dispossessed of the cities. But it should be understood that this is not simply a class problem or a power problem—although economic and political elements are pivotal. A decisive element in distinguishing class from mass in Brazil is race. There is a very high correlation between those outside the class structure and monetary system and those outside the population defined as "white." According to the 1940 census reports, 63.5% of the population is defined as white (*branco*), 14.6% as black (*preto*), and 21.2% as brown (*pardo*).* However, not a few in the category designated as white have a considerable admixture of Indian and Negroid features and ancestry. As T. Lynn Smith has pointed out: "The number of those classed as black, or Negro, certainly is the absolute minimum. Any changes in the criteria used would inevitably have the effect of in-

---

* The remaining 1% is comprised of people of Asian stock, primarily of Japanese and Chinese ancestry.

creasing their numbers." The 60-40 division in those in and out of
the money economy has as its direct counterpart the racial divisions in Brazil. Money itself sometimes serves to "define" a person
as white, while the absence of any appreciable wealth can serve
the opposite function of "proving" that one is black. In plain
words, the colored people of Brazil are dispossessed and directly
subject to the feudal order.

The racial dimension in class exploitation is revealed by the
composition of racial types by areas. In the industrial South, in
São Paulo, Paraná, Santa Catarina, and Rio Grande do Sul, the average population defined as white is over 85% according to the
1940 census, and over 90% according to the 1950 census. In the
North and in the Northeast, the white population averages only
40% to 45%. And while the ruling groups in the northern States
are also white, it is clear that the colored problem is the key to the
feudal problem. Smash racialism and the feudal order crumbles.

Teixeira's "masses" are thus *colored* masses, while his "classes"
are *white* classes. The system of paternalism, the "easygoing" aspects of racialism, should not blind observers to the fact that the
"race question" is directly linked to the urban-rural bifurcation.
And if no revolution can be genuine or successful which fails to
incorporate the peasantry, so, too, no revolution can be considered
authentic or meaningful which fails to promote the colored people
to leadership capacities. This is especially so because both peasantry and *preto* turn out to be one and the same social sector.
Every society has hidden, informal measurements of freedom. In
Germany it is the treatment of its Jewish community; in the
United States it is the treatment of the Negro people; in Turkey it
is the treatment of national minority groups. In similar fashion, the
"secret" definition of freedom in Brazil begins and ends with the
treatment of the "browns" and the "blacks."

The colored population of Brazil, which is increasingly seeking
to escape from the racialism of the feudal North and Northeast,
which searches in vain for Freyre's wonderful world of racial
comity, goes to the big cities. But this urban migration has only
served to make for black ghettos, the *favelas*. The semi-proletar-
ianization of the blacks and the browns thus does not in and of
itself alleviate racial antagonism. Frank Bonilla, discussing Rio's
favelas, gives the following pertinent data. According to the 1960
census, 13% of Rio de Janeiro's population was Negro. In a present

estimated population of about 3 million, that would give about 400,000 *pretos*. If the present *favela* population is close to 900,000 as estimated by the police, and the proportion of *pretos* among *favelados* is still close to 40%, practically all of Rio's Negroes, must live in *favelas*. Such a picture makes clear why the response of the colored peoples of Brazil to political organization is something less than enthusiastic. The effort by some elitist commentators to attribute the absence of political passions of the colored people to their ingrained sluggishness or downright stupidity is simply an attempt to justify and rationalize the supreme exploitation of the masses—of the "de-classed."

In his study of *Race and Class in Rural Brazil*, Charles Wagley summed up the racial situation most candidly:

Most Brazilians and most foreign students of Brazil wonder that the upper class is composed almost exclusively of European whites or people in whom the traces of Indian or Negro blood are infinitesimal. The middle class is also predominately Caucasoid, though numerous *mesticos* of various racial backgrounds have been able to ascend into this group. It is in the lower classes that the large mass of Negroes, of mulattoes, of people with American Indian characteristics, and of *pardos* are found. Although a process of "bleaching"—or progressive tendency of the Brazilian population toward a generalized Caucasoid appearance—is probably taking place, the homogeneous "Brazilian race" predicted by many authors is still in the future. Today, class lines generally divide the more Caucasoid Brazilians from those who might be called "people of color." As yet, economic opportunities and educational advantages have not been extended to the rural masses nor even to all the urban poor; thus, the majority of the "people of color" remain in the lower class. *It is thus still a general rule throughout Brazil that the people of the upper class are almost exclusively Caucasian in appearance, and the majority of the "people of color" are found in the middle and lower classes.* [italics by Wagley]

Brazil is renowned throughout the hemisphere for its racial harmony. But in good measure this represents a confusion between the long process of miscegenation between the three chief racial strains due to special factors of Brazilian Manorial living, such as the Conquistador origins of Portuguese settlements, and something much more idealized—racial democracy. There is a different import to sexual intercourse between Negro males and white females because the Negro male is supposedly "more virile" than the white male, and the import of sexual unions between races which are a consequence of a general indifference to racial type or stock. One can speak of the "equality of races" or "racial democracy" only where there is a correlation between the anthropological evidence for the natural equality of races *and* the sociological acceptance of and action upon this doctrine. But if Brazil at least has the merit of accepting the anthropological side of the coin, it nonetheless remains a nation in which there is an acute awareness of social distance, of race as a sociological designation of superiority and inferiority. Indeed, the Brazilian tends to have a highly refined racial sensibility. Such accidental properties of human biology as intensity of skin pigmentation count most heavily in defining class membership. For example, one might be a "brunette" (*moreno*); but more likely he or she will be called *moreno escuro* (dark brunette) or *moreno claro* (light brunette). And there is no doubt that from the point of view of both power and prestige, it is better to be light brunette than dark brunette. The lighter-skinned of the species is clearly held superior in virtues to the darker. All of which yields a picture at best of high racial interaction—much more than exists in the southern portion of the United States, for example—but not anything even approximating racial democracy. What has often been confused is racial paternalism and racial equality. But to elevate the former to the latter is simply to compound a basic untruth.

There is a powerful system of stereotypes operating to hold each race in check. The stereotypes undulate between a pattern of negative sentiments about other races, that is, races other than one's own, to a series of paternalistic sentiments about "responsibility" for races other than one's own. Thus the Negro is considered by the whites to have ugly facial characteristics. The Negro is held to be lazy and a false friend. And, of course, the stock argument against educating the Negro population is that "white education" makes the black-skinned proud and impossible to bear. At the same time, the area in which the Negro "rates highly" on a status scale comes close to that of John Dollard's description of attitudes in the American South in *Caste and Class in a Southern Town*—sex. Negroes are said to be passionate lovers. White women are necessary as marriage companions, but Negro women are good as sexual companions. The whole psychology of illicit behavior, and the excitement such behavior creates, is thus transferred into a general designation of the races. The fact that Negroes are held to be the least honest, the least truthworthy, and the least ethical only further feeds this paternalistic stereotype. Since illicit sexual unions are taboo, such fusions between the races serve to reinforce the stereotype. The general statement, "carrying on like a Negro," indicates a low-class person. Status tends to define racial identity in part. "Money lightens skin color" throughout Brazil. Thus self-identification, and identification for others, is often determined not by ancestry or pigmentation but by occupation and social status.

Despite the fact that the criterion of race is often crucial in determining social ranking and economic occupation, there is a relatively low degree of racial *conflict* and competition of the kind characteristic in the southern United States. There appear to be four distinct reasons for this racial comity: (a) the absence of actual physical segregation according to racial types in such public institutions as schools, residential districts, and public buildings; (b) the absence of racial discrimination in such affairs of state as voting; (c) the colored peoples of Brazil identify their nationality as Brazilian first, and only secondarily as people of color, i.e., the absence of "dual allegiances"; (d) prejudice operates mainly in terms of social class rather than anthropological race, and, as such, color "lightens" as social rank "changes."

Basic to all of these factors is the general acceptance on the part of the colored peoples of their inferior socio-economic position. They are taught the "naturalness" of subordination in the public school texts, they are compelled to "work the system" of a highly paternalistic set of masters and *patrãos*, and, in truth, they often dislike the social responsibilities imposed by industrial and urban relations. Since there is little consciousness of racial exploitation, there are hardly any organizations of Negroes or Indians which are limited to people of a specific racial type. The Brazilian government has made a concerted effort to preserve its ethnic heterogeneity by the most enlightened Indian policy in the hemisphere, in this way avoiding the sort of *Rassenkampf* found in British Guiana. Poverty is what groups people. Race is simply held to be a property of the condition of being poor. People of color thus frequently see themselves as being providentially ordained to occupy a subordinate social position. Hence, racial relations are quite "good" throughout Brazil, based, as these relations oftentimes are, on a joint acceptance of feudal mores, of white supremacy and black subordination. How economic development will affect such traditional societal patterns is yet to be seen. If the United States is any example, industrialization does not of itself automatically "solve" the problem of racial differentiation. For racial democracy to be learned, racial mythology must first be unlearned. And this is not a spontaneous event, but one which takes place only when social ascription gives way to social achievement as the measure of a man.

The concept of paternalism is fundamental not only to racial relations, but to social relations in general. In its best form, it is a symbolic representation of the ethic of feudal responsibility, while in its less noble effects, paternalism serves to reinforce traditionalist patterns of exploitation. As Charles Wagley indicates, "the *patrão*-worker relationship was something more than economic. It involved a sense of noblesse oblige and paternalism on the part of the employer toward the worker which had survived out of the paternalism of slavery and monarchy." Similarly, the relationship between the rulers and the ruled of Brazil also entails something more than political domination. Here, too, a social ethic was operative which serves to smooth out the ragged edges of dictatorship and political tyranny. One cannot simply say this is part of the Latin Catholic ethic, since paternalism is far more widespread in Brazil than in the Hispanic nations. The more likely explanation is the decisive role of the plantation system in Brazil, and the capacity of the plantation owners to exercise an inordinate amount of political and military influence. Other nations in South America revealed an urban-rural dichotomy of a far sharper variety, e.g., Buenos Aires' historic competition with the rest of Argentina. Thus, the tardiness of Brazilian industrial development, as well as the unique plantation form of agriculture, helps to explain the widespread acceptance of paternalism as a social ethic.

Paternalism, expressed as a benevolent despotism during the Empire period and as Presidentialism during the Republican period, is a thin but powerful veil disguising the elementary fact that Brazil has historically been a command society, a society founded and grounded on the leadership principle. The "mediative power" of the state is supposed to steer clear of the *Scylla* of revolution and the *Charybdis* of stagnation. Because Brazil is ostensibly a nation where things are done by elites on behalf of the people, it is little wonder that the supreme example of active paternalism in Brazil is its armed forces. The military of Brazil has traditionally convinced itself that it is the ultimate repository of order and progress. The authoritarian democracy of Brazilian political leadership thus dovetails nicely with the general orientation of the military establishment. This can perhaps best be seen by the military attitude toward the national oil and electrical monopolies (*Petrobrás* and *Eletrobrás*). The military would no more tolerate a denationalization of these industries than the government. These industries represent Brazil's "basic honor," and, as such, must be protected by the guardians of that honor. Again, to see how different the situation is elsewhere, we may cite the role of the Argentine military, whose fundamental commitments are to specific upper classes and to specific imperial powers. The Argentine military show little of the fervor in regard to maintaining YPF (Argentina's national oil monopoly) that is displayed by the Brazilian guardians.

The ideology of Brazilian militarism derives from a unique blend of positivism and Catholicism. It is an attempted pragmatic synthesis of both. During the lengthy tenure of Getúlio Vargas (himself a civilian), initially made possible by the military *junta* which nullified the 1930 electoral victory of Júlio Prestes, and then ensured by the crushing of the *Paulista* revolt in 1932, we observe the perfect functioning of a command structure, based on authoritarian notions of giving the people democracy. From the positivistic tradition, the military elite sought the rationalization of the economy and society. The corporate state, or the *Estado Novo,* was a cross between Comte's grand design for a society of technical proficiency and Mussolini's early fascism, which was to balance the play of social forces through the direct intervention of state authority. From the papal encyclicals of 1891 and 1931, from *Rerum Novarum* and *Quadragesimo Anno,* the military confirmed its paternalistic ideology of guardianship. The state was held to have definite social responsibilities to specific cultural, economic, and political groups, *all* of which were somehow to be miraculously woven into a harmonious fabric free of strife. The *casa grande* of the feudal barons was moved to the presidential palace where the military barons held court. But this shift was not simply a movement in the locus of power. It was more profoundly an early acceptance of the need for national cohesion.

By the elimination of parliamentary obstacles, notorious in Brazil, where legislation can be introduced without ever being acted upon, the military sought to win a mass following for its plans for democracy from above. However anti-democratic this procedure was, Brazilian militarism performed a democratic service, since parliamentary rule invariably meant the open and direct rule of the traditionalists and the latifundists. The military was anchored in the large urban centers and thus had to derive its mass support from labor and commercial interests, an ambiguous position which led to paradoxical consequences. The Vargas regime, and later the Kubitschek government, instituted a comprehensive system of social security and labor benefits, including minimum-wage and maximum-hour legislation. Under the auspices of this federal *casa grande* system, the workers were urged to organize into trade unions, but were in turn denied the right to strike. Mediation of labor-employer disputes was made mandatory, and was handled by special labor courts set up for this singular purpose. The "great compromise" never became more than a slogan for maximizing state power.

During the Vargas regime occurred the coupling of the industrial upsurge with a maximum amount of military paternalism, a strange phrase, but one which at least serves to distinguish Brazil's military from that of other parts of the continent. The social consequences were vast. Mass education was developed, and school enrollment and school building more than doubled between 1930 and 1945. Traditionalist classes developed urban values (for themselves, at least) and flowered under the tutelage of the military. Throughout this period of initial industrial buildup and productivity, the military viewed itself as the chief instrument for orderly social process. That it was also faced with the ineluctable dilemma of using anti-democratic tactics and principles to bring "democracy to the people" was less important than it might have been were Brazil to have used other social methods for maintaining a high industrial growth rate in the face of popular disinterest.

The military theory of guardianship, which initially supported Vargas' effort at social legislation and industrial reform, had as its upper limits any real initiative from below. As was the case with Peronism in Argentina, Vargas' regime created the instruments of its own self-destruction, by transcending the parochialism of the poor and the paternalism of the rich. Vargas gradually saw his

Partido Trabalhista Brasileiro (the party machinery now operated by Goulart) become an instrument for vast social legislation that inevitably would have taken Brazil along a socialist path. Vargas' chief source of power in his successful bid for re-election in 1950 was the industrial classes, while his chief loss of support was from the military. At the time, Vargas was quoted as having favored "the socialization of water-power resources, mineral deposits, electrical supply facilities, and means of transport—in short, the program that the British Labour Party is carrying out." Nonetheless, despite the radicalization of Brazilian politics, the military, although withdrawing actual support from Vargas, still maintained the need for legality. One can see parallels in the more recent governmental upheavals. When Quadros resigned, the military, which by this time had become disengaged, if not thoroughly disenchanted, with the PTB, still held firm to the principles of legality. Despite their misgivings, they did not prevent Goulart from assuming the Presidency late in 1961.

But while the Brazilian military is still bound to a general ethos of legality and guardianship, it has grown in power during the modern period. It has therefore tended to reinterpret its guardianship in more activistic terms. During World War II, the Brazilian military received $300 million in Lend-Lease equipment as "part payment" for sending a token expeditionary force to Italy during the latter stages of the war in Europe. The result was to build up the prestige of the officer corps, so that when it returned to its traditional political role after the war, the military began making and breaking governments. As has now become clear, the growth of hemispheric "defense pacts," and the sending of modern arms to Brazil which this entailed, only further strengthened the military pivot in relation to civilian rule. The military arrogated to itself the right to depose Vargas once more, although he had been freely elected and had a clear popular mandate.

By the early fifties it had become clear that Vargas viewed the military not as an objective mediator but as a group with a partisan interest in maintaining the *status quo*. For its part, the military viewed Vargas' power with alarm, because it saw Vargas as creating a semi-fascist countervailing force. Hence, army influentials saw themselves not as conservative defenders of the past but as guarantors of democratic rights they felt would be abrogated by Vargas' continuation in power. But whatever the facts were in the Vargas dispute with the Army, it is clear that civilian government in Brazil was never permitted to alter the armed forces' traditional role as the ultimate arbiter of political disputes, or to interfere with their pay, benefits, discipline, and promotions. Reform regimes were obliged to confine their reform of the bureaucracy to non-military echelons. In light of this, civilian rulers sought to extend their reform policies by first convincing the military of the need for such policies. Once the military hurdle had been cleared, as in the case of *Petrobrás* and *Eletrobrás*, the road to reform was made infinitely easier.

The problem of the Brazilian military differs somewhat from that in such adjacent countries as Argentina, Chile, and Peru. The budget for the armed forces is much less that of Brazil's Hispanic neighbors, and therefore the drain on the national economy is correspondingly smaller as well. The Brazilian Army shows a kinship with its neighbors in the ideology of paternalism, in the belief of its officer corps that the basic sphere of military operations in a developing nation is and should remain political. Unlike Mexico, the political elite was never able to effect a clear separation between military professionalism and civilian politics. Hence, while it cannot be said that militarism in Brazil rules the political roost, it does nevertheless act as policy formulator, perhaps as the ultimate arbiter when things political become "ultimate." But if Brazil has not been able to thoroughly harness its military, it has at least invalidated the old dictum that the last step in a military career in Latin America is the Presidency of the republic.

What places strict limits on the Brazilian military is not so much the strength of democratic processes as the tardiness of development of its military sector in relation to other interest groups. During the nineteenth century, when *caudilhismo* was already entrenched in other portions of the continent, Brazil was still without much of a military force. Feudalism prevented centralized authority from developing. Each latifundia might boast of its gunmen, of its private army of overseers, but without a clearly defined national policy there could be no well-developed military arm. Furthermore, the very vastness of the country made it impossible for the typical Latin American parochial army to execute its self-defined mandate of national solidarity. Geography, regional differences, logistics, all of the natural forces mitigated against a strong centralized regime with a well-defined military caste. For a powerful standing army to have been developed in Brazil would have necessitated an abandonment, or at least a long-range postponement, of any efforts to enter the modern world. This sacrifice was too great to make, even by the more ambitious militarists.

Another critical factor which has continued to keep the military from exercising an inordinate amount of power is the simple fact of urban diversification in Brazil. Buenos Aires is the capital city and center of military operation in Argentina; Lima is the capital city and center of military operations in Peru; Santiago is the capital and center of military operations in Chile. Such a situation does not prevail in Brazil. The capital city is now Brasília, while the leading cultural and industrial centers are Rio de Janeiro and São Paulo respectively. *Coups d'état* are much more difficult to engineer in such a situation. Regionalism in Brazil, unlike anywhere else on the continent, is not a simple struggle between rural and urban interests, since each of the "United States" of Brazil also boasts a major city. A "march" on Brasília would be risky, and probably the least successful way to conduct a counterrevolution or a revolution from above. Hence, one of the special factors preventing an inordinate amount of power from falling into the hands of the military is functional diversification, a factor likely to increase in significance as Brazil, in the process of development, achieves new States, cities, and regions of major importance.

In no country in Latin America can the military be said to be united *qua* military. Precisely because the military functions as a political pressure group, it often reflects the powerful schisms within each nation. Brazil is no exception to this rule. Indeed, it might even be an exaggeration of it. Between the senior officers and the junior officers the struggle became manifest after World War I. The junior officers, who came to be known as the *tenentes,* reflected the rising discontent of all Brazilian sectors which saw salvation in terms of national unity; this included the industrialists, professional groups, and urban labor. The old military guard, whose power derived in large measure from the rural and regionalist political domination of the wealthy States of Minas Gerais and São Paulo, sought to maintain Brazil as a huge agricultural and mineral-rich picking-grounds. The new military corps, recruited as it was from middle-class sectors, resented this feudal strain in Brazilian life.

In addition to ideological disputes, the young army officers were responsible for two major uprisings which, though failures in the immediate sense, ultimately resulted in the Vargas revolution. One *tenente* uprising occurred in 1922 in the Rio de Janeiro garrison in protest against the obviously manipulated election of President Artur Bernardes. Loyal troops, with some difficulty, crushed this movement. However, a far more serious challenge to orthodoxy took place in 1924 when the young *tenentes* captured the key city of São Paulo. They held the city for almost a month before government forces compelled them to flee westward. For three years under the command of Luís Carlos Prestes, this fighting force, reduced to hundreds, wandered across the vast interior of the country, arousing the peasantry to heed its demands for constitutional, economic, and social reforms. The legendary exploits of the Prestes column did more than legitimize the ideas of *Tenentismo;* in the figure of its heroic leader Prestes, it helped insure a favorable reception among the military for radical change in both urban and rural Brazil.

A significant factor in the left turn the Vargas New State took after 1935 can be attributed to the first attempt at a communist revolution from above to take place in the Western hemisphere. On November 27, 1935, red flags were displayed in a number of military barracks in the major cities of Rio de Janeiro, Natal, and Recife. While the uprisings of the military rebels were crushed, the Vargas regime was made aware of the powerful forces aligned against him. A second wave of military communism was prevented just prior to the 1937 elections only by the use of open terrorism and, finally, the dissolution of all political parties. It is thus extremely important to realize that the present strength of the left-wing bloc in the army has powerful historical antecedents.

Whether the Vargas era was a true social revolution or simply a counterrevolution with constitutional trappings, the fact remains that the military of Brazil, rather than forming any single segment of the power elite, reflect the schisms within the Brazilian power structure from the twenties until the present. While it is true that many of the young *tenentes* soon became old *tenentes,* tired of failure and anxious for a modicum of power, another section became still more radical in its demands. Left *Tenentismo,* in part at least, drifted into national communism. And there is little doubt that among military men, a residue of sympathy for Prestes' brand of national communism remains in evidence. The military leaders of the 1940's who supported Vargas, and again in the 1960's, those supporting Goulart, were men who had been associated with Prestes during the period of the long march.

With or without communist support, the radical wing of the Brazilian military prevailed throughout the fifties, and is now firmly implanted in the highest echelons. The military elite in the early fifties supported the nationalization of the oil and electrical industries. The *Centro de Estudos e Defesa do Petróleo* succeeded in getting twelve generals, a vice admiral, and various lesser officials to sign its proclamation against foreign investment in Brazilian basic industries. The "Vargasista" candidates in the mid-fifties, Juscelino Kubitschek and João Goulart, were victorious. But there was a strong effort on the part of the most reactionary segments of the landed classes and their supporters in the commercial sectors to invalidate the election. It was the military which forestalled any *coup d'état*. Chief of Staff, General Teixeira Lott, led a move which placed Nereu Ramos temporarily in the Presidential Palace, until the Kubitschek-Goulart forces were able to take office. Thus, the military assured both nationalism and legalism, and in this way functioned to keep Brazil from going on the low-road of modernism through foreign aid, and kept it on the road to structural social change initiated, one-sidedly to be sure, under Vargas.

With the assumption to presidential power of João Goulart, again with the strong support of the "left" faction in the army, the nationalist wing of the military was immeasurably strengthened. Under the leadership of the First Army Commander of Rio's garrison, General Osvino Alves Ferreira, the military has increased the pressure for political and social reforms. It is now the turn of the more conservative wing of the Army to decry the direction of events. In November 1962, more than thirty old-line generals supported General Decio Escobar's appeal to keep the armed forces free of *Tenentismo*. He declared that "politics in the Army or the Army in politics are an evil and must be combated without truce. Military pressure for political and social reforms is as odious as the pressure from organized labor." Thus it is clear that the Brazilian military can hardly be said to be a unified pressure group. At best, it applies pressure in contrasting

directions. In personal terms, for every Denys there is a Lott.*
All the schisms accounted for, it remains a fact of Latin American history that military solutions to social problems tend to be extremely narrow in scope and limited in vision. The military leadership, of both the nationalist-radical and anti-nationalist conservative varieties, provides little in the way of an independent working program for solving Brazil's basic internal problems. Its attitudes toward class and race, toward the needs for land reform and industrial reform, remain shrouded in abstractions and clouded by self-doubts as to the legitimate role of the military. The comments on this score offered by Edwin Lieuwen, in his work on *Arms and Politics in Latin America,* deserve serious attention.

Revolutions were most sweeping when the regular army, the ultimate guardian of social order, was overwhelmed, as in Mexico in 1914, Bolivia in 1952, and Cuba in 1958–59. These, however, were not primarily planned revolutions, but spontaneous outbursts of popular antagonism manifested in violent uprisings. Only in these three countries, moreover, was it possible in the aftermath of victory to deal with the basic problem of land reform, a matter which even the most radical military reformers elsewhere avoided. Genuine agrarian reform in Latin America was perhaps impossible without the destruction of the officer corps, recruited as it was from the middle and upper-middle social ranks which believed firmly in the sanctity of private property. A reform regime that attacked the latter soon forfeited the good will of the officers, as was demonstrated in Venezuela in 1948 and Guatemala in 1954.

Nonetheless, it is possible that the Brazilian military will prove an exception to this rule. There is a solid segment of its armed forces that is either quite willing to join the forces of national revolution or, failing that, act as a corps to smash the regular army. One fact is certain: the divisions within the armed forces are real enough to create a counter-force balance—in this way making possible the implementation of political and social decisions, if not with the outright support of the Army, at least without their outright interference, as in the cases of Venezuela, Guatemala, and, more recently, Argentina and Peru.**

* *See* Hélio Jaguaribe's paper in this volume for the details of military factionalism in the transition from Quadros to Goulart.
** The most recent example of this left tendency in the Brazilian armed forces is the decision of João Goulart to use Army personnel to carry out

A recent summation of the general characteristics of the "new elite" in developing areas, made by the sociologist, R. F. Behrendt, helps to shed considerable light on the contradictory panorama offered by the Brazilian military. Behrendt offers four points, each of which can be found in the Brazilian military establishment. First, in consequence of the widening divergence of interests, old and new elites begin to exhibit a distinct ideological polarization. Second, the new elite reveals a marked disassociation from the masses, and in this way formulates policies in the "general interest" rather than responds to mass pressures as such. Third, the new elite is national in character, rather than traditionalistic or regionalist in loyalties. Its concentration is in the sphere of political power rather than landed wealth or commercial activities. This gives the new elite a consciousness of purpose often absent in the old elite. Fourth, the new elites become supporters of dynamic national development. They distinguish themselves from the old elite in that their function is not to maintain conventional lines of social stratification and political order, but to work for a fluid reformation of social goals and political ends. Thus, the Brazilian military represent in their existence, no less than in their aims, a circulation of elites which will serve to redefine the goal of society and the structure of power without involving Brazil in a long and costly civil war.

The total picture then is one in which urbanism, a "society of the masses," is rapidly replacing rural feudal patterns of domination. The only real question on this score is whether the industrial revolution can move rapidly enough, freely enough, to overcome the need for a "redemptive" civil war. The lines of intersection are the rate of feudal decay versus the rate of industrial growth. The consequences of continued feudal entrenchment and resistance to change could be serious, and, from the point of view of the national bourgeoisie, most damaging—since in any outright physical combat, there is little question that "stage-skipping" socialism would burst the limits of reform, and the capitalist sector

---

his agrarian reform plan. Military leaders agreed to supervise the plan, under which the state would have the right to expropriate lands lying up to six miles on either side of federal highways. Besides executing the agrarian reform, the armed forces are responsible for making surveys of lands to be expropriated and studies of the climate and economy of the areas involved.

would be hard-pressed to keep the revolution from affecting itself no less than the feudal classes.

The division of races and the absence of mobility among the colored and Indian populations of the country also contribute to the imbalance which currently prevails in the Brazilian social order. While the likelihood of racial struggle is very slim, almost non-existent, these sectors would undoubtedly cast in their lot with the revolutionary factions in any showdown effort—with the disadvantage of seeing the industrial upsurge seriously slowed down at the expense of the agricultural sector. In addition, the destruction of racial barriers, the equalization of opportunities of employment for each race, is itself a contributing element in the destruction of the feudal latifundiary system and the paternalistic ideology it has so assiduously cultivated over the centuries.

The military apparatus, divided in class loyalties, torn between old elites and new elites, confused in ideology, and rendered quiescent by internal dissension, represents a force that can either support or oppose the nationalist sentiments of the political leaders of Brasília. In itself, the military establishment cannot possibly rule.

It can act as a stabilizing lever for social order. Thus, the extent to which the military replaces low-middle-class private-property consciousness with nationalistic aspirations will at best affect the tempo and style of the revolution in Brazil, but it can no longer (indeed, if it ever could) prevent such a social revolution from taking place.

This synopsis of class, race, and power in the Brazilian social structure reveals, more than anything else, that the Brazilian Revolution is not an item for some far-off agenda, but is a present-day, on-going reality. The unsettled and perhaps unsettling questions concern tactics: is the revolution to be accompanied by military counterforce, by peasant uprisings, or is it to come about through political channels and through a negotiated settlement of the outstanding claims of each social sector of the Brazilian future? The romantic should be cautioned in the thought that only violence can establish a thoroughgoing revolution. Likewise, the pacifist should be cautioned in his belief that only non-violence can tumble the old order of things. Matters of violence and non-violence are at the level of heuristic devices, tactics, as they are conventionally labeled. Matters of revolution and counterrevolution are at the level of structural alterations, principles. Whatever the devices may be, the fact is that Brazil's insistence on equal partnership among the world's great nations is being supported by continuing social revolution that will insure its greatness in fact—however tardy the recognition that in the Western hemisphere there are now two great nations.

X
BRAZIL CONFRONTS
THE CLASH OF WORLD SYSTEMS

. . . in which Gilberto Freyre asks whether Brazil is becoming
a tropical China; Jacob Gorender gives a communist view of
Brazil's problem, and Luís Carlos Prestes attacks the United States
and wonders whether Brazil ought not to become a tropical Russia; this is followed by Roberto de Oliveira Campos' distinction
between neutralism and independence in foreign policy; and by
João Goulart's statement before the United States Congress that
Brazil's destiny is in its own hands.

I. WHY A TROPICAL CHINA?

Gilberto Freyre *

WHY IS IT that some observers speak of Brazil as a tropical
China when, aside from extension of territory, power of cultural
absorption, and a few Chinese traits to be found in Brazilian civilization, Brazil seems so unlike modern or ancient China? Probably
because there has always been in Brazil something Oriental in
contrast to its Western characteristics; something "Moorish"—as
it was pointed out à propos of its architecture—in contrast to its
Roman or Latin traits; something different from Republican
America, due to the fact that Brazil remained a monarchy until
1889 (even at present there are two inheritors to a Brazilian
throne, two real princes, two authentic Orleans-Braganças).

Also, perhaps, because of the present tendency on the part of a
considerable number of Brazilians to consider their tropical Ama-
zonian forests and all that they contain, especially their oil and
minerals, almost sacred values that only Brazilian hands should

* Gilberto de Mello Freyre was born in Recife and received his university
training in the United States. He is Professor (Honoris Causa) of the University of Recife, and is well known for his many writings, particularly
The Masters and the Slaves and *The Mansions and the Shanties*.

touch. For this sort of nationalism is taking the aspect of an intense Yankeephobia. Because, also, of the attitude of other Brazilians, not to be included among narrow economic nationalists, who think that there is something specific in certain values, social and cultural, peculiar to Brazil or to tropical America, which should be preserved from American standardization of a Yankee type.

If it is true that a member of the medical research staff of a United States pharmaceutical firm who has spent years studying diseases in Latin America—especially in central Brazil—is inclined to believe that there are places in that tropical part of the American hemisphere which are free of some of the diseases that so plague the so-called civilized world or affect other tropical areas, he is right when he points out the urgent need for the proper scientific study of this situation, a study to be carried on by a multi-talented crew of scientists: a biological chemist, an anthropologist, a zoologist, a clinician, and other specialists. This is an urgent need because settlements in which immunity to these diseases seems to exist are "in the path of rapidly advancing industrial civilization" and "their isolation will soon be over and their natural immunities may be a thing of the past." Now, what happens—if it happens—in connection with immunity to "civilized" or "tropical" diseases may happen in connection with the preservation of social and cultural values by certain Latin American communities of the less industrialized sub-areas of that part of the American continent. Proper scientific study of the conditions under which they flourish might indicate a way of saving them, or some of them, or parts of them, from blind standardization.

If a study of this type had been made in proper time of why Brazil became independent, remaining a monarchy and avoiding a republican form of government, monarchy might have been preserved in Brazil for the possible advantage of the Brazilian people in particular, and of the Pan American commonwealth in general. For it certainly meant immunity to some of the political diseases that seem to have been acquired by Brazilians when, to modernize or Pan Americanize their country, they adopted the republican form of government. Even today, the Republic in Brazil is safer from political diseases when its methods of dealing with Brazilian problems are a careful modernization of the traditional Brazilian monarchical and, at the same time, democratic methods instead of being a mere copy of what Anglo-Americans have done in the United States or of what the Germans did when they founded their lyrical, unrealistic Weimar Republic—also copied in some points by Brazilian idealists.

Some Brazilians think today that inter-Americanism should not mean a mechanical and narrow form of standardization with emphasis on the massive, quantitative or monolithic Pan American aspects of values and cultural styles, but a healthy, though difficult, combination of differences and even of antagonisms within a dynamic inter-American structure or system. Just as Latin Americans should take from the United States and adapt to their different regional or national conditions some United States values and techniques, so the Americans of the United States might profit from Latin American suggestions and examples instead of rigidly adopting the attitude that because they lead in industrial progress, they are, or should be, the absolute leaders of everything in hemispheric culture, that hemispheric culture should follow their example in every human or cultural activity.

There seems to be a tendency among certain Anglo-Americans to use disparagingly the words "Latin American," under the impression that in America what is Latin is always inferior to what is Anglo-Saxon or Nordic. It is a tendency similar to the one of using disparagingly the adjectives "medieval" or "feudal" or "Chinese" or "Moorish" in their relation to modern civilization, as if the Middle Ages or the East had not given mankind values superior to the ones that came to man from the generally glorified age of Enlightenment or that have come to him only since the commercial and the industrial revolutions in the West, including, as Professor George Sarton, a specialist in the subject, reminds us, such apparently modern values as money, economy, banking, and extensive trade, an invention of the Crusades. In other words, a two-way cultural policy should be encouraged between the Americas, with reciprocal appreciation for Latin and Anglo values and inventions. If this is not done, Brazilians and other Latin Americans should close themselves against American standardization of a Yankee type to the point of appearing "Chinese."

When there is, as at the present time, a wave of "anti-Yankeeism" in Latin America, an acute manifestation of an almost always latent Yankeephobia—for as some Anglo-Americans know, to most Latin Americans, all Americans from the United States are Yankees—Americans of the United States should consider this situation a good reason or pretext for a really scientific study of their relationship with Latin America, investigations that should take into consideration not only political or economic matters, through statistics and figures, but also social, cultural, and psychological aspects of the same total and complex situation. One might say that the United States-Latin America relationships need a sort of Kinsey report to magnify the intimate, hidden psychological factors that make them unhappy.

It may be that the present-day unpopularity of the United States in Latin America comes largely from the fact that the "North American colossus," as Latin Americans sometimes call the United States, is now, to Latin American eyes, a big power practically without competitors—the French, British, German, Japanese competitors, against whom the Latin Americans until some years ago might divide the somewhat feminine resentment of semi-colonial peoples faced by imperial, masculine, or economically aggressive nations. Now all the resentment is concentrated on or against the United States, with a weak France, a weak Germany, a weak Japan, a weak Great Britain considered almost angelic nations for whom some Latin Americans even begin to feel nostalgic, nostalgic for the days when they were powerful nations and, in their competition for Latin American markets, used subtle, suave, and, at the same time, masculine, methods of economic penetration that some of the modern North Americans of the United States do not seem to consider necessary to use in Latin America, where they have no strong competitor to fight or destroy. Only in the Near East and in Africa do they feel that they have to deal with powerful Chinese or Soviet competition. Therefore, they seem to have neglected Latin America—a sort of legitimate wife—for exotic adventures of economic and political donjuanism in Africa, Asia, and Europe. Only now is Soviet Russia beginning to make its presence felt in Brazil as a strong competitor of the United States.

It is true that each one of us, Anglo- or Latin Americans, should consider some of these Anglo-American adventures in distant Eastern lands as activity essential for Pan American and even pan-human, democratic development, and not a mere adventure in the exclusive interest of the United States. But exclusiveness of action in this respect may do considerable harm to inter-American relations, in a phase still too plastic and delicate for Latin Americans to be left alone in their struggle to develop industries and an agriculture that depend, to a large extent, upon united financial help—a help that should not take the aspect of domination or imposition of Anglo-American values upon their Latin neighbors.

Would it not be possible for such Anglo-American activities to go on in the East and Africa as well as in Europe without an apparent or real neglect of Latin America by the United States, especially if one remembers that the United States had, during its tremendous war effort against Nazism, Fascism, and Japan, the loyal and valuable co-operation of some of the Latin American countries—especially Brazil? Should not some United States leaders refrain from showing, in their relationship with Latin America, an immediacy of aim that has been disappointing to Latin Americans who are beginning to contrast what seems to them to be an extremely opportunistic, dynamic, restless, striving, or Faustian policy on the part of the United States or of the United States leaders with what they now idealize, through a nostalgic mood, as the reliable, classical, regular policy of the British, the French, or the Germans when they were powerful in Latin America and used methods—so the idealization of a recent past goes—notable for their sobriety and elegance and for their distrust of the unusual, the eccentric, the exuberant? Too often, it seems, United States forays into Latin America are almost immediately and totally followed by neglect or indifference or by a strict "business-is-business" or "time-is-money" attitude.

More than once the parent-child relation has been applied by sociologist and social psychologists to the study, analysis, and interpretation by analogy of the political, social, and psychological relations between human groups. Perhaps the male-female concept may be applied in the same way and with the same reservations to the study and analysis of the political and economic and social relations between the United States and the Latin American nations, with the United States as the male partner in this conjugal situation. These relations seem to be, on a national scale, those of a sociological male in regard to a sociologically feminine, that is, dependent, Latin America. The America south of the Rio Grande sees in the United States a masculine power that some of the most feminine Latin American nations are inclined to consider unstable, exuberant, and irregular in its masculine, that is, protective, behavior toward them. Hence the need of a careful scientific study of the situation, a task for not only a multi-talented, but also a multi-national crew of social scientists from North and South America.

Sociologists tell us that in our time nationalism is one of the observed facts of life which no scientist can neglect. It is a potent fact in Latin American life, but so far no comparative study of the various expressions of nationalism in that part of the world has appeared. One of the results of neglect of this study is that outsiders have a tendency to oversimplify Latin American reality, neglecting its diversity.

Some time ago in Paris, in a UNESCO meeting of social scientists, I suggested not only a revision of history books used in schools—a suggestion already extended from Europe to Latin America by some of the late League of Nations idealists and pacifists—but also an attempt at a reinterpretation of the national heroes of Europe, Asia, and America, through comparative biographies, or through biographies written not by one single writer, but by three or four, representing two or three or four special sciences and two, three, or four areas more deeply affected by the projection of the hero considered, for sometimes a hero to one nation can be a villain to a neighboring nation. That has been the case of the Brazilian Caxias as viewed by most Paraguayans and of the Paraguayan Solano López as viewed by most Brazilians, the case of more than one Mexican hero when seen by Mexicans or considered by Mexico's Anglo-American neighbors.

A similar task might be attempted with regard to certain elements in the culture of a people considered noble by the Anglo-American group of Americans and inferior by the Latin Americans. They too might be studied, analyzed, and interpreted in a comparative and co-operative way. For instance, most of the modern Anglo-Americans seem to regard a political career as an inferior activity, while in countries like Brazil politics is still regarded as a high and noble form of human activity in which some of the best intellectuals of the nation are engaged or desire to be engaged. Brazilians and other Latin Americans still look down upon a purely business career and find it difficult to understand why the United States should send merely successful businessmen as ambassadors to Latin American Republics. Why the two attitudes? How do they affect the relations between the two Americas? For they are bound to affect these relations and to make them difficult and delicate.

Another study that I consider essential for the improvement of political, cultural, and economic relations between Anglo-Americans and Latin Americans is a careful psychological and sociological study of time: their different attitudes toward time or tempo. The rigid Anglo-Saxon attitude—"Time is money"—with an almost mystical cult of minutes and seconds on account of their practical, commercial value, is in sharp contrast to the Latin American attitude, a sort of "more-or-less" ("*mais ou menos*") attitude. It is easier to understand why a Nordic was so shocked in Spain to know that a Spanish or Latin American guest in a hotel asked the desk to call him next morning not exactly at ten or ten-fifteen, as an Anglo-Saxon or an Anglo-American would have asked, but at ten or eleven: the "more-or-less" attitude in regard to time in contrast to the strictly mathematical one, a contrast that makes simultaneity as difficult between peoples or nations engaged in a common activity as between man and woman in love relations, for instance, when the male partner does not take into consideration the difference of time values of his female companion. When instead of a people or an individual enjoying as much as possible the flow of living, there is concern and eagerness for immediate achievement on the part of an individual in relation to another individual or on the part of a people in relation to another people, the relations between the two become extremely difficult. An adjustment has to be found between *speed-up* and *ralentie:* a sort of third *tempo*, a third psychological and sociological *tempo*, has to be found which will be lived by the two with full reciprocity.

According to the French sociologist Georges Gurvitch, each national culture has its own time or rhythm. Anglo-Americans and Latin Americans certainly have two very distinct attitudes toward time, and this is important not only in political and business but also even in social and cultural activities. Anglo-American sociologists say that the predominant time dimension of the United States Americans "is the future." Most of the Latin American groups are inclined to celebrate the present, and some of them the past, rather than to "live in the future." São Paulo in Brazil and present-day Venezuela may be exceptions to this predominance and be as future-oriented as any progressive or faustian Anglo-American group. But São Paulo is only São Paulo and not all of

Brazil. Present-day Venezuela is far from being typical of normal Latin Spanish America, where one generally finds, among some groups, an excessive attachment to the past, and among many a perhaps excessive taste for present enjoyment. As a result of this, one finds less inclination among Latin Americans than among Anglo-Americans to sacrifice almost everything in one's life to rapid collective progress, "mortgaging the present for the future," as an Anglo-American sociologist puts it.

It is easy to see how these two different attitudes toward time may cause social and psychological distance between two human groups, not only in regard to business and political matters, but also in dealing—I repeat—with diplomatic and cultural matters of the most subtle kind. A people taking a definite pleasure in mere activity in the present or in celebrating the past finds it difficult to understand, admire, and like a civilization that seems to specialize in disregarding the past and even the present, to value and glorify only the future. Perhaps the ideal Pan American time should be— I insist on this point—a combination of these two attitudes. But this combination will come about only if both groups become conscious of the problem through psychological and sociological analysis of each other's excesses. Hence the need of a scientific study of the differences that separate Latin Americans and Anglo-Americans as if they were two sociological, cultural sexes.

One hears more and more often that Africa is no longer an isolated, static continent, but what someone has aptly described as a quick-changing area whose fate is intimately connected with that of the free world and whose development has an immediate effect on the national interest of the United States and not only of Western Europe. Latin Americans agree with this: they too see the importance of Africa, as well as that of Asia. But they think that still more important in its social and cultural dynamics and in its closeness to the interests of the free world and particularly of the United States is now-neglected Latin America, if it be considered as an area or a region whose general development has been and is today, even more than African development, an expression or an evidence of the capacity of a group of peoples, largely non-European in ethnic composition and in their folkway, to grow in modern civilizations and to organize themselves as nations of a modern type in largely tropical or semi-tropical spaces.

Books written on Latin America by Europeans and Anglo-Americans as recently as the first decades of the twentieth century hardly admitted, with one or two exceptions, that such a development was to be expected from non-European peoples, from peoples, like most of the Latin Americans, largely non-European in their ethnic composition, who added to this tragic deficiency—tragic to the eyes of a number of European and Anglo-American sociologists—the equally fatal inferiority of being inhabitants of tropical or quasi-tropical areas, a condition common to the majority of Latin Americans. That being so, it was natural for political and commercial Anglo-American leaders, and for missionaries and diplomats of the United States, when sent to tropical Latin American countries as to positions so difficult and unpleasant that they felt the need of being recommended to the special benevolence of God Almighty and of their almost as powerful governments or companies, to act in these positions like the British, the Germans, and even the French in similar situations. They considered themselves biologically, culturally, and totally superior to the strange peoples they found in such un-European and, to their eyes, absolutely inferior surroundings—physically and culturally inferior. There has been a considerable change of mentality in this respect both in Europe and in the United States, but even today one finds that Latin America suggests to the typical Anglo-American "inferior race," "unhealthy climate," "degenerate mestizos," "yellow fever," and "malaria," rather than any positive values.

I have just read in a New York magazine these words of a citizen of the United States apropos of a national problem now being widely discussed in newspapers and magazines of the dynamic Anglo-American Republic: "Look at South America, where all the races have intermarried, and what have they got? Lazy, unproductive, backward people." Latin Americans hesitate to express themselves on any strictly domestic problem of Anglo-America. But some of them feel inclined to remind Anglo-Americans or citizens of the United States who think of South America, Latin America in general, or Brazil in particular as being made entirely of "lazy, unproductive, backward people" that there are notable exceptions to this generalization. Anglo-Americans will find places in Latin America where people are so progressive, creative, and modern that even north Europeans or Anglo-Americans of the most dynamic type have been surprised at their progress and achievements, achievements obtained by them without doing violence to their essential Latin traditions. Of course, Latin or South America is no paradise. But is there a perfect paradise in the modern world? Are not orthodox Christians right when they consider the Paradise an unearthly reality?

Nevertheless, one finds persons in modern South Africa, for instance, who look at South America as if it were almost a paradise. Four years ago I heard from a South African in South Africa: "I wish we had followed the same ways as South America." As a South or Latin American I was greatly pleased to hear him, but I could not avoid telling him: "But do not think that in South America we live in a paradise." Of course, we do not. South or Latin America has had a tragic history. Earthquakes and revolutions have been numerous, some of them devastating. Great presidents of great republics—great on the Latin American scale —have committed suicide. Great political crimes have attracted the attention of the world even to small republics. But in spite of the generalization that Latin Americans are lazy and unproductive, incapable of self-government and civilization, positive values are increasing in number and quality among Latin Americans. Some of the Latin Americans have even reached political maturity.

Most of the Latin American peoples are going through an aggressive anti-European or anti-Anglo-American phase of nationalism which places them in almost the same sociological situation as some of the modern Asians and Africans. And that fact gives some basis to the remark that Brazil is becoming a tropical China. But some of the Latin Americans have preceded by more than a century of political development these modern Asians and Africans who are now in the first and crudest phase of nationalistic adolescence, if not political childhood disguised by a few expressions of precocious modernity. National maturity has been reached by comparatively small groups in the Latin American populations, not by any of these populations as national wholes. Not even in a politically progressive country like the small Republic of Uruguay—a sort of Latin American Switzerland—is this the case. Argentina, after years of development as an electoral democracy that seemed to be so cosmopolitan in its spirit that one of its political leaders was enthusiastically applauded when thirty years ago he suggested that the "Argentinian Doctrine" surpassed the

Monroe Doctrine—America for the Americans—in being a much broader claim: America for Humanity—a few years ago adopted a narrowly nationalistic policy. This is also the case of modern Brazil, whose tradition, developed under a democratic and politically advanced monarchy, was one of harmonizing national interests with international and continental responsibilities, so much so that as a very young independent nation it became famous for the opportunities it gave naturalized Brazilians, or to the sons of naturalized Brazilians, to rise to the highest positions in the Empire and even to become diplomats or officers in the international service of Brazil. This was the case of Varnhagen, for instance—he was the son of a German—who was given the very national title of Baron of Porto Seguro, and of Taylor, an Englishman, who became a naval leader at the service of the Brazilian national cause.

If countries like Brazil and Argentina have sometimes acted in international matters as if they were still adolescent nations excessively afraid of the maturer ones and eager to rival or surpass the maturer ones in the expression of their national "power" or of their national "vitality," that is because their process of becoming politically mature has not really advanced much beyond adolescence as far as their national wholes are concerned; and this may be true even of the United States in regard to international politics. And adolescence seems to be as difficult a phase in the life of a nation as in the life of an individual. As unpleasant to the adolescent as to the maturer members of his family who have to understand an individual who does not understand his own contradictions of feeling, thought, and behavior.

Still, this understanding is necessary, and Latin America has to be understood by outsiders—especially by Anglo-Americans who, as a national whole, are politically maturer than the other American nations, though not perfectly mature—as a dynamic, changing area whose problems are not entirely national, but international; but whose international behavior is to a large extent an expression of difficult national problems that each Latin American nation is facing, and has to face, through ways and methods that have to correspond to its culture, its past, and its particular psychology. In the midst of these difficulties—the difficulties of growing cultures, growing economies, growing national systems—they now see the United States as a fully developed nation that does not

seem to know how to deal with adolescent members of the same
continental family; or—to come back to a previous analogy—as a
male nation that does not know how to deal with psychologically
female nations, eager, as nations, for the equivalent of full sexual
experience as well as for the sociological equivalent of a sexual
equality that will not imply that female nations are necessarily
inferior to male ones.

One of the recent expressions of this attitude of Latin American
nations in regard to their powerful Anglo-American neighbor has
been economic nationalism; and one of the manifestations of economic nationalism has been, in some of the Latin nations of the
continent—especially in recent years Brazil—an eagerness for industrialization that has meant a systematic hostility to the super-
industrialism of the United States. The United States, being, in
relation to its hemispheric neighbors, a super-industrialized nation,
must be treated as an enemy whose purpose, open or disguised,
would be to preserve the same neighbors as inhabitants of mere
agricultural areas so as to be only buyers and markets for its industries. Not only this, but the United States is seen by some
Latin American nationalists as being diabolically active in Africa,
doing much more than it should be doing, if it were a loyal member of the American community of nations, to stimulate African
agricultural production to surpass that of Brazil and other Latin
American countries. And this, with a United States financial help
that some Brazilians think should have been given to Brazil. Thus
stimulated and assisted by United States financial and technical
help, Africa will become—Latin American nationalists fear—a
competitor to Latin America, not by natural means but through
the intervention in her favor of a nation whose duty should be to
help its Latin neighbors in their agricultural production as well as
in their industrialization.

However, restrictions against foreign—Anglo-American, included—enterprise in countries like Brazil, rather than being a
Latin American reaction against this Anglo-American assistance to
Africa, have to be considered acts that preceded the present-day
United States policy of extraordinary economic activity in Europe, Asia, and Africa, with concomitant neglect of Latin America. These acts seem to deprive Latin Americans of the right to
complain against what is considered by many of them an unfair
attitude of the United States. As the hemisphere's leading nation,

its main activity should be to stimulate economic development in the hemisphere and not outside of it.

One of the reasons is that Latin Americans were made to feel by some of their economists, as early as the thirties (when, during the effects of crisis the United States went through after 1929, some of the most respectable Anglo-American banks and industries with agencies in Latin America acted in these countries in what was considered by some Latin Americans a very inelegant and unethical way) that they were depending too much on foreign—especially Anglo-American—bankers, middlemen, industrialists, and shipping and insurance interests. They should free themselves from such a dependence instead of merely freeing themselves from European financial and industrial power to fall under the cruder dominance of "Yankee" industrialism and "Yankee" financial lords.

As the Second World War made clear that the United States would emerge as the great imperial super-power of a new phase in the history of capitalism, fear of "Yankee" financial and industrial lords began to increase among Latin Americans. Latin American nations should concentrate their nationalism in economic issues instead of satisfying themselves with mere political appearances of independence. Hence, the numerous Latin American restrictions and measures put into effect since the thirties and intensified after the end of the Second World War, measures against exploration of mines and water power by foreigners; against the establishment of deposit banks and insurance companies with shares held by foreigners; against the ownership by foreigners not only of agricultural land (until the foreigners have established permanent residence as farmers), but also of enterprises considered national in their purposes; of restrictions even against the practice by foreigners of liberal professions—restrictions that in some cases have been considered incomplete by some exaggerated and even morbid Latin American nationalists, because they do not include naturalized citizens of some of these young republics as well as pure foreigners.

Similar measures have been taken in Latin America during the last decades to protect native labor against foreign intrusion, a typical law specifying that foreigners shall not constitute more than one-third of the employees or receive more than one-third of the wages or salary of any industrial, commercial, or public-utility enterprise except in certain industries. Besides this, measures have been taken against foreign intrusion, to favor so-called industrialization programs, making them expressions of an intensive economic nationalism. Privileges of almost sacred value have been claimed by industrialists and patriots during recent decades, in Latin America in general, and in Brazil in particular, for domestic manufactures as opposed to imported commodities that once were exalted as angelic marvels and are now considered diabolical when imported from the United States. Through their influence in the press, industrialists have been able to create in some parts of Latin America a sort of industrialist *mystique* or fad that has meant, in more than one case, the neglect of agriculture—for agriculture should be left to colonial peoples—and, almost always, hostility toward the United States, now the only super-industrial power whose influence is seen as an immediate "danger" by economic nationalists in some Latin American areas.

How have Anglo-Americans faced this situation in Latin America? With Franklin D. Roosevelt, the "Good Neighbor Policy" manifested itself through ways and means that gave even some of the most fanatic economic nationalists in Latin America confidence in the more experienced and economically and technically more mature neighbor. It is a fact that United States financial and technical aid was then extended to Latin America to assist not only non-competitive, but even competitive new industries—competitive with United States industries. The United States government made itself felt, through this assistance, as an influence—a corrective influence—that was above narrowly competitive or "imperialistic" private United States interests or groups in their relations with the Latin American republics eager to pass from a "colonial" status to a really national one, through industrialization. In connection with this, really constructive work—economically and psychologically constructive—was done through such agencies as the Export-Import Bank and the Inter-American Development Commission, organized in Washington in 1940, as a working unit of the Inter-American Financial and Economic Advisory Committee, to "assist in the development of the republics of the Western Hemisphere by promotion of trade, development of agriculture and industry, improvement of transportation facilities and conservation of forests."

As a concrete economic achievement of this now historical

commission, the stimulation of interest in increased production of high-grade tapioca starch (manioc), a product so typical of tropical Latin America, including tropical Brazil, may be pointed out. Other concrete economic achievements might be pointed out in connection with vegetable oils and minerals. But the work of the commission was also successful from a psychological point of view because it gave Latin Americans, suspicious of United States economic imperialism, a healthy confidence in the United States government as a force that stood above narrowly private interests and threw all its influence in favor of a policy of continental economic co-operation.

It seems that those in the United States who have advocated the abolition of all governmental agencies as instruments for such co-operation, leaving private interests free to act, forget the psychological aspect of the problem as viewed by Latin Americans. The neglect of this aspect of the problem seems to be contributing, to a large extent, to the deterioration of inter-American relations. The recent pre-eminence of private interests in these relations has become an easy target for Communists—so active now in Brazil and so systematic in their efforts to stimulate a sort of nationalistic religion among Brazilians, especially among the Brazilian military forces—in their eagerness to do away with all the valuable remains of the "Good Neighbor Policy." Now, they point out, Anglo-American "big business" of "the worst kind" is free to do what it pleases with Latin America, and Latin America must intensify its economic nationalism so as to protect itself against this type of "big business."

At the same time, some Latin American nationalists point out that Europe and Africa have been receiving technical and financial assistance of a type that Latin Americans should not fear, but welcome, as really beneficial to its young industries and its archaic agriculture. A contradictory attitude. But the second attitude seems to indicate that there is, latent among Latin Americans, a feeling of solidarity with Anglo-Americans which reacts in a somewhat feminine way to what appears to some Latin Americans to be a sort of male disloyalty of the United States to its sister republics of the South, neglected for the sake of Europe, Asia, or Africa. This psychological situation—which makes some Latin Americans nostalgic for F. D. Roosevelt, and this is only one aspect of a complex problem—should not be overlooked by Anglo-

Americans, but should be considered carefully and, if possible, studied not only through statistics, but also through more subtle, psychological methods. Psychological and ecological, for—being a European civilization developed in the tropics, adapted to the tropics, changed by the tropics, perhaps deformed, in some respects, and in other respects reformed, by the tropics—Brazil has to be studied, analyzed, and interpreted in the light of its tropical situation.

A prominent Brazilian business leader, Senhor Bazílio Machado of São Paulo, has recently expressed the attitude of a large number of Brazilian businessmen in regard to what they consider the neglect of Brazil by the United States in favor of a policy of an increasing concession of advantages to tropical Africa. Senhor Machado has anticipated the possibility of Brazilians refusing to co-operate with the United States if an international crisis similar to the 1941 crisis arises, on the basis that the United States should ask them, not Brazilians, but Africans for military co-operation and for the concession of naval and air bases, with all the serious disturbances to national life that such concessions mean. A similar stand has been taken by Senator Lourival Fontes, who was a close associate of Vargas and is an able specialist in international problems from a Brazilian point of view. These facts indicate that the present Yankeephobia in Brazil has sources besides shrewd Russian-Communistic propaganda against the United States in all tropical countries. Mistakes are being made by the United States in regard to Brazil that seem to be as effective in stimulating this Yankeephobia as Communistic propaganda ably carried on against the "Yankees" and "Imperialists" as if Soviet Russia were not an imperialistic power.

According to an Anglo-American author, Mr. Charles Morrow Wilson, in his book *The Tropics: World of Tomorrow* (New York, 1951), the tropics inevitably will have most to do with deciding whether the United States or Soviet Russia will lead the world tomorrow. He writes: "For at least twenty years past, the views and strategies of the Comintern have tended to accept this truth." Hence, a systematic policy of the Kremlin to penetrate the tropics and "win them, not by costly trade lines nor costly conquests, but rather by words, gestures, and implications, by exploitations of grievances, prejudices, and emotion, and by other superbly skilful devices of play-acting." Of course, this tropics-minded policy includes Brazil, considered by some a tropical China or, rather *the* tropical China. Consequently, as Mr. Wilson points out, writing from a United States point of view in the final passages of his book, "now is the time to play well and look South."

Is the United States playing well in regard to Brazil? Scarcely a single Brazilian thinks so. Most Brazilians—even some of those who are known as sincere friends of the United States—think that their country has been, or is being, used by the United States for its narrowly national purposes without reciprocity or any special consideration for what has been Brazil's traditional policy of co-operating with the United States. Some Brazilians have even reached the conclusion that Argentina has been wiser in its policy in regard to the United States: a policy of roughness, arrogance, brutal "realism." They think that this policy seems to be more fruitful than the Brazilian one. For them, the United States takes Brazilian willingness to co-operate as passive submission allowing Anglo-Americans to consider Brazil a submissively friendly nation and then give special facilities to tropical nations that follow the Argentinian method of dealing with the United States.

There may be something in these arguments and there are facts that seem to back them.[1] One thing is certain: for the first time in history of the relations of Brazil with the United States, Yankeephobia is becoming a potent factor. The famous anti-United States letter signed by Vargas before his tragic death—I say signed by him because it is so badly written, so grossly demagogical, so deficient in the very qualities that made Vargas known and admired, that, having known him personally, I refuse to believe that he himself wrote it—has contributed enormously toward intensifying Yankeephobia in Brazil. It is time now for the United States to have an exceptionally able ambassador to Rio de Janeiro —a second Edwin Morgan, who will add personal charm to a

[1] In a recent book, *Um Estadista da República* (Rio, 1955), Professor Affonso Arinos de Melo Franco, a member of the Brazilian House of Representatives, pointed out a significant example of a situation in which the United States refused to take a stand in favor of Brazil in an international issue, as asked by the Brazilian Foreign Office in its traditionally suave way, and then, immediately after this refusal, acted in favor of Argentina on the same issue (III, 1517-23). This is why Senator Lourival Fontes, in his *Discurso aos Surdos* (Rio, 1955), argues for the adoption by Brazil of an international policy that will go farther than "international courtesy" (p. 34).

deeper knowledge of economic and social problems—so that Brazil will not go on becoming a tropical China in some of the undesirable aspects of that concept.

Yankeephobia is becoming something of a religion among less well-educated Brazilians, well known for their predisposition to fall victims to emotional appeals. In connection with this, Vargas has become, after his death even more than while he lived, an example of the classic charismatic leader of Weber's definition: one who in an epoch of unrest stands at the beginning of a revolutionary, emotional, sectarian movement. He is finding adherents, as a typical charismatic leader would anywhere, because he is believed to have been the one who knew what was really needed for Brazil. And according to some Brazilian nationalists, nothing was more important in this knowledge than the fact that Brazil has been, or is being, exploited by the United States under the disguise of friendship. Hence the attitude of those sectarian nationalists who now claim for Brazil a position similar to that of China, that is, a position of aggressive resistance toward the United States and of receptive tolerance toward Soviet Russia, the only rival power of the United States at present.

One thing, however, should be taken into consideration in connection with an anti-United States *mystique* in present-day Brazil as part of a projection of Vargas's charisma over a large part of the Brazilian population, a charisma intensified by his tragic death. This is that Vargas reduced Communism in Brazil to a movement whose only hopes of attaining power are now through infiltration into the army, the navy, and the air force. As a force among the proletarian and the poor, the Vargas cult in Brazil became much more important than Communism; and perhaps to attain this, Vargasism had to outdo Communism in hostility to the United States as the symbol of the worst form of "bourgeois capitalism" and "imperialism."

When this is taken into consideration, one becomes prepared to accept the possible rise to presidential power of Vargas's successor as leader of the "worker's cause" in Brazil, Senhor Jango Goulart—now Vice President of the Republic—as a Brazilian Ngo Dinh Diem, to use an Asian, though not Chinese, point of reference. On the other hand, this may happen with another man, perhaps General Teixeira Lott, possibly Governor Jânio Quadros or Mayor Ademar de Barros, taking the role of a President of the

Republic who will probably be anti-United States in some of his nationalistic attitudes, though, like Vargas, any one of them will probably also be an obstacle to new attempts by the Communists, inspired by Soviet Russia, to transform Brazil into a tropical China according to their taste.

While Brazil waits for a new election for the Presidency, a physician who has become a politician, something unusual in the West, but not in the East—and in this, as at other points, Brazil presents a striking similarity to the Eastern world—is intensively engaged, as President of the Brazilian Republic, in establishing a new capital for the Republic in the very center of the country. This is indeed a monumental task, and if its foundations are definitely laid by President Juscelino Kubitschek during his presidential term, he will become a historic figure while still a young man with a face that reminds us of a Chinese or an Oriental with a European or Anglo-American training: he has non-European blood.

The plan to establish the capital of the Brazilian Republic in central Brazil involves a very complex group of problems. The architectural ones are being attended to by the two ablest modern Brazilian architects: Senhor Lúcio Costa and Senhor Oscar Niemeyer. Senhor Cândido Portinari, the painter, will probably be asked to decorate new buildings with adequate murals. But some critics fear that urbanistic problems of a sociological character are not being considered as they should be, though one of the assistants to Senhor Lúcio Costa has stated that the idea of a Brazilian sociologist that towns should have special zones for "social interpenetration" is being used by urbanists in the planning of the new capital. Nobody knows of any plans for European immigration of farmers—good farmers for tropical areas, such as the Portuguese of the Madeira Island—to provide for the needs of the new capital, establishing themselves as communities of families, an ideal opportunity for this type of colonization in an almost virgin part of tropical Brazil.

Numerous other problems of social relevance, for the orientation of whose solutions anthropologists, sociologists, economists, and educators should be consulted, seem to be neglected, with the risk of enormous mistakes being made by politicians with the help only of engineers and architects. Perhaps in the treatment of some of these problems, modern Chinese and Oriental leaders are being wiser than Brazilian politicians, most of whom have not yet realized that the task of modernizing such a tropical China as Brazil is in some respects a very complex one, not to be accomplished only by politicians, engineers, and architects. A broader vision of problems is needed and also a technique of planning similar to that followed in the United States in regard to the Tennessee Valley.

As in China, industrialization in Brazil has meant, for a large part of the peasant population, the "physical and spiritual dislocations . . . that have undermined existing institutions" which an Anglo-American expert in non-Western problems points out in a recent book, *The Nature of the Non-Western World*.[2] In China, according to the same observer, these dislocations left "a vacuum" in which Communism "has proved the most powerful element of reintegration." Will Brazil have to depend upon so radical and violent a solution for its problems of social reintegration? Objective analysis of the problem seems to point to different means for Brazilians to achieve reintegration between rural and urban, industrial and agrarian activities. Here as in face of other difficulties, the choice would not be "either-or," between this and that, but in the direction of a complementary policy, for which a Brazilian student of the problem has adapted, from the English language, the word "rurban," giving it a new and broader implication than the one it has had so far; and meaning by it a dynamic adjustment between two apparent contraries.

Brazil would thus develop, in possibly a more dynamic way than China—for its population is in a more plastic condition than that of China—in a "rurban" civilization, more rurban than that of the United States. For this development would profit from ultramodern technical facilities favoring decentralization of industries, with modernisms usually associated only with cities taken to rural communities. The capital of Brazil, changed from Rio de Janeiro to Brasília, would be a decisive step toward the development of Brazil as a "rurban" civilization of the most dynamic type, with agriculture and industry as complementary activities and not as the antagonistic ones they have been in Brazil and in other countries. This would be a check on the tendency of some Brazilian leaders to make the cause of "industrialization" and that of "na-

---

[2] Chapter II, *The Nature of the Non-Western World* (New York, 1957), by Vera Micheles Dean. An interesting book, though rather deficient on Latin America.

tional independence" a single cause, a messianic cause. Of course, it is not. Brazilian experience is already evidence in favor of what Mr. Eugene Staley writes in *The Future of Underdeveloped Countries*, that "unless agriculture does modernize substantially, industrial expansion in most undeveloped countries is likely to be cut short by lack of markets, for the great majority of the population will not have the necessary purchasing power."

Although apparently an absolute enthusiast for industrialization, Getúlio Vargas was convinced that industrialism by itself was not the solution for a "tropical China" like Brazil. A few days before he committed suicide, his secretary telephoned me from Rio to Recife, saying that the President wanted to see me at once. It was very urgent. I took the first plane going from Recife to Rio, and was immediately received by Vargas; with him I had an old personal friendship, though not political affinities. He told me that he had for me what he considered a very important mission from a Brazilian or a national point of view, more important than any of a constructive character which he could think of at the moment. He told me that I should not fear that it would be a political mission: it was something far above politics. He wanted to begin at once an agrarian reform in Brazil. It would mean the modernization of agriculture and the decentralization of industries, which he knew I thought essential for Brazil. But to do this he wanted from me something more than suggestions or ideas: he wanted me as head of a national organism that would be more important than any post in his cabinet and that would give him the basis for a policy of immigration and colonization, for he agreed with me that nothing could be done in the way of an agrarian reform without European immigrants of the "right sort" who would stay as farmers.

I refer to this because it seems to indicate that Vargas had a clear vision of Brazilian problems even though at the end of his career he was a politician surrounded by politicians, some of whom saw only in him the charismatic leader they needed in order to stay in power. And the easiest way for politicians to stay in power in Brazil was then, and still is, to be, or to appear to be, narrowly nationalistic, to see a panacea in industrialization, and to flirt so much with Communism as to make it possible for Communists of the sectarian type who follow Russian instructions— and now so weak in Brazil among intellectuals, students, and laborers as to be insignificant as such—to attempt to take control of the country, through penetration of the army, the navy, or the air force. This is a risk; and an adventure of this kind may happen, a repetition of the bloody adventure of 1935, led by a Brazilian Communist trained in Russia and himself a former officer in the Brazilian Army. The technique followed then was Russo-Asiatic: it caused indignation among Brazilians—even among those who were leftist. But this was in 1935, and a small group of sectarian Communists under the same Russo-Asiatic spell of Communism may take advantage of present-day political and military leaders who think it a safe game for them to use Communism against "Yankee imperialism" and against liberals of what they consider a *démodé* type (and some of these liberals are really *démodé* in imagining that what is good for them is good for non-bourgeois Brazilians).

Communism, especially of an Oriental or Asiatic type, would be no solution for Brazilian problems. Brazilian civilization, though not European or passively sub-European, is too Western and, from a sociological point of view, too Christian to admit that solution. More than recent nations like India or Pakistan or Ceylon, Brazil offers an example of a blending of European with non-European ideas, customs, and traditions, with a predominance of the European or Western ones. What has been said of India and Pakistan—that their blend of non-European ideas with modern Western ideas of social welfare into a workable synthesis represents "the most telling challenge yet discovered to totalitarian Communism"—may be said much more aptly of Brazil. It is a nation in search of its own solution for its own problems, a solution that socially is already beginning to be a workable synthesis of the European and non-European elements of its civilization. Only in its political aspect is this synthesis still deficient.

But even under this aspect, the present Brazilian situation, though damaged by an almost tragic absence of able leadership, is plastic enough to admit a readjustment between advanced thought in regard to labor—advanced here not meaning Communist—and a serious effort toward industrialization and mechanization of agriculture, in which so-called free enterprise may take an active part. The 1946 Constitution of Brazil is certainly wise on this point: the opening paragraph of its paragraphs on the "social and economic order" is one of conciliation between those who wanted to give absolute emphasis to the so-called "valorization" of labor and those who wanted to emphasize free enterprise. As an independent member of the National Assembly that was charged with the task of drawing a new constitution for Brazil—entirely independent from any political party, economic group, or ideological sect, for he was elected through the initiative of university students—the author of this book took what he considers a decisive part in the wording of that paragraph, a paragraph extremely important for the social and economic development of Brazil. He feels happy in having succeeded in defeating then a Brazilian version of Perón's "justicialism," in which there was also something of Communism— Soviet Communism—but he feels happy also in having contributed to defeat a "free enterprise" entirely antagonistic to the welfare state in a country like Brazil. Though this may sound like a sociological paradox, Brazil needs both. The conflict between the desire to preserve "traditional values" and the desire to live in harmony with "twentieth-century conditions," so well observed by a number of modern students of non-Western countries, is not peculiar to Oriental or African peoples. It is also found among Brazilians and other Latin Americans. And one of the expressions of this conflict is found in a Yankeephobia that identifies the United States with a capitalism considered to be disdainful of everything, including the improvement of the cultural conditions of workers, that does not mean profit for capitalists.

It is the conviction of some Brazilian students of the Brazilian situation that it will be possible through conciliation of technical development and some of the traditional values characteristic of Brazil and which may be preserved among workers, for this Latin American nation to develop a civilization that can be modern in its technical aspects without becoming in other aspects sub-European or sub-Yankee. Some of these students envisage this civilization— peculiar, in the American hemisphere, to Brazil, with this peculiarity not meaning absence of affinities with the other republics of America—as a Luso-tropical, that is, Portuguese-tropical, civilization that, if recognized as such, would be a vast civilization more wide-spread even than that of China—in America, Africa, the Orient, islands of the Atlantic, and Europe itself, in spaces either tropical or quasi-tropical. If such a unified civilization is really developing, then Brazil may be considered the potential leader of a significant modern civilization. A "tropical China" whose extension is considerable, and whose language—the Portuguese language —is spoken today by almost eighty million people.

II. THE BRAZILIAN PROBLEM: A COMMUNIST VIEW

Jacob Gorender *

Capitalist development in Brazil has proceeded at an accelerated rate in the past three decades, gaining particular momentum in the '50s. This has resulted in a marked increase in industrial production.[1]

Industrial production, which until 1930 was about half that of agriculture in terms of value, has almost drawn level with the latter. As regards the output of consumer goods, it is now nearing the level of the latter and there is every indication that it may even surpass it.

There is no doubt that the economy of Brazil has undergone big changes both in volume and in structure.

This development has produced a crop of diverse theories. Bourgeois apologists, and especially the advocates of the so-called "theory of development," claimed that capitalist expansion would of itself lead to economic independence for the country and to prosperity for the people. The revisionists argued that the growth

* Jacob Gorender is Secretary of the Brazilian Communist Party, and is considered to be its leading theoretical spokesman.

1	1941	1950	1960
Electric power (1,000 kwh)	1,232.7	1,882.5	4,800.0
Steel (1,000 tons)	155.4	768.6	2,300.0
Oil (1,000 tons)	10.4†	44.3	3,871.0
Cement (1,000 tons)	767.5	1,385.8	4,442.6
Automobiles (1,000)		30.7**	133.1
Cotton fabrics (million meters)	989.7	No data	1,272.9***

† Data for 1945.
** Data for 1957. As in 1960, they include the output of automobiles, trucks, and other vehicles.
*** Data for 1958.

would automatically solve the tasks of the anti-imperialist and anti-feudal revolution. But the growing contradictions in Brazilian society are the refutation of these arguments.

An analysis of objective data shows that the development of capitalism in Brazil, far from having solved the basic tasks of the anti-imperialist and anti-feudal revolution, has, on the contrary, underscored their urgency. One feature of the development is that by stimulating the growth of the productive forces it has intensified the old structural discrepancies and has given rise to new ones, thereby hastening the maturing of revolution.

The first thing to note is that economic progress has not rid the country of imperialist domination; it has merely compelled imperialism to adapt itself to the new conditions in which its domination became even more oppressive. Let us examine the more basic aspects of this question.

Expansion of foreign capital. Unlike the situation in the '30s and the '40s, direct foreign investment shot up in the '50s. The foreign investment was computed to be around $3,500,000,000 in 1959. According to the same estimates, foreign capital accounted for 25% of the total invested in industry and trade in 1957, 31% in 1959, and 32% in 1960. These figures relate only to direct investments. It follows, then, that as a result of the plowing back of profits and increased investments from abroad, particularly in 1957–60, foreign capital, far from declining, showed a rapid increase.

The figures cited here do not, of course, give the whole picture. They do not take into account the credits issued by Brazil banks (State banks included) to foreign-owned undertakings and the recent mobilization of local capital through numerous investment companies or direct partnership between foreign and Brazil capitalists. The Brazilian economist Aristóteles Moura, who has studied this question, cited the data for 1950 published by the U.S. Department of Commerce, showing that 36% of the capital of U.S.-controlled undertakings in Latin America was of local origin.[2] If we assume that the same proportion (which is undoubtedly understated) applies to over-all foreign investments in Brazil, we can safely conclude that the imperialists directly control over 40% of all investment in industry and trade.

[2] A. Moura, *O Capital Estrangeiro no Brasil* (São Paulo: Ed. Banas, 1961).

The capital invested in manufacturing industry directly belonging to foreign capital was distributed approximately as follows in 1959: in the cellulose industry 22%; in the paper industry 15%; 62% in the pharmaceutical industry; 17% in iron and steel; 38% in engineering; 57% in the production of spare parts; 69% in the automobile industry; 37% in the chemical industry; and 28% in plastics production. Of the total for the same year 37.5% was U.S. capital, Canadian 17.7%, Federal German 9.3%, British 7.4%, Benelux countries 5.6%, French 5.5%, and Italian 4.5%. Actually, however, the United States share is bigger considering that about one-fourth of the shares in the Traction, Light and Power Company, the biggest Canadian company in Brazil, are held by U.S. interests. The past few years have also witnessed big inroads by Japanese capital, particularly in the form of loans and credits.

In what way does the present foreign capitalist expansion in Brazil differ from the earlier process, and especially before the '40s?

Unlike the earlier period when foreign capital was channeled chiefly to public utilities (including electric power), transport, trade, and other non-manufacturing branches, it is being concentrated more and more in the manufacturing industry, particularly heavy industry. According to the Foreign Trade Department of the Banco do Brasil, new direct foreign investment, registered in the form of import of equipment, totaled $511,200,000 between 1955 and 1961. Of this sum $379,500,000 was invested in heavy industry, the remaining $131,700,000 in light industry.

The explanation for this is not so much the initiative displayed by the foreign capitalists as the economic headway made by the country. For a long time the imperialists did their utmost to prevent the industrialization of Brazil, which was engendered by the internal forces of capitalist development. Another contributory factor was the two world wars, and also the economic crisis of 1929–33 which compelled the country to cut down sharply on imports. During the period of rapid economic development, which covered the '30s, the '40s, and the first three years of the '50s, the direct foreign investment (excluding reinvestment) and foreign loans did not play a very significant role. In the '50s, however, when industrialization forged ahead, the imperialist monopolies, changing their tactics, took part in the industrialization with a view to controlling the key positions in industry and gaining the maximum out of it.

To this end the foreign monopolies were granted preferential terms in the sphere of legislation, credits, currency operations, taxation, etc. The government itself sought to attract foreign capital. The so-called National Goals plan, for example, drafted by the Kubitschek government to develop the key sectors of the national economy, provided that direct foreign investment loans and credits would reach the sum of $2,318,500,000 over the period of 1957-61. In fulfillment of this plan, foreign capital investment and financing totaled $1,836,200,000 between 1957 and 1960. The National Goals plan embodies the conciliatory policy of the bourgeoisie, which, although favoring economic development, wants to achieve this in collaboration with imperialism. Thus it swings from intransigence to agreement, the outcome being mutual concessions. And it is undeniable that this policy of the bourgeoisie has, to a certain extent, been instrumental in forcing imperialism to modify its position.

This is particularly evident in the case of U.S. finance capital. According to U.S. Department of Commerce estimates, direct American investment in Brazil's public utilities and transport totaled $96,900,000 in 1929, and in the manufacturing industry, $45,-700,000. By 1959 U.S. capital investment in Brazil had reached $1,201,000,000. Of this sum $86,700,000 was invested in public utilities and transport, $970,100,000 in manufacturing industry, and $470,100,000 in the engineering and automobile industries alone. Characteristic, too, is the position of the West German monopolies whose direct investment in 1959 totaled $320,200,000. Of this sum $200,500,000 was invested in the engineering and automobile industries and $30,700,000 in the iron and steel industry. U.S. capital began to display greater interest in heavy industry only after the West European monopolies, especially the Federal German, began to gain a foothold there. Although the imperialistic powers have common interests in exploiting the Brazilian market, they at the same time compete with each other.

Fetters of the foreign debt. Another form of imperialist exploitation is associated with the foreign debt which in the '50s reached vast dimensions. This is due to a number of factors, among them the increased transfer abroad (legally and illegally) of capital held by foreigners, payments for patents, increased imports of raw materials, equipment, and fuel, necessitated by the industrialization, which are accompanied by a chronic deficit in the trade balance, compelling the country to resort to foreign loans and credits; the growing import-export price gap, especially since 1954, arising from the fall in the price of coffee and other export products, which, in turn, led to a decrease in the amount of foreign currency earned; [3] and lastly, the illegal "flight" of Brazilian capital to Western Europe and the United States. These factors forced Brazil to indulge in heavy foreign borrowing and on very onerous terms. By the beginning of 1961, its liabilities in convertible currency reached the sum of $3,515,300,000; in 1961 alone, Brazil had to pay $1,166,900,000 on its debts.[4] As a result of negotiations in the United States and Western Europe, the Quadros government was granted a deferment on payments and additional credits. In exchange for this the government, submitting to the dictatorial attitude of the International Monetary Fund, introduced reforms in the exchange rate, thus abolishing even those small protective barriers the country still had in the sphere of exchange and completely surrendering the money market to the mercies of foreign capital.

As might have been expected things became worse; 1962 saw a big deficit in the trade and payments balance. Hence the outlook is pretty bleak, especially when we bear in mind that foreign capital, which is rapidly growing, will siphon out of the economy bigger and bigger profits. This will make it still easier for the imperialist monopolies to make big reinvestments at the expense of the working people and to continue to pay big dividends to their shareholders. Hence the persistence displayed by imperialism through its organizations like the IMF, to get Brazil to accept the policy of "free" exchange, so essential to unhampered import-export of foreign capital. The steady shrinking of exports and the chronic deficit in the balance of payments will confront the country with more difficulties in importing essential goods. It will, therefore, have no choice but to seek more foreign loans on still more onerous terms. What is more, a sizable part of these loans will have to be used to pay the old debts. *The end result is a*

---

[3] According to a statement made by ex-President Kubitschek last December, in the period from 1954 to 1962 the country lost $500,000,000 as a result of the fall in the price of coffee. "The Latin American states are in a peculiar position," he commented in connection with U.S. aid under the Alliance for Progress plan. "It reminds one of a sick person who is given a blood transfusion in one arm with the blood taken from another."

[4] *Relatório do Banco do Brasil* (1961).

vicious circle which fetters and deforms the national economy and forces the people to pay a colonial tribute to their foreign exploiters.

Much of the foreign debt has to be paid to the United States. Of all the credits extended to Brazil as of September 30, 1961, 51.3% came from the United States. If we add to this the credits extended by the International Bank for Reconstruction and Development and the International Monetary Fund, both of which are under the control of U.S. finance capital, the figure will be about 70.8%. U.S. imperialism thus has a powerful weapon for bringing pressure to bear on the Brazilian government and compelling it to make political and economic concessions. In the light of this it is clear why the Ministry of Finance, irrespective of who is the republic's President, has for many years been a sort of patrimony of the big bankers and industrialists closely associated with U.S. monopolies or with their top men in Brazil.

An end to the policy of compromise. The development of capitalism in Brazil, while it has strengthened national capital, both state and private, has done little to abolish the imperialist domination. Just the reverse. It has pursued a policy of compromise with imperialism, especially U.S. imperialism. The outcome is that it has intensified the contradictions between the people, on the one hand, and U.S. imperialism and its domestic agents on the other. Politically this is expressed in the intensification of the mass struggle for national liberation. This struggle is supported by those sections of the bourgeoisie whose interests have been hurt by the policy of betrayal of the country's interests and compromise with imperialism. But their nationalism notwithstanding, these sections are inconsistent and hesitate to take a definite stand.

Important gains have been won in the struggle for national independence, such as the establishment of a state oil monopoly, some positive changes in the country's foreign policy—the establishment of diplomatic relations with the U.S.S.R. and other socialist countries, support for Cuba's right to self-determination, etc.

The big bourgeoisie is using these gains of the people to strengthen its own bargaining positions with imperialism. Thus, in the State of Rio Grande do Sul the government has taken over the subsidiaries of the two U.S. companies, the American and Foreign Power Corporation and the International Telephone and Telegraph Company. While this measure did not greatly injure the more influential concessionaires, it did have the effect, since it was carried out in terms that were favorable to the nation, of raising anew the question of nationalizing those foreign-owned utilities that were not keeping pace with the growing requirements of the national economy. Meanwhile, President Goulart, who was constantly under U.S. government and press fire, although his policy has essentially been one of compromise with imperialism, hastened to propose his plan for a general take-over of foreign-owned public utilities. Goulart's plan, however, provided that their owners be suitably compensated and enabled to transfer their capital to more profitable and "sounder" branches of the Brazilian economy. This anti-national decision was confirmed in the joint statement by Goulart and Kennedy, signed in April 1962 during the latter's visit to Brazil, in which the Brazilian President declared that his government would provide safeguards enabling private capital to play a vital role in advancing Brazil's economy, and that agreements with private companies on conveying public utilities to the state would be based on the principle of fair compensation and the investments involved transferred to other branches essential for the economic development of Brazil. President Kennedy, the statement said, evinced much interest in this policy.

The foregoing clearly shows up the compromising attitude of the Brazilian bourgeoisie.

In August 1962 the National Congress, yielding partly to the nationalist movement, passed a law imposing certain restrictions (it is true, weak and inadequate) on foreign capital, particularly as regards the outflow of profits. But even this law, though it falls short of what is needed to protect the national economy, is in danger of being curtailed because of the campaign started by foreign capitalists with the support of the conciliators both inside and outside Parliament.

However that may be, the compromising attitude of the bourgeoisie is powerless to prevent the aggravation of the antagonisms between the national interests and the interests of imperialism. As the masses in town and country begin to take a more active part in the political life of the country, under the revolutionary leadership of the proletariat, the policy of betrayal and of compromise will be defeated and its place taken by national liberation and independence.

*   *   *

Nor has the development of capitalism brought with it corresponding changes in the agrarian structure inherited from the times of colonial slavery and founded on the domination of the latifundists. Not only has this structure been preserved, it is being buttressed and adapted to capitalist conditions. An indication of this is the growth of the number of tractors from 7,000 in 1950 to 66,000 in 1960. On the vast coffee, cocoa, and sugar-cane plantations, and the livestock ranches (the main branches of latifundist agriculture), capitalist methods go hand in hand, to a lesser or greater degree, with semi-feudal survivals. More capitalist in the South and more feudal in the North and Northeast, the latifundia with their parasitic forms of exploitation of labor and the land are the obstacle to a rapid development in agriculture.

According to the 1950 census there were about 2,000,000 farms in the country. Of these 3.4% were farms of 500 and more hectares and occupied 62.3% of all privately owned land (under the census of rules the concept "farm" does not necessarily imply ownership, for it may refer to the farm of a leaseholder or a settler who has no title deed on the land). But 22.2% of the farms were of less than five hectares each, in other words (discounting rare high-yielding crops), not enough for the peasant to sustain his family. These data give an idea of the degree of land concentration in Brazil.[5]

Only a small part of the 1960 census figures for agriculture have been published, which makes it difficult to draw a comparison with the census figures for previous years. But even they show a considerable growth in the number of farms: from 2,064,600 in 1950 to 3,319,200 in 1960, that is, by 60.8%. It does not necessarily follow from this, however, that the growth has taken place at the expense of the latifundia. The organ of the National Confederation of Industrialists, *Desenvolvimento e Conjuntura*, in its issue of June 1962 commented as follows on this process: "In general the increase in the number of farms took place without breaking up the big and medium-sized estates which are not being touched. The cultivation of new areas in Maranhão, Bahia, Espírito Santo, Paraná, Goiás, Mato Grosso, and other States, was accompanied by a tendency to set up small farms."

In reality, the increase in the number of farms is due to the crisis

[5] Rui Facó, *Brasil século XX* (Rio de Janeiro, 1960).

in the agrarian structure, which is driving the peasants en masse from the latifundia-dominated districts to the towns and also to areas where there is unused land. A large part of the new farms belongs to the so-called *posseiros*, that is, peasant squatters who cultivate it themselves but who have no legal right to it, because the government has made it well-nigh impossible for them to obtain this right. But only to a limited degree can the new areas serve as an outlet to lessen the congestion caused by the latifundist monopoly. The thing is that the latifundists and speculators of all hues are trying, with government connivance, to entrench themselves in the areas after the small farmers have brought them under cultivation. Hence the frequent agrarian conflicts in the past few years, conflicts which often grow into armed clashes between the peasants and the retainers of the latifundists.

An indication of the slow penetration of capitalism into agriculture can be seen in the fact that in the decade between 1950 and 1960 the rural population increased by a bare 6,000,000—from 33,-000,000 to 39,000,000. Although the rural population is declining in proportion to the population as a whole, it is increasing in absolute ratio. In other words, we have here a process the reverse of that typical for countries where agriculture has undergone technical reconstruction. And this absolute growth of rural population aggravates the contradictions between the exploited peasant masses and the ruling clique of latifundists.

Preservation of the latifundists' land monopoly is depressing the already low standard of living of the peasants and, consequently, hampers the development of the productive forces not only in agriculture but in industry as well. Whereas output of means of production has created its own market, having replaced imports and substantially expanding in the last ten years the market for its goods, production of consumer goods is encountering difficulties precisely because of the restricted home market. Such industries as textiles and footwear, for example, despite growth of production taken over a long period, have been stagnant for years.

The latifundist monopoly is felt also in food consumption. Whereas the production of foodstuffs for the home market increased approximately 48% between 1950 and 1960, the growth in population for the same period was 36.6%, reaching 70,967,000, the rural increase being 17.5% and that in the urban population, 70.3%. (In 1950 the urban population totaled 18,000,000, or 36.2%

of the total; by 1960, according to preliminary census figures it had reached 32,000,000, or 45.1% of the total.) Although food production is outstripping the total population growth it is lagging behind the urban growth and behind the demand for foodstuffs. To make matters worse, the latifundist monopoly either excessively inflates the price of land or allows soil exhaustion, thus more and more pushing the agricultural producing areas into the hinterland, away from the big cities along the coast, causing transportation costs to go up and leading to a waste of agricultural products. Food prices, as a consequence, are constantly rising, there are frequent interruptions in supplies which are further aggravated by profiteering, especially on the part of the wholesalers who are organized on monopoly lines.

The land monopoly, the high prices for agricultural and animal products, the penetration of capitalist relations into agriculture— these factors are sending up the prices of land near the towns, that is, in the very places where latifundists hold sway. This has greatly increased the rent extracted by them and intensified their social parasitism. It is only natural, therefore, that the growing contradictions in agriculture should be reflected in the sweeping peasant movement and in the popularity of the demand for a radical agrarian reform.

In order fully to appreciate how capitalist development is adversely affecting the conditions of the working people, mention should be made of another of its features, viz., the chronic inflation, the greatest, perhaps, in the world.

Inflation in Brazil has its source in the complex of trade and financial relations with imperialism, which has led to chronic devaluation of the cruzeiro, especially since the Second World War. The exporters (the latifundists and wholesalers) view the devaluation of the cruzeiro as a means of compensation (advantageous to them but at the expense of the economy) for the fall in the prices of their exports. Inflation is also the result of the latifundist structure which, as we have said, is causing agricultural prices to soar. Another inflationary factor in the past five years is the policy of piling up coffee in the warehouses. According to the president of the Brazilian Coffee Institute the government had in its warehouses as of July 12, 1962, 52,000,000 sacks of coffee for export. In terms of the average price for the period from January to April 1962 inclusive, this mountain of coffee was valued at $2,079,000,000; this was paid for in cruzeiros which aggravated the inflation.

Despite world coffee overproduction and the fall in coffee prices on the world market (this was evident in 1957), the coffee plantations were enlarged from 3,672,000 hectares in 1957 to 4,420,000 hectares in 1960. In other words, another 748,000 hectares were cultivated to replenish existing supplies, although the people are short of cereals and other primary products. But the coffee growers do not have to worry. They are assured credits from the Banco do Brazil and their coffee crop is guaranteed a market at profitable prices in cruzeiros, the government buying the surpluses left over from export. With calamity now knocking at the door the government intends to carry out a costly and bureaucratic plan of destroying the unprofitable coffee plantations. This is the price the nation has to pay for the preposterous waste of material values and labor—a glaring example of irrational management of the economy.

The foregoing, however, are not the only factors responsible for the inflation. There is also the inflation policy, deliberately pursued by the bourgeoisie, especially in the last decade, through the state system of note emissions and credits. The Brazilian economist Celso Furtado, an advocate of the "theory of development," frankly writes in his book *Development and Underdevelopment*: ". . . There can be no doubt that the industrialization was aided by inflation. The latter did not stand aside from the process of industrialization; it served it as a means for removing obstacles." Another economist, J. P. de Aemeida Magalhães, stated that ". . . in countries like Brazil, inflation can for an indefinite period play a positive role." This positive role, we are told, is that by compelling the working people to economize it could increase investment. The author holds that theoretically it is possible to get rid of the inflation gradually, in the course of a few years, without hurting investment, *provided the workers voluntarily agree to economize, that is, agree to wage cuts.* Here we have in a nutshell the bourgeoisie's idea of an inflationary policy. In some instances state capitalism in Brazil is of a progressive nature, but its financing was promoted by big inflationary emissions, from which private capital received and continues to receive generous state credits. In the final analysis this means that part of the working people's income is used, without compensation, for investments in state and private undertakings. The bourgeoisie has used inflation as an instrument to intensify the exploitation of the working class, to clamp exorbitant prices on the consumer, and to realize, in the end, a kind of primary accumulation of capital.

An idea of the scale of the inflation can be gleaned from the cost-of-living index in Rio de Janeiro, which according to the journal *Conjuntura Econômica* increased tenfold between 1948 and 1961. Even the bourgeoisie who have waxed rich on the inflation are taking fright at its gallop. The cost of living in Rio de Janeiro and São Paulo in 1954–57, according to the journal *Desensolvimento e Conjuntura* (February 1962, p. 57), rose at a rate of 20% annually, and in 1959–61 the rise exceeded 33%.

Inflation has seriously affected the conditions of the working class. Average real wages in Rio de Janeiro, according to official data, have never topped the 1920 level, and in the '50s they were rarely higher than the 1940 level. The short-lived rise in wages in 1956–58 was followed by a drop in real wages, as shown by the data of the Inter-Trade Union Department of Statistics and Social-Economic Research, and the Economic Department of the National Confederation of Industrialists. Even the official statistics can not conceal the fact that the economic law of the relative and absolute impoverishment of the working class under capitalism, discovered by Marx, is operating in Brazil. To prevent a further worsening of their conditions the working people are putting up a fight against the intensification of labor, from which the bourgeoisie—national and foreign—are amassing huge profits.

The contradictions between the proletariat and the bourgeoisie, which are becoming more acute, are reflected in the class struggle which is growing sharper as the proletariat gains in strength organizationally and politically. Although these contradictions cannot be radically solved at the present stage of the revolution (it not being a socialist revolution as yet), they are, nevertheless, leaving their imprint on developments.

It is difficult in the limits of one article to examine all aspects of the economic development in Brazil, for example, the development of state capitalism, the restriction of foreign trade, the uneven development in the different States, etc. Our purpose has been to give the reader a picture of a system rent by contradictions, a system that is highly unstable.

*　　*　　*

How to solve the contradictions caused by imperialist domination and the monopoly of the latifundists—this is the subject of a political debate that revolves around the problem of so-called radical or structural reforms. The compromising sections of the bourgeoisie and landowners want them to be reforms that will not lead to a break with imperialism, but, on the contrary, will help to win some concessions from it without essentially affecting foreign monopoly capital's plunder of the country. These reforms should not, in their view, abolish the latifundia, but rather assist in running them on capitalist lines, with only minor concessions being made to the peasantry (settlement on state-owned lands, easier terms of leasing and subleasing, etc.).

Abroad this attitude of compromise dovetails with Kennedy's Alliance for Progress which, aside from everything else, aims at coming to terms with the bourgeoisie by promising it more credits on favorable terms. At the same time this plan holds out the bait of pseudo-reforms designed solely to reduce the social and political tension in Latin America and to protect U.S. investments from an advance of the national-liberation movement which might follow the splendid and inspiring example of the Cuban Revolution. A subtle hoax, designed to preserve and consolidate imperialist domination, the Alliance for Progress has, for all that, brought its initiators rather discouraging results in the first year of its operation.

The united nationalist and democratic front now taking shape in Brazil is represented in the main by the working class, peasantry, and middle sections in the towns, and also by the national bourgeoisie whose interests, despite its inconsistency and tendency to compromise with foreign capital, are linked with general national aims.

The reactionaries, who are resisting revolutionary changes and structural reforms, are steadily losing ground, exposing themselves in the eyes of the masses. This is borne out by the unsuccessful military coup d'état of 1961–62, and by the results of the general election in October 1962 and the national plebiscite on January 6, 1963, at which the overwhelming majority of the people (over 75%) voted in favor of restoring the executive power of the President, curtailed by the reactionaries and military clique during the political crisis in the summer of 1961.

The revolutionary forces, headed by the working class, hold

that radical reforms should bring with them the complete liberation of the country, the abolition of latifundism, and structural reorganization of the social and economic system; this reorganization should accord with the radical tasks of the profoundly popular, anti-imperialist and anti-feudal revolution that will pave the way to the independent social and economic development of Brazil from which the working people of town and country will stand to gain. In conditions of the consolidation of socialism on the world arena, and with due regard to national peculiarities, such a revolution, led by the working class, will save the people of Brazil from the torments of capitalist development and enable them to pass on directly to socialism.

III. THE UNITED STATES, THE SOVIET UNION,
AND COMMUNISM IN BRAZIL

Luís Carlos Prestes *

The grand success achieved in building socialism in the Soviet Union has, naturally, aroused real enthusiasm both in Brazil and in the other countries of our continent. This is expressed in the admiration with which the numerous Brazilian M.P.s, scientists, artists, and athletes who in recent years have visited the Soviet Union speak of it, and also in the spontaneous manifestations of welcome for the Soviet people who have visited us. Although there are no diplomatic relations between our countries, the Brazilian and Soviet people have found common ground in the joint struggle for world peace, in initiating and extending cultural exchanges. And the more success the Soviet Union achieves in developing its economy, science, technology, and culture, the more effective will that rapprochement be.

Consequently the recently published theses of the report to be delivered at the Twenty-First Party Congress will add to the interest in Soviet achievements. In Brazil people are following this progress with keen interest.

Brazil, like other Latin American countries, is still an underde-

* Luís Carlos Prestes has long been the titular and spiritual leader of the Brazilian Communist Party. Before that he was the military hero of the *Tenentismo* movement.

veloped country. It yearns for progress and prosperity. Now we
are witnessing the awakening national consciousness which insists
on economic development, industrialization, and national liberation. We are in dire need of technological and financial aid, of
modern industrial equipment. All this is still monopolized by the
North Americans, who use their economic superiority to plunder
our natural wealth and keep our country in political subjugation.

Thus, there are sharpening contradictions between the people
of Brazil and the U.S. imperialists and their stooges. As long as
these contradictions remain unsolved we will suffer from low
prices for our exports and depreciation of our currency (last year,
within a few months the *cruzeiro* declined by one-half). In conditions of the general crisis of capitalism and the present economic
crisis in the United States, the imperialist drive against our national interests acquires an open and cynical character. Because of
pressure from the International Monetary Fund there is a widening gap between what we get for our exports and what we pay
for our imports from the United States. U.S. investors are demanding further privileges and "guarantees" for themselves, and
renouncement of our national investment in the basic branches of
the economy. At the same time they are demanding that measures
be taken against the working class and to the detriment of the
entire nation.

The direct result of this is a worsening of the conditions of the
working people, a rising cost of living, and lowering of the already miserable real wages.

The acute internal contradictions make necessary an independent solution of the problem of developing the national economy. It
is necessary to extend the foreign market. The bleeding of our
country, expressed in the pumping out of profits, without any
control, must be ended. The situation in Brazil is, in one way or
another, typical of all the Latin American countries. N. S. Khrushchev was quite correct when he said in a recent interview with
the Brazilian journalist Murilo Marrokin that "for decades the
American, British, and other foreign monopolies, like giant leeches,
have been clinging to the living body of Latin America, greedily
sucking dry and plundering its natural wealth, ruthlessly exploiting its peoples, distorting their economies, and retarding their
independent development."

Even the ruling classes in Brazil seek an outlet from this situation which cannot continue forever. An attempt in this direction was made by former President Juscelino Kubitschek, when he proclaimed the "pan-American operation," expressing the desire for economic development, to abolish the semi-colonial status and enable our countries to have an equal say in international affairs. This initiative, even though it did not go beyond the confines of obedience to the United States, suffered complete fiasco. Nor did the dramatic warning sounded by August Frederico Schmidt, the Brazilian delegate in the "Committee of 21" in Washington, to the effect that Latin America would be forced to seek more trade with the Soviet Union and People's Republic of China unless Washington rendered substantial aid to its southern neighbors, have any effect on the U.S. representatives.

The people of Brazil, however, like the other nations of Latin America, fully determined to carry on their fight for an independent national economy, are seeking new ways which would rule out the constant dependence on United States imperialism. These aims are supported by Oswaldo Aranha, former Minister of Foreign Affairs, and others who in the press and in public lectures have spoken in favor of direct business contacts between Brazil and the Soviet Union; by Assis Chateaubriand, Brazilian Ambassador to London, who wants closer ties with the East European countries and who in pursuit of this aim visited Prague.

These politicians realize that the socialist countries could be a vast market for our exports, that they could supply, on favorable terms, the machinery and equipment which now eat up our scanty currency reserves. That is why the *Cruzeiro* interview with Premier Khrushchev met with a wide response. Khrushchev reaffirmed that the Soviet government was prepared to aid the industrialization of Brazil by supplying us with machinery and equipment, training Brazilian specialists in the Soviet Union, and by giving us the benefit of its rich technological experience.

We know that all this is feasible, that we are not alone in the struggle which the Latin American nations are waging against backwardness and for economic emancipation. The Soviet Union's all-round support to all peoples striving for their liberation is meeting with growing sympathy in our countries. People are keenly interested in the fact that the Soviet Union is building an iron and steel plant in India which, when completed, will turn out 2.5 million tons of steel a year, and this without any share in capital, profits, or management, without any strings, either economic or political; in other words, the reverse of the practice of other countries. We have been favorably impressed by the U.S.S.R.-Egypt agreement on the construction of the Aswan dam, the Soviet Union granting a credit of 400 million rubles at very low interest to be paid off over a long period, and this again with no strings. We know that similar agreements have been concluded with other Asian and African countries, and recently with Argentina, not to mention the fraternal aid given by the Soviet Union to the people's democracies building socialism, and especially to the industrialization program of the Chinese People's Republic. Consequently, when the Soviet Union, confident of its strength, of the selfless and valiant labor of its people, launches another majestic plan for economic development, this evokes trust in the U.S.S.R. among the working people and intellectuals of our countries. This is also true of the national bourgeoisie and of the groups of capitalists and landlords who are antagonistic toward U.S. imperialism.

Foreign trade can become the cornerstone of a fruitful policy of rapprochement between our country and the Soviet Union. At present our foreign trade is virtually monopolized by the United States. This is one of the most striking manifestations of the North American parasitism in our economic life. Americans exercise their monopoly through U.S. domination of the world market in coffee, sugar, cocoa, cotton, and other products, which account for 80% to 90% of our traditional exports, and an even greater percentage of other agricultural produce. Over half of our coffee, sugar, and cotton exports, our chief sources of foreign currency, go to the United States. Abolition of this monopoly would be most beneficial for our entire economic activity.

Hence we place particularly big hopes on extending the market for our produce, especially when a new area with a population of over 900 million, including the U.S.S.R. and China, is opening before us. Hence the prospects which we see in the Seven-Year Plan, summed up in the theses. In view of the realization of the previous economic plans which transformed the Soviet Union into a leading world power, no one doubts that the targets of the new Plan, bold though they are, will become a reality. This Plan will greatly enhance the might of the world's first socialist state, and through an unprecedented rise in the national income and in purchasing power, will create better conditions for the people.

In this way the Soviet Union will have still greater facilities for rendering aid to the underdeveloped countries, who repose great hopes in it. We are one of those countries. We ardently want to get rid of our poverty and backwardness, the main result of our economic dependence on the U.S. monopolies.

Our existence as a sovereign nation depends on our free economic development. We are confident that the theses of Premier Khrushchev's report to the Twenty-First Congress of the C.P.S.U. will render another great service to the progressive forces in Brazil and in the other Latin American countries in the fight for their noble aims, for the realization of their dream of freedom, progress, and prosperity.

IV. THE UNITED STATES AND BRAZIL: A DIPLOMATIC VIEW
Roberto de Oliveira Campos *

I

"We are in the midst of a nation brought to the very verge of moral, political and material ruin. Corruption dominates the ballot box, the legislature, the Congress and even touches the ermines of the bench. Business is prostrated; our houses covered with mortgages; labor impoverished; and the land concentrated in the hands of capitalists. The fruits of the toil of millions are boldly stolen to build up . . . the fortunes for the few . . . we have witnessed for more than one quarter of the century the struggle of the two great parties for power and plunder. Neither do they now promise any substantial reform . . . they propose to sacrifice our homes, lives and children on the altar of Mammon."

This text is not a description of the turmoil and trials of the present transition in the Congo. It is not a stricture by conservative New York financial papers on the situation of economic chaos which in their view is confronting Latin America. The country described in the above quotation is the United States of America, and the diatribe is nothing less than the platform of the Populist Party, in its Omaha convention of July 4, 1892.

* Roberto de Oliveira Campos is the present Ambassador of Brazil to the United States. He was formerly a director of the Banco Nacional do Desenvolvimento Econômico.

Despite the objurgation of the Populist Party that displayed a singular lack of historical perspective, the United States grew to be a mighty nation with a sound economy and fair standards of social justice.

I wonder whether the U.S. financial circles as well as the press are not at this moment afflicted by a similar lack of historical perspective in examining the Brazilian reality.

The performance of a society both in times of glory and trouble must be judged by various indicators of a political, social, and economic nature. In the recent Brazilian case an obsessive focusing on the inflationary upsurge has led many analysts to disregard unreflectingly significant achievement in other areas.

With the onset of a profound constitutional crisis, brought about by the resignation of President Quadros, in August 1961, the nation was faced with a number of priority social objectives. First and foremost was upholding the fabric of an open and democratic society. Second was the preservation of a high rate of economic growth. Third, the attainment of a greater measure of autonomy in development decisions, and fourth, the maintenance of a reasonable degree of price stability.

The first objective appears to have been substantially achieved in the face of major internal tensions. Brazil is approaching the end of the constitutional crisis, with the scheduling for January 6 of the plebiscite to decide on the restoration of the presidentialist regime (which is likely to be the choice of the electorate) or the continuation of parliamentarianism. An open and freely debating society, untarnished by any military takeover, suspension of constitutional rights, or imposition of authoritarian controls, has been preserved.

The second objective is almost as important. For only a dynamic economy can provide the job flexibility, the opportunity for social promotion, and the widening of horizons needed to abate social tensions and make for ultimate viability. What is now the record? For the decade of the fifties as a whole, the Brazilian growth rate—5.8% per year in real terms—was the highest of Latin America. In 1960–61, despite the political crisis and adverse terms of trade, the increase in the gross national product was 7.2%. While in 1962 the rate of expansion seems to have abated, there are good prospects that 1963, when heavy investments in electricity and steel will come to fruition, will mark another upsurge in production.

In the history of the recent growth of the Brazilian economy, another important feature is that the expansion throughout the decade of the fifties has been achieved with practically unchanged imported inputs, since imports did not increase while the real GNP expanded by 31%. A comparable performance is hard to find in the non-socialist world. For in the majority of the developing countries, economic growth has been accompanied by a more than proportionate increase in imported inputs.

In the Brazilian case, the enhancement of the coefficient of autonomous growth has been made possible by the rise of import-substituting industries and particularly by the diversification and increasing sophistication of the domestic production of capital goods. In the last few years an entirely new motor-vehicle and shipbuilding industry has been created; steel production has expanded at an annual cumulative rate of 13%, and about 50% of the needs of capital goods are now met by domestic production. In the short run, this rapid pace of import substitution adds to the inflationary pressures of the economy. In the long run, it makes for structural flexibility and renders development decisions less dependent on vicissitudes of foreign trade and aid.

The sharpness of the inflationary advance in Brazil is incontrovertible evidence that we did not succeed in maintaining a reasonable degree of price stability. Nothing is further from my mind than to condone inflation or deny the serious social attrition or economic dislocations that come in its wake. There is in fact a general clamor from all sectors of the population in Brazil for measures to control inflation. Some have already been taken, such as the passage of a tax-reform bill designed to increase Treasury revenues by a minimum of Cr$130 billion. The Executive has also been authorized to present to Congress a program for reducing non-fixed government expenditures by 45% during 1963. The specific tax on electricity consumption has been converted into an "ad valorem" tax to provide non-inflationary financing for power programs. Proposals for readjusting public utility, transportation, and fuel rates are under study for enforcement as part of an over-all anti-inflationary program. Much ampler financing of the budget deficit through sale of escalator-clause Treasury bills is also contemplated.

While the seriousness of the inflationary problem in Brazil and in many other Latin American countries cannot be denied, it is equally true that the current analysis of this problem on the part of international financial organizations and banking circles in this country is far from balanced. There is, in the first place, a proneness to regard inflation from a moralistic and not a sociological viewpoint, as if it were simply a display of moral laxity and not the result of irresistible distributive pressures (claims on consumption) and growth pressures (claims on investments) in an environment characterized by adverse trade conditions for exporters of primary products.

There is, secondly, the view that inflated countries are necessarily violating the principle of self-help. This may be true if inflation is not accompanied by growth and is eating up large foreign resources through overspending on imports. Those are certainly not the characteristics of the Brazilian inflation, where growth has been maintained and the diet of imports has been meager. If anything, this proves self-help. For resources are being squeezed out from a poor economy, even though by cruel and brutal means. These comments are in no way a defense of inflation nor is it claimed that inflation played a causal role in the process of growth. In fact, given an adequate political context and efficient tax administration, economic development can be achieved and has been achieved with only moderate inflationary pressures.

They are, however, a plea for a balanced view of the problem and for recognition of the Brazilian performance in relation to other important social and political objectives.

The inner workings of the Anglo-Saxon mind are often mysterious. Somehow, countries that maintained price stability and fiscal discipline, even when suffering from low growth rates or stagnation, are held up as prime examples of self-help and conformity to the Alliance for Progress philosophy. But surely in the philosophy of the Alliance, growth takes precedence over stability; and if self-help means anything it means mobilization of resources which, in turn, cannot be meaningful if it does not translate itself into growth and expansion. These thoughts should make one more sober in words and less harsh in judgment when assessing the economy performance in underdeveloped countries.

There is justified apprehension in this country concerning the dangers of inflation in Latin America. But those sorely miss the point who do not recognize that an even greater danger is stagnation. When there is growth there is a continuous dilation of the economic horizon, and the correction of social injustices, though often slow, can be made without social explosion. When there is stagnation there is nothing left but a bitter fight for a share in the common misery.

In Latin America only two countries have managed in recent years to reconcile moderate inflation with an acceptable rate of expansion of the Brazilian economy in the last decade.

The seriousness of the stagnation problem in Latin America has been pungently underlined in the recent report of the Joint ECLA-OAS Secretariat to the Ministerial Meeting of the LAECOSOC in Mexico City. While during the period 1950–57, at least seven of the Latin American countries had attained 2.5% yearly rate of per-capita growth, during more recent years— 1957–61—in the light of available data only Brazil managed to accomplish the minimum growth objective set forth in the Punte del Este Charter.

There is now in this country fatigue and disenchantment in relation to foreign assistance. The *disenchantment* is perhaps based on a false analogy. Quick results were attained through massive infusion of funds for European recovery. No similar speed was or can be attained in the economic development field. For the job goes beyond the reconstruction of the physical plant and the setting in motion of existing skills. The job is one of promoting social transformation, creating new skills, and modernizing the whole fabric of society. Quite outside the fact that the scale of resources mobilized for the Alliance for Progress is but a fraction of those poured into Europe, the nature of the task does not lend itself to dramatic short-run achievements.

The *fatigue* stems perhaps from an overestimation of the real burden placed on the American economy by programs of foreign aid to underdeveloped countries in general, and to Latin America in particular. Those programs now absorb less than 1% of the GNP as compared to nearly 2% during the Marshall Plan, and the American economy has at present vast underutilized human and plant resources. More important still, there is a related underestimation of the subtle savings accruing to the consumer-taxpayer from the steady decline, since 1953, of the prices of imported primary products, a decline which, in the case of Latin American export products, has been sufficiently large to frustrate expected beneficial effects from aid.

This point which tends to be neglected in current discussions has been adequately emphasized in a recent speech by Mr. Edwin Martin, Assistant Secretary of State for Inter-American affairs, given at the Institute of World Affairs, in the University of Southern California.

Between 1953 and 1960 Latin American exports other than oil grew in quantity by thirty per cent but brought in only four per cent more foreign exchange. If prices had stayed at 1953 levels, Latin American earnings from exports would have been $1.3 billion larger than they were. You can understand how much difference this would have made.

Their exports are largely products whose prices fluctuate widely in response to small variations of supply. Accordingly, if they had exported much more of those products they would probably have earned less rather than more. Even as it was, the average price in 1961 of coffee and cocoa was only about sixty per cent of the 1953 level, bananas eighty-five per cent, and fibers—cotton and wool—about eighty per cent. These products alone accounted for one fourth of Latin American export earnings in that year.

Meanwhile, U.S. wholesale prices—a rough guide to their import cases—had increased ten per cent. This four-per-cent increase in export earnings fell substantially. And since government revenues are greatly affected by both export levels and the amount of imports export levels permit to be bought, as well as by related domestic business prosperity, they have increasingly fallen short of the demands made upon them.

Mr. Martin has underlined two aspects of the declining trend of Latin American terms of trade. The first is the resulting pressure on the balance of payments, which made it necessary to devote roughly 40% of the funds disbursed during the first year of operation of the Alliance for Progress for direct or indirect balance-of-payment loans. If the relationship between aid and trade were placed in proper perspective, the unqualified condemnation of balance-of-payment loans as indicating wastefulness or laxity in aid administration would appear quite irrational. Mr. Martin called attention also to the inflationary effect of declining trends of trade in those cases where tax revenues of the government are heavily dependent on export taxation. A similar effect, it might be added, occurs if the loss of exchange revenue forces a reduction of imports that might otherwise abate the inflationary pressure.

In the last few months a number of objurgations were heard, both from informed and uninformed sources, concerning the supposed wastefulness of assistance to Brazil in view of persistent inflation and recurrent balance-of-payments crises.

In the light of this it might not be ungracious or impolite if some comments were made in order to place the assistance given to Brazil in proper perspective. There is an altogether exaggerated idea concerning the net volume of resources transferred to the Brazilian economy. This results partly from the utilization of gross figures relating to commitments and authorization, rather than to actual disbursements, and from disregarding the reverse flow of amortization and interest payments.

A second reason is the substantial increase in disbursements since the inception of the Alliance for Progress, which coincided with particularly adverse foreign-trade conditions. In *net* terms, and viewed in a long perspective, from 1940 to 1956, the net transfers of governmental assistance to Brazil in various forms—loans, grants, food supplies—from all sources—Eximbank, ICA, AID, Food for Peace, Peace Corps, Social Development Trust Fund, PL 480—have amounted to roughly $1 billion, or to be precise, $1,024 million. Spread over the entire period, this would mean less than $50 million per year, although as said before, the net flow of funds increased substantially since the inception of the Alliance for Progress. It can hardly be said that this assistance has been wasted, for this would be inconsistent with the high rate of growth maintained by the Brazilian economy. But the important thing is that, in welfare terms, the burden of assistance has been greatly reduced by the savings accruing involuntarily to the American consumer-taxpayer through cheaper prices paid for our primary exports. A simple calculation will bring this out. If the cumulative value of Brazilian exports at current prices from 1955 to 1961 is adjusted by the terms-of-trade ratio prevailing for the period 1950–53, the additional export earnings would have amounted to $1.4 billion in the last six years alone. During the same period of time, the accumulated deficit of the Brazilian balance of payments was roughly $966 million, substantially less than the decline in export earnings.

The purpose of this statement is not to belittle the good will and forbearance of the American taxpayer, who feels directly the real burden of the tax, while his saving as a consumer of Latin American products is distant, unrequested, and diffused. The purpose is *not* to ascribe guilt to the United States for the deterioration of the Latin American terms of trade. For just as the rising prices of primary products from 1949 to 1954 were not due to the generosity of the American trader, the price decline since 1955 does not prove his exploitive bent. The purpose is *not* to deny that the betterment of the terms of trade for the industrial producers benefited Europe as well as the United States, and while the latter endeavors to alleviate the problem of primary producers by foreign-aid programs or by sponsoring commodity agreements such as that of coffee, the Western European countries have dragged their feet both in regard to loan assistance and to the improvement of trade conditions of the underdeveloped countries. The purpose is *not* to imply that there is any moral obligation on the part of the developed nations to restitute the gains from trade, although this might be commendable in their own self-interest, just as within most industrialized countries protection is given to farm prices in order to maintain markets for industrial goods and to avoid socially painful and politically dangerous income inequalities.

But when all is said and done, the fact remains that there is little justification for a self-righteous attitude on the part of the lending countries, as if inflation and balance-of-payment troubles in Latin America were plain lack of guts or love of vice, and not the symptoms of a difficult travail in face of adverse winds of trade, impatience of consumers, and confused aspirations for the fruits of progress before the tree has matured to yield.

Another image deformation results from the loose utilization of the word "communist" to describe various strains of leftist movement in Latin America in general, and in Brazil in particular. In a pluralistic society, facing the enormous task of reform, there is bound to be profound divergences as to methods and intensity of the required social change.

The left in Brazil encompasses a wide spectrum—the Catholic left, the nationalist left, the utopian socialist left—which are not communist-oriented. In fact, the communist apparatus appears to be losing ground steadily, bitterly split as it is among three factions

—the Stalin-Marxist dogmatists, the Khrushchevian revisionists, and a small residuum of the old Trotskyite movement.

It is true that communism remains a danger despite its numerical insignificance because of (a) the frustrations of underdevelopment and the temptation to correct still prevailing social injustices by revolutionary means; (b) the uncanny ability of the party for infiltration and sabotage; and (c) the communists' skillful manipulation of popular reform movements which they seek to twist and poison in order to serve anti-democratic objectives and to perturb the march of development within Western institutions.

But we cannot fight this danger by indiscriminately labeling as communists all those who favor an enlargement of the area of state ownership or practice the sport of anti-Americanism, wrong as they may be from the viewpoint of maintaining economic efficiency and unfair as they may be in interpreting American motivation and ideals. (Painful as this is, the Americans have to recognize that the price of power is solitude, and that the glory of leadership and wealth breeds respect but also evokes resentment.) In particular, one must not defeat the purpose of social reforms—which is at the very core of the Alliance for Progress—by an unwarranted assimilation of the reformists to the revolutionaries.

In my view the traditional political vocabulary of right, center, and left is outmoded and quite meaningless in the Brazilian landscape. It would be better to speak of the *conservatives,* who desire to preserve the *status quo;* the *reformists,* encompassing a broad political spectrum, ranging from right of center to a large segment of the left, who may disagree on the type and intensity of reforms but agree on the basic postulate that they should be instituted through the democratic mechanism; and finally the *revolutionaries* who advocate violent change by totalitarian methods, encompassing the communists, the ultramontane nationalist left, and a small residuum of rightist revolutionaries.

It is time we realize that communism, as Guy Mollet, the French socialist, once said, is neither to the right nor to the left but rather to the East.

The changing face of Latin America is full of paradoxes. Some of the countries, relatively stable on the surface and able to maintain satisfactory financial discipline, may conceal explosive elements; while less disciplined countries, exhibiting the superficial turmoil characteristic of pluralistic societies with diffused power, may be endowed with greater resilience and enduring strength.

The crucial criteria are whether the masses are being brought to increased participation in the political process, whether the areas of social promotion exceed the areas of rigidity, and whether the rate of development is sufficient to render the more dynamic groups interested in advancing through the surgery of revolution.

These factors, much more than banking measurements of credit-worthiness, price stability, or budget discipline, so obsessively inspected by lending agencies in Washington, will ultimately determine both the political and the economic viability of the society.

One should not be disturbed by the often hesitant and confused workings of the democratic process, even though at times vitiated by demagoguery and apparently misguided economic policies. For recent history has proved that communist revolutions have only been successful when projected against authoritarian states, in which access to power is the privilege of a class or a group. (Czechoslovakia was an exception, but their revolution was imposed from without.) Democracies, even when poor and imperfect, have managed to survive, for they never present a target sufficiently rigid to permit a successful revolutionary impact.

Having heard in the last few months so many dire predictions of chaos in the Brazilian economy and so many exhortations on formulas of salvation, I cannot resist the temptation of closing my speech where it began—by recalling the Populist platform's castigation of the American impending economic disaster and political disintegration at the turn of the century.

Let us not confuse a historical perspective, which may bring recipes of wisdom, with a hysterical perspective, which may bring decisions in anger and poison the wells of understanding.

II

What do you think about the controversy over neutralism and independent foreign policy? Isn't Brazil turning away from her diplomatic traditions?

I find this debate filled with personal elements, sometimes harmfully so. It seems to be incorrect as well as unjust to identify the neutralist policy, as practiced by Egypt, Ghana, or Yugoslavia, with the independent policy of Brazil or Mexico.

There are three fundamental differences. The neutralist nations are systematically unaligned. They seek, whenever possible, to maintain a symmetrical attitude in relation to the two poles of the cold war. Our independent policy accepts all the commitments of the Inter-American system. It is, therefore, a policy of "selective alignment," without any attempt to seek symmetry in our attitude toward the two poles of the cold war. (A symmetry which is indeed unacceptable, since the United States represents a system of values—representative democracy, political freedom, acceptance of private property—much closer to ours than the totalitarian values of the Soviet system.)

The second difference is that the neutralists are obsessed with the idea of a third bloc and construction of a third force. For us, this is secondary. We do not seek to replace the two contenders but only avoid our own destruction.

The third difference is that the neutralists are, in the great majority, countries without any institutional stability. Politically they have not yet chosen representative democracy, but are experimenting with various degrees of guided democracy or one-party systems, when they are not actually under authoritarian regimes run by charismatic leaders like Nkrumah, Tito, or Nasser. And with some exceptions they have made no clear choice between capitalism and socialism.

Now it cannot be said that Brazil and Mexico are in the same state of institutional instability as the countries cited above. Perhaps they practice both democracy and capitalism imperfectly, but they certainly chose both. Therefore, in my opinion, the identification of the independent policy with neutralism is hasty, if not actually vicious. If it is very true that the United States, as the leader of the Western system, deserves our support in all fundamental questions of preservation of human liberty, her idealistic motives are naturally at times mixed with very powerful self-interests. We may disagree with these, as well as with methods and solutions applied in different incidents of the cold war. As for the Foreign Office turning away from its traditions, the phenomenon of the cold war is a new challenge to which old answers not do apply.

Why does the Foreign Office insist that Brazil is not part of any politico-military bloc, when the Treaty of Rio de Janeiro is exactly that? We are part of the American politico-military bloc.

Perhaps there has been too much semantical hair-splitting. If we wish to describe the Treaty of Rio de Janeiro as constituting a politico-military bloc, I see no conflict with an independent policy. We have gone to great lengths to differentiate between the Treaty of Rio de Janeiro and treaties of NATO, SEATO, and CENTO. But in my opinion the fundamental difference lies not in the fact that the latter creates politico-military blocs and the former does not, but in the fact that the latter is a specific by-product of the cold war and is designed to contain Soviet expansion. The Treaty of Rio de Janeiro antedates the cold war and was not established in connection with the present ideological conflict. It was designed to protect the Latin American countries themselves from aggression by their own neighbors as well as an aggressive resurrection of European Nazism. It is evident that the Treaty of Rio de Janeiro also protected us against Soviet aggression, but it was not primarily conceived for this. It is, indeed, imperfect for the conditions of the cold war, where the danger comes less from conventional aggression than from subversive infiltration.

Don't you think that the support given by the Foreign Office to the thesis of peaceful coexistence is too close to Khrushchev's line? If the confessed objective of the Soviet Union is to bury capitalism, why should we ingenuously accept coexistence?

In the first place, coexistence is not a choice, it is an imposition —an imposition resulting from the nuclear balance of the two great powers. We cannot escape this fact, but if we don't like the word "coexistence," somewhat debased by the harangues of Mr. Khrushchev, we can talk about "competitive coexistence." Now it does not seem strange to me that underdeveloped countries, whether "independent" or "neutral," should view the cold war somewhat differently from the United States and Western Europe. These countries achieved a high living standard and a satisfactory degree of social integration within the institutional system which they adopted, thus establishing its value and efficiency. Internal threats having been overcome; the socialist bloc is the last great remaining threat to those institutions. Therefore the East-West conflict is basic, unrelenting, and obsessive.

For the underdeveloped countries, the sharpness of the East-West breach is somewhat dulled by the North-South breach, which separates the underdeveloped from the industrialized countries. Internal threats still exist for capitalist-democratic institutions which have not yet been consecrated by success. The external threat creates a problem of internal security; the remedy is development.

But there is also a certain degree of selfishness on the part of the underdeveloped countries in contemplating "competitive coexistence" with more equanimity and tolerance than the Western leaders. The fact is they secretly hope that this competition, by offering them alternative development techniques, will oblige the West to become ever more deeply involved in assisting the underdeveloped. Jealousy and imitation are powerful spurs. It is by no means certain that this reasoning is correct. In the absence of the cold war, the vast expenditures for armaments which burden the West could be easily diverted to development, if only for the purpose of creating markets and maintaining a high level of economic activity. It would be easy . . . but would the West take advantage of the opportunity?

Doesn't this attitude of complacency toward coexistence constitute a danger for the West in general, and principally for the underdeveloped countries?

Khrushchev prophesies that coexistence will prove the superiority of communism over capitalism, eventually burying the latter. But there are reasons to believe, paradoxically, that coexistence with communism will perfect capitalism and guarantee its survival. It will force capitalism to worry much about maintaining a high growth rate (a preoccupation already aroused in the United States) and will make it more conscious of the problem of social justice, and thus more capable of survival. One of the advantages of capitalism is that it is not a rigid dogma, but a collection of social attitudes. It can absorb enormous changes, such as the establishment of the income tax and the rise of the balancing factor of labor unions, without the trauma which has accompanied every revision of the Marxist dogma, such as the deviationism of Trotsky, the revisionism of Tito, and now the further revisionism of Khrushchev.

There does exist a certain danger that developing countries may overestimate the effectiveness of communism as a social technique. It is alarming to note the superficiality with which even rightists and conservatives among us accept the fallacy that capitalism is better at organizing production but communism is better at solving the problem of distribution. Nonsense: there is more social equality and better distribution in income in Switzerland, Holland, or Denmark than in Russia itself. And as far as the United States is concerned, I have no hesitation in stating that after the income tax collectors have done their work, the difference in income between an unskilled worker and the manager of the company is one to 17, while in the Soviet Union it is one to 40. The truth is that the Western social democracies have adequately resolved the problem of production as well as that of social distribution, and if Marx were to be resurrected today he would be the first to abandon the theory of labor-value and the inflexibility of salaries.

Another fallacy is the belief that the Soviet system was the exclusive discoverer of the formula for rapid economic development. Nothing is more questionable. Russia did indeed become a great industrial power in a relatively short period of time. But according to the Rostow theory (and ever-increasing statistics confirm this), Russia had already passed the "take-off" stage before the Russian Revolution, and was growing at a rate of 8% per year, despite an obsolete agrarian structure and a disintegrating political regime. In view of the extraordinary wealth of her soil and the scientific bent of her people, it is probable that Russia would be a great power today, with or without communism. In fact Alexis de Tocqueville prophesied exactly that a century and a half ago (much before Marx) when he predicted that the United States and Russia would be the great powers of this century, one based on freedom and the other on oppression.

No, the Soviet system has not demonstrated superior effectiveness, neither as an instrument of economic equality nor as an instrument of development. Yes, it has achieved impressive results as a technique for promoting one aspect of development—industrialization. Or, if you prefer, it has proven extremely effective in promoting unbalanced development. China jumped ahead industrially, but now we find out that Chinese stomachs are also jumping.

And while we are exorcising the various inferiority complexes which the West has inexplicably acquired, let us clear up another semantical misconception. I believe the Western countries are conceding too much when they accept and repeat the term "socialist countries" to designate those behind the Iron Curtain. Some of the most solid democracies in the West, like Sweden and Denmark, are socialist countries in the true sense of the word. It is high time we clarified this distinction between socialist and communist countries. They may at times appear very similar in their system of property organization, but there is an enormous difference. The ideology of true socialist countries offers no danger of subservience, contagion, or proselytism, while communism (basically a form of state capitalism rather than socialism) is essentially subversive and expansionist.

How did the North Americans view the Brazilian position taken at the Punte del Este Conference? Did they feel they had been betrayed by Brazil?

The initial reaction was one of disappointment. Cuba is not only a political problem; it is also an emotional one. More than 300,000 Cuban refugees in the United States are a daily reminder of the drama of Castro. Furthermore, in view of the disproportion between forces, the Cuban question would not even exist if the United States decided to really use its strength. They refrained from doing this and referred the problem to the collective action of the Organization of American States. When this organization refused to act, even in a moderate form, a feeling of national humiliation in the face of the Cuban challenge revived in the United States, and a feeling of impatience with the attitude of the abstaining countries.

Gradually, however, they began to understand that the position of Brazil and of certain other countries was not only more a question of method than fundamentals, but also had considerable practical value. And here we must make a distinction. Many North Americans became impatient with the strictly juridical arguments which we advanced—inapplicability of Article 8 of the Treaty of Rio de Janeiro, lack of any provisions in the charter of the OAS for expulsion of members, etc.—based on the point of view that juridical accuracy is a valid standard of conduct within the Western ideology, but is irrelevant when dealing with the Soviet ideology, which completely divorces policy from morality.

But if the North Americans became impatient with juridical arguments, they did recognize substantial validity in two practical arguments, one domestic and the other foreign. The domestic argument concerned the trouble-making potential of leftist minorities in certain key positions, which could result in strikes, street incidents, and general disturbances at a time when Brazil and other countries were in a delicate state of political convalescence and needed normalization of economic life—that this fear was well founded was proven by events in certain South American countries.

The second practical argument concerns the unworkability of the measures proposed in Punte del Este. Commercial sanctions would be meaningless in view of the insignificance of trade between Cuba and the rest of Latin America. The breaking off of diplomatic relations would not protect us from infiltration, since we would continue to maintain relations with other communist countries, and would only prevent us from keeping up with the real situation in Cuba, protecting refugees, and eventually facilitating a reconciliation with the West—a remote but desirable possibility. Many moons have passed since Punte del Este, and the Brazilian position of remaining faithful to the principles of the Inter-American system, while disagreeing on the measures to be adopted in isolated cases, is better understood today in the United States. The important thing now is to concentrate more on the Alliance for Progress and less on an obsessive preoccupation with the revolutionary experiment on a small Caribbean island.

How do the North Americans understand the Brazilian controversy over "entreguismo" (handing over Brazil's natural resources to foreign interests)?

They don't understand it. Indeed, it isn't easy to understand. It would be more accurate to speak in terms of *recebismo* (receiving). From the American viewpoint the granting of loans is hardly a state of affairs which could be described as looting. As for our natural resources, our problem is to find them and not to hand them over. Wealth under the earth isn't wealth—it isn't anything. As for petroleum, there is world overproduction; we still haven't found oil in sufficient quantity and we have to import it, running up bills to increase the deficit in our balance of payments. Iron, manganese, uranium? The first two are in overproduction throughout the world and our problem is to find buyers. As for the latter, it is also in overproduction, and we only have a poor cousin—thorium—whose technology is still insufficient. Hand over what? Many people see in this epithet *entreguista*, with which we insult some of our greatest patriots and finest technicians, an example of bad faith. It is not even that. It is an example of simply stupidity.

V. BRAZIL AND THE UNITED STATES *
João Goulart **

Mr. Speaker, Mr. Vice President, Senators, and Congressmen, I feel greatly honored to speak from this rostrum and transmit to the representatives of the American people the greetings of the government and the people of Brazil. This is the second time that such a privileged opportunity has been accorded me by act of fate. The first occasion was in 1956 when, as Vice President of my country, I came here at the invitation of your own Vice President at that time, the distinguished Mr. Richard Nixon, and today I do so again in compliance with another invitation, which I have had the honor of receiving from the eminent President of the United States, Mr. John F. Kennedy. The relations between our two countries go back to the era of our independence, and they have been intensified in more recent times, as we have fought side by side in the two World Wars, in defense of democracy and freedom.

Never have those relations been dimmed by attritions or by misunderstandings, even though at times we may have supported divergent views.

It is my deep conviction that good and well-defined relations between Brazil and the United States are both desirable and neces-

---

* Delivered to joint session of United States Congress, Washington, D.C., April 4, 1962.

** João Goulart is President of the Republic of Brazil. Elected as Vice President in the last general elections, he succeeded to power upon the renunciation of Jânio Quadros. He is a disciple of the late Getúlio Vargas, and heir to the leadership of Brazil's Labor Party.

sary. It seems to me essential, in terms of a democratic continental affirmation, that there be always a perfect understanding between the two greatest nations on this hemisphere.

Brazil and the United States shaped their democratic conscience over the course of their struggles for independence, and ever since they have been engaged in a century-old effort to implant and perfect a form of representative government, based on the supremacy of a written constitution, on respect for the autonomy of states, and on the guarantees of individual rights.

While this similarity in political organization breeds identical sentiments as to the defence of legality and the preservation of public freedoms, there is, at the same time, between our two countries a profound diversity in socio-economic conditions which has led us down different paths, at a different pace, to achieve identical objectives.

The government and the people of Brazil have spared no sacrifices in order to overcome backwardness and underdevelopment. We are trying to establish a harmonious development throughout the country to correct regional imbalances and avoid a state of destitution in certain areas and raise them to the level, for instance, of the State of São Paulo, where the per capita income is higher than that of some of the highly industrialized countries.

In the struggle for development and for our economic emancipation, we have suffered the influence of adverse factors, which we are determined to overcome. There are permanent imbalances in the system of trade relations between countries having an adverse economic development, with prejudicial reflexes on the economically weaker countries. We can eliminate or at least attenuate these imbalances, through conventions and agreements based on friendly arrangements and the adoption of realistic formulas.

The monetary inflation in Brazil, of which so much has been said both in our country and abroad, is not a local phenomenon; it coincided with the wartime economy, when the old economic-financial structure suffered the impact of abrupt changes in our allies' supply and demand.

During the war years the prices of our export products were frozen at levels that were much below their real value. When normal trade conditions were re-established, it became possible for the countries of Europe, and others whose economies had been ravaged by war, to eliminate inflation and restore prosperity. To this end they were favored during the period 1948–52 by the massive help received from the American economy which sustained, through loans and grants, not only the former Allies but also the former enemies, allowing them quickly to recover and even to surpass their previous levels of agricultural and industrial production. Once their industries were rebuilt, those countries began to trade under the particularly advantageous conditions under which the exporters of manufactured goods operate.

The Latin American countries, with their war-born inflation, remained devoid of any plan of international cooperation for the recovery of their agriculture and the development of their industries, depending exclusively upon the export of their primary products for the restoration of their trade. The story of the growing deterioration of the terms of trade of commodities with manufactured goods is well known to all. From year to year, the same number of bags of coffee or of cocoa or of cotton buys a lesser quantity of the same type of equipment or of manufactured products. While our primary products have remained exposed to a continuing fall in prices, the index of growth of our population has increased at such levels that Brazil is expected to possess 200 million inhabitants by the end of this century. Notwithstanding such adverse factors, Brazil has been maintaining a growing rhythm in the increase of its per capita income and of the national product. This notable effort for development is due above all to the unlimited reserves of energy and sense of patriotism of the Brazilian people.

It is true that we have secured appreciable bank loans at normal rates of interest and for regular terms, granted chiefly by financial agencies of the United States—and of this the Brazilian people is fully aware, as it is also aware that the eradication of the difficulties which we are now undergoing depends upon our work, our energy, and our sacrifice.

We feel, gentlemen of the Congress, that our destiny is in our own hands, and we keep our eyes open to find the adequate solutions for the development of Brazil. The political awareness of the leaders in government and of the people themselves is keenly awake to the fact that the fight for development is the fight of the people. In pursuance of this purpose, we are engaged in the realization and implementation of basic reforms, among which the agrarian reform is paramount. We recognize the importance of the foreign contribution to the process of our development.

I have repeatedly said that we nourish no prejudice against foreign capital and the technical collaboration of the more advanced countries. We desire this cooperation and will assure its full freedom within the legal limits established and under the inspiration of Brazilian ideals. Only a short time ago I reaffirmed these very same concepts, in an address which I made to the American Chamber of Commerce in Rio de Janeiro where I was guest of honor at a reception organized on the occasion of my departure from Brazil.

As a country now in a phase of full expansion, Brazil offers broad possibilities to foreign private enterprise desirous to cooperate loyally for its development. In the matter of public utilities services, there are certain areas of friction which should be eliminated, all the more so because through a natural phenomenon, besides creating disagreements between the granting authority and the concessionary, they are not rarely a source of misunderstanding between friendly countries.

Brazil hailed with confidence the announcement of the new policy of the United States toward Latin America, as expressed by President Kennedy in the Alliance for Progress and having "Operation Pan America," a Brazilian initiative, as one of its historic milestones. We see in the Alliance for Progress the formulation of a plan for global cooperation, which Latin America has awaited since the termination of the Second World War, and which, once carried out, should have for our hemisphere the proportions and significance which the Marshall Plan had for the countries of Western Europe. The lack of initiative of this magnitude made it extremely difficult for the countries of the hemisphere to stabilize their economies. Thus, the Alliance for Progress has significantly been placed within the framework not only of its economic aspects but also of its social aspects as your Chief Executive emphasized in these highly significant words, "those who make peaceable revolution impossible will render violent revolution inevitable." I cannot conceal, however, my fears as to the difficulties in implementation. If the Alliance for Progress is to depend upon an effort by the Latin American countries to achieve global planning with absolute technical precision in the economic and social fields and to eliminate beforehand certain factors of instability, we can introduce hindrances capable of impairing the urgency of solutions which cannot be put off.

Such difficulties will mount if the Alliance fails to reflect, principally, the spirit of reciprocal trust and respect between the countries which comprise it, in line with the purpose expressed by the eminent President Kennedy. I wish to reaffirm the identification of my country with the democratic principles which unite the peoples of the West. Brazil forms no part of any politico-military bloc, but it abides by its freely assumed international commitments. Brazil's international action responds to no other objective than that of favoring, by all means in our power, the preservation and strengthening of peace. It is our belief that the ideological conflict between East and West cannot and must not be decided by military action, for in the event of a nuclear war, even if we managed to save our own lives, whether in victory or in defeat our very reason for living would be obliterated. The end of the dangerous emulation in armaments in comity of relationships must be sought through negotiations.

Brazil believes that a non-inimical contact between the democratic world and the socialist world can be beneficial to the knowledge and coordination of experience of all. It is our hope that these contacts will make it evident that representative democracy is the most perfect of all forms of government and the only one compatible with the protection of mankind and the preservation of human freedom.

Gentlemen of the Congress, I have used simple and direct language to express the thought of the government and the people of Brazil on the more timely problems in our relations as good and longstanding friends. This is the same kind of language used by two great Presidents—President Franklin Delano Roosevelt and President Getúlio Vargas—in times that were crucial for the history of mankind, when they found efficient and friendly forms of mutual understanding. I place my trust in God, and I feel certain that we can contribute to the peace and happiness of the world, eliminating economic slavery, despotism, and fear, and guaranteeing popular freedoms and personal security within a democratic and representative political system.

XI
BRAZIL
AND
THE SINO-SOVIET DISPUTE

... in which the main facts in the present rupture between Russian and Chinese communism are raised, with special emphasis on the strategic character of left-wing politics in Brazil; this is followed by an attempt to assess long-range strengths and weaknesses in both the Soviet and Chinese attempts to influence Brazil's pluralistic socialism.

THE EMERGENCE of Brazil as a world power is nowhere illustrated more clearly than in the present rift within the communist bloc concerning the strategies and tactics of revolution. Indeed, the ideological dialogue now under way in the Brazilian extreme left is a microscopic condensation of the Brazilian issues as such: *why* should rapid development be prized? *What* price should be paid to secure such development? *Who* should provide the leadership in this struggle? *Which* nation should provide the model of emulation? *How* can a unified political body emerge under polycentric conditions?

This is not solely a problem for Brazilian leftists, but for the nation as a whole. The "opening to the world" in terms of economic and cultural exchange has thus far meant more in terms of Russo-Brazilian relations than Sino-Brazilian affairs. Yet over the past three years the acceleration in Chinese cultural contacts with South America has had its greatest impact on Brazil. While at the present jockeying stage neither the Soviets nor the Chinese can possibly demand any sort of allegiance, it is clear that as time passes, and the Sino-Soviet dispute hardens into alternative political styles, Brazil will be compelled to decide just how extensive its opening to the world ought to be. More precisely, Brazil has to decide upon the advantages of looking West to Russia or East to China, without for a moment losing sight of the United States to the North.

The single most decisive political event of 1963 was the acknowledged split between the Soviet Union and China. Not even summitry proposals of the kind which Premier Khrushchev submitted to Chairman Mao Tse-tung, could possibly do more than provide an ideological gloss to a fundamental political corrosion of the two largest communist nations on earth. The charges made by Peking come down to six essential propositions:

(1) Soviet leadership has permitted technological-military innovations (thermonuclear weapons) to betray fundamental political facts (the need to carry on an active multi-national campaign against imperialism and colonialism).

(2) The Khrushchev leadership is adventuristic and opportunistic. This was shown by the installation of Soviet bases in Cuba without regard for Cuba's safety, and then the withdrawal of these bases under United States threat, once again in total disregard for the sovereignty or safety of Cuba.

(3) The Soviet Union abandoned the principles of international communist solidarity in its relations with China. This was demonstrated by the steady withdrawal of economic assistance (thus crippling Mao's ability to expand the collectivization of agriculture and industry) and its later neutralist posture in connection with the India-China border warfare, which in its call for immediate settlement had the effect of equating the interests of a socialist state with those of a capitalist state.

(4) The Soviet policy is nationalistic rather than communist. It works to increase consumer satisfaction of the Russians at the expense of a continued struggle against colonialism.

(5) By its acceptance of the principle of "three worlds" (capitalist, communist, and neutralist) the Soviet Party apparatus has destroyed the integrity of Marxism-Leninism and negated the historic drive toward international socialism.

(6) The Soviet Union has encouraged groundless illusions among the citizenry by asserting that full communism can be achieved in one country and in the present generation. This slogan of total communism only hides the betrayal of the proletarian character of the Soviet Party apparatus.

*　　　*　　　*

The replies of the Soviet Communist Party have been couched in language which is considerably more moderate than that of Peking. But, nonetheless, they are indicative of the serious nature of the schism in world communism. In essence, the Soviet position can be summed up as follows:

(1) Thermonuclear weaponry is indeed a powerful enough variable to change traditional Leninist postures. A fully escalated nuclear war would lead to the decimation of vast numbers of people, and socialism no less than capitalism would be jeopardized in the process.

(2) The installation of the missile bases in Cuba was at the behest of the Castro government, and the handling of the situation by the Soviets in the crisis week preserved the Cuban Revolution by forestalling an all-out United States military invasion.

(3) The principles of international communist solidarity were violated by Mao and not by Khrushchev, since it was the Chinese Party which refused to abide by the decisions made by the collectivity of Communist Parties. Indeed, Khrushchev, in a special memorandum, has indicated that the Chinese communists are moving toward a *Rassenkampf* (race struggle) in place of a *Klassenkampf* (class struggle) attitude. This is expressed in the Russian reference to "Yellow Communism" of an All-Asian type. It is reinforced by the publication of a memorandum dated April 30, 1963, reiterating the danger. The memorandum is by Boris Ponomarenko, a secretary of the Soviet Communist Party.

(4) The Soviet policy is, and has traditionally been, the defense of wage-workers all over the world, so that its nationalism is but a form of internationalism.

(5) The integrity of Marxism-Leninism remains intact, since the notion of an "uncommitted bloc" is viewed as a transitional phase, a prelude to socialism in the developing nations. It is Maoism which is really revisionist, since it substitutes the theory of peasant revolution for proletarian revolution, and in so doing, corrupts the working-class character of communism.

(6) The Chinese Communist Party has encouraged the growth of sectarianism and cultism within its apparatus. They are attempting to foist upon the world communist movement the practices, forms, and methods of the leadership which are no longer appli-

cable. Socialism is not a consequence of inner-party strife, but of the economic freedom and abundance of the people.

This, then, is the setting for current Latin American disputes over the nature of the Sino-Soviet split. If we take the cases of Brazil and Cuba as our models, it will be seen that the long-range future of Latin America will in considerable measure be fashioned out of the crucible of the Great Communist Debate of 1963.

It has long been clear that the Chinese communists have sought to aid and abet the "national revolutionary movements" in Latin America directly; that is, by direct contact with men like Francisco Julião, rather than through the Communist Party apparatus. The famed *Proposal Concerning the General Line of the International Communist Movement,* issued June 14, 1963, alludes to this in a general way. It notes that "the attitudes taken toward the revolutionary struggles of the people in the Asian, African, and Latin American countries is an important criterion for differentiating those who want revolution from those who do not and those who are truly defending world peace from those who are abetting the forces of aggression and war." Translated into political action this means that the Chinese consider national movements such as Julião's more central than any political apparatus.

The Chinese have stepped up their activities throughout Latin America, with particular success in the Communist Party machinery of such Central American countries as Panama and El Salvador. But in countries such as Brazil, where the Soviet orientation remains firmly intact, the Chinese have adjusted their tactics to the situation. Portuguese-language broadcasts beamed to Brazil from the China mainland are heard nearly eight hours daily, while Chinese folklore groups, circus performers, journalists, and representatives of the arts have come to Brazil in increasing numbers. The Chinese have carried their case in a more directly political manner, taking an active part in the Conference of Students from the Underdeveloped World held in Bahia, Brazil, during July 1963. This was a meeting of radical youth from developing nations throughout the world, but mostly from Central and South America. The leader of the Chinese delegation, Chu Liang, took advantage of a speech devoted to the denunciation of American imperialism to criticize the Soviet Union for "allowing themselves to be deceived" by Western arms-control plans. Underlying most of these Chinese efforts is a warning to the Latin revolutionaries that the Soviet Union is not really interested in their respective national liberation efforts. The "hard" Peking line is now a political reality in Northeast Brazil.

The text of the Soviet *Open Letter to all Party Organizations and Communists of the Soviet Union*, dated July 14, 1963, in reply to the Chinese communists alludes more directly to the situation in Brazil. It notes that the Chinese were supporting factions and groups expelled from the Brazilian Communist Party, directly interfering with the affairs of a foreign party. But the real hub of the Soviet position is that the Chinese are in search of easy victories. The Chinese have effectively divorced, in theory, the movement of national liberation from the tasks of the international socialist movement. And in giving priority to the former, the Chinese Communist Party is attempting to isolate the communists from the nationalists. And while the Chinese have had extremely limited successes in most Latin American Communist Parties, the Chinese have registered important inroads among the radical elements of Brazil. So that it can rightfully be said that Brazil represents a fundamental testing ground for the ideas being propagated by both Moscow and Peking.

Even prior to the Sino-Soviet schism, there was a growing disparity between revolutionary currents in Latin America and official communist organization. In nation after nation, from the Rio Grande to Tierra del Fuego, the Communist Parties offered a contradictory spectacle. As the work of Robert J. Alexander has shown, the communists opposed Perón's bid for power at the outset, but supported him when he was already on the way out. Similar confusions of policy were manifest during the last stages of the Vargas regime in Brazil.

The quest for legitimization and legality interfered with and compromised revolutionary directions. The need to keep communist policy in tune with Soviet foreign policy often led to absurdities such as an emphasis on peace campaigns *at the expense of mass political organization*. Communist shibboleths about the "united-front approach" led some Latin Communist Parties to neglect problems of the very poor peasantry and overemphasize the need for the cooperation of the urban middle sectors. The final straw came with the Cuban Revolution. *Fidelismo* was considered a form of "revolutionary romanticism," when, as a matter of fact, Communist Party policy in Cuba had degenerated into "revolutionary rhetoric."

Thus it is quite understandable that "marginal" radical opinion would eventually hold the Soviet Union in large measure responsible for the absence of a cohesive and powerful Left in Latin America. Even under the most "correct" policies emanating from abroad, matters would be difficult. The countries of Latin America are still defined by their mass peasant base, their low standards of industrial development, their feudal and epi-feudal character, their poor educational and cultural facilities. The idea of a socialist revolution as necessarily anchored to the factory-worker class, to a relatively *contented* portion of the population, thus seemed a clear anachronism. It is not simply that the proletariat was not interested in leading a revolution, but that as a social class it was neither large enough nor poor enough to get beyond a "trade-union" ideology. The Goulart regime, with its factory-labor base, is a perfect illustration of the revolutionary impulse of the blue-collar workers of Latin America exhausting itself in economic gains. The model for Goulart is legal socialism rather than violent revolution.

A final factor is the classic ethnocentrism of the Latin American revolutionary. Being outside the chief nuclear-power blocs, his concern with questions of disarmament and deterrence was never high to begin with. And the continued emphasis of the Soviet Communist Party on a peace posture reduced itself to empty slogans devoid of charismatic possibilities. As the Uruguayan educator, Vas Ferreira, once put it, we have the spectacle of South Americans weeping over war casualties when we have had none, and writing novels about the agonies of wars fought eight thousand miles away. Of course, such forms of Marxology left basic issues up in the air, while matters of a rather tenuous and distant nature occupied the exclusive energies of communist leadership. Involved was a continuous postponement of the time of the revolution and a steady frustration of radical energies which desired to provide political foundations for a new beginning. Indeed, perhaps the Latin is "shortsighted" about the dangers of an all-out nuclear conflict (I have actually had revolutionaries tell me that after a thermonuclear war, Latin America would finally emerge from its slumbering underdevelopment), but this psychological condition is a factor which worked decisively against communist "internationalism" of the Soviet variety.

Given these historical and theoretical antecedents, the growth of schisms in Latin American communism was inevitable, whether or not a Sino-Soviet schism occurred. The Communist Party of Brazil has been split into two parts. The "official" Soviet branch of the party, headed by Luís Carlos Prestes and Jacob Gorender, supports the policies of Goulart. It sees this support as contingent on a wider trade basis with the Soviet Union, better cooperation politically with the Soviet Union, legalization of the Communist Party, and respect for the need to industrialize Brazil as rapidly as possible. Prestes, in a recent comment, hailed Soviet economic achievements, not simply in the name of Brazilian laborers, but no less "in the name of the national bourgeoisie and of the groups of capitalists and landlords who are antagonistic toward U.S. imperialism." Prestes' rather unique faith in class harmony concluded with the belief that Soviet industrial achievement, its rise in national income and purchasing power, would better the conditions of Brazilians as well:

In this way the Soviet Union will have still greater facilities for rendering aid to the underdeveloped countries, who repose great hopes in it. We are one of those countries. We ardently want to get rid of our poverty and backwardness, the main result of our economic dependence on the U.S. monopolies.

Just how Soviet economic affluence would lessen Brazilian dependence on the United States is not resolved. Nor does Prestes account for the simple fact that Soviet growth in the past did not exactly add to the salaries or liberation of Brazilian workers.

The lesser, breakaway faction in the Brazilian Communist Party reflects the depth of discontent with the formerly unchallenged myth that what is good for the Soviet Union is *ipso facto* good for Brazil. Prestes' Machiavellian effort to link communist aspirations to the "national bourgeoisie of Brazil" drew special fire in the publication of the factionalists, *Classe Operaria*:

This resolution will draw the militants of the Brazilian Communist Party, honest as most of them are, behind the opportunistic and traitorous policy of President Goulart's Labor Party which compromises with imperialists and with our own reactionaries. Those who, like ourselves, see no real difference between politicians such as Goulart, who always want to make a deal, and the reactionary leaders of the traditional parties, will be called sectarians and dogmatists. But at least we shall not be the ones who fool the workers.

This breakaway phenomenon is not restricted to Brazil. Similar splits are to be observed in Mexico, Bolivia, and Chile. Long-smoldering tendencies, which were formerly "resolved" by the expulsion of communist deviants, can no longer be contained or ignored. The magnitude of the schism makes containment impossible, while the strength of the deviants makes an expulsion policy extremely risky—particularly at a time of theoretical crisis within world Marxism, and an organizational decentralization within the bloc nations.

Before turning directly to the impact of the Chinese communist position, perhaps we should underscore the fact that Soviet-style Communist Parties were already suffering serious setbacks. Fidel Castro "repaid" his pre-1959 communist critics by completing the *absorption* of the Communist Party into the Cuban revolutionary front—and not, as some in Washington feared and others in Moscow hoped for, the other way around! In Castro's 1962 speech against sectarianism, this process of absorption is made with perfect clarity and candor:

The tendency to mistrust everybody who could not claim a long record of revolutionary militancy, who had not been an old Marxist militant, the sectarianism of believing that the only revolutionaries, the only ones who could have positions of trust, the only ones who could hold a post on a People's Farm, on a Cooperative, in the government, anywhere, had to be an old Marxist militant . . . That policy introduced extraneous matters into the integration process [of merging the three Cuban revolutionary movements]. And so, many months after the forces had been officially integrated, one found someone who would come out and say: "He's not a member of the Party." To what Party was he referring, if there was already a new organization here? . . . To what did such a state of affairs give rise? To vanity, to the domination of influence, to privilege. What would this engender but conditions which would earn the old Communists the antipathy and suspicions of the masses?

Thus, this schismatic propensity existed before the Sino-Soviet split became manifest. What, in effect, the Great Split has done is to crystallize "anti-Soviet communism," and, as a matter of fact, for the first time in the history of the Communist Party system, place the burden of proof, the burden of pattern-maintenance, and the burden of ideology on the Soviet apparatus—on the Revisionist Marxism of Khrushchev and his West European supporters. This burden is multiplied a hundredfold by a common Latin socialist consensus that Russia has "joined the West" in terms of being a "have" nation, and in terms of its unwillingness to take risks which any revolutionary must be willing to brave if he wishes to earn the respect of the great unwashed.

Enter China. It is a commonplace that the handbook of guerrilla warfare written by Ernesto "Ché" Guevara had as its inspiration and source the writings of Mao Tse-tung on peasant warfare. Cuba and China share in a have-not brand of revolutionary common-man-ism. And "have-nots" simply tend to be unworried about long-range consequences, material defeats, or human sufferings—for the very obvious reason that little is being risked. "Nothing ventured, nothing gained" might well be the motto of the Chinese "dogmatists," a view which has been reinforced by the highhanded, "big-power" resolution of the Cuban missile crisis. There is increasing evidence that the Russian rockets were put there by Khrushchev as the price of other forms of aid, and not "requested" by Castro. The willingness of the Soviet Union to grant on-site United Nations inspection of Cuba, over the objections of the Castro Establishment, certainly did not endear the Soviet political elite to the Cubans. The further willingness of old-line communists like Blas Roca to go along with Soviet "prudence" only further alienated the Cuban revolutionary leadership. The temper of Cuba remains revolutionary—in a continued state of agitation to which the United States policy of supporting invasion contributes in no small measure. It is hard to imagine Khrushchev turning away an offer of safety in a crisis situation. It is hard to envision either Mao or Castro accepting such an offer. Guevara reports that when strategies were being mapped in the event of a full-scale invasion of Cuba from United States shores, and an offer of safety for "*el maximo lider*" was presented, Castro replied "that if the United States invaded Cuba and Havana, it would be defended as it should be defended, hundreds of thousands of men, women, and children would die before the impetus of Yankee arms, and that the leader of a people in a revolution could not ask to be sheltered in the mountains; that his place was there, where the cherished dead were to be found, and that there, with them, he would fulfill his historic mission." It would be dangerous and erroneous to assume this to be rhetoric. This is precisely the way things would be—and neither American nor Russian leaders were willing to assume the risks of invasion and defense of the "island."

What must be particularly attractive about the Chinese position from a Cuban vantage point is that the country is already in a state of permanent ideological warfare with the United States. It is hard to accept the canons of *realpolitik* for a nation that considers itself persecuted, economically strangled, and politically threatened by at least one partner to the delicate balance of terror. And surely the month-long visit by Soviet Deputy Premier Anastas Mikoyan, with its inconsequential results, indicates that Cuban *sentiments* are not with the Soviets—even if its economic and military sustenance remains necessarily anchored to the Russian deterrent.

But the connection between China and Cuba remains tenuous not simply on functional grounds, but on ideological grounds as well. The turn away from Russian communism is toward another and further freedom, and not toward the Mao type of dogmatism. Castro's frequent comment that "abstract art is not the enemy of the Cuban Revolution, imperialism is . . ." or that "Cuba is the only free country in the world" moves in an orbit having little to do with the higher dialectics which forms the basis of Mao's polycentric communism. And Cuba's avoidance of the fetishism of growth rates further emphasizes its unique status.

As has been remarked in the first chapter, parallels between China and Brazil are being drawn even by wide strata of the intellectuals. There are enough geographical as well as economic similarities to lend some credence to the idea that Brazil is the China of the Western world. The idea of peasant revolution combined with military leftism serves to further stimulate organizational models derived from the Chinese. The rhetoric of Maoism is also well suited to rouse the peasantry to action against their masters. The Soviet position, like the American position, has grown sophisticated in the crucible of two decades of Cold War. The highly moralistic-religious world of rural Brazil is better serviced by the messianic fervor of the Chinese message. And it is undoubtedly the case that even if parallels in the economic and political structures of feudal China and rural Brazil could not be sensibly drawn, there are sufficient ideological reasons for imagining a linkage between the Chinese Revolution and contemporary Brazil to invite patterns of emulation.

Differences between China and Brazil are clear to the close observer. Suffice it to say that Brazil is still "Western" in everything from politics to religion. But revolutionists, such as Francisco "Junior" Julião, are too busy making preparations for "operation abolition" to worry about refinements in analogies. The point is that the comparison between China and Brazil is being made by many "orthodox" economists and intellectuals. It would be asking too much for the Brazilian revolutionary not to feel a kinship with the Chinese "have-not" revolutionist. At a recent meeting, in northeastern Brazil, Julião, the acknowledged leader of more than two hundred thousand peasants (some already carrying small arms), had this to say about China:

Brazil's problems are very much like those of China, and in any case it is almost certain Mao is right. The Soviet Union is moving closer to the satisfied nations, and Brazil is an unsatisfied nation. I respect the Chinese and the Orientals in general for their logic and their patience. They recognize that Khrushchev's liberalization policy is doing the world revolutionary movement great damage, but they can wait for time to prove them right and the Moscow revisionists wrong.

The Brazilian Julião has been shuttling back and forth between Havana and Recife so often that the suspicion grows that the entire Latin American radical complex may be readying itself to overthrow the ballast of Soviet-styled leadership. When and if this takes place, the position of Khrushchev in the Soviet hierarchy will be seriously compromised. And Julião's statements in Cuba during his last visit to the island in March 1963 do little to encourage the Soviet aim of domestic liberalization and international pacification. Julião considers his present task the transformation of his *Ligas Camponesas* (Peasant Leagues) into agrarian unions. On his last visit to Cuba he said, "I wish there were other ways than force, but against the landholder and the imperialists, it is only force that can win." To underscore this, he added parenthetically that: "By the measure one publicizes, one makes revolution." It is interesting that the Prestes branch of the Communist Party has seen fit to compete rather than cooperate with Julião to organize the peasantry. They are trying to capitalize on a peasant consciousness given definite shape by Julião and in the past much neglected by communist leadership. The internecine strife between Prestes and Julião is hardly less intense than that between the "great men" of Moscow and Peking themselves.

The "officialist" Communist Parties are counting on a reduction of tensions between the United States and the Soviet Union to press for a broader type of coalition politics. Thus Soviet-style communism sees its greatest possibilities in electoral terms. Allende of Chile, Goulart of Brazil, the Peronists in Argentina, are some of the groups with which the communists would like closer political ties and working bureaucratic connections. What for the Chinese-style communists appears as opportunism is for the old-guard groups an iron necessity. Underlying this Soviet-styled view is that social change in Latin America will be relatively slow —political change will emanate from an existing power apparatus rather than through the emergence of new elite groups from the peasantry—and, ideologically, Latin America is still committed to constitutionalism and legality, rather than to militant direct action. To be sure, the Soviet-type approach is risky. But in the views of official Latin communism, the option provided by men like Julião is riskier still, both in terms of possibilities of victory and, no less, in terms of the fuzziness in the long-range ambitions of the anti-officialists. It should be understood that a complete socialization and neutralization of Brazil, through Goulart, would go far in vindicating Khrushchev's approach to "popular front" politics.

Under such circumstances, whatever measure of success which accrues to the Brazilian communist apparatus will go to that faction displaying the greatest flexibility, that is, the Soviet-oriented faction. On the other hand, any worsening of the position of Goulart vis-à-vis rightists such as Lacerda will provide the Chinese-oriented extremists with an opportunity to capture the sympathies and organizational loyalties of the communist sector. It should be recalled that the Brazilian communists went from a major political force in the forties to virtual oblivion in the fifties. The "renaissance" of the communists rests upon the linkage of socialism to nationalism in politics, and leadership of union demands for autonomy in economics. It is unlikely therefore that

Brazilian communism will revise its tactics to suit either Julião or Mao.

The appointment to Cabinet positions by Goulart of "national communists" such as Evandro Lins e Silva (Foreign Minister), Paulo de Tarso (Minister of Education), Armando Oliveira Brito (Minister of Mines and Energy), Abelardo Jurema (Minister of Justice), Amaury Silva (Minister of Labor), and Darcy Ribeiro, Rector of the University of Brasília, as Chief Civil Advisor to the President, represents an exceptional opportunity for the sort of quiet revolutions which the Soviet Union would like to see occur in Latin America. It must be further appreciated that the quiet revolution may not bring any upsurge in romantic rhetoric; but it will also not bring on any invasion from North American shores in the name of the Monroe Doctrine.

On the basis of the foregoing, it would be foolish to counsel Latin Americans to turn their backs on revolutionary solutions. Indeed, the very schisms in the Sino-Soviet bloc serve to accelerate experimentation with new and more feasible forms of socialist theories and programs. Latin American nationalism has never been easily straitjacketed by imported notions of socialist revolution. The State Department tendency has always been to equate revolutionary potential in Latin America with communist electoral strength—a mortal equation and a wrongheaded one. Never has the potential for revolution been closer to realization than now—and American foreign policy must be prepared for an *increase* in revolutionary ferment.

But this revolutionary activity will, in all likelihood, be determined by area requirements, by Latin American conditions, and not by either China or the Soviet Union. If Soviet-style communism is disintegrating, the hopes of those looking for a China-style communism are essentially ludicrous. Too many sectors of Latin society are firmly committed to the need for rapid industrialization without violent forms of revolution to allow the Julião types of peasant revolutions to conquer. Julião's peasant communism may be well intentioned, but in a nation with Brazil's potential for industrial achievement and technological growth, it is also economically backward, and not likely to attract the urban masses of Rio de Janeiro, São Paulo, Santos, and, still less, those in the political center of gravity, Brasília.

If one were to summarize the reasons why the Sino-Soviet split will further encourage in Latin America an independent and large-scale socialist movement at the expense of both Soviet and Chinese varieties of communism, five points would have to be entertained: (a) Latin American nationalism is an overriding factor in the politics of the region. (b) Social revolution is seen in terms of industrial development rather than force of arms. (c) There is a growing resentment toward Communist Party structures of any variety, from any bloc nation. (d) Area homogeneity is a basic political variable and more magnetic than ideological affinities with communist-bloc nations. (e) Certain "bourgeois" features of Latin American socialism, such as legality and individuality, which are a consequence of the double inheritance of an easygoing Catholicism and an Enlightenment-inspired libertarianism, sharply curtail the effectiveness of big-power communism of any sort.

The United States has not been able to exploit the Sino-Soviet rift, because it is committed to a political posture of such a rigid and reactionary variety that it cannot fill the ideological void now in existence. Our policy is still predicated on the assumption that Latin American communism is undifferentiated and homogeneous—without the faintest realization that the Soviet-style Communist Party is being rapidly absorbed into more broad-scaled revolutionary movements. Our policy is still predicated on "exploiting" the Sino-Soviet rift for the purpose of maintaining the *status quo* or restoring the *status quo ante* in Latin America. The menacing growth of military despotisms in Peru, Guatemala, and Ecuador (in the last years), and the gradual changeover from tacit United States support for such forms of "anti-communism" as *Alianza* grants and Peace Corps projects to a notion of massive aid for a few "buffer" nations having firm military establishments such as Venezuela, hardly help us to manipulate or utilize the schism in world communism. Our sheepish "unofficial" embarrassment over the "rising tide of militarism" is meaningless—particularly in the face of our growing condemnation of the "rising tide of revolution" in Brazil, Chile, and Mexico.

The United States expects a great deal for its projects and slogans. It expects of Brazilians a firm commitment to the policy of eliminating Castroism from the Western hemisphere, and it expects support for the Alliance for Progress even though both nations know that it promises much more than it can hope to deliver. In the meanwhile, on pivotal issues of land reform, future expropriation, nuclear-free zonal policies, the United States has been plainly procrastinating. There is a mindlessness to foreign-policy pronouncements that must only serve to confirm the present course of the Goulart administration.

The rift in the Sino-Soviet bloc serves therefore to give a diffuse quality to the Latin American revolutionary ferment. We can only look forward to a period of intensified anti-United States policies and sentiments—especially in such pivotal nations as Brazil, Chile, and Mexico. There is already a spread of revolutionary fervor among sectors of the Latin American population who have resisted the blandishments of older, more authoritarian radical forms. What has made this eminently plausible is the double process of breakdown: the disintegration of Great-Power communism, and the continued disparity between American domestic prosperity and American foreign promises. These, then, are the effects of the Sino-Soviet split upon Latin America—effects which broaden not only the problems, but also the choices for the people of Latin America, and bode evil both to those who live by clutching at totalitarian straws and those clinging to straw militarists.

XII

AMERICAN CAPITALISM,
SOVIET COMMUNISM,
AND THE BRAZILIAN "MIX"

. . . in which alternative models for the Brazilian Revolution are discussed; the right and the wrong way for critics to make criticisms; contradictions in a solution based on American capitalism; contradictions in a solution based on Soviet communism; the socialist alternative; when giants clash—the shape of future United States-Brazilian relations; proposals for the American champion and the Brazilian challenger.

THE DIFFICULTY with a survey, however intensive, is that conclusions tend to be as arbitrary as initial remarks. For the Brazilian sub-giant we have been discussing does not admit of endings—happy or tragic. What we must here take up is the issue of new beginnings, of alternative models for the conduct of the Brazilian Revolution. It is plain that social, political, and economic revolution is both a present necessity and a future certainty. Those who continue to argue the reverse, who argue that Brazil is simply in for more of the same no matter who rules or what form of economy is evolved, will simply be ensconced in their own limitations. With such critics there can be no meaningful discussion, since whatever happens is simply interpreted as part of a vast metaphysical continuum. The difficulty with the anti-historical bias which so characterizes social science empiricism is that it can never explain or predict social change. It can only trivialize and de-emphasize its extent. And when this is no longer feasible, as in outright cases of fierce and open political or military violence, these same analysts profess impotent amazement at events, often followed by denunciatory rhetoric that the revolution, which could never happen, did not proceed according to established or acceptable blueprints.

There appears to be a "natural history" of the blind critic. First, he declares that revolution is impossible given the backward condition of the populace or the corruption of the leadership. Second, he insists that those changes which are observable are really not decisive breaks with the past, but only adjustments of the old regime making possible a more perfect maintenance of the social structure. Third, when it is no longer possible to deny the evidence of the senses common and uncommon, when it can no longer be maintained that the present is simply a continuation of the past, these same blind critics are found pushing and shoving each other to be first in line to denounce the "forms" of the revolution. Finally, the blind critic reveals the nostalgic yearning for the past that underlies the theory of social cycles by passing over from a criticism of the "forms" of revolution to the critique of the "contents" of the revolution, that is, to revolution as such. We must therefore flatly declare that *the first rule for the critic is to remember that he is an observer first and makes criticisms last; and this means honesty with respect to events that are unforeseen no less than those foreseen.* He should remember a proverb claimed by both Brazilians and Argentines: "In the country of the blind, the one-eyed man is king."

Another phenomenon which has developed, particularly with reference to those men of learning working in Latin American "programs" and "area studies," is a confusion of roles. Oftentimes, the man of learning is less interested in understanding social change in the developing societies than in controlling such change. Thus, too many critics, sophisticated enough not to be deceived by dream-like thoughts that all goes well in Latin America, carry their sophistication to the point of manipulation. This, too, happens in stages and by imperceptible degrees. At first the novitiate is sent on his field trip to earn his advanced degree. Then, once acquiring his academic credentials, he finds himself besieged by offers from foundations and government agencies to pursue his researches further. Enriched (or inflated) with a sense of his importance, plugged into philanthropic and federal sponsorship, he then begins to present "policy recommendations" rather than scholarly research papers. If these recommendations receive attention in government circles, the scholar-manipulator then feels a part of the American Establishment rather than a part of the American academic community. And at this stage the critic is divested of his intellectual functions and forms a solid phalanx with public relations men against any further understanding of unsanctioned social changes. For those whose "policy recommendations" are ignored, there is either a sort of an alienated disenchantment with politics as such, or a heightened desperate effort to get right into the policy-making apparatus and abandon the pose of objective critic and researcher altogether. Thus, *the second rule for the critic is to clarify his own role before settling affairs of state; and that means making sure that commitment does not pass over into celebration, that meaningful research is not abandoned in favor of a manipulated consensus.*

An additional type of critic is the academic monopolist. Only he has a perfect understanding of the situation. Only he can say truly what is happening, because of such reasons as years of service in the field, intimacy of personal contacts, and past training in one discipline rather than another. To be sure, while these may indeed be genuine elements in critical understanding, they just as frequently operate as inhibiting factors. The "expert" builds up a pet theory with which he is loathe to part company despite changing circumstances. And the "expert" is furthermore the last one willing to make generalizations, to take a significant perspective of the situation, since he is usually committed to one geographic area, one discipline, one way of doing research. He develops a vested interest in his "specialty," a vested interest which can only lead to a situation in which all those who fail to share the identical vision (and very few are even allowed to share such a vision) or enter the discipleship are considered "mavericks," out to upset well-established research practices. The "expert" is generally the last one to see his own obsolescence. He thinks of serving time in the field, in the area, as in and of itself giving rise to wisdom. This "type" rarely takes the trouble to re-examine his own premises, the fundaments of his own training. He becomes an academic reactionary without ever so much as casting a forward glance. Thus, *the third rule for the critic is to be open to criticism, to make sure that time served is not substituted for understanding gained.*

It might appear strange and quarrelsome in a work on Brazil to dwell at length on what are essentially "internal" problems of research. However, so many "area studies" of Brazil reveal clear-cut shortcomings, not to say downright misinformation, that one is forced to conclude that some reasons for these shortcomings have nothing whatever to do with problems intrinsic to research; rather they have much to do with problems intrinsic to the researchers. But there is an additional reason for clearing the intellectual air in this fashion: if we are to give sober thought to revolution in Brazil, and to its relations with American capitalism and Soviet communism, then such thought must take place by liberating ourselves as much as possible from the debilitating effects of pseudo-expertise, cynicism about the reality and worth of social change, and scholarship turned rancid with manipulative ambitions. Once liberated from the canons of *extraneous* ideological considerations (not necessarily ideological moorings as such), the task of defining the course of the Brazilian Revolution can be seen as meaningful in its own right.

The first basic problem is the examination of the forms of the Brazilian Revolution: Will this revolution necessitate civil war? Will it take a violent, militaristic form? Will basic party structures be altered? Will the main role in the revolution be played by peasants? Only after some preliminary settlement of these questions will we be in a position to determine the content of the Brazilian Revolution, its root economic structure and the type of political organization that can be expected to emerge from it.

It should be pointed out, to friend and foe of the Brazilian Revolution alike, that it cannot be stopped, bartered away, rolled back, or forced into prefabricated molds. Too often, the question of revolution is confused and confounded with the question of civil war or insurrection. It need only be said that civil war may indeed be a result of efforts to *prevent* Brazil from entering the twentieth century—either through domestic masters having a stake in the epi-feudal society or through foreign traders and businessmen having a stake in the *status quo* as such. In this connection, Americans should remember their Civil War of 1861–65, and Russians ought to recall their Civil War of 1918–21. In both instances, violence was not the *cause* of the revolutionary impulse to free Negroes from the slave system or to free the Russian peasantry from an iniquitous serfdom and czardom, but the *consequence* of abortive (and pacific) attempts to prevent the inevitable from happening. In retrospect, everyone can see ways in which violent civil war could have been averted—abstractly, in principle. But can anyone seriously attempt to show how the disastrously uneconomical slave system, or a kulak system that left the land prey to banditry, could fail to be toppled by these earlier American and Russian "revolutions of rising expectations"? To be sure, the Brazilian Revolution is taking place at a much later "take-off" period, and in conditions in which it must contend with exacting world factors and not simply national factors. However, its basic impulse is precisely what it has been elsewhere, to liberate the bulk of the population from a grinding serfdom, and to join in the general path of technological-industrial development.

In this connection the fact that this is taking place in 1963 and not in 1863, as in the United States, is of supreme importance. For the forms of revolutionary striving, the forms for realizing a modern industrial-technological complex come from planning, through socialism, and not from free-market or mercantile capitalism. On the other hand, the very existence of a socialist economic sector considerably lessens the need for absolute terrorism as in Russia between the World Wars. It must be expected that resistance to the Brazilian Revolution will be forthcoming, not only from the decadent feudal sectors, but from the semi-developed capitalist sectors, particularly from that portion of the middle classes that has imbibed the commercial and cultural values of capitalism and the free-enterprise system. This resistance, and not the trend to revolution as such, makes the conditions for civil war, if not omnipresent, then at least everpresent.

It might be asked why can't the Brazilian Revolution take a capitalist form? The answers are complex, but nonetheless clear: (a) Brazilian experience and contact with American capitalism have on the whole been negative, since American capitalism entered Brazilian affairs as an imperial force with little interest in accelerating the "take-off" point of Brazilian industrial growth. (b) The "free enterprise" notion is rejected by even the modern Brazilian capitalists. There is a general recognition that the "public sector," the government-regulated sector of the economy, is a necessary political and even economic posture if Brazil is to achieve a successful national revolution. (c) It is furthermore recognized that given the backward state of Brazilian capitalism, the development of such essential fields as mineral exploration, advances in hydroelectric energy, petroleum fuels, atomic energy, etc., must be performed on a massive scale, with massive dosages of economic investment that can only come from the public sector. (d) One must also face the fact that a high degree of planning often signifies a high degree of organization and centralized authority; so that the politics of socialism are more nearly representative of the economics of rationality than is the free-market, free-enterprise system (a "system" which is largely mythic even in the most advanced capitalist nations). (e) A final factor in the basic rejection of capitalist solutions has been the incapacity of Brazil to gain prosperity under a free-market arrangement. As the present Brazilian Ambassador to the United States pointed out in a recent conference on Tensions in Development in the Western Hemisphere, the average price of Latin American exports to the United States had declined by 20% as compared with 1953—Latin American exports to the United States in 1961 measured in 1953 prices would have earned $1000 million more than they actually did. He concluded by noting that this represents a sum greater than the total of all aid funds to Latin America in 1961. Given the fact that Brazilian exports have been particularly hard hit in the free-market economy, one can readily understand the widespread disillusionment with capitalist solutions even amongst the middle-class sector.

But while the Brazilian economic and political "mix" unquestionably and increasingly favors the public sector, the socialist sector, this does not mean that Soviet communism will be, or even must be, duplicated. The leaders of the Brazilian Revolution, whether from peasantry, proletariat, or middle class, all realize the absurdity of blueprinting their revolution on a Soviet model. Socialism has itself become a world system, "polycentric" in character rather than "monolithic." The rise of alternative socialist formations has unleashed an experimental attitude, a search for yet new and distinctive types of socialism. What makes socialism so exciting and enticing a prospect for uncommitted Brazilians is precisely its experimental nature, e.g., Poland, China, Egypt, Russia, Czechoslovakia, and, above all, Cuba in the Western hemisphere. At a time when capitalism is becoming more "monolithic," more bound to multi-national economic communities, socialism is exhibiting that variety of forms that has classically characterized Western-style economic liberalism and political pluralism! This fact must be recognized as a partial explanation for the Brazilian drive toward socialism and, at the same time, its insistence upon retaining an experimental flavor.

The Brazilian tradition of political libertarianism, as a matter of fact often bordering on political anarchism, makes the establishment of bureaucratic (*in contrast to decentralized*) forms of socialism most difficult to envision. Again, what makes socialism so natural an alternative to traditional bourgeois democracy is precisely the absence not only of a two-party system, but of a firm adhesion to the party system as such. The very absence of traditional bourgeois modes of polity makes possible a direct form of producer socialism, and thoroughly bypasses the problem of the constitutional party system as it exists in the United States or Western Europe. The paradox is "dialectical": presidentialism makes possible the institution of a socialism from above, while the absence of a middle-class political party structure makes possible a socialism from below. The problems that will emerge once the economic phase of the revolution is unfolded will thus more likely be a conflict between the political elite on one side and the economic mass on the other, with neither resorting to industrial terrorism or "forced collectivization" as a form of accelerating social change.

The Brazilian Revolution will be taking place in the Western hemisphere under the watchful eyes and close scrutiny of the United States. This in itself must undoubtedly play a significant part in the character of social development. The United States will clearly block, by whatever means it deems necessary, any direct embrace by Brazil of the Soviet Union. However weakened the economic position of the United States vis-à-vis Brazilian capital becomes, it will retain sufficient military and political influence over the area to make any direct commitment to Soviet communism well-nigh impossible (even if this were the desire of Brazilian revolutionary leaders, which is clearly not the case). Of course, this can and to some extent already does have a built-in boomerang effect, since the very compelling United States "presence" in the hemisphere is itself an irritant, a major source for socialist agitation in the Brazilian sub-continent. If Brazilian policy at any given time leans too heavily in the direction of either the Soviet Union or the United States, one can count on the pressure from either of these goliaths to restore a sort of equilibrium, and compel Brazil to be relatively neutral with respect to the geopolitical struggles going under the name of the "Cold War." But again it must be reiterated that whatever the character of the East-West struggle at any moment, the socialist direction of Brazilian politics seems quite assured. And there is a warranted assertability that the United States would respect the establishment of a socialist Brazil, however much this might affect its own financial empire. On record are United States compromises with Mexico over the petroleum question during the 1938–40 period, and its compromise with Bolivian socialism—however much Bolivia's "socialism" is largely a matter of political labels rather than economic operations. But it is not the sufferance of the United States alone that Brazil will be guided by. Size and power are important. Brazil is a powerful nation-state. Barring overt military intervention, it is hard to conceive that the United States could do other than acquiesce in the thrust of the Brazilian people and polity toward a socialist nation-state.

A basically separate factor, but one quite organic to any discussion of the on-going Brazilian Revolution, is the theory and practice of the Brazilian communist movement. We must start with the fundamental paradox of communist policy in Brazil: whether to base itself on the peasant rural mass or upon the urban proletariat. From the time of the First International, socialist politics have been plagued with this necessity of choice. Karl Marx referred to the peasants as "native barbarians" and "troglodytes," and declared that, since they did not form a conscious class, they were incapable of defending their own interests as a class. The rural population, to Marx, was always a bulwark of economic backwardness and political counterrevolution. The main opposition to this view at the time came from Michael Bakunin. In his view, sooner or later, peasant revolution was inevitable; and the longer it was deferred, the more terrible and more destructive it would be. In Bakunin's view, if the peasants of Western Europe had appeared comparatively indifferent to the need for socialist revolution it was because socialist revolutionists had made the enormous mistake of exclusively concentrating their efforts on the city proletariat.

The relative failure of orthodox revolutionary socialism in France, Italy, England, and, above all, Germany—where a large class-conscious urban proletariat has existed for the past two centuries—and, contrariwise, the relative successes of peasant revolution in China, Cuba, Ghana, Algeria, and even India, could not fail but to make its impress. The Communist Party of Brazil has been badly torn ideologically on this matter. For while its draft programs speak of "raising the question of forming the democratic united front of the country's patriotic popular and democratic forces, with the working class in the van," Prestes and his party remain troubled by the failure of this "van" to move in a communist direction. In a desperate effort to erect a "united front," Prestes still speaks of the Brazilian capitalist classes with the sort of longing and lingering hope not uncharacteristic of the directors of the Pan American Union! Prestes' Soviet-styled apparatus *asks* the middle sectors to "show their support of the people"—whatever that might mean. Or failing to support the proletariat openly, at least to adopt a position of "benevolent neutrality." This strikes a peculiarly nostalgic note in a Brazilian context—reminiscent as it is of the *patrão*-worker relationship and of the life history of Brazilian paternalism. The cry for "benevolent neutrality," made as an attempt to root out "left sectarianism" in the Brazilian Communist Party, is, as a matter of fact, strikingly like Vargas' falangist insistence on class cooperation as the high road to socialist revolution—an amazing outcome for a Party which so bitterly denounced Vargas' "betrayals" at every opportunity.

The left socialist leadership, such as Julião, Brizola, Arrais, Furtado (amorphous as it may be), has thus tended to veer increasingly to the views first enunciated by Bakunin on the peasant question, and now commonly associated with the Chinese faction within the international communist movement. They have attempted to orient their theories about a program which would have a common appeal to urban workers and rural peasants alike (often inclining toward the latter). The problem with proletarian "vanguardism" is its tendency to adopt bureaucratic and dictatorial means of achieving socialist objectives. The strictly communist solution is intrinsically unappealing to the mass of peasants, since it would mean an acceleration of the process of industrialization at the expense of the peasant sector as such. Thus, a "Soviet" solution would only intensify the process of agricultural de-emphasis already marked in "bourgeois" efforts at industrialization. On the other side, the devotees of peasant socialism must face the fact that such a form of socialism often deteriorates into a sabotage of the industrial process as such. A peasant solution without coercive features, without an industrial program such as a Julião is proposing, has the functional defects of Gandhism, and few of its ideological or ethical refinements.

This emphasis on fundamental defects in Brazilian communism ought not to lead to a distorted perspective. The communist movement at present remains a basic, albeit minority, factor in the evolution of Brazilian socialism. It has earned this status through diligent effort and self-sacrifice. The basic formation of Brazilian communism came about through its support of the nationalist claims of *Tenentismo* in the twenties; its assistance of basic labor and peasant reform in the thirties; its steady opposition to the Vargas dictatorship in the forties; and its anti-imperialist, pro-nationalist posture throughout the fifties. This is not a matter of whether the communist position is or has been consistently "right"; only a recognition that the Communist Party of Brazil has historically not been as badly compromised as the Western European parties of France, England, or Italy, and not as badly fragmented as the Latin communist movement has been in such pivotal Hispanic countries as Mexico and Argentina.

Indeed, strange as it might seem to North Americans, the generally consistent opposition of the Communist Party of Prestes to the Labor Party of Vargas (which contrasts most decisively with the wavering confusions of the Argentine Communists in relation to Perón and Peronism), has tended to fix an image of communist conservatism in the minds of many Brazilian urban workers and intellectuals. The Vargas movement in retrospect is now considered the basic political assurance which enabled Brazil to launch its industrial development program. Most labor factions, including present government leaders as well, consider the Vargas New State as equivalent to the Roosevelt New Deal in the United States—only of a more radical nature. Thus the overthrow of Vargas, and the relatively consistent opposition to Vargas by the Communists, is seen in retrospect as a negation, if not outright betrayal, of the social revolution. This is why communism tended to remain stagnant in the aftermath of the Vargas collapse. And this is also why Brazilian socialists view with some caution and suspicion the "radical" posture of the Brazilian communist movement.

To be sure, the Brazilian Communist Party has been deeply compromised by the often competing and conflicting claims of Brazilian "nationalism" and Soviet "internationalism." During the fifties, when Brazilian socialists were tooling up for the long pull of getting the industrialization process in the public sector, communists were busy collecting signatures in defense of world peace. During the early sixties, when Brazilian socialists were seeking yet new curbs on Brazil's capitalist sector, the communists were calling for class indulgence and cooperation. The fact is that the prime allegiance of Brazil's industrial labor force is *not* to class but to nation; not to internationalism but to extreme nationalism. What this has accomplished is to make the Brazilian communist movement considerably less effective, even with its return to a semi-legal status under Dutra, than might otherwise have been the case. These ambiguities, occasioned by the mechanical identification of Brazilian needs with Soviet interests, has doomed the Communist Party to a prolonged minority status. But perhaps more significantly, the minority status has an accepted niche in the Brazilian power structure. This can be seen by failure to prosecute the Communists and a general absence of persecution irrespective of their "legal status." Thus the Communist Party, to the extent that it has been absorbed into middle-class politics as such, is not a revolution-making agency. The relative impotence of the Party to act in "non-legal" ways, and its search for parliamentary strength and juridical recognition, make clear the non-revolutionary nature of the communist faction, and, furthermore, have accelerated the demand for non-communist agencies to initiate radical social change.

Finally, however popular a hero Luís Carlos Prestes might be in the eyes of many, he lacked either the independence or the political *savoir faire* necessary for the conduct of *majority* politics. The *mystique* of Prestes, the "Cavalier of Hope," detracted from the concept of collective Party leadership. The sin of Stalinism passed directly over into *Prestismo*. And a top-heavy party apparatus developed along the French communist model of Duclos and Thorez, an apparatus essentially unresponsive to actual political needs. The Communist Party turned inward during the Stalin era, developing the concept of "class struggle" in such a corrupted and stupid form that it became equivalent to "inner-party struggle." Hence, the entire field of social reform was left to the independent socialists and peasant reformers. The formal proclamations were usually "correct" in terms of abstract considerations of Marxian formulas, but the specific activities of the Communist

Party were directed toward the purification, maintenance, and rationalization of the Party apparatus—and not focused on the conduct of the social revolution it ostensibly was dedicated to achieve.

What then is the likely outcome of the Brazilian Communist Party? While at this stage of revolutionary progress, prognostication is difficult and exceedingly tentative, everything points to the use of the Soviet-styled Party during the revolution, and its relatively quick absorption by the larger socialist complex after a period of political consolidation. This definitely happened in Yugoslavia in 1949, in Algeria in 1961, and as we have seen in the last chapter, in Cuba in 1962. It provides a firm model on which the Brazilians can build. Socialism is, furthermore, extremely powerful in Brazil, while the Soviet communist variety of socialism is relatively weak. If an analogy could be made, one would have to say that Goulart's movement, however amorphous and multi-party its strength is at present, resembles the basic platform of the English Labour Party on matters of politics and the Yugoslavian Communist Leagues on matters of party organization. Given this continuation of present tendencies, it is highly doubtful that a Communist Party which remains a Soviet-oriented Party could long survive a socialist revolution in Brazil; while it is even dubious that a Chinese-patterned Communist apparatus could make enough headway even to participate in the revolution.

Precisely the delays in the completion of the revolution, precisely the continuing strength of reactionary factions, precisely the continued pressures from the "Giant of the North," give sustenance and substance to the Brazilian Communist Party. We must once again assert a paradox: the surest way to minimize Soviet political influence in Brazil, that is, the way most certain to reduce the influence of the Communist Party, is through the maturation of an authentic economic breakthrough—authentic enough not to be bought out by the empire of oil, and powerful enough to absorb (not crush) the elite and rank and file of the Communist Party. This does not mean that American entrepreneurs will gain any clear-cut advantage in their own private war with the devils of socialism; quite the reverse. But it does imply that the rise of Brazilian socialism will probably spell *finis* for the Soviet-oriented political apparatus in Brazil—a development which will probably increase the long-run pacification of the struggle between East and West.

The supreme fact, moreover, is not the political decline of the Communist Party movement, but the political incline of the socialist party movement. It would be foolish to expect a "movement of national redemption" to stop within strictly capitalist limits; such a proposal would not be taken seriously even by conservative Brazilian politicians. We must learn to live with a socialist Brazil. And a socialist Brazil will not be an abortive political maneuver as it has been in Bolivia during the fifties, or as it was in Mexico during the thirties. It will be an economic transformation of both hemispheric weight and international consequence. Any United States approach which fails to recognize this simple fact will be doomed beforehand. Whatever else is negotiable in Brazilian-American relations—the connections with the Soviet power bloc, an independent nuclear striking force outside of United States supervision, the forms of expropriation and indemnification, etc.—one item is non-negotiable, and that is the drive of Brazil to enter the modern industrial world, a drive whose basic economic content is rapidly becoming socialistic.

Socialist parties exist in virtually all the countries of Latin America. The membership of these parties is generally dominated by middle-class intellectuals with a strong interest in Marxism. Despite their avowed interest in problems of the working classes, the socialists of Hispanic America have, in fact, developed little genuine influence with the masses. This Hispanic pattern is not the case in Luzo-America, in Brazil. Socialism in Brazil has not been converted, at least not on a widespread basis, into a heuristic device for cutting into communist strength (widespread suspicions exist elsewhere that socialist parties are simply rhetorical devices for holding revolutionary impulses in check). Between the Socialist Party and the Labor Party, socialist sentiment can claim a sizable minority, and within organized labor, perhaps a majority. Whatever the repressive character of the Vargas regime in the thirties and the *Caudillo* aspects of the Goulart regime in the sixties, each possessed the distinct advantage of not being "officialist." The *Queremistas* have created a self-image of socialism, and in some measure are now obligated to deliver socialist, and not simply social, reforms. The present demands of the urban proletariat are for a functional autonomy that thus far no Brazilian government has tolerated.

The difficulty with most North American proposals for a "solution" to the Brazilian "problem" is that they are mortifyingly naïve, well intentioned, and thoroughly petit bourgeois! In one monumental treatise on the land system and demographic factors in Brazil, we find two mouse-like recommendations put in elephantine form: First "above all, Brazil should seek to put large acreages of public lands into the hands of those who themselves will till them adequately"; and second: "Brazil should start sending students to foreign universities for technical training and developing teachers for secondary schools." Now both of these statements or recommendations are patently meaningless. The question is not putting "public lands" (which have been badly depleted by murderous land speculators through the centuries) into the hands of peasants, but of abolishing *private latifundias*. Furthermore, the solution to the Brazilian land problem is not individual proprietorship of small *miniplots*—this has been tried and found wanting over and over again—but of the rationalization of agricultural production through technology, irrigation, and farm machinery. The Brazilian land problem will be solved when 10% of the people are engaged in farming and the other 90% in trade, commerce, and industry—and not by making half the population over into petty farm holders tilling unprofitably for no sensible reason except imagined psychological needs of proprietorship. As for the education of the people, this is simply like declaring one's allegiance to Truth, Goodness, and Nobility. The facts of the matter are that education in a situation of rigid social stratification, education where mobility patterns either do not exist or are not rewarded on the basis of merit, simply intensifies the agony of the intellectual classes, and makes the poor even more discontented. To educate the Brazilian public while leaving intact the basic social structure is simply to accelerate the patterns of alienation and discontent, and ultimately, to accelerate the revolutionary process itself—something those who prattle about educational reforms in Latin America never seem to grapple with.

But there is a new kind of approach heard with increasing frequency. It is an approach based on revolutionary rhetoric, with the contents of fundamental social change quite thoroughly emasculated and spayed. It is a position which sees the social revolution as a fact of Latin American life, but does not provide us with the least inkling of the economic and political contents of that revolution, which does not admit in effect what the backward Brazilian peasant knows—that the social revolution is by necessity transforming itself into a socialist revolution. This kind of position, which poses as radical, which proposes "a carefully designed massive attack on the problem of guided social change," leaves unanswered *who* is going to "design" this "massive attack," and *who* is going to "guide" the "guided social change." It is, furthermore, a posture which reeks with double-talk, which speaks of the "rights of self-determination" while calling for "mutual intervention" by a team of "carefully selected" (by who?) and "highly trained" Latin American and Anglo-American specialists. But this sort of truncated Platonism assumes much and delivers little. It assumes that a Brazilian solution must be a hemisphere-wide solution. It assumes that only by "mutual intervention" can progress be made. What can such a solution deliver? Only a greater expenditure of foundation monies, academic armies, and social workers to frustrate the real development of the revolution.

American scholarship has not come up with either "solutions" or "policy recommendations" for the simple reason that solutions to Brazil's problems cannot be exported by intellectual salesmen. It is undoubtedly true that revolutions cannot be exported. But it is doubly true that arbitrary solutions based on the threats of a foreign power also cannot be exported. The constant demand that Brazil conform to United States business and political policies, or face an end to Congressional aid, only further embitters even those Brazilian sectors friendly to American society. Thus, this work will end, must end, not with proposals to Brazilians on the conduct of their revolution, but with proposals for Americans on the conduct of their reaction to this revolution.

What then are these proposals for Americans? In the rough, they are proposals that can be made for American attitudes vis-à-vis the entire Latin American complex. They are urgings for the support of national sovereignty, accelerated social change, a replacement of a social stratification system exhibiting peaks of very rich and very poor with a structural change that would permit social mobility and maximize social equality at the same time. But this is still on the level of rhetoric. A sharper and more precise understanding of the Brazilian situation yields a more specific and hence more readily realizable set of proposals.

(1) In the first place, the United States should support, and not try to counter (through the Alliance for Progress), the agrarian reform policies of Julião, Arrais, Furtado, Mello, and other leaders of the Brazilian Northeast. The United States need hardly feel threatened as to its own interests, on this score at least. The latifundists, the historical drag on development in Brazil, the perfect complement to our own slaveholding caste of the *ante-bellum* South, represents a form of backwardness alien to the American democratic tradition no less than to Brazilian freedom movements. This is one area where an authentic show of support for the revolution in Brazil could have vastly beneficial results. The recent elections (October 1962) in the Northeast showed the temper of the public. Conservative UDN candidate João Cleofas de Oliveira, backed by the sugar-planter oligarchy, lost to left-wing candidate Miguel Arrais, who was backed by the Communist Party, socialist and labor groups, and the Peasant Leagues of Francisco Julião. It is no secret that the fear of "communism" led the United States State Department to give indirect support to the conservative candidate. Our government had committed nearly $200 million in aid funds to prevent the very event which occurred, a leftist victory. Might it not be wiser to recognize that a "leftist" regime would only achieve by 1965 what the United States had secured in 1865, a formal victory over serfdom?

(2) Intimately connected to the problem of agrarian reform is the general issue of economic development. The United States must come to realize that Brazil, unlike any other Latin American country with the possible exception of Mexico, has reached a new plateau in its industrial development. It is now at a stage where investment coupled with technical and marketing know-how is often more important to the further development of a specific industry than capital itself. Brazil has a special need for electronics, chemical, and metallurgical manufacturing, industries which woud enable Brazil to improve its export position, and hence resolve the paradox of high consumption with low production that in large measure is aggravated by American corporate and marketing policies. In this sense, there is little point to United States government policy recommendations based on bolstering the *cruzeiro* by direct monetary subsidization—which in the monetary cycle

only flows back to our country in the form of payment for secondary goods.

The mythic dimensions of "poor nations and rich nations" often translates itself into stereotyped thinking. This is particularly true of any number of policy reports by American teams and missions. Even if we restrict ourselves to the Northeast, an area often described in terms of drought and disease, we find "pockets" of real wealth and expansion. Drought years do exist. Diseases do take countless life in genocidal fashion. But neither defines nor exhausts the central issues. The demand for land redistribution makes sense precisely because the potential resources of the area are capable of immediate realization. If this were not the case, land reform would be a farce, an ideological gimmick, as it often is even in such "advanced" areas as Mexico and in less advanced areas of Latin America such as Bolivia.

The need for technical assistance, specifically of United States assistance, must be expanded from its present parochialism, to a type which takes account of the socio-economic variables—of the need to install new forms of redistributive justice, even if it involves the outright confiscation of large landholding estates or middle-sized foreign enterprises. Thus far, it is precisely at this point that American foreign aid has broken down. *It views technical aid as a substitute for, rather than a complement of, expropriation and confiscation.* If at any point along the political axis the United States might follow a correct policy rather than a costly policy, it is in the sphere of land reform and industrial production. The promise of the Alliance on this count remains essentially unfulfilled, not so much because of the minimal funds at its disposal, but due to its ideological limits, that is, a concept of land reform unconnected to class reform. At some point, it might be found that United States policy would be better served by full-scale political support for the final and inevitable Brazilian assault on feudalism, than by a costly and thus far largely inept outflanking maneuver. The feudal sector may have retreated a bit under the weight of United States agricultural and industrial policy, but neither the rate at which it has done so nor the real change in class forces over the past several decades warrants any undue optimism for the pacific, non-confiscatory policies of the United States.

The problem of transforming the Brazilian Northeast is less tied to direct massive doses of monetary assistance than most Americans care to grant. It is far more intimately tied to the general and over-all development of the Brazilian economy. The present "uneven" tendencies in its development are real features, but not necessarily desirable features. And the process of "evening out" such development, entailing as it must high-level planning, confiscation of latifundias, and expropriation of foreign investments, can only be faced by the Brazilians themselves. The ambiguous foreign policy of the United States does little to enhance matters: on one hand we find an encouragement of legally elected representatives, while on the other scandals arise concerning American corporations purchasing Brazilian Federal Deputies; on one hand, we encourage the growth of expertise, while on the other we consider recommendations which violate sacred cows of policy to be intolerable; on one hand there is a search for a democratic alternative to communism, while on the other any steps leftward are defined as communistic. The American public ought to be informed that the oversimplified rhetoric of anti-communism, upon which the politics of ambiguity are built, is played out, and that the present course of action can result in a right-wing coup which would only accelerate the schisms within Brazilian society and hasten the revolutionary process in the long run.

(3) The United States as a sovereign government should clearly distinguish itself from private corporate United States investors, and not, as is now done, attach Congressional "rider" amendments which would cut off all federal funds to Brazil if any further expropriations are made. It must develop an anti-imperialist legislation comparable in strength to the anti-monopolist legislation of the 1890's. There can be little question that the free-wheeling corporate empires operating in Brazil constitute perhaps a greater threat to the foreign-policy posture of the United States than did the military excursions of our government in an earlier epoch. As matters now stand, the Brazilians can hardly distinguish the United States government from the United States business empire. Congressmen and State Department officials threaten an end to federal aid if private corporations are tampered with in the slightest, while Standard Oil executives lecture Brazilians on the meaning of the United States free-enterprise systems. This utter "bourgeoisification" of American foreign policy has only heightened Brazilian nationalist aspirations, so that it now has be-

come an anti-American consciousness as such. If the respect of Brazil's policy-making elite, not to mention its public, is to be maintained or, better, restored, there must be some sign from the United States government that it is not captive to the economy and ideology of the private investors.

This absence of difference between American policy and American business contributes substantially to the frustration of sound structural development of the Brazilian economy. It does this by converting loans into unproductive consumer channels. United States loans tend to be squandered in the importation of luxury goods, or in the purchase of goods manufactured by United States corporations. Thus, instead of the loans having a salutory effect, they only further increase the wealth of American corporate investors, and decrease the possibility of use of these funds in developing a form of production which would have long-run benefits for the Brazilian mass, and would at the same time lead to a stable economic equilibrium. American policy-makers must cease playing deaf, dumb, and blind to the American manufacturers who sap Brazilian wealth.

(4) The United States must demand from its own agencies the strictest adhesion to democratic norms of polity. The customary theory that military rule, or military-controlled rule, is the most reliable "friend" of the United States and the most vigorous opponent to communism is dangerous for the future of Brazilian polity, and, worse than that, based on the thinnest kind of evidence. We have shown in earlier chapters that the position of the military of Brazil, while it offers little in the way of an escape from Bonapartist rule, also offers little consolation to United States' attempts to secure hemispheric hegemony. The role of the military may be anti-communist to be sure, but it does not therefore signify a positive orientation toward United States' interests and over-all needs. Guatemala offers evidence that "communism from above" may actually be sponsored by the military.

Present tendencies in the Brazilian military afford ample evidence that a large portion and perhaps even the majority of the military elite favors a vigorous anti-United States and extremely pro-nationalistic political and economic program. It may well be that the present American myth about the anti-communism of the Latin military will prove precisely the factor which leads Brazil at every level farther away from an orientation toward the

United States. The Brazilian military are largely recruited from the petty bourgeois families of the cities, particularly in its lower staff echelons—and this sector as a social force has every reason to promote an "anti-American" campaign in the belief that an end to American hegemony in the area might lead to the growth of a countervailing military and political force in the southern hemisphere. Given the additional fact that the higher echelons have been strongly influenced by left-nationalist and even socialist currents since the days of the "long march," the blind faith in and support of militarism as the basic tool of anti-communism must be seen as a naïve and dangerous fiction.

(5) The United States should allow, and even encourage, the Quadros-Goulart policy of an "opening to the world." Brazilian efforts at becoming a world power in the economic sense rest almost entirely on ambitions normal to a healthy and vigorous middle class. It is in keeping with the historic impulse of the manufacturing classes to reach for new and greater markets. If we imagine a normal evolution of this Brazilian process, what would be the result? Would the United States have a new competitor? Most certainly yes. But it would also have a new competitor in a strictly commercial sense, in the same sense as Japan or Western Germany. In short, the economic loss to American business firms would not entail, but would make far more difficult, the political penetration of communism or, for that matter, even socialism. Unfortunately, it sometimes seems that to expect such far-sightedness on the part of State Department experts or Congressional whips is to ask for miracles. The more likely prospect is that the United States will vigorously oppose this Brazilian middle-class movement of an "opening to the world" on the fantastic premise that any trading with Soviet-bloc nations would render Brazil inept in the struggle against communism—although why this same "logic" does not obtain in Canadian dealings with the Soviet-bloc nations (including Cuba) is simply never explained. One can expect an ever-increasing radicalization of the middle sectors as their efforts to join the world financially come up against a shortsighted mercantilism and protectionism characteristic of American business attitudes. The very social sector and the very economic program best calculated to avoid a communist *coup d'état* are now being fearfully and timidly opposed. The only possible consequence will be a strengthening of the bonds

between Brazilian capital and labor, a strengthening which will also accelerate the revolutionary process toward socialism.

(6) The United States, which for so long has counseled "education" as a solution to Latin American ailments, might well see the virtues of this approach in reverse. What is needed is some basic education in the realities of Latin America and Brazilian America in our own schools and colleges. As matters now stand, the greater portion of the American population could probably not tell an inquirer what the capital of Brazil now is, or even was. It would be an interesting experiment to ask our Post Office to determine the number of letters sent annually to "Rio de Janeiro, Argentina" or to "Buenos Aires, Brazil." And how could this be otherwise? Our "social studies texts" still claim rubber is Brazil's "basic export"; and our language teachers are thoroughly unfamiliar with Latin America as a cultural entity, much less a political entity. The case of Brazil is particularly acute. Portuguese is rarely taught in American high schools or colleges, and the cultural contributions of this great country are shrouded in obscurity. The first step might be a massive translation project of Brazilian classic writers such as Ruy Barbosa, Euclydes da Cunha, Machado Assis. A second step might be increased attention to the work of Brazilian social scientists and popular political writers. The initial stage is to educate the educators. Then, perhaps we will have a more sensitive political cadre and a better informed public. Certain developments in this direction are already apparent. The tragedy, or perhaps the comedy of it all, is that only under the gun, only with the threat of an "uncontrolled" revolution, has the beginnings of consciousness of the Brazilian complex come to the fore. If it takes "communism" to extract the long overdue recognition, then we can be assured that "communism" it will be, if not in fact, then at least in threats.

This education of the American public must be an honest one. It must not be an "anti-communist' crusade that substitutes orientation for information; for such education is simply miseducation, a demented result of the public's need for knowledge.

It would be the height of utopian imagination to think that even these six points will be transformed into policies. For the United States government to support the agrarian reform movement, divest itself of its image as defender of business interests, adopt an anti-militarist approach, allow Brazilian business interests to develop in an unfettered fashion, and initiate a massive educational campaign would require substantial changes in the attitude of the American electorate. The present political climate in the United States offers little encouragement. In a climate of opinion where words must be measured on such "controversial" subjects as foreign policy, where a violation of the consensus means potentially or actually to place oneself outside the protection of the Establishment, and where politics has been abandoned in favor of elitist policy decision, it would be foolhardy to anticipate anything but extreme intransigence, and anything but outright hostility to any change in the prevailing norms. We are witnesses to the consequences of our own fear, our own paranoid reaction to any social changes which we do not inspire, guide, or control. We have lost the capacity to think outside of stereotyped guidelines of communism and anti-communism. And the strange part of it all is that this smacks strongly of a self-fulfilling prophetic mode of thought and action. We so limit the alternatives of the Hispanic and Brazilian peoples that, in order to escape our clutches, they do indeed flee to the communist siren waiting off-stage. We have put Brazil between the devil and the deep blue sea, between the Eagle and the Bear. To demand virginity, if not downright loyalty, under such conditions is national egocentrism. It is a tribute to the maturity of the Brazilian political leadership that it has managed to assert its independent claims in a forceful way, in terms of the politically possible. It would be wise to bend every effort to expand the possible, instead of our present course which seems hell-bent on closing out all options. Then perhaps the six-point program herein outlined might have a chance of success.

Clearly much of what has been said in this chapter is applicable to United States relations with other nations of South and Central America. While it is undoubtedly true that Brazil is "different" from the other nations of Latin America—given its distinctive geography, its different language, and its racial and ethnic composition and intermixture—the attempt to create a theory of Brazilian exceptionalism is a dangerous form of political romanticism. Brazil is very much a part of Latin America—and becoming more so as its continental leadership becomes pronounced. Cuba can move into the Soviet orbit and not carry a single other nation in the hemisphere with it. Can anyone seriously claim that the same political indifference or intransigence would result were Brazil firmly to enter the Soviet camp—or, for that matter, develop into a socialist nation of the third camp on the order of Yugoslavia or India? Clearly not.

For the Brazilians, the supreme fact is that the United States is, and shall for a long while into the future, remain the central military, economic, and political power of the hemisphere. Any attempt to challenge this supremacy by a frontal assault, by an alliance with the Soviet Union in the military sense, will invite the most severe troubles and may well result in a loss of prestige rather than a gain of sovereignty. Willy-nilly, socialism has become "negotiable" in the hemisphere. But, by the same token, it should now be clear that any military alliance of Brazil with the Soviet bloc would be considered "non-negotiable." This may be mistaken by the reactionary clique in the United States as a surrender of American hegemony and supremacy. This is partially correct. Such a position does involve the equalization and normalization of political and economic relations and a surrender of pretentious and outmoded notions of superiority. This may also be taken by Brazilian super-nationalists and super-Sovieteers as a limitation placed on the rights of Brazil to negotiate whatever sort of military or political pacts it deems necessary or desirable. This, too, is partially correct. Such a position does entail a realistic appraisal of the political context in which Brazil must live. The "third position," the "third force," is a real entity; so, too, is the military division of the world between the first two forces, between the United States and the Soviet Union. The third force is a protest against the thermonuclear diplomacy of the big powers. In this linkage of Brazil with the third force, it can perform a great and vital service in any future political thaw. We have seen, in the sort of brinkmanship conducted by the major powers over Cuba and Germany, what happens when fundamental thermonuclear realities are surrendered to revolutionary romanticism or, for that matter, to nostalgic reactionism.

The scope for political independent actions has never been more evident than now. However, such latitude should not be mistaken for cowardice and weakness. It should be taken as part of the slow, painful maturation of American foreign policy. Backward "slips," attempts to re-establish Monroeism, attempts to violate the sovereignty of any Latin American nation, should be resisted, and resisted to the maximum degree. But the Brazilian, too, should not make dangerous "slips," should not allow himself to become a pawn or a tool in any international power struggle. The greatness of Brazil can only be assured by Brazilians—not by Americans and not by Russians. And there is little question that, as the Brazilian social revolution gains momentum and registers large-scale successes, this fact will increasingly impress itself on the minds and hearts of the Brazilian people, and on the calculations of the world powers.

BIBLIOGRAPHY

This bibliography is both restrictive and selective: restricted to the field of social and political sciences; and selected in terms of those works and essays which had particular value to the execution of this volume. A most unfortunate situation greets the English-speaking reader interested in finding out the Brazilian point of view. Basically, the work of the most important social scientists and political analysts is not available in English. Thus, for the reader concerned with the writings of such critical and pivotal contemporary Brazilian figures as Furtado, Costa-Pinto, Jaguaribe, Bastide, Carneiro-Leao, et al., one must be able to read some Portuguese (or, at the least, Spanish, since a good number of Brazilian writers have been translated into that language). The best primary sources for information on Brazil are the publications issued by commercial and industrial agencies, especially *Brazilian-American Survey, Brazilian Business,* and the reports issued by the *Instituto de Aposentadoria e Pensões dos Industriarios,* and by the Getúlio Vargas Foundation, *Conjuntura Econômica (Economics and Business in Brazil).*

An indispensable bibliographical tool is the *Inter-American Review of Bibliography.* This publication of the Pan American Union not only supplies up-to-date and relatively complete information on new and forthcoming books in Portuguese and Spanish, but also offers a great many leads for further bibliographical sources. An additional vital source for information of this sort is contained in the monthly publication, *Hispanic American Report,* published by the Hispanic American Society and edited by Ronald Hilton. It must also be noted that this publication is indispensable for news of current interest in Hispanic America, gathered from the newspapers and periodical literature of each country in the Americas.

The periodical literature available to an English-speaking audience on Hispanic American subjects has grown enormously during the post-World-War-II period. *The Journal of Inter-American Studies,* perhaps the most recent entry into the field, is also the most important from the viewpoint of those with a social science interest. Edited by Robert E. McNicoll and A. Curtis Wilgus, it places a strong emphasis on Brazilian affairs, unlike other Hispanic journals. Another major source of information is the bulletins published by the American Universities Field Staff. Its Brazilian representative, Frank Bonilla, offers first-rate on-the-spot coverage. An additional good source of direct information is *Atlas: The Magazine of the World Press*, which often contains important articles from Brazilian newspapers and popular weeklies.

There are a number of journals catering to specialized interests in the history and social structure of Latin America. The most notable of these are: *The Hispanic American Historical Review; Hispania; Revista Iberoamericana; Hispanic Review;* and *Revista Interamericana de Ciencias Sociales.* Certain of the more general scholarly publications give particularly strong coverage to South America, if not to Brazil as such. Among the most notable in this category are: *The Annals of the American Academy of Political and Social Science; Comparative Studies in Society and History; The World Today; Current History;* and *The South Atlantic Quarterly.* Thus, while literature concerning Brazilian developments is often most difficult to come by for the general reader, it is there to be dug out. What is urgently needed is a greater effort on the part of the mass weeklies and monthlies, as well as the newspapers, to make this information more widely disseminated. Newspaper reporting on Brazil is, with the proud exceptions of *The New York Times* and *The Christian Science Monitor,* seriously deficient. It is to be imagined that the growing problems in Inter-American affairs, if not their ever-increasing importance, will change this situation.

I hope that this note explains, and perhaps excuses, the obvious gaps and shortcomings in the following bibliography. I should also like to mention in conclusion that those items in the bibliography preceded by an asterisk (*) are included in the essay portions of this book. In certain instances, the titles of the essays have been slightly changed for purposes of maintaining stylistic and literary balance.

ILH

Aleixo, Pedro. *Imunidades parlamentárias.* Belo Horizonte: Faculdade de Direito, Universidade de Minas Gerais, 1961.
Alexander, Robert J. "Brazilian Tenentismo," *Hispanic American Historical Review,* Vol. XXXVI, No. 1 (May 1956), pp. 229-42.
————. "Luiz Carlos Prestes and the *Partido Comunista do Brasil,*" in *Communism in Latin America.* New Brunswick: Rutgers University Press, 1957. Pp. 93-134.
Amado, Jorge. *The Violent Land.* Trans. by Samuel Putnam. New York: Alfred A. Knopf, 1945.
————. *Vida de Luís Carlos Prestes, o Cavaleiro da esperança.* São Paulo: Livraria Martins, 1946.

Andrade, Manuel Correia de. *A terra e o homem no Nordeste*. São Paulo: Livraria Brasiliense, 1963.

Araujo Castro, João Augusto. "Time Is Running Short," *New University Thought*, Vol. III, No. 3 (December-January 1963-64), pp. 57-69.

Azevedo, Fernando de. *Canaviais e engenhos na vida política, do Brasil*. Rio de Janeiro: Instituto do Açúcar e do Álcool, 1948.

————. *Brazilian Culture: An Introduction to the Study of Culture in Brazil*. Trans. by W. R. Crawford. New York: The Macmillan Co., 1950.

Baratz, Morton S. "The Crisis in Brazil," *Social Research*, Vol. XXII, No. 3 (October 1955), pp. 347-61.

Barbosa, Ruy. *Ruínas de um govêrno*. Rio de Janeiro: Editora Guanabara, 1931.

————. *Ditadura e república*. Rio de Janeiro: Editora Guanabara, 1932.

Bastide, Roger. *Imagens do nordeste místico em branco e prêto*. Rio de Janeiro: Seção de livros da emprêsa grafica, 1948.

————. "Religion and the Church in Brazil," in *Brazil: Portrait of Half a Continent*. Ed. by Smith and Marchant. *Loc. cit.*, pp. 334-55.

————. *Les Religions africaines au Brésil*. Paris: Presses Universitaires de France, 1960.

Bastos, Humberto. *A Marcha do capitalismo no Brasil: ensaio de interpretação, 1500-1940*. São Paulo: Livraria Martins, 1944.

————. *A economia brasileira e o mundo moderno: ensaio geopolítico sobre a estruturação do capitalismo brasileiro*. São Paulo: Livraria Martins, 1948.

Berle, Adolph A. "Latin America: The Hidden Revolution," *The Reporter* (May 28, 1959), pp. 17-20.

————. "The Communist Invasion of Latin America," *The Reporter* (July 7, 1960), pp. 23-25.

Bohan, Merwyn (head of "a group of experts"). "Northeast Brazil Survey Team Report." Washington, D.C., February 1962. (Mimeographed)

Bonilla, Frank. "Rio's 'Favelas': The Rural Slum within a City," *Dissent*, Vol. IX, No. 4 (Autumn 1962), pp. 383-86.

————. "Rural Reform in Brazil," *Dissent*, Vol. IX, No. 4 (Autumn 1962), pp. 373-82.

Borges da Fonseca, Herculano. "The Economic and Financial Situation of Brazil," *Brazilian American Survey*, No. 16 (Rio de Janeiro, 1962), pp. 7-13.

Botsford, Keith. "Brazil's New Language," *The New Leader* (September 3, 1962), pp. 6-9.

————. "Conversation in Brazil" (with Gilberto Freyre), *Encounter*, Vol. XIX, No. 5 (November 1962), pp. 33-41.

Boxer, C. R. *The Golden Age of Brazil, 1695-1750: Growing Pains of a Colonial Society*. Berkeley: University of California Press, 1962.

Buarque de Holanda, Sergio. *Raízes do Brasil*. 2nd ed. Rio de Janeiro: José Olympio, 1948.

Calmon, Pedro. *História da Civilização Brasileira*. 2nd ed. São Paulo: Companhia Editora Nacional, 1935.

————. *História Social do Brasil*. São Paulo: Companhia Editora Nacional, 1940.

————. *Curso de Direito Constitucional Brasileiro*. Rio de Janeiro: Lirravia Freitas Bastos, 1947.

Calógeras, João Pandiá. *A History of Brazil*. Trans. by P. A. Martin. Chapel Hill: The University of North Carolina Press, 1939.

Camacho, J. A. *Brazil: An Interim Assessment*. 2nd ed. London and New York: Royal Institute of International Affairs, 1954.

Camargo, José Francisco de. *Êxodo rural no Brasil, formas, causas e consequências economicas principais*. Rio de Janeiro: Conquista, 1960.

Cardoso, Fernando Henrique. "Tensões sociais no campo e reforma agrária," *Revista Brasileira de Estudos Políticos*, No. 12 (Belo Horizonte, 1961), pp. 7-26.

Carneiro, Leão Antonio. "Problems in Rural Society and Rural Education," in *Educational Yearbook*. New York: Teachers College of Columbia University, 1938.

————. *Sociedade Rural: seus problemas e sua edução*. Rio de Janeiro: Editora a Noite, 1940.

————. *El sentido de la evolucion cultural del Brasil*. Buenos Aires: Editorial Americalee, 1945.

————. *Nabuco e Junqueiro*. Porto: Livraria Lello, 1953.

————. *Panorama sociologique du Brésil*. Paris: Presses Universitaires de France, 1953.

Carvalho, Edgardo. *Brasil, un continente hacia la revolucion*. Montevideo: Ediciones Presente, 1962.

Carvalho, Orlando M. *Problemas Fundamentais do Município*. São Paulo: Companhia Editora Nacional, 1937.

————. *A crise dos partidos nacionais*. Belo Horizonte: Kriterion, 1950.

Castro, Josué de. *La alimentación en los trópicos*. Mexico, D.F.: Fondo de cultura economica, 1946.

————. *Fatores na Localização da Cidade do Recife*. Rio de Janeiro: Imprensa Nacional, 1948.

————. *The Geography of Hunger*. Boston: Little, Brown and Co., 1952.

————. *A cidade do Recife: ensaio de geografia urbana*. Rio de Janeiro: Livraria-Editora da Casa do Estudante do Brasil, 1954.

————. "Colonialism, Hunger and Progress," *World Marxist Review*, Vol. IV, No. 10 (October 1961), pp. 67-70.

Comissão Econômica para a America Latina. "A Inflação no Brasil," *Revista Brasileira de Ciências Sociais*, Vol. II, No. 1 (Minas Gerais, March 1962), pp. 274-300.

Cooke, Morris L. (ed.). *Brazil on the March, a Study in International Cooperation*. New York: McGraw-Hill Book Co., 1944.

Costa-Pinto, L.A. "A Estrutura da Sociedade Rural Brasileira," *Sociologia*, Vol. X, No. 2-3 (São Paulo, 1948), pp. 156 ff.

————. *Pesquisa sobre a padrão de vida do comerciário no distrito federal*. Rio de Janeiro (privately printed), 1949.

————. *Migrações Internas no Brasil*. Rio de Janeiro, 1952.

————. *O negro no Rio de Janeiro*. São Paulo: Companhia Editora Nacional, 1953.

————. *O comércio metropolitano do Distrito Federal*. Rio de Janeiro: Serviço Nacional de Aprendizagem Comercial, 1957.

————. *Recôncavo: laboratório de uma experiência humana*. Rio de Janeiro: Centro Latino-Americano de Pesquisas em Ciências Sociais, 1958.

————. *As ciências sociais no Brasil: estudo realizado para a CAPES*. Rio

de Janeiro: Campanha Nacional de Aperfeiçoamento de Pessoal de Nivel, Superior, 1958.
————— (ed.). *Resistências à mudança: Factôres que impedem ou dificultam o desenvolvimento*. Rio de Janeiro: Centro Latino-Americano de Pesquisas em Ciências Sociais, 1960.
—————. "O desenvolvimento: seus processos e seus obstáculos," *Journal of Inter-American Studies*, Vol. IV, No. 3 (July 1962), pp. 297-312.
*————— and Waldemiro Bazzanella. "Economic Development, Social Change and Population Problems in Brazil," *The Annals of the American Academy of Political and Social Science*, Vol. CCCXVI (March 1958), pp. 121-26.
Coutinho, Lourival. *O general Góes depõe*. Rio de Janeiro: Coelho Branco, 1956.
Crawford, William Rex. "Three Thinkers of Brazil," in *A Century of Latin-American Thought*. Rev. ed. Cambridge: Harvard University Press, 1961.
Cunha, Euclydes da. *À Margem da História*. Porto: Livraria Chardon, 1922.
—————. *Rebellion in the Backlands*. Trans. by Samuel Putnam. Chicago: University of Chicago Press, 1944.
Dantas, Nelson. "O Brasil e o petróleo," *Leitura* (Rio de Janeiro, May 1962), p. 444.
Ferguson, J. Halcro. *Latin America: The Balance of Race Redressed*. London: Oxford University Press, 1961.
Fernandes, Florestan. *Mudanças Sociais no Brasil*. São Paulo: Difusão Europeía do Livro, 1960.
—————. *A sociologia numa era de revolução social*. São Paulo: Editôra Nacional, 1963.
Ferrari, Fernando. *Minha campanha*. Rio de Janeiro: Editôra Globo, 1961.
*—————. "Panorama político del Brasil," *Combate*, Vol. IV, No. 21 (San José, Costa Rica, March-April 1962), pp. 9-13.
Fischlowitz, Estanislav. "Êxodo Rural en Latinoamérica," *Combate*, No. 15 (San José, Costa Rica, March-April 1961), pp. 9-17.
Fitzgibbon, Russell H. "What Price Latin American Armies?" *The Virginia Quarterly Review*, Vol. XXXVI, No. 4 (Autumn 1960), pp. 517-32.
Frank, Andrew Gunder. "United States-Latin-American Economic Relations: The Case of Brazil." March 1963. (Mimeographed)
—————. "A Pré-Revolução Brasileira de Celso Furtado." April 1963. (Mimeographed)
—————. "Integração econômica da América Latina," *Revista Brasiliense*, No. 48 (July-August 1963), pp. 6-10.
Frazier, E. Franklin. "The Negro Family in Bahia, Brazil," *American Sociological Review*, Vol. III (August 1942), pp. 465-78.
Freyre, Gilberto. *The Mansions and the Shanties*. Trans. by Harriet de Onis. New York: Alfred A. Knopf, 1963 (first published in 1936).
—————. *O Nordeste*. Rio de Janeiro: José Olympio, 1937.
—————. *Brazil: An Interpretation*. New York: Alfred A. Knopf, 1945.
—————. *The Masters and the Slaves: A Study in the Development of Brazilian Civilization*. Trans. by Samuel Putnam. New York: Alfred A. Knopf, 1946.
—————. *Nação e exército*. Rio de Janeiro: José Olympio, 1949.
—————. "Slavery, Monarchy, and Modern Brazil," *Foreign Affairs*, Vol. XXXIII, No. 4 (July 1955), pp. 624-33.

————. *Sugestões para uma nova política no Brasil*. Recife: Secretaria de Educação e Cultura, 1956.

*————. "Why a Tropical China?" *New World in the Tropics: The Culture of Modern Brazil*. New York: Alfred A. Knopf, 1959.

Furtado, Celso. *A economia brasileira: contribuição à análise do seu desenvolvimento*. Rio de Janeiro: Editora A Noite, 1954.

————. *Formação ecônomica do Brasil*. Rio de Janeiro: Editora Fundo da Cultura, 1959.

————. *Desenvolvimento e Subdesenvolvimento*. Rio de Janeiro: Editora Fundo da Cultura, 1961.

*————. "Reflexões sôbre a pré-revolução brasileira," *Revista Brasileira de Ciências Sociais*. Vol. II, No. 1 (Minas Gerais, March 1962), pp. 40-56.

————. *The Economic Growth of Brazil: a Survey from Colonial to Modern Times*. Berkeley and Los Angeles: University of California Press, 1963.

* Gorender, Jacob. "Brazil in the Grip of Contradictions," *World Marxist Review: Problems of Peace and Socialism*, Vol. VI, No. 2 (February 1963), pp. 27-32.

*Goulart, João. "Brazil and the United States," *Vital Speeches*, Vol. XXVIII, No. 14 (May 1, 1962), pp. 425-27.

Haring, C. H. *Empire in Brazil: A New World Experiment with Monarchy*. Cambridge: Harvard University Press, 1958.

Harris, Marvin. *Town and Country in Brazil*. New York: Columbia University Press, 1956.

Hauser, Philip M. (ed.). *Urbanization in Latin America*. Paris: United Nations Educational, Scientific and Cultural Organization, 1963.

Heare, Gertrude E. *Brazil: Information for United States Businessmen*. Washington, D.C.: Department of Commerce (Government Printing Office), 1961.

Herring, Hubert. *Good Neighbors: Argentina, Brazil, Chile and Seventeen Other Countries*. New Haven: Yale University Press, 1941.

————. "Brazil," *Yale Review*, Vol. XXXVI, No. 2 (Winter 1947), pp. 304-19.

————. "Brazil: Empire and Republic," *A History of Latin America*. Rev. ed. New York: Alfred A. Knopf, 1961. Pp. 723-85.

Hill, Lawrence F. *Diplomatic Relations between the United States and Brazil*. Durham: Duke University Press, 1932.

———— (ed.). *Brazil*. Berkeley and Los Angeles: University of California Press, 1947.

Hilton, Ronald. "Brazil's Independent Foreign Policy," *Sequoia* (Stanford University, Autumn 1962), pp. 1-11.

Hirschman, Albert O. *The Strategy of Economic Development*. New Haven: Yale University Press, 1958.

————. *Journeys Toward Progress: Studies of Economic Policy-Making in Latin America*. New York: The Twentieth Century Fund, 1963.

Horowitz, Irving Louis. "Sociology and the Philosophy of History in Latin America," *History and Theory*, Vol. II, No. 1 (1962), pp. 85-89.

————. "The Revolt Against Political Mythology," *The Nation*, Vol. CXCIV, No. 13 (March 1962), pp. 281-84.

————. "Latin American Communism," *Liberation*, Vol. VIII, No. 3 (May 1963), pp. 11-15.

————. "Palace Revolutions and Political Realities: A Latin American Casebook," *Trans-Action*, Vol. I, No. 3 (March 1964).

Hutchinson, Bertram. "Social Grading of Occupations in Brazil," *British Journal of Sociology*, Vol. VIII, No. 2 (June 1957), pp. 176-89.

————, et al. *Mobilidade e Trabalho*. Rio de Janeiro: Centro Brasileiro de Pesquisas Educacionais, 1960.

Hutchinson, Harry W. *Village and Plantation Life in Northeastern Brazil.* Seattle: University of Washington Press, 1957.

Jaddad, Jamil Almansur. *Revolução cubana e revolução brasileira.* Rio de Janeiro: Editora Civilização Brasileira, 1961.

*Jaguaribe, Hélio. "A renúncia do Presidente Quadros e a crise política brasileira," *Revista Brasileira de Ciências Sociais*, Vol. I (University of Minas Gerais, Belo Horizonte, 1961), pp. 272-311.

————. *Burguesia y Proletariado en el Nacionalismo Brasileño.* Buenos Aires: Editorial Coyoacan, 1961.

————. "Desarrollo Economico Programado y Organizacion Politica," *Desarrollo Economico*, Vol. II, No. 1 (Buenos Aires, April-June 1962), pp. 5-64.

————. *Desenvolvimento Econômico e Desenvolvimento Político.* Rio de Janeiro: Editora Fundo da Cultura, 1962.

James, Preston. *Latin America.* New York: Odyssey Press, 1942.

————. *Brazil.* New York: Odyssey Press, 1946.

Jobim, José. *Brazil in the Making.* New York: The Macmillan Co., 1942.

Johnson, John J. "Brazil, Late Bid for Power," in *Political Change in Latin America: The Emergence of the Middle Sectors.* Stanford: Stanford University Press, 1958. Pp. 153-79.

————. "Brazil: New President, Old Problems," *Current History*, Vol. XL, No. 236 (April 1961), pp. 201-206.

————. "Politics and Economics in Brazil," *Current History*, Vol. XLII, No. 246 (February 1962), pp. 89-95.

Johnson, Paul. "The Plundered Continent: The United States and Latin-American Nationalism," *New Statesman* (September 17, 1960), pp. 380-91.

*Julião, Francisco. "A Alforria do Camponês," *Que São as Ligas Campo-nesas?* Rio de Janeiro: Editora Civilização Brasileira, 1962.

*————. "Cartilla del campesino," *Escucha Campesino.* Montevideo: Ediciones Presente, 1962.

*————. "Carta de Ouro Preto," *Marcha*, Vol. XXIII, No. 1107 (May 1962), pp. 16-17.

Júnior, Caio Prado. "O Estatuto do Trabalhador Rural," *Revista Brasiliense*, No. 47 (May-June 1963), pp. 1-13.

Kahl, Joseph A. "Careers, Values and Social Change in Brazil." Latin American Center for Research in the Social Sciences. United Nations Economic and Social Council, December 1960. (Mimeographed)

————. "Urbanização e Mudanças Ocupacionais no Brasil," *América Latina: Centro Latino Americano de Pesquisas em Ciências Sociais.* Vol. V, No. 4 (October-December 1962), pp. 21-30.

Kuznets, Simon, Wilbert E. Moore, and Joseph J. Spengler (eds.). *Economic Growth: Brazil, India, Japan.* Durham: Duke University Press, 1955.

* Láfer, Horácio. "The Survival of Mankind: United Nations Not a Super-State," *Vital Speeches*, Vol. XXVII, No. 1 (October 15, 1960), pp. 19-21.

412 BIBLIOGRAPHY

Lambert, Jacques. *Os Dois Brasis*. Rio de Janeiro: Centro Brasileiro de Pesquisas Educacionais, 1959.

Lamego, Alberto Ribeiro. *O Homem e o Brejo*. Rio de Janeiro: Serviço Gráfico do Instituto Brasileiro de Geografia e Estatística, 1945.

————. *O Homen e a Guanabara*. Rio de Janeiro: Conselho Nacional de Geografia, 1948.

Leeds, Anthony. "Brazil and the Myth of Francisco Julião." 1962. (Mimeographed)

————. "Brazilian Careers and Social Structure." Revised version of paper read before the Anthropological Society of Washington, D.C., 1962. (Mimeographed)

Lieuwen, Edwin. *Arms and Politics in Latin America*. Rev. ed. New York: Frederick A. Praeger, 1961.

————. "The Military: A Revolutionary Force," *The Annals of the American Academy of Political and Social Science*. Vol. CCCXXXIV (March 1961), pp. 30-40.

Lima, Hermes. *Introducão à ciencia do direito*. 5th ed. rev. Rio de Janeiro: Editora Nacional de Direito, 1949.

Lipson, Leslie. "Government in Contemporary Brazil," *The Canadian Journal of Economics and Political Science*, Vol. XXII, No. 2 (May 1956), pp. 183-98.

Livermore, H. V. (ed.). *Portugal and Brazil*. London: Oxford University Press, 1953.

Loewenstein, Karl. *Brazil under Vargas*. New York: The Macmillan Co., 1942.

Lopes, Juarez Rubens Brandão. "Motivações e atitudes do operário," *Boletim*, Vol. III (Centro Latino-Americano de Pesquisas em Ciências Sociais, May 1960), pp. 15-23.

————. "A fixação do operário de origem rural na indústria," *Educação e Ciências Sociais*, Vol. II (November 1957), pp. 203-22.

Machado, Augusto. *Caminho da Revolução Operária e Camponeza*. Rio de Janeiro: Calvino Filho, 1934.

Madariaga, Salvador de. "Challenge in Latin America," *Saturday Review* (March 25, 1961), pp. 14-16, 37-38.

————. *Latin America Between the Eagle and the Bear*. New York: Frederick A. Praeger, 1962.

Manchester, Alan K. "Brazil in Transition," *South Atlantic Quarterly*, Vol. LIV, No. 2 (April 1955), pp. 167-76.

————. *British Preeminence in Brazil, Its Rise and Decline: a Study in European Expansion*. Chapel Hill: University of North Carolina Press, 1933.

Marchant, Alexander. *From Barter to Slavery*. Baltimore: Johns Hopkins University Press, 1942.

Marshall, Andrew. "Brazil: The Reawakening of the Giant," *The World Today*, Vol. XVII, No. 8 (Royal Institute of International Affairs, August 1961), pp. 336-43.

Meijer, Hendrik. *Rural Brazil at the Cross-Roads*. Wageningen: H. Veenman, 1951.

Mello, José Luiz de Anhaia. *O Estado federal e as suas novas perspectivas*. São Paulo: M. Limonad, 1960.

Mielche, Haakon. *The Amazon*. London: Hodge, 1949.

Montenegro, Abelardo F. *História do fanatismo religioso no Ceará.* Batista Fontenele: Fortaleza, 1959.

Moog, Clodomir Viana. *Bandeirantes e pioneiros: Paralelo entre duas culturas.* Rio de Janeiro: Editora Globo, 1955.

Moraze, Charles. *Les trois ages du Brésil: Essai de politique.* Paris: A. Colin, 1954.

Morse, Richard M. *From Community to Metropolis: A Biography of São Paulo, Brazil.* Gainesville: University of Florida Press, 1958.

————. "Some Themes of Brazilian History," *The South Atlantic Quarterly,* Vol. LXI, No. 2 (Spring 1962), pp. 159-82.

————. "Contrast and Modulation: A View of Brazilian History," *História* (Rio Piedras, Puerto Rico, January 1962), pp. 5-34.

Mosher, Arthur T. *A Case Study of the Agricultural Program of ACAR in Brazil.* Washington, D.C.: National Planning Association, 1955.

————. "The Program of ACAR in Brazil," in *Technical Co-operation in Latin American Agriculture.* Chicago: University of Chicago Press, 1957. Pp. 136-80.

Motta Lima, Pedro. "Marxism-Leninism and Its Influence on Cultural Life in Brazil," *World Marxist Review* (Prague, October 1962), pp. 19-25.

Nabuco, Carolina. *The Life of Joaquim Nabuco.* Trans. and ed. by Ronald Hilton. Stanford: Stanford University Press, 1950.

Nascimento, Benedito Helorz. "Acumulação capitalista e salários," *Política Operária* (São Paulo, October 1962), pp. 24-26.

Niemeyer, Oscar. *Minha Experiência em Brasília.* Rio de Janeiro: Editorial Vitória, 1961.

Normano, J. F. *Brazil: A Study of Economic Types.* Chapel Hill: University of North Carolina Press, 1935.

Oliveira Campos, Roberto de. "Foreign Policy of Brazil," *Brazilian Business* (Rio de Janeiro, November 1962), pp. 43-46.

Parente, Agenor B. "Atualização de normas da consolidação trabalhista," *Revista de estudos sócio-econômicos* (May-June 1962), pp. 27-36.

Pereira de Queiroz, Maria Izaura. "Classifications des messianismes bresiliens," *Archives de Sociologie des Religions,* No. 5 (January-June 1958), pp. 111-20.

Pereira, L. C. Bresser. "The Rise of Middle Class and Middle Management in Brazil," *Journal of Inter-American Studies,* Vol. IV, No. 3 (July 1962), pp. 313-26.

Pierson, Donald. *Negroes in Brazil: A Study of Race Contact in Bahia.* Chicago: University of Chicago Press, 1942.

————. "The Educational Process and the Brazilian Negro," *American Journal of Sociology,* Vol. XLVIII, No. 6 (May 1943), pp. 692-700.

————. "Research and Research Possibilities in Brazil with Particular Reference to Culture and Cultural Change," *Sobretiro de Acta Americana,* Vol. V, No. 1-2 (1947), pp. 19-82.

————. *Cruz das Almas: A Brazilian Village.* Washington: U.S. Government Printing Office, 1948.

Pilla, Raúl. "Será parlamentar o nosso sistema de govêrno?" *Síntese Política, Econômica, Social* (October-December 1961), pp. 5-11.

Pinto, Heráclito Sobral. *As fôrças armadas em face de momento político.* Rio de Janeiro: Editorial Ercilla, 1945.

Poppino, Rollie E. "Imbalance in Brazil," *Current History,* Vol. XLIV, No. 258 (February 1963), pp. 100-105.

Prado, Caio. *Formação do Brasil Contemporâneo.* 2nd ed. São Paulo: Editora Brasiliense, 1945.
————. *Evolução política do Brasil.* 2nd ed. São Paulo: Editora Brasiliense, 1947.
Prestes, Luís Carlos. *Os comunistas na luta pela democracia.* Rio de Janeiro: Edições Horizonte, 1945.
————. *Organizar o povo para a democracia.* Rio de Janeiro: Edições Horizonte, 1945.
————. *Documentos de Luís Carlos Prestes.* Buenos Aires: Ediciones Tiempo Nuevos, 1947.
————. "On the Program of the Communist Party of Brazil," *Political Affairs,* Vol. XXXIV, No. 4 (April 1955), pp. 55-65.
*————. "Brazil, the Soviet Union and Communism," *World Marxist Review,* Vol. II, No. 1 (January 1959), pp. 16-18.
Price, Paul H. "The Brazilian Population at Mid-Century," *Inter-American Economic Affairs,* Vol. X, No. 1 (Summer 1956), pp. 66-78.
Putnam, Samuel. *Marvelous Journey: Four Centuries of Brazilian Literature.* New York: Alfred A. Knopf, 1948.
*Quadros, Jânio. "Brazil's New Foreign Policy," *Foreign Affairs,* Vol. XL, No. 1 (October 1961), pp. 19-27.
Ramos, Alberto Guerreiro. *A crise do poder no Brasil.* Rio de Janeiro: Zahar Editores, 1961.
Ramos, Arthur. *The Negro in Brazil.* Washington, D.C.: The Associated Publishers, 1939.
————. *Las Poblaciones del Brasil.* Mexico, D.F.: Fondo de Cultura Economica, 1944.
————. *Introdução à Antropologia Brasileira.* Two vols. Rio de Janeiro: Casa do Estudante do Brasil, 1947.
————. *Le Métissage au Brésil.* Paris: Hermann et Cie, 1952.
Ribeiro, René. "Brazilian Messianic Movements," in *Millennial Dreams in Action.* Ed. by Sylvia L. Thrupp. Supplement II of *Comparative Studies in Society and History.* The Hague: Mouton and Co., 1962.
Rios, José Arthur. "Assimilation of Immigrants from the Old South in Brazil," *Social Forces,* Vol. XXVI (December 1947), pp. 145-52.
Robock, Stefan H. "Northeast Brazil: A Developing Economy." Washington, D.C.: The Brookings Institution, November 1962. (Mimeographed)
*Rodrigues, José Honorio. "The Foundations of Brazil's Foreign Policy," *International Affairs,* Vol. XXXVIII, No. 3 (July 1962), pp. 324-38.
Rosen, Bernard C. "Socialization and Achievement Motivation in Brazil," *American Sociological Review,* Vol. XXVII, No. 5 (October 1962), pp. 612-24.
Saldanha, P. H. "Race Mixture among Northeastern Brazilian Populations," *American Anthropologist* (August 1962), pp. 751-59.
Salgado, Plínio. *Direitos e deveres do homem.* 2nd ed. Rio de Janeiro: Livraria Clássica Brasileira, 1953.
————. *Psicologia da revolução.* 4th ed. Rio de Janeiro: Livraria Clássica Brasileira, 1953.
Schmidt, Carlos Borges. "System of Land Tenure in São Paulo," *Rural Sociology,* Vol. VIII (September 1943), pp. 242-47.
————. "Rural Life in Brazil," in *Brazil: Portrait of Half a Continent.* Ed. by Smith and Marchant, *loc. cit.,* pp. 165-87.

————. "Tropas e Tropeiros," *Journal of Inter-American Studies*, Vol. I, No. 2 (April 1959), pp. 103-22.

Schurz, William Lytle. *Brazil: The Infinite Country*. New York: E. P. Dutton & Co., 1961.

Siegel, Bernard J. "Themes and Variations in Brazilian Culture," *Pacific Spectator*, Vol. IV, No. 1 (Winter 1952), pp. 98-112.

Simão, Asis. "Industrialização e Sindicalização no Brasil," *Revista Brasileira de Estudos Políticos*, No. 13 (January 1962).

Simonsen, Roberto C. *História Econômica do Brasil*. Two vols. São Paulo: Companhia Editora Nacional, 1937.

————. *Brazil's Industrial Evolution*. São Paulo: Escola Livre de Sociologia e Política, 1939.

Singer, Leonardo. "Brazil Stands on the Brink," *Atlas: The Magazine of the World Press*, Vol. IV, No. 5 (November 1962), pp. 349-53.

Smith, Thomas Lynn. *Brazil: People and Institutions*. Rev. ed. Baton Rouge: Louisiana State University Press, 1954.

————. "Patterns of Living in the United States and Brazil: A Comparison," *Sociologia: Revista Dedicada a Teoria e Pesquisa nas Ciências Sociais*. Vol. XXI, No. 3 (August 1959), pp. 236-46.

————, and Alexander Marchant (eds.). *Brazil: Portrait of Half a Continent*. New York: The Dryden Press, 1951.

Sodré, Nelson Werneck. *Oeste*. Rio de Janeiro: Livraria José Olympio, 1941.

————. *Formação da Sociedade Brasileira*. Rio de Janeiro: Livraria José Olympio, 1944.

Souto, Claudio. "Um projeto de lei agrária para o estado de Pernambuco," *Estudos Universitários* (Recife, July-September 1962), pp. 29-42.

Spiegel, Henry W. *The Brazilian Economy: Chronic Inflation and Sporadic Industrialization*. Philadelphia: Blakiston Co., 1949.

Stein, Stanley J. *The Brazilian Cotton Textile Industry*. Cambridge: Harvard University Press, 1957.

————. "Freyre's Brazil Revisited," *Hispanic American Historical Review*, Vol. XLI, No. 1 (February 1961), pp. 111-13.

Sternberg, Hilgard O'Reilly. "The Physical Basis of Brazilian Society," in *Brazil: Portrait of Half a Continent*. Ed. by Smith and Marchant, *loc. cit.*, pp. 52-85.

Suárez, Luis. "Julião, el líder místico del marxismo en Brazil," *Siempre* (Mexico City, August 15, 1962), pp. 30-31.

*————. "Reportaje en Brasil: La crisis de fondo en las ultimas crisis políticas," *Cuadernos Americanos*, Vol. CXXV, No. 6 (November-December 1962), pp. 15-29.

Tannenbaum, Frank. "The Political Dilemma in Latin America," *Foreign Affairs*, Vol. XXXVIII, No. 3 (April 1960), pp. 497-515.

Tavares de Sá, Hernane. *The Brazilians: People of Tomorrow*. New York: John Day and Co., 1947.

Teichert, Pedro C. M. *Economic Policy, Revolution, and Industrialization in Latin America*. University, Mississippi: Bureau of Business Research, 1959.

Telles, Jover. *O movimento sindical no Brasil*. Rio de Janeiro: Editorial Vitória, 1962.

Troncoso, Moises Poblete, and Ben G. Burnett. *The Rise of the Latin American Labor Movement*. New York: Bookman Associates, 1960.

Vallier, Ivan A. "Roman Catholicism and Social Change in Latin America:

From Church to Sect." Paper read before American Sociological Association, Los Angeles, California, August 26-29, 1963. (Mimeographed)

Vargas, Getúlio. *A Nova Política do Brasil.* Two vols. Rio de Janeiro: Livraria José Olympio, 1938.

—————. *A campanha presidencial.* Rio de Janeiro: Livraria José Olympio, 1951.

—————. *O govêrno trabalhista do Brasil.* Rio de Janeiro: Livraria José Olympio, 1952.

Viera, Dorival Teixeira. "The Industrialization of Brazil," in *Brazil: Portrait of Half a Continent.* Ed. by Smith and Marchant, *loc. cit.,* pp. 244-64.

Von Gersdorff, Ralph. *Saving, Credit and Insurance in Brazil: Their Contribution to Economic Development.* Barbados, W.I.: Government Printing Office, 1962.

de Vries, Egbert, and José Medina Echavarría (eds.). *Social Aspects of Economic Development in Latin America.* Paris: United Nations Educational, Scientific and Cultural Organization, 1963.

Wagley, Charles. "Regionalism and Cultural Unity in Brazil," *Social Forces,* Vol. XXVI, No. 4 (1948), pp. 457-64.

—————. "Brazil," in *Most of the World: the Peoples of Africa, Latin America and the East Today.* Ed. by Ralph Linton. New York: Columbia University Press, 1949. Pp. 212-70.

—————— (ed.). *Race and Class in Rural Brazil.* Paris: United Nations Educational, Scientific and Cultural Organization, 1952.

—————. *Amazon Town: A Study of Man in the Tropics.* New York: The Macmillan Co., 1953.

—————. "The Brazilian Revolution: Social Changes since 1930," in *Social Change in Latin America Today: Its Implications for United States Policy.* Introduction by Lyman Bryson. New York: Harper and Brothers. Published for the Council on Foreign Relations, 1961.

—————— and Eduardo Galvão. *The Tenetehara Indians of Brazil.* New York: Columbia University Press, 1949.

Walker, Harvey. "The Vargas Regime," in *Brazil.* Ed. by Lawrence F. Hill, *loc. cit.,* pp. 107-22.

Willems, Emílio. "Assimilation of German Immigrants in Brazil," *Sociology and Social Research,* Vol. XXV, No. 2 (1940).

—————. *Assimilação e populações marginais no Brasil.* São Paulo: Companhia Editora Nacional, 1939.

—————. "Some Aspects of Cultural Conflict and Acculturation in Southern Rural Brazil," *Rural Sociology,* Vol. VII (December 1942), pp. 375-84.

—————. *Buzios Island: A Caiçara Community in Southern Brazil.* Locust Valley, N. Y.: J. J. Augustin, 1952.

—————. "The Structure of the Brazilian Family," *Social Forces,* Vol. XXXI, No. 4 (May 1953), pp. 339-45.

—————. *Brasil: período indígena.* Mexico, D. F.: Instituto Panamericano de Geografia e História, 1953.

Wyckoff, Theodore. "Brazilian Political Parties," *South Atlantic Quarterly,* Vol. LVI, No. 3 (Summer 1957), pp. 281-98.

Wythe, George, Royce A. Wight, and Harold Midkiff. *Brazil: An Expanding Economy.* New York: Twentieth Century Fund, 1949.

Zweig, Stefan. *Brazil: Land of the Future.* London: Cassell Ltd., 1942.

Subject Index

197; control, 347; and corruption, 98; dangers of, 349; and economic growth, 219; and economy, 199; eliminate, 363; high, 199, 243; extended, 223; and masses, 159; monetary, 362; negative aspect of, 221; persistent, 351; policy, 338; problem of, 348; and rapid growth, 196; and redistribution of wealth, 220; solution to, 198; warborn, 363
intellectuals, 73, 86, 195, 285, 325, 344, 375-76
intelligentsia: and Lott, 158; and masses, 159; nationalist, 157; revolutionary, 283, 287; scope of, 91
International Telephone and Telegraph, 81, 215, 264, 333
investments, 20, 207, 220, 338; in Brazil, 81n; claims on, 348; British, 119; capital, 217, 263; foreign, 202, 212-13, 216, 262, 264, 329, 330-31, 398; group, 218; and pot-of-gold philosophy, 196-200; premium on, 64; types of, 222; United States, 83, 208, 216, 340; *see also* capital; capitalism
Italy, 296, 388; Communist Party of, 390; corporativism in, 92

Japan, 108, 211-12, 308-309, 400
Jéca, Tatu, 11, 257

labor, 11, 295, 326; aristocracy, 29; and capital, 92, 125; cheap, 201; as creator of wealth, 138; domestic, 212; exploitation of, 335; intensification of, 339; legislation, 134; movement, 95; organization and ideology of, 242-56; organized, 300; parties, 137, 177, 195; power, 274, 288; pre-capitalist, 268; progressive forces of, 157; protection for, 317; reformism, 137; role of, 224; sector, 93; slave, 68, 89, 117, 201; surpluses, 222
labor party, 393; Goulart's, 11, 372; Vargas', 390
labor union, 47, 50, 53, 220, 242-56, 357; and latifundists, 44; rural, 44n, 49, 54; urban, 256
land: concentration, 335; distribution, 172, 183; enslavement of, 38; expropriation of, 54, 204; monop-

oly, 337; ownership, 171, 193, 205, 267, 335; and peasantry, 27; and prestige, 174; problem, 34, 71, 202-204, 279; rational utilization of, 272; redevelopment, 203; redistribution, 15-16, 33, 204, 397; reform, 268, 287, 380, 397; rent, 20, 63-64, 202; tenure, 23; *see also* agrarian reform; agriculture
landowner, 36, 38n, 39, 44, 49, 203, 234; and bourgeoisie, 340; and capitalists, 267; and farmers, 174; interests of, 131; middle range, 50; and parliamentary agents, 220; profits of, 52; and slaves, 184; and workers, 268
latifundias, 13, 16, 21, 33-37, 43, 46-48, 51, 202-206, 209; abolishing, 394; and *capanga,* 60; confiscation of, 397-98; corruption of, 58; division of, 268; dominated districts, 336; exploitation, 335; fight against, 50; internal migration from, 284; in Northeast, 89, 171; and paternalistic syndicalism, 268; and plantations, 90; and power, 267; private army of, 297; system of, 15; and traditionalism, 171; undeveloped, 57; and the vote, 54
law, 22, 23, 51, 56, 72, 153, 245, 317; change of, 39; civil, 147; economic, 209, 339; electoral, 165; of excess profits, 132, 263; and freedom to strike, 253; and mass, 41; structure of, 242, 244; violation of, 145

Maranhão, 167, 259, 335
Marxism, 65; revisionist, 372
Marxism-Leninism, 69, 367-68; *see also* communism
Marxist, orthodox, 30, 70, 179
Marxist-Leninist: bias, 71; revolutionary techniques, 30, 69; type of revolution, 68, 70-71
masses, 10, 62, 63, 68, 143, 159 196, 223, 288; colored, 289; exploitation of, 290; and inflation, 159; and military, 302; mobilization of, 155; and participation, 354; proletarian, 154; and Quadros, 157, 162; rule of, 81; rural, 137, 290; society of, 96, 209, 211; in underdeveloped